Stalin's Terror

Also by Kevin McDermott:

THE CZECH RED UNIONS, 1918–1929

THE COMINTERN: A History of International Communism from Lenin to Stalin (*co-author*)

POLITICS AND SOCIETY UNDER THE BOLSHEVIKS (*co-editor*)

Stalin's Terror
High Politics and Mass Repression in the Soviet Union

Edited by

Barry McLoughlin
Lecturer
Vienna University

and

Kevin McDermott
Senior Lecturer in Political History
Sheffield Hallam University

palgrave
macmillan

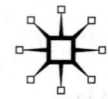

Selection, editorial matter and Chapter 1 © Barry McLoughlin and Kevin McDermott 2003
Chapter 6 © Barry McLoughlin 2003
Remaining chapters © Palgrave Macmillan Ltd 2003

All rights reserved. No reproduction, copy or transmission of this publication may be made without written permission.

No paragraph of this publication may be reproduced, copied or transmitted save with written permission or in accordance with the provisions of the Copyright, Designs and Patents Act 1988, or under the terms of any licence permitting limited copying issued by the Copyright Licensing Agency, 90 Tottenham Court Road, London W1T 4LP.

Any person who does any unauthorised act in relation to this publication may be liable to criminal prosecution and civil claims for damages.

The authors have asserted their rights to be identified as the authors of this work in accordance with the Copyright, Designs and Patents Act 1988.

First published in hardcover 2003

First published in paperback 2004 by
PALGRAVE MACMILLAN
Houndmills, Basingstoke, Hampshire RG21 6XS and
175 Fifth Avenue, New York, N.Y. 10010
Companies and representatives throughout the world

PALGRAVE MACMILLAN is the global academic imprint of the Palgrave Macmillan division of St Martin's Press, LLC and of Palgrave Macmillan Ltd. Macmillan is a registered trademark in the United States, United Kingdom and other countries. Palgrave is a registered trademark in the European Union and other countries.

ISBN 1–4039–0119–8 hardback
ISBN 1–4039–3903–9 paperback

This book is printed on paper suitable for recycling and made from fully managed and sustained forest sources.

A catalogue record for this book is available from the British Library.

Library of Congress Cataloging-in-Publication Data
Stalin's terror: high politics and mass repression in the Soviet Union/edited by Barry McLoughlin and Kevin McDermott.
    p. cm.
    Includes bibliographical references and index.
    ISBN 1–4039–0119–8 (cloth) — ISBN 1–4039–3903–9 (paper)
    1. Political purges – Soviet Union. 2. Kommunisticheskaĕĭ partiĕĭ Sovetskogo Soĕĭza – Purges. 3. Stalin, Joseph, 1879–1953. 4. Soviet Union – Politics and government – 1936–1953. I. McLoughlin, Barry, 1949– II. McDermott, Kevin, 1957–

DK267 .S6955 2004
947.084'2–dc22   2004044355

10 9 8 7 6 5 4 3 2 1
13 12 11 10 09 08 07 06 05 04

Printed and bound in Great Britain by
Antony Rowe Ltd, Chippenham, Eastbourne

*To Susanne and Susan
and our fantastic kids Siobhán, Frances and Alex*

Contents

Notes on Contributors	ix
Preface and Acknowledgements	xii
Glossary of Terms and Abbreviations	xv
List of Archives and Archival Abbreviations	xviii

1 Rethinking Stalinist Terror 1
   Barry McLoughlin and Kevin McDermott

Part I: The Politics of Repression 19

2 Party and NKVD: Power Relationships in the Years of the Great Terror 21
   Oleg Khlevniuk

3 Ezhov's Scenario for the Great Terror and the Falsified Record of the Third Moscow Show Trial 34
   Wladislaw Hedeler

4 Dimitrov, the Comintern and Stalinist Repression 56
   Fridrikh I. Firsov

Part II: The Police and Mass Repression 83

5 Social Disorder, Mass Repression and the NKVD during the 1930s 85
   David Shearer

6 Mass Operations of the NKVD, 1937–8: A Survey 118
   Barry McLoughlin

7 The "Polish Operation" of the NKVD, 1937–8 153
   Nikita Petrov and Arsenii Roginskii

Part III: Victim Studies 173

8 Foreign Communists and the Mechanisms of Soviet Cadre Formation in the USSR 175
   Berthold Unfried

9	Stalinist Terror in the Moscow District of Kuntsevo, 1937–8 *Aleksandr Vatlin and Natalia Musienko*	194
10	The Fictitious "Hitler-Jugend" Conspiracy of the Moscow NKVD *Hans Schafranek and Natalia Musienko*	208
11	Terror against Foreign Workers in the Moscow Elektrozavod Plant, 1937–8 *Sergei Zhuravlev*	225

Select Bibliography 241

Index 244

Notes on Contributors

Fridrikh Firsov has over 40 years' experience of extensive research in the history of the Comintern. Among his many publications are: 'Stalin and the Comintern', *Voprosy istorii*, nos 8 and 9 (1989); 'Die "Säuberungen" im Apparat der Komintern', in *Kommunisten verfolgen Kommunisten* (1993); *Dimitrov and Stalin, 1934–1943: Letters from the Soviet Archives*, co-edited with Alexander Dallin (2000).

Wladislaw Hedeler has translated the prison writings of Nikolai Bukharin and Dimitrov's diary into German and co-edited three volumes of documents on the "purging" of the Marx-Engels Institute in Moscow in the 1930s. He is currently researching the history of the Karaganda Gulag complex.

Oleg Khlevniuk is the internationally acclaimed expert on Stalin's leadership during the 1930s and is currently working in the Department of Public Administration at Moscow State University. His studies of Stalinism have been translated into English, French, German, Italian, Japanese and Chinese. At present he is preparing a volume of documents on the history of the Gulag system up to 1941.

Kevin McDermott is Senior Lecturer in Political History at Sheffield Hallam University. He is the author of *The Czech Red Unions, 1918–1929* (1988), co-author of *The Comintern: A History of International Communism from Lenin to Stalin* (1996), and co-editor of *Politics and Society under the Bolsheviks* (1999). He is at present working on a study of Stalin.

Barry McLoughlin is Dozent at the Institute of Contemporary History, Vienna University, where he offers seminars on Irish and Soviet history. He has co-authored two volumes on the history of Austrian political refugees in the Soviet Union and has written articles on the history of the Comintern and its schools. Dr McLoughlin is currently working on a biographical study of Irish victims of Stalinist terror.

Natalia Musienko studied German at Moscow University and is a teacher of the German language. She collaborated with other volunteers in compiling the data of victims shot in Moscow during the late 1930s. She is preparing a book of documents on the history of the Karl

Liebknecht secondary school in Moscow, which lost most of its teachers and not a few pupils to the Stalinist terror of 1936–8.

Nikita Petrov is Vice-Chairman of the Board of 'Memorial', the most prominent Russian organisation dedicated to uncovering the crimes of Soviet communism. He has co-edited volumes of documents on the Gulag system, and on the leading cadres and structures of Stalin's secret police. His study (together with Marc Jansen) of Nikolai Ezhov will appear shortly in the English language.

Arsenii Roginskii is Chairman of the Board of 'Memorial' and the editor of the historical almanac *Zven'ia* (*Links*). His most recently published work, based on intensive research in the archives of the former KGB, centres on the annihilation of foreigners and non-Russian ethnics in 1937–8.

Hans Schafranek is a freelance historian in Vienna. His most important publications focus on Austrians in Stalin's Russia, especially those handed over to the Gestapo in 1939–41 or the young inhabitants of Children's Home No. 6 in Moscow (together with Natalia Musienko). At present he is completing a research project about Soviet parachutist agents behind German lines during the Second World War.

David Shearer is Associate Professor of History at the University of Delaware, USA. His publications include *Industry, State, and Society in Stalin's Russia, 1926–1934* (1996/7) and articles on Soviet historiography and social history of the 1920s and 1930s. Professor Shearer is currently working on two monograph-length research projects: social order and repression in the Soviet Union under Stalin and the history of Siberia during the first half of the twentieth century.

Berthold Unfried lectures at Vienna University on cultural studies in the Stalinist era, specialising in the phenomenon of "speaking about oneself" in Catholic and Communist cultures. He recently published (with Brigitte Studer) the volume *Der stalinistische Parteikader*.

Aleksandr Vatlin is Senior Lecturer in the Department of Modern History at Moscow's Lomonosov University. His studies on the history of the Comintern have appeared in German and English. Dr Vatlin has written extensively in the Russian press about the Great Terror in the Moscow region.

Sergei Zhuravlev is Senior Researcher at the Institute of Russian History of the Russian Academy of Sciences in Moscow. He has co-authored volumes of documents on everyday life under Stalin, including *Stalinism as a Way of Life* (2000), and published a monograph on foreign workers in the Moscow electro-technical plant *Elektrozavod*, which will shortly appear in a German translation. Dr Zhuravlev is continuing his social history studies of everyday life in the Soviet Union.

Preface and Acknowledgements

Three hundred years ago Lord Orrery, the planter magnate, observed that the Ireland outside his estate walls was like "Vulcan's forging-shop, enlivening to observe but death to live in". A decade ago that seemed an apposite description of post-communist Russia; that is, until one recognised that sensationalist Western reports about the former USSR underplayed the resilience of the Russian people to survive by adapting, as so often in the past, to conditions over which they had little control. For an historian from western Europe, working in the new Russian Federation was not only enlivening in respect of the untold bounties made possible by access to archival documents. Equally rewarding was the exchange of opinion with Russian colleagues, in particular with those involved in studies of Stalinist mass repression. Such volunteers, frequently activists of the human rights association Memorial, were assembling data from the secret police files opened on the victims of the Great Terror. In Moscow, Lidia Golovkova, Svetlana Bartels, Natalia Musienko and Zhenia Lubimova provided us with the first national lists of victims executed in the Moscow suburb of Butovo in 1937–8.

What had started as collaboration in researching into the fate of Austrian political refugees shot in Moscow gradually transcended the field of Comintern studies and confronted us with that most traumatic, and in many respects inexplicable, biennial in Soviet history. We therefore had the good fortune of being able to reverse the usual procedure of historical investigation: by going from specific exile studies to general questions centring on the nature of, and motivations behind, the mass repression unleashed in the USSR shortly before the Second World War.

The initial stimulus to compile a collection of essays on the Great Terror was provided by Reinhard Müller, the noted German expert on Stalinism employed by the *Hamburger Institut für Sozialforschung*. In February 1998, he organised a workshop in Hamburg on the Great Terror in the Soviet Union, which was attended by most of the contributors to this volume. Reinhard's interest accompanied us throughout the many drafts of the text, variants of compilation that had to take account of the constant stream of new findings. This proved to be a strenuous challenge, which led to intense collaboration between the contributors and the editors. Barry McLoughlin translated the texts from Russian and German, and Kevin McDermott supervised the editing. In the end, the exigencies of book production made difficult decisions unavoidable: what had commenced as a collection of studies on foreigner groups targeted by the Stalinist repressive apparatus in the 1930s changed to a more general, and we believe more focused, collective description and analysis of "purging" throughout Soviet society.

Barry McLoughlin is grateful to the Cultural Department of Vienna City Council (Dr Hubert Ch. Ehalt), and to the main Austrian scientific funding agency *Fond zur Förderung der wissenschaftlichen Forschung* (Project P-11197-HIS, supervised by Dr Wolfgang Maderthaner), for financing the first phase of his research programme. Kevin McDermott wishes to thank the British Academy for the Small Research Grant awarded in 1997–8, which funded the employment of a Research Fellow, Dr Aleksandr Vatlin, and a study trip to the Moscow archives.

Apart from the Memorial activists and the State Security officers who generously gave us of their time and knowledge, we wish to thank the contributors for their patience and encouragement. We are also indebted to the staff of the State Archive of the Russian Federation (GARF) and the former Central Party Archive (RGASPI). Over the years we have become constant, and importunate, visitors to the fourth and fifth floors of the RGASPI building. However, Director Kyrill M. Anderson and his diligent co-workers, especially Andrei Doronin, Galina Gor'skaia, Elenora Shakhnazarova, Ludmilla Karlova, Raisa Paradisova and Svetlana Rozental', met us with forbearance, good humour and inventiveness in helping to find and reproduce documents. A special vote of thanks is also due to library staff, especially Boris Derenkin and Alena Kozlova (Memorial Moscow) and Ina Shchekotova, Natalia Rytsk and Tamara Gnilitskaia (Sakharov Centre), who placed valuable collections of rare publications at our disposal. The authors also owe a debt of gratitude to Fred Firsov, Slawa Hedeler, Rolf Binner and Marc Junge for providing archival documents and publications in the Russian language.

Veronika Seyr of the Austrian Embassy, the Vatlin family, Vadim and Rita, Natalia Musienko and Svetlana Bartels provided us with accommodation, good company and the delights of Russian cuisine during our frequents visits to the Russian capital.

Kevin McDermott would like to give special thanks to John Morison, recently retired from the School of History, University of Leeds, who, for over 25 years, has provided generous and unstinting academic and other support: a true friend.

Finally, but by no means least, we wish to acknowledge our editors at Palgrave, Luciana O'Flaherty and Jen Nelson, whose encouragement, patience and guidance have been much appreciated.

The editors and publishers also wish to thank the following for permission to use copyright material: Les Editions de l'Ecole des Hautes Etudes en Sciences Sociales, for an amended version of David R. Shearer, 'Social Disorder, Mass Repression, and the NKVD during the 1930s', *Cahiers du Monde russe*, vol. 42, nos 2–4 (2001), pp. 505–34.

Note on transliteration: the editors have adopted the Library of Congress transliteration system with the exception of well-known names such as Trotsky (Trotskii), Zinoviev (Zinov'ev) and Yeltsin (El'tsin).

Barry McLoughlin (barrymc@utanet.at)
Kevin McDermott (k.f.mcdermott@shu.ac.uk)

Glossary of Terms and Abbreviations

aktiv	activists (politically-active members of an organisation)
anketa	questionnaire
antisovetchik	anti-Soviet activist
apparat	bureaucratic machinery or staff of an organisation
CC	Central Committee (of Communist Party)
Cheka	Extraordinary Commission; name for secret police, 1917–22
chekist(y)	secret police officer(s)
chistka	purge (cleansing) of Communist Party
Comintern	Communist (or Third) International
CP	Communist Party
CPSU	Communist Party of the Soviet Union
CPUSA	Communist Party of the United States of America
dvoika	two-man sentencing board
ECCI	Executive Committee of the Communist International
edinolichnik(i)	individual peasant farmer(s)
Ezhovshchina	'the time of Ezhov' (mass terror of 1937–8 named after NKVD boss, Nikolai Ezhov)
FSB	Federal Security Service
Gosplan	State Planning Commission
GUGB	Main Administration of State Security (of the secret police)
Gulag	Main Administration of Corrective Labour Camps
GURKM	Main Administration of the Worker-Peasant Militia
iacheika	party cell
ILS	International Lenin School
inokolonia	foreigner colony
KGB	Committee of State Security
Kharbintsy	Russians repatriated from the Manchurian city of Harbin to the USSR during the 1930s
knigi pamiati	remembrance books
kolkhoz	collective farm
kolkhoznik(i)	collective farm worker(s)

Glossary of Terms and Abbreviations

kombinat	group of enterprises
komendant	commandant
Komsomol	Communist Youth League
KPD	German Communist Party
KPÖ	Austrian Communist Party
KPP	Polish Communist Party
krai	administrative region
kulak	better-off peasant
KUNMZ	Communist University for Western National Minorities
KVZhD	Chinese Eastern Railway
limity	arrest quotas (of NKVD)
lishentsy	disenfranchised persons
massoperatsii	mass arrest operations (of NKVD)
MOPR	International Organisation for Aid to Revolutionary Fighters (International Red Aid)
MTS	Machine Tractor Station
MVD	Ministry of Internal Affairs
Narkomindel	People's Commissariat of Foreign Affairs
NATI	Scientific Research Institute for the Car and Tractor Industry
NKTP	People's Commissariat of Heavy Industry
NKVD	People's Commissariat of Internal Affairs
nomenklatura	list of key administrative appointments approved by the Party
oblast'	administrative region
OBKhSS	Department for the Struggle against the Misappropriation of State Property
OGPU	Unified State Political Administration; appellation for secret police, 1927-34
Okhrana	Tsarist Secret Police
OMS	Department for International Communications (of the Comintern)
ORPO	Department for Leading Party Organs
OSO	Special Board (of the NKVD)
PCF	French Communist Party
PCI	Italian Communist Party
perebezhchiki	defectors
piatërka	quintet (of Soviet leaders)
Politburo	Political Bureau (of Russian Communist Party)
polozhenie	statute

Glossary of Terms and Abbreviations xvii

POUM	Workers' Party of Marxist Unity (Catalonia)
POV	Polish Military Organisation
Profintern	Red International of Labour Unions
prokuror	public procurator
proverka	verification (of party documents)
raion	administrative district
RKM	Worker-Peasant Militia (regular police force)
ROVS	Russian General Military Union
RSFSR	Russian Soviet Federative Socialist Republic
seksoty	secret police informers
sotsvredelementy	socially harmful elements
Sovnarkom	Council of People's Commissars
spetsposelki	penal resettlement colonies
SRs	Socialist Revolutionaries
TASS	Telegraphic Agency of the Soviet Union
Torgsin	shop trading in hard currency
troika	three-man sentencing board
udarnik	shockworker
UGB	State Security Administration
ugolovnyi rozysk	Criminal Investigation Department
UNKVD	local administration (of secret police)
valiuta	hard currency
VKP(b)	All-Union Communist Party (Bolsheviks)
VOKS	All-Union Society for Cultural Relations
VSNKh	Supreme Council of the National Economy
VTsIK	All-Russian Central Executive Committee (of the Soviets)
VTsSPS	All-Union Central Council of Trade Unions
ZAG	Civil Registry Offices

List of Archives and Archival Abbreviations

APRF	Archive of the President of the Russian Federation
Arkhiv UFSB MO	Archive of the Administration of the Federal Security Service for Moscow and Moscow District
GANO	State Archive of the Novosibirsk Region
GARF	State Archive of the Russian Federation
ITs GU MVD MO	Information Centre of the Main Administration of the Ministry of the Interior for the Moscow Region
RGAE	Russian State Archive of the Economy
RGANI	Russian State Archive of Contemporary History (see TsKhSD below)
RGASPI	Russian State Archive of Socio-Political History
RGVA	Russian State Military Archive
TsAFSBRF	Central Archive of the Federal Security Service of the Russian Federation
TsAOD	Central Archive of Social Movements
TsKhSD	Centre for the Preservation of Contemporary Documentation (renamed RGANI)
TsMAM	Central Municipal Archive of the City of Moscow
f.	*fond* (collection)
op.	*opis'* (inventory)
d.	*delo* (file)
l.	*list* (folio)

1
Rethinking Stalinist Terror

Barry McLoughlin and Kevin McDermott

In June 1992 the Russian security establishment was still firmly ensconced in the rows of buildings behind the ochre block of the Lubianka in central Moscow. In what was once an aristocrat's villa, the Rehabilitation Group of the Ministry of Security for Moscow City and Region was coming to terms with the new post-communist Russia. Their office was an important address for those who now had the right to find out what had happened to relatives arrested in the Soviet era. At the reception desk in the rundown villa on Bolshaia Lubianka, or in the reading room of the Central Archive of the Ministry of Security on Kuznetskii Most, most of the scholars represented in this book first got to know each other, forging links of friendship and collaboration that were renewed at conferences in Russia and Germany.

In time we learned that the ex-KGB officers seconded for this "rehabilitation" work not only dealt with requests from the general public, but also had to carry out their own historical research. A directive passed by the Supreme Soviet of the USSR on 16 January 1989 ordained that local government bodies were obliged to locate the mass graves of the executed and erect memorials there.[1] The Rehabilitation Group in the capital succeeded in narrowing down the number of potential sites where mass executions, and mass burials, had taken place in the Moscow Region before the Second World War. It transpired that the shooting squads of the Stalinist secret police, the NKVD (People's Commissariat of Internal Affairs), had discriminated between rulers and ruled to the very end: prominent victims, such as leading party cadres, ex-NKVD staff and former Red Army officers were shot before open pits on the State Farm Kommunarka some 20 kilometres south of the city centre; the "ordinary" victims sentenced to death in batches of hundreds during 1937–8 were shot and buried nearby, in an enclosed zone in the village of Butovo.[2]

The rehabilitation of the victims of Soviet state repression was comprehensively detailed in a law signed by President Yeltsin on 18 October 1991. Survivors of the Gulag were thereby entitled to social and medical benefits and they now received the right to view their own files. In the majority of cases, of course, the victim was long dead, so the right to read the personal files of the prisoner was extended to the families or persons of their trust. Two further demands of Russian democratic groups were included in the new legislation: firstly, the Federal Security Service (FSB), the successor organisation of the KGB, was obliged to inform the victim's family when and where the prisoner had died and to disclose the place of burial; secondly, the deeds of the perpetrators in the legal system or secret police who had broken the law (use of torture, falsifying evidence, etc.) were to be published in newspapers and journals.[3] The dissemination of knowledge about Stalinist terror was given further legal support less than six months later when the Supreme Soviet of the Russian Federation approved a regulation directing the rehabilitation commissions set up at central, republican and regional level to publish lists of the repressed in "remembrance books" (*knigi pamiati*).[4] The pyramid of new evidence subsequently assembled rested on a solid basis – millions of investigation-prosecution files (*sledstvennye dela*) of the local State Security Administration (UGB) of the NKVD.[5]

The historians who benefited from the Rehabilitation Law were getting a bird's-eye view of the Ezhovshchina, the rule of terror under Stalin's police chief Nikolai Ezhov in the years 1936–8. Yet despite the horrific and unequivocal contents of the victim documentation, which traced the fate of individuals from party expulsion and other forms of social ostracism to the death verdict executed at night in Butovo, much of the plot seemed to be missing in 1992–3. It was not until the eve of the new millennium that the reams of new evidence had congealed into an empirically based *topos*, namely that the Stalinist leadership launched and directed the mass arrests of 1937–8, which were carried out in a series of discrete campaigns by the secret police and targeted specific groups in the population.[6]

It also emerged that the countrywide state terror was not random, had a beginning (August 1937) and an end (November 1938), and originated in what the Bolshevik leadership considered to be an immediate pre-war situation that called for emergency measures against real or potential internal enemies. The wholescale repression, then, had a pre-emptive or prophylactic character. Its dynamic nature stemmed from the arrest and conviction tactics adopted by the secret police and sanctioned by the Politburo. In a series of distinct mass operations (*massoperatsii*), those in the native population marked down for extinction were arrested and convicted on the basis of quotas that were originally fixed after consultations between leading party and police organs, but which could be increased on application to Moscow. The second type of mass operation was aimed at foreigners and suspect ethnic minorities and, while not quota-driven, was renewed time and again. The third thrust of the repression campaigns beginning in 1937 was directed at party, administrative and industrial elites, who, in statistical terms at least, constituted a fraction of all victims arrested during Ezhov's rule.

It is no accident that the contributors to this collection, with two exceptions, are outside the Anglo-American community of scholars writing on Stalinism. The strong Russian presence is largely due to the fact that foreigners, in general, are refused access to sensitive archival materials, especially those of the leading party bodies and NKVD. The second group of contributors, including the Irishman Barry McLoughlin who lives in Vienna, comprises historians who profited from the serendipities of liberal access to Russian archives in the early 1990s. Even after archival rules were tightened from 1994, the German speakers represented in the following pages were able to complete their remit: to reconstruct the lives and fates of exiles in pre-war Russia.[7] Starting their researches in the voluminous NKVD and Comintern documents *ad personam*, our contributors from Central Europe focused initially on the repressed, an orientation based on cooperation with victims' families and the willingness of the latter to issue letters-of-attorney in order to allow third parties to view and copy hitherto top-secret materials held in FSB and other State archives. Hence, "victim studies" of the Ezhovshchina years informed public and scholarly debate on the Stalinist system in the German-speaking lands, which, to a varying degree, had experienced both Communist and National Socialist forms of dictatorship. Moreover, and of greater import in our context, groups and political parties in such countries had strong historical or ideological ties to the USSR, whither many of their citizens had emigrated in the inter-war years. Studies on Stalinism in the German language are therefore influenced by national debate and knowledge of personal loss and betrayal ("the revolution devouring its children").

By contrast, in the polities of the Anglo-Saxon sphere, stable democracies without the moral mortgage of Communist or Nazi oppression, a "national" perspective on Stalinist terror was perforce absent. Unlike Central Europeans, relatively few Britons or Americans emigrated to

Soviet Russia and fewer still fell prey to the meat-grinder of state repression. Soviet experts writing in English tended towards a "history from above" methodology, which placed greater weight on high level decision-making than the grassroots experience of terror. More recently, the main thrust of Anglo-American scholarship on Stalinist state violence has been on the social processes and repressive policies in place *before* the mass operations were unleashed in the summer of 1937.[8]

Our volume attempts to bring these national strands of research together in a study highlighting a relatively short period of Soviet history. The emphasis is on ideologically motivated repression and how it was implemented at different levels of the social hierarchy. Special attention is given to victims who left no memoirs, the great mass of native-born or foreign "ordinary folk" who perished in Stalin's empire on the eve of the Second World War.

The origins, processes and outcomes of Stalinist terror have preoccupied scholars for many decades. Not surprisingly, there is no consensus. Historians disagree on Stalin's personal role in the carnage, his motivations, the influence of other key actors and institutions, the intended targets of state violence, the number of victims, and the short- and longer-term impact of mass repression on Soviet society. In the 1980s and into the 1990s adherents of the rival "totalitarian" and "revisionist" schools slugged their way through a cantankerous, and ultimately sterile debate, the former stressing the terroristic essence of the Stalinist state and Stalin's controlling hand, and the latter concentrating on the chaotic and dysfunctional elements of the Stalinist system and its manifold interactions with Soviet society.[9] Neither of these two paradigms was "right" or "wrong": both elucidated fundamental "truths" about Stalinism. The "totalitarians" correctly identified the monist urge of the Bolsheviks to gain mastery over social processes and human destinies. The "revisionists" accurately concluded that intention "from above" was often foiled by unforeseen reaction "from below", which in turn demanded ever more draconian "solutions" from the leadership.[10]

In the last few years the cutting edge of research has moved the goalposts still further. No longer motivated by essentially politico-historical perspectives, many contemporary scholars, some influenced by post-structuralist and post-modernist theories, focus on socio-cultural and ideological themes, including gender, consumption, popular culture and opinion, and the construction of social and national identities.[11] These methodologies have enriched our knowledge of the diverse means of Stalinist social integration and shifted attention away from purely coercive and disciplinarian impulses.

A significant drive behind these new approaches has been the partial opening of Russian archives and the publication of an impressive array of primary sources since the collapse of communism. The chapters presented in this collection benefit greatly from these developments, although the authors' methodological starting-point is that of political, not the "new" cultural, history.[12] How does this volume of essays by leading Russian, German, Austrian, American and Irish experts contribute to our understanding of the mechanisms and dynamics of Stalinist mass repression in the 1930s? Firstly, it must be noted that the authors approach the terror phenomenon from different positions. While many emphasise the signal role played by the central party and secret police leaders in organising and overseeing the mass repressions of 1937–8, others speculate on the input of local and regional NKVD bosses and touch on the sensitive topic of popular participation in the maelstrom of events. However, the weight of argument is on the former – "high politics", the interventions of the "centre" and the primacy of Stalin. The dominant interpretation is that the Great Terror was carefully planned, coordinated and executed by the Stalinist political and secret police leaderships as a programme of extermination of clearly defined targets, the whole process being closely overseen by Stalin himself. This conclusion conflicts fundamentally with the view that mass repression emerged unevenly and in an essentially *ad hoc* fashion as a response to intense inner-Party conflicts, centre–periphery tensions and real fears on the part of the Stalinist elite, culminating in a largely arbitrary and blind lashing out against an array of ill-defined "enemies".[13]

Published and unpublished archival sources lend credence to the "intentionalist" perspective. We know that Stalin anathematised "slothful" party-state bureaucrats for their inefficiency and insubordination. In a letter to Lazar Kaganovich, dated 21 August 1934, Stalin berated the People's Commissariat of Foreign Affairs (Narkomindel or NKID) for its conciliatory attitude to Japanese anti-Soviet accusations: "We need to flog the NKID for its somnolence, blindness and myopia. But instead we lag behind the yawners from NKID... . You can't yawn and sleep when you're in power."[14] His repeated demands in the late 1920s and early 1930s for the verification of these "Menshevik" officials had, by 1936–7, taken on far more ominous connotations. Organisational incompetence was now tantamount to disloyalty to the party leadership and a perceived threat to Stalin's personal position. "Self-admiring and smug" bureaucrats were "enemies of the people" to be arrested *en masse*. It could be speculated that Stalin's vengeance was exacerbated by an awareness that he was dependent on the bureaucracy to implement state policy. Here was a despot whose power had grown inordinately, but one who was still reliant on seemingly idle, recalcitrant and cliquish strata of functionaries, whose inclination was to follow the path of least resistance. Stalin must have regarded this dependency as an insufferable curb on his personal power. If so, his decimation of the party-state organs and managerial elites has its origins not so much in psychological phenomena – relevant though these certainly are – but in the ineluctable dilemmas of twentieth-century dictators whose grandiose plans for state-building are modified and impeded by a cowed, but resilient and self-protecting bureaucracy.

Aside from new information on Stalin and central policy-making, four other key themes are addressed: the "national" operations of the secret police directed against specific foreign and ethnic contingents; the "social cleansing" of "alien elements" and "class enemies"; the nature of repression at the micro-level, including the role and fate of individual perpetrators and victims; and the complicity of strictly speaking non-Soviet institutions, such as the Comintern and its various front organisations. The volume thus establishes beyond all reasonable doubt that Stalinist terror should no longer be interpreted as a unitary phenomenon, possessing a singular overriding aim. Rather, it was a multi-faceted process, composed of separate but related political, social and ethnic dimensions, the origins and goals of which were differentiated, but which coalesced in the horrific mass repressions of 1937–8.[15] Another important conclusion of the book relates to the targets of repression. McLoughlin argues that, contrary to received notions, the communist elites were not the main victims. In numerical terms, the majority of those arrested and executed were "ordinary" proletarians and peasants. He is not alone in this thesis. Hiroaki Kuromiya in his study of the terror in the Donbas maintains that "the untold numbers of files on repressed workers, peasants, and other 'ordinary' people in the former KGB archives" are evidence that "the bulk of the terror victims were these *narod*".[16]

While the printed and archival sources now permit scholars to delineate more precisely the temporal breakdown of the Great Terror and to identify its victims in an individual and collective sense, the reasons for, rather than the occasion of, the murderous initiatives of 1937–8 are subject to interpretation and controversy. A framework for future discussions can be borrowed from studies of Nazi exterminatory policies: was the Holocaust "intentional" or "functional"? That is, did the National Socialists intend, from the very outset, to physically eliminate the Jews or was such a "final solution" thrust upon them by the exigencies of war following the invasion of the USSR in June 1941?[17] Viewing the Soviet terror of 1937–8 in this model would, as in the German case, not produce unanimity but differentiated arguments indicating that both elements of motivation were applicable: the "intended" victims were the "traditional suspects" (peasants, clergy, political opponents from 1917–21, supporters of the Old Regime); the "functional" ones, on the other hand, were invented in the specific context of developments in late 1936 and early 1937 and consisted of replaceable elite cadres and alien nationals (denoted by ascribed nationality or passport). War or its expected imminence, therefore, radicalised repressive policy in both dictatorships.

The work raises further perplexing questions: firstly, should the Ezhovshchina be located within established policies of Soviet repression dating from the Civil War through forced collectivisation and "dekulakisation", or should it better be seen as a radical departure from Bolshevik norms of "revolutionary legality"?; secondly, were Stalinist methods of social control intrinsic to Soviet "totalitarianism" (or indeed by extension Russian autocracy), or are they comparable to broader, pan-European "modernising" trends of increasing state intervention, surveillance of citizens, and even "ethnic cleansing"?; finally, should we take for granted the negative *de*structive elements of "terror" (an appellation never used in Stalinist Russia), while ignoring the official Soviet perception of social and political "cleansing" as a necessary *con*structive stage in the building of a new socialist state and society, which may have gained fairly widespread popular support.[18] Should we attach any credence at all to this Stalinist rhetoric, or should it continue to be dismissed as crass justification of indefensible and morally corrupt state violence?

This anthology offers no definitive answers to these intractable historical dilemmas, and nor should it. They will long remain highly contentious battlegrounds among historians and no amount of archival revelations will satisfactorily resolve the disputes. Nevertheless, several authors imply that the Great Terror was inextricably linked to Stalinist policies from 1928–9 onwards. The intense social flux and dislocation, the rising crime levels, the peasant resistance to collectivisation, the urban tensions attendant on rapid industrialisation, the limited success of the initiatives on the "nationality question", and the contradictory pressures on the bureaucracies and other elites, which engendered insubordination, deceit and local and regional self-defence cliques and networks, all these "outcomes" of the Stalinist "revolution from above" created conditions that were propitious for the hunt for "enemies". Add in Stalin's personal motivations and paranoia, the in-built need for scapegoats to "explain" the dire state of Soviet material consumption, and the threatening international context of the mid-to-late 1930s and the origins of mass repression become more explicable.

*

The present volume is divided into three parts: the politics of repression, the police and mass repression, and victim studies. The first part, consisting of chapters by Oleg Khlevniuk, Wladislaw Hedeler and Fridrikh Firsov, focuses on the directing hand of the central authorities in the terror process. These papers reconfirm, on the basis of a wealth of recently declassified archival material, one of the pivotal premises of the totalitarian model, that Stalin, supported by Ezhov and prominent Politburo members, carefully planned the assault on leading Party, state and Comintern officials as well as former oppositionists. Khlevniuk argues convincingly that in 1936–8 the traditional relationship between the Communist Party and the secret police was disrupted, the latter gaining a temporary supremacy over the former. Stalin is portrayed as a conscious manipulator and shaper of these developments, skilfully shifting between policy extremes in an attempt to play off the party and NKVD one against the other. Khlevniuk's is essentially an "intentionalist" interpretation, from which it is but a short step to suggest that Stalin carried out a well-planned coup against the party, the main aim of which was to remove whole layers of "double-faced" officials and perceived "fifth columnists", and install a new generation of cadres totally loyal to the "boss".[19]

In similar vein, Hedeler's contribution focuses on Ezhov's pernicious role in the organisation of the terror, in particular the preparation of the Show Trials. Ezhov is depicted as a long-time supporter of Stalinist coercive measures and a fanatical believer in the existence of conspiratorial anti-Soviet "plots", "sabotage" and "wrecking". His response was invariably to purge the culprits.[20] Hedeler claims that Ezhov's text "From Fractionalism to Open Counter-Revolution and Fascism" (1935–7) provided key material for the selection of defendants in the three Show Trials and for the final indictments against them. At the same time, Hedeler shows that Stalin's was the dominant hand, editing and adding to Ezhov's tract, orchestrating propaganda campaigns in the press, and emphasising specific points in the prosecution case in the Bukharin–Rykov trial.

Another prominent Stalinist who played a significant, though subsidiary, role in the purges, was Georgi Dimitrov, the Bulgarian General Secretary of the Comintern. The Comintern and its various affiliates were formally internationalist bodies, independent of the Soviet government. In reality, the Executive Committee of the Communist International (ECCI), based in Moscow since its creation in 1919, came under ever-increasing Bolshevik hegemony and the international communist movement after 1928 experienced a fierce "Stalinisation" process that more or less wiped out all vestiges of autonomy and critical thinking.[21] As such, the Comintern and those foreign cadres who were employed in its vast apparatus could not escape the worst excesses of the Stalinist terror. Firsov's essay shows conclusively that the Comintern was both a helpless victim and a major accomplice in the mass repression of Soviet and foreign communists in 1937–8. Numerous ECCI officials were arrested, whole departments destroyed. Basing his study primarily on Dimitrov's diaries, Firsov concludes that the "leading organs of the Comintern strictly followed Stalin's orders", dutifully supporting the official Soviet "line" on the three Show Trials, excoriating world-wide "Trotskyism", and demanding that all communist parties trumpet the same tune.

But the Comintern leadership did more than simply act as apologist for Stalin's murderous campaigns. Dimitrov, Dmitrii Manuilskii and other luminaries instigated so-called "cadre reviews" of exiled foreign communists to seek out "enemies" and they kept the NKVD informed of their findings. The ECCI Cadres Department provided compromising biographical material to "the neighbours" (secret police) on countless political immigrants, including leading figures in foreign communist parties, who were then invariably arrested. Although Dimitrov and several other Comintern bosses occasionally appealed on behalf of detained comrades, and possibly harboured private doubts about the scale of the carnage, their efforts were usually in vain.[22]

The second part of the book elucidates the origins and mechanisms of NKVD mass repression. David Shearer's important contribution examines the inter-relationship between, on the one hand, social disorder and evolving NKVD strategies to contain it in the early to mid 1930s, and, on the other, the onset of mass arrests in 1937. By shifting our attention from the overtly political and "national" to the equally significant social origins of the terror, Shearer has performed a highly valuable service. He demonstrates that the threat of social instability posed by criminal recidivists, hooligans, other "socially harmful elements", and even armed bandit gangs, was taken extremely seriously by NKVD chiefs. By

1937 the lethal triumvirate of "social disorder, political opposition, and national contamination" had raised fears among the increasingly xenophobic political and police elites of a broadly based anti-Soviet "fifth column", linked to foreign agents and spies. In response "the police launched the massive purge of Soviet society in 1937 and 1938 in order to destroy what Stalinist leaders believed was the social base for armed overthrow of the Soviet government." To this extent, mass repression under Stalin was not solely a means of combating the state's enemies; it became a "constitutive part of Soviet social policy."

Barry McLoughlin's essay discusses in some detail the "mass operations" carried out by the secret police in 1937–8, both at the Moscow and provincial level. He argues convincingly that the mass arrests were a crusade against simple citizens, not an assault on the Soviet elite. This comparative approach not only broadens our geographical knowledge of the Great Purges, but also illuminates the vexed question of the relative weight of central and regional inputs in the terror process: to what extent did the scope of the arrests depend on local NKVD initiative?; how much latitude did subordinate *chekisty* have in interpreting central orders and in arbitrarily expanding target numbers?; how far were the selection of victims, the form of indictments and the use of coercive interrogation methods the products of over-zealous secret police officers?; and why were some NKVD headquarters more inclined than others to under- or over-fulfil their quotas? Answers to these questions probably depend on the nature of the archives consulted by scholars. Central party documents in Moscow may well suggest the determining hand of a smoothly functioning leadership, whereas regional evidence may reveal a picture of disorganisation, confusion and *ad hoc* responses and over-responses as local officials scurried to fulfil the flood of central directives. McLoughlin concludes his paper with a persuasive overall assessment of the origins and nature of the terror, stressing its multi-faceted essence, the proximate and longer-term internal and external factors that influenced its architects, and the existence of inter-related, but ultimately distinct, forms of purging: "elite" and "mass" repression.

In their study, Nikita Petrov and Arsenii Roginskii focus on NKVD Order No. 00485, ratified by the Politburo on 9 August 1937, which in essence depicted all ethnic Poles living on the territory of the USSR as "spies", "saboteurs" and "wreckers". By late 1938 almost 140,000 had been sentenced under the terms of the "Polish order", over 111,000 of whom were shot. Such was the pressure of numbers that new methods had to be initiated by the NKVD to expedite the sentencing process – the so-called "album" procedure. Terse information sheets (*spravki*) were drawn up by local secret police officers outlining the investigation and charges. These sheets were collated and then lists of accused were typed up every ten days and presented for sentence to a local NKVD dignitary and public prosecutor, the *dvoika*. Their decision was either death or five to ten years in the Gulag. The lists, bound into albums, were in turn sent to Moscow to be formally sanctioned by Ezhov, Vyshinskii or their deputies. But, according to Petrov and Roginskii, these worthies never "cast a glance" into the contents of the albums, preferring to delegate the task to subordinates in the central NKVD *apparat*. Only after these officials had "mechanically approved the draft" did Ezhov and Vyshinskii sign the documents, which were then returned to the regional NKVD offices for sentencing to be carried out. These simplified procedures characteristic of the "Polish operation" became the norm for all other "national sweeps" undertaken by the Soviet secret police between autumn 1937 and summer 1938.

Petrov and Roginskii's paper acts as a bridge between the second and final part of the book, which is devoted to the fate of the numerous victims of Stalinist terror, many of whom were foreign nationals. Berthold Unfried addresses the important and controversial theme of Stalinist mechanisms of "thought-control" over foreign communist cadres. He focuses on the "intrinsic components of Soviet political liturgy", the practices of "criticism" and "self-criticism". Unfried shows how Soviet attempts to mould ideologically pure Stalinists out of European clay met with a deal of incomprehension and resistance from many émigré communists, in particular those from the English-speaking democracies. The ritualised self-accusatory repentance sessions organised at grassroots level during the *chistki* (party purges) of the mid-to-late 1930s were deemed to violate "Western notions of individuality and ignore boundaries between what were private and public domains". Indeed, before the onset of the Great Terror the most common accusations against foreigners were linked to "petit-bourgeois" behaviour in the home: wife-beating and promiscuity, for example. Thereafter, political "deviancy" and "contacts with abroad", a euphemism for spying, became the usual source of "self-criticism". Unfried concludes that, regardless of the resistance evinced by many European communists, the Stalinist urge to reconstruct the political identity of foreign cadres did prove "successful" and permanent to the extent that loyal party members were coerced, by their uniformed torturers, to take on the persona of "agents", "saboteurs" or "Trotskyites".

The paper by Aleksandr Vatlin and Natalia Musienko provides fascinating details on the micro-level functioning of terror in Stalinist

Russia. The authors concentrate on the Moscow rural district of Kuntsevo. We are told that NKVD units often lacked sufficient staff and facilities for mass arrests, and that inordinate pressure was placed on local secret police commanders to fulfil central directives. Refusal meant certain arrest. Transcripts of interrogations carried out by the NKVD in Kuntsevo in March 1938 reveal the absurdity of the charges brought against innocent citizens, such as strewing weeds over a *kolkhoz* field, and illuminate the mechanisms by which individual cases were amalgamated, for example, into entire "Trotskyite conspiracies". Beatings and other forms of physical and psychological torture were common practice. Vatlin and Musienko's evidence also corroborates the idea, frequently found in western historiography, that one of the main impulses behind the terror was "scapegoating". The horrendous economic and social consequences of the regime's policies had to be shifted onto the shoulders of "wreckers", "saboteurs" and "double-dealers". This "scapegoat logic" filtered down from the leadership to all levels of the hierarchy, republican, regional and district.

As noted above, whole national contingents were identified by the NKVD for victimisation. Among the worse effected were Central and East Europeans, most often loyal communists who had sought refuge from fascist (or neo-fascist) oppression by emigrating to the "socialist fatherland", the USSR. But by mid-1937 the Soviet sanctuary had turned into a prison house, even an execution chamber. Countless thousands of Poles, Germans, Balts, Finns, Romanians, Yugoslavs, Bulgarians, Italians, Hungarians, Austrians and others found themselves trapped in the meat-grinder. How can the arbitrary arrest of hundreds of thousands of foreign residents in the USSR be explained? Perhaps there is no "explanation" outside of Stalin's pathological xenophobic attitudes, which, as Hans Schafranek and Natalia Musienko in their paper on the fictitious "Hitler-Jugend conspiracy" imply, were widely replicated among NKVD officers for whom "all persons of 'German blood' were *ipso facto* potential spies and fifth-columnists." This psycho-historical reasoning will not satisfy all scholars, but Petrov and Roginskii are in no doubt that ultimate guilt lies with the Gensek. As war loomed, Stalin's perverted logic transformed "class brothers" exiled from the countries bordering the Soviet Union into "agents" of hostile states and intelligence services. They represented a "fifth column" engaged in an undeclared state of war against Soviet power and communism, and as such had to be eliminated. The Poles were especially badly hit for several reasons. Poland was believed to be the Soviet Union's most dangerous neighbour, there were more Polish refugees than any other single nationality, and hence Polish Intelligence had a "natural" pool of recruits within the USSR to draw on. It might also be speculated that Stalin's antipathy towards the Poles was exacerbated by his controversial military failures during the Russo-Polish War of 1920. The experience of foreigners in the USSR in the 1930s raises the significant issue of the relationship between pre-existing social attitudes among Soviet workers and the terror process. Those foreign labourers and political émigrés who sought refuge in the Soviet Union did not always receive a comradely welcome. During the First Five-Year Plan many Soviet workers, and indeed party officials, came to perceive foreigners as arrogant, privileged and overpaid aliens, who disrupted established patterns of labour and productivity. Sergei Zhuravlev describes such sentiments in his micro-study of foreign operatives in the Elektrozavod plant in Moscow. How far, then, did these tensions between Soviet and immigrant workers help to rationalise the subsequent victimisation of the latter? To what extent did the state-sponsored anti-foreigner campaigns of 1937–8 find a willing audience in the shape of popular xenophobia? Was the Stalinist propaganda of ubiquitous spies and agents readily comprehensible to a population pre-disposed to a kind of siege mentality? The point is not to absolve Stalin and his cronies by suggesting the "national" operations of the NKVD were somehow fuelled by popular chauvinist sentiment. Indeed, as Zhuravlev concludes, foreign workers "were repressed solely on 'national' criteria, victims of a prophylactic policy of mass repression in a pre-war emergency." Nevertheless, by placing the terror in its social and cultural, as well as its political, context researchers may be able to achieve a more holistic understanding of this most complex of phenomena.

*

Where does the evidence presented in this volume leave us in our understanding of the Stalinist terror and what avenues of research should be followed in the future? As we have seen, many of the authors powerfully reaffirm the "primacy of Stalin" in the mass repressions of the late 1930s. As Robert Tucker wrote several years ago, he was the Great Terror's "director general".[23] But this observation does not imply that "centre–periphery" tensions and regional variations should be overlooked. Clearly, even as "omnipotent" a tyrant as Stalin could not inspire or control everything that occurred in his vast domain. Indeed, much recent research has attempted to shift attention from the decision-making processes in Moscow to the implementation of those decisions in the provinces, demonstrating unintentional, and sometimes contradictory, outcomes.[24] Should we also take ideological concerns more seriously than hitherto? To what extent was the mass purging motivated not only by Stalin's desire to strengthen his power base, but also to "revolutionise" and transform Soviet society by crushing once and for all counter-revolutionary "socially harmful elements" and "class enemies" (*kulaks*, priests, recidivist criminals)? Likewise, was the attack on the sprawling bureaucracies an attempt to smash the "bourgeois" and "Menshevik" lethargy of party-state functionaries?[25]

We need to know far more about how the terror was received by different sections of Soviet society. Did "ordinary" citizens perceive the mass arrests of communists as an essentially positive phenomenon: the despised "them" devouring each other? How far did the language and images of "enemies", "wreckers" and "spies" reflect a society, still largely rural, in which traditional notions of evil spirits and nefarious demons were deep-rooted?[26] From a longer-term perspective, what was the psychological and demographic impact of mass repression on Soviet wartime performance and popular attitudes? One prominent "revisionist" has asserted that the morale of the Red Army, and of the Soviet people in general, during the Great Patriotic War was not unduly undermined by the terror of the late thirties, though this hypothesis requires closer inspection.[27] Neither should scholars ignore the web of interconnections between foreign and domestic policy in the 1930s. To what extent did reverses in the European and Asian arenas, in particular the lessons of the Spanish Civil War, induce an atmosphere of panic in the Kremlin and incite the Stalinists to seek "enemies" at home and abroad?[28] Finally, much more clarity is needed on the winding down of the Terror in the course of 1938. Why did Stalin and Molotov decide to rein in Ezhov and the NKVD and limit mass arrests? The evidence presented in this volume suggests that the Stalinist leaders had become aware of the dysfunctional aspects of repression and sought to restore a modicum of "normality" to party and economic life. These are just a few of the themes that will engage scholars in the immediate future. Two things are for sure – the "great debate" on Stalin, Stalinism and the terror will continue for a long time to come and we should expect no definitive answers regardless of archival "revelations".

Notes

1 E. A. Zaitsev (ed.), *Sbornik zakonodatel'nykh i normativnykh aktov o repressiiakh i reabilitatsii zhertv politicheskikh repressii* (Moscow, 1993), pp. 186–7. This

volume is an indispensable collection of laws and directives about state repression and the rehabilitation of its victims.
2 For details of Moscow's "killing fields", see *Memorial-Aspekt* (Moscow), vol. 1, no. 3 (1993), p. 4; *Trud*, 9 July 1993; *Stolitsa* (Moscow), no. 47 (1992), pp. 16–17; *30 Oktiabria* (Memorial, Moscow), no. 3 (2000), p. 7.
3 For the text of the Rehabilitation Law, see Zaitsev (ed.), *Sbornik*, pp. 194–204.
4 The resolution of the Supreme Soviet of 30 March 1992 is reproduced in Iu. V. Olovianov (ed.), *Ne predat zabveniiu*. *Kniga pamiati repressirovannykh v 30-40-e i nachale 50-kh godov, sviazannykh sud'bami s iarovslavskoi oblast'iu* (Iaroslavl', 1993), pp. 420–2.
5 For details of the structure of *sledstvennye dela*, see B. McLoughlin, 'Documenting the Death Toll: Research into the Mass Murder of Foreigners in Moscow, 1937–1938', *Perspectives* (American Historical Association Newsletter), vol. 37 (1999), pp. 29–33.
6 A seminal collection of archival documents relating to the terror can be found in J. Arch Getty and O. V. Naumov, *The Road to Terror: Stalin and the Self-Destruction of the Bolsheviks, 1932–1939* (New Haven and London, 1999). For an insightful review of this volume, see E. A. Rees, 'The Great Terror: Suicide or Mass Murder?', *Russian Review*, vol. 59 (2000), pp. 446–50; O. W. Chlewnjuk, *Das Politburo. Mechanismen der Macht in der Sowjetunion der dreißiger Jahre* (Hamburg, 1998). The volume is more comprehensive than the original Russian text: *Politbiuro. Mekhanizmy politicheskoi vlasti v 1930-e gody* (Moscow, 1996); R. G. Pikhoia, A. I. Kokurin and N. V. Petrov, *Lubianka. VChK-OGPU-NKVD-NKGB-MVD-KGB 1917–1960. Spravochnik* (Moscow, 1997); A. Kokurin and N. Petrov, 'NKVD: struktura, funktsii, kadry (1934–43)', *Svobodnaia mysl'* (June, July, August 1997); N. V. Petrov and K. V. Skorkin, *Kto rukovodil NKVD 1934–1941. Spravochnik* (Moscow, 1999); A. V. Kvashonkin, L. P. Kosheleva, L. A. Rogovaia and O. V. Khlevniuk (eds), *Sovetskoe rukovodstvo: perepiska 1928–1941* (Moscow, 1999); L. S. Eremina (ed.), *Repressii protiv poliakov i pol'skikh grazhdan* (Moscow, 1997); I. L. Shcherbakova (ed.), *Nakazannyi narod. Repressii protiv rossiiskikh nemtsev* (Moscow, 1999); O. F. Suverinov, *Tragediia RKKA 1937–1938* (Moscow, 1998); Iu. Stetsovskii, *Istoriia sovetskikh repressii*, 2 vols (Moscow, 1997).
7 The following list of works by European scholars, based on primary Russian sources, is not exhaustive: R. Müller (ed.), *Die Säuberung. Moskau 1936: Stenogramm einer geschlossenen Parteiversammlung* (Reinbek bei Hamburg, 1991); R. Müller, *Die Akte Wehner. Moskau 1937 bis 1941* (Berlin, 1993); R. Müller, *Menschenfalle Moskau. Exil und Stalinistische Verfolgung* (Hamburg, 2001); H. Weber, *'Weiße Flecken' in der Geschichte. Die KPD-Opfer der Stalinschen Säuberungen und ihre Rehabilitierung* (Frankfurt-am-Main, 1990); W. Neugebauer (ed.), *Von der Utopie zum Terror* (Vienna, 1994); P. Huber, *Stalins Schatten in die Schweiz. Schweizer Kommunisten in Moskau: Verteidiger und Gefangene der Komintern* (Zurich, 1994); H. Schafranek, *Zwischen NKWD und Gestapo. Die Auslieferung deutscher und österreichischer Antifaschisten aus der Sowjetunion an Nazideutschland 1937–1941* (Frankfurt-am-Main, 1990); H. Schafranek (with N. Mussijenko), *Kinderheim Nr 6. Österreichische und deutsche Kinder im sowjetischen Exil* (Vienna, 1998); C. Tischler, *Flucht in die Verfolgung. Deutsche Emigranten im sowjetischen Exil 1933 bis 1945* (Münster, 1996); H. Weber and U. Mählert (eds), *Terror. Stalinistische Parteisäuberungen*

16 Stalin's Terror

    1936–1953 (Paderborn, 1998); H. Weber and D. Staritz (eds), *Kommunisten verfolgen Kommunisten. Stalinistischer Terror und 'Säuberungen' in den kommunistischen Parteien Europas seit den dreißiger Jahren* (Berlin, 1993); B. McLoughlin, H. Schafranek and W. Szevera, *Hoffnung-Aufbruch-Endstation. Österreicherinnen und Österreicher in der Sowjetunion 1925–1945* (Vienna, 1997); DÖW (Dokumentationsarchiv des Österreichischen Widerstandes), *Österreicher im Exil – Sowjetunion 1934–1945. Eine Dokumentation. Einleitung, Auswahl und Bearbeitung: Barry McLoughlin und Hans Schafranek* (Vienna, 1999); A. Natoli and S. Pons (eds), *L'età dello stalinismo* (Rome, 1991); R. Caccavale, *La speranza Stalin. Tragedia dell' Antifascismo italiano nell'URSS* (Rome, 1989).

8 For recent Anglo-American analyses, see footnote 15 below.

9 The fierce polemics engendered by the totalitarian-revisionist controversy can be found in S. Fitzpatrick, 'New Perspectives on Stalinism', *Russian Review*, vol. 45 (1986), pp. 357–73, the discussions that followed at pp. 375–413, and in *Russian Review*, vol. 46 (1987), pp. 375–431. The debate has latterly been enjoined by Russian historians. See I. V. Pavlova, 'Sovremennye zapadnye istoriki o stalinskoi rossii 30-x godov. (Kritika "revizionistskogo" podkhoda)', *Otechestvennaia istoriia*, no. 5 (1998), pp. 107–21.

10 The classical work on Stalinist terror from the totalitarian perspective is R. Conquest, *The Great Terror: Stalin's Purges of the Thirties* (Harmondsworth, 1971), up-dated as *The Great Terror: A Reassessment* (London, 1990). Other important works that stress Stalin's dominant role in the Terror are R. A. Medvedev, *Let History Judge: The Origins and Consequences of Stalinism*, 2nd ed. (Oxford, 1989) and R. C. Tucker, *Stalin in Power: The Revolution from Above, 1928–1941* (New York, 1990). The prime examples of 'revisionist' work are J. Arch Getty, *Origins of the Great Purges: The Soviet Communist Party Reconsidered, 1933–1938* (Cambridge, 1985); G. T. Rittersporn, *Stalinist Simplifications and Soviet Complications: Social Tensions and Political Conflicts in the USSR, 1933–1953* (Chur, 1991); J. Arch Getty and R. T. Manning (eds), *Stalinist Terror: New Perspectives* (Cambridge, 1993); and R. W. Thurston, *Life and Terror in Stalin's Russia, 1934–1941* (New Haven and London, 1996).

11 The pioneering study of this socio-cultural approach to Stalinism was V. S. Dunham, *In Stalin's Time: Middleclass Values in Soviet Fiction* (Cambridge, 1976). The most influential recent works in this genre include S. Fitzpatrick, *The Cultural Front: Power and Culture in Revolutionary Russia* (Ithaca, 1992); L. H. Siegelbaum and R. G. Suny (eds), *Making Workers Soviet: Power, Class and Identity* (Ithaca, 1994); S. Kotkin, *Magnetic Mountain: Stalinism as a Civilization* (Berkeley, 1995); S. Davies, *Popular Opinion in Stalin's Russia: Terror, Propaganda and Dissent, 1934–1941* (Cambridge, 1997); C. Kelly and D. Shepherd (eds), *Constructing Russian Culture in the Age of Revolution: 1881–1940* (Oxford, 1998); T. Martin, 'The Origins of Soviet Ethnic Cleansing', *Journal of Modern History*, vol. 70 (1998), pp. 813–61; and E. Osokina, *Our Daily Bread: Socialist Distribution and the Art of Survival in Stalin's Russia, 1927–1941* (Armonk, 2001). A compilation of path-breaking work on Stalinism can be found in S. Fitzpatrick (ed.), *Stalinism: New Directions* (London, 2000). See also S. Fitzpatrick, *Everyday Stalinism: Ordinary Life in Extraordinary Times: Soviet Russia in the 1930s* (Oxford, 1999).

12 Access to Russian archives improved considerably after 1991, although an unwelcome measure of retrenchment had taken hold by the mid-1990s.

The two most important "open" archives for the study of Stalinist terror are the Russian State Archive of Socio-Political History (RGASPI – the former Central Party Archive) and the State Archive of the Russian Federation (GARF). Key documents relating to the terror are housed, it must be assumed, in the Presidential Archive of the Russian Federation (APRF) and in the archives of the former KGB (TsAFSBRF), both of which are essentially inaccessible to scholars. For a relatively recent study of the situation in Russian archives, see P. Grimsted, *Archives of Russia Five Years After: "Purveyors of Sensations" or "Shadows Cast to the Past"?*, International Institute of Social History Research Paper, No. 26 (Amsterdam, 1997).

13 This view is most eloquently expressed by J. Arch Getty, '"Excesses are not permitted": Mass Terror and Stalinist Governance in the Late 1930s', *Russian Review*, vol. 61 (2002), pp. 113–38, and J. Arch Getty, 'Afraid of Their Shadows: The Bolshevik Recourse to Terror, 1932–1938', in M. Hildermeier and E. Müller-Luckner (eds), *Stalinismus vor dem Zweiten Weltkrieg: Neue Wege der Forschung* (Munich, 1998), pp. 169–91.

14 RGASPI, fond 81, opis' 3, delo 100, list 158. Verbal assaults on party-state officials proliferate in Stalin's letters to Kaganovich. See for instance f. 81, op. 3, d. 99, ll. 16, 35, and 42–3. Evidence of Stalin's vindictive anti-bureaucratic proclivities can also be found in L. T. Lih, O. V. Naumov and O. V. Khlevniuk (eds), *Stalin's Letters to Molotov, 1925–1936* (New Haven and London, 1995).

15 This conclusion is consistent with much recent research. See D. R. Shearer, 'Crime and Social Disorder in Stalin's Russia: A Reassessment of the Great Retreat and the Origins of Mass Repression', *Cahiers du Monde russe*, vol. 39 (1998), pp. 119–48; S. Davies, 'The Crime of "Anti-Soviet Agitation" in the Soviet Union in the 1930s', *Cahiers du Monde russe*, vol. 39 (1998), pp. 149–68; Martin, 'The Origins of Soviet Ethnic Cleansing'; and P. Hagenloh, '"Socially Harmful Elements" and the Great Terror', in Fitzpatrick (ed.), *Stalinism*, pp. 286–308.

16 H. Kuromiya, 'Workers under Stalin: The Case of the Donbas', in Hildermeier and Müller-Luckner (eds), *Stalinismus vor dem Zweiten Weltkrieg*, p. 94.

17 See the contributions in I. Kershaw and M. Lewin (eds), *Stalinism and Nazism: Dictatorships in Comparison* (Cambridge, 1997), especially O. Bartov, 'From Blitzkrieg to total war: controversial links between image and reality', pp. 158–84, and M. von Hagen, 'Stalinism and the politics of post-Soviet history', pp. 285–310; see also C. S. Maier, *The Unmasterable Past: History, Holocaust, and German National Identity* (Cambridge, Mass, 1988), pp. 71–84.

18 This observation is derived from D. Shearer, 'From Divided Consensus to Creative Disorder: Soviet History in Britain and North America', *Cahiers du Monde russe*, vol. 39 (1998), p. 583.

19 See also O. V. Khlevniuk, 'The Objectives of the Great Terror, 1937–1938', in J. Cooper, M. Perrie and E. A. Rees (eds), *Soviet History, 1917–1953: Essays in Honour of R. W. Davies* (Basingstoke, 1995) pp. 158–76.

20 For another interpretation of Ezhov's role, see B. A. Starkov, 'Narkom Ezhov', in Getty and Manning (eds), *Stalinist Terror*, pp. 21–39.

21 For a general text on the Communist International, see K. McDermott & J. Agnew, *The Comintern: A History of International Communism from Lenin to Stalin* (Basingstoke, 1996).

22 Documents and commentaries on the terror in the Comintern can be found in W. J. Chase, *Enemies within the Gates?: The Comintern and the Stalinist Repression, 1934–1939* (New Haven and London, 2001); see also M. Panteleev, 'Repressii v Kominterne (1937–1938 gg.)', *Otechestvennaia istoriia*, no. 6 (1996), pp. 161–8; on Dimitrov's and Manuilskii's role, see 'Riad sektsii Kominterna..okazalis' tselikom v rukakh vraga', *Istoricheskii arkhiv*, no. 1 (1993), pp. 220–1.
23 Tucker, *Stalin in Power*, p. 444.
24 For local and regional studies of the terror, see J. Arch Getty, 'Party and Purge in Smolensk, 1933–1937', *Slavic Review*, vol. 42 (1983), pp. 60–79; H. Kuromiya, 'Stalinist Terror in the Donbas: A Note', in Getty and Manning (eds), *Stalinist Terror*, pp. 215–22; R. T. Manning, 'The Great Purges in a Rural District: Belyi Raion Revisited', in Getty and Manning (eds), *Stalinist Terror*, pp. 168–97; F. Benvenuti, 'Industry and Purge in the Donbas, 1936–37', *Europe-Asia Studies*, vol. 45 (1993), pp. 57–78; S. Fitzpatrick, 'How the Mice Buried the Cat. Scenes from the Great Purges in the Russian Provinces', *Russian Review*, vol. 52 (1993), pp. 299–320; R. Weinberg, 'Purge and Politics in the Periphery: Birobidzhan in 1937', *Slavic Review*, vol. 52 (1993), pp. 13–27; Kotkin, *Magnetic Mountain*, pp. 280–354; K. Sanukov, 'Stalinist Terror in the Mari Republic: The Attack on "Finno-Ugrian Bourgeois Nationalism"', *Slavonic and East European Review*, vol. 74 (1996), pp. 658–82; D. Shearer, 'Policing the Soviet Frontier: Social Disorder and Repression in Western Siberia during the 1930s', unpublished paper, 1998; J. R. Harris, 'The Purging of Local Cliques in the Urals Region, 1936–7', in Fitzpatrick (ed.), *Stalinism*, pp. 262–85; M. Ilic, 'The Great Terror in Leningrad: A Quantitative Analysis', *Europe-Asia Studies*, vol. 52 (2000), pp. 1515–34; L. A. Rimmel, 'A Microcosm of Terror, or Class Warfare in Leningrad: The March 1935 Exile of "Alien Elements"', *Jahrbucher für Geschichte Osteuropas*, vol. 48 (2000), pp. 528–51; M. Ellman, 'The Soviet 1937 Provincial Show Trials: Carnival or Terror?', *Europe-Asia Studies*, vol. 53 (2001), pp. 1221–33. For remarkable insights into the conduct of one of Stalin's itinerant provincial purgers, see the telegram correspondence between A. A. Andreev, Secretary of the Central Committee, and the "boss" in RGASPI, f. 73, op. 2, d. 19, ll. 16, 22, 72 and 106; see also Kvashonkin et al. (eds), *Sovetskoe rukovodstvo*, pp. 364–7, 371–5, 377–80, 383–9 and 393–7.
25 For a recent general text which seeks to integrate ideas and political practice in the USSR, see M. Sandle, *A Short History of Soviet Socialism* (London, 1999).
26 See G. T. Rittersporn, 'The Omnipresent Conspiracy: On Soviet Imagery of Politics and Social Relations in the 1930s', in Getty and Manning (eds), *Stalinist Terror*, pp. 99–115; and S. Davies, '"Us" against "Them": Social Identity in Soviet Russia, 1934–41', in Fitzpatrick (ed.), *Stalinism*, pp. 47–70.
27 See Thurston, *Life and Terror in Stalin's Russia*, pp. 199–226.
28 For the impact of the Spanish Civil War and other international events on thinking in Moscow, see O. V. Khlevniuk, 'The Reasons for the "Great Terror": The Foreign-Political Aspect', in S. Pons and A. Romano (eds), *Russia in the Age of Wars, 1914–1945* (Milan, 2000), pp. 159–69.

Part I
The Politics of Repression

2
Party and NKVD: Power Relationships in the Years of the Great Terror

Oleg Khlevniuk

At the February–March 1937 Plenum of the Central Committee of the All-Union Communist Party (Bolsheviks) [VKP(b)], Ezhov declared that Stalin held the state security organs to be "the armed vanguard of our Party".[1] Stalin, sitting beside Ezhov in the presidium of the plenum, did not contradict his police chief. The open identification of the Communist Party with the punitive organs of the state reflected real tendencies in the development of the Stalinist system. This close relationship manifested itself in the practice of exchanging cadres and executing certain tasks together: Komsomol or VKP(b) members entered the ranks of the secret police and Chekists were given party posts, and both party officials and NKVD officers supervised the purging of VKP(b) cells. Ezhov's definition of the NKVD mirrors another stage in this cooperation that had special significance in the years 1937–8: a shift in the balance of power which placed the NKVD in a position of ascendancy over the party.

The manipulation of these links was one of the most important methods in building the Stalinist dictatorship. However, the history of the interaction between the Soviet party and state security organs is largely unwritten, save for one aspect: the portrayal of the party as "victim", the countless members it lost through the terror waged against alleged "oppositionists". This classical theme – the revolution devours its offspring – has given rise to various interpretations on how Stalin's "revolution from above" proceeded. Such a one-sided view of mass repression ignores many questions that need examination in their historical context. The links between the power structures of the VKP(b), including its Politburo, and the secret police OGPU-NKVD at the different geographical and administrative levels is a huge field of research. In the following pages we must confine ourselves to the question how this relationship functioned generally during the years of the Great Terror.

The evidence to date indicates that the secret police was subordinate to the party up to the mid-1930s. Until then Stalin seems to have considered the opinions of his colleagues in the party and state leadership and they still exercised considerable influence. Moreover, the OGPU-NKVD commissars Menzhinskii and Iagoda were absent from the centre of power, not being members of the Politburo. In other words, the secret police was under party supervision, with Stalin being responsible for such matters within the Politburo. From 1935 Ezhov, at the time secretary of the Central Committee and chairman of the party's Control Commission, was appointed to succeed Stalin in this role of overseer. A commission of the Politburo "for political matters" examined the lists of those sentenced to death by shooting and it also monitored the major show trials. Sometimes, the conflicts between the State Prosecutor's Office and the NKVD were arbitrated by party councils. It must also be emphasised that the leading bodies of the OGPU-NKVD were under Stalin's direct orders throughout the period. This was an important source of Stalin's power and it afforded NKVD leading personnel a privileged status towards high-ranking officials of other People's Commissariats (Ministries), allowing the former to ignore "proper channels" when carrying out the tasks assigned to them by the dictator.

Relations between party leaders and the heads of NKVD administrations and departments at local level were usually harmonious. To date no evidence has surfaced to document conflict scenarios between party officials and NKVD officers in the provinces before 1938. As is known, sharp clashes did often occur between party bodies on the one hand and the administration of MTS (machine tractor stations), local government officials and emissaries from the party's Control Commission on the other. In some places, especially after Kirov's murder, disputes flared up between judicial staff in the public courts or the prosecutor's office and the secret police.[2] Judges and state prosecutors intervened in cases under investigation by the NKVD, sometimes ensuring that the charges were dropped or that the suspects were acquitted. Complaints sent by local NKVD commanders to Moscow about such practices often led to further investigations and charges against judicial staff. Holders of important party posts – from members of the Politburo down to regional secretaries of the VKP(b) – supervised the "unmasking of enemies" and the purges conducted within the party organisation. They naturally endeavoured to exclude their immediate political or official environment from NKVD scrutiny and arrest operations.

This situation changed fundamentally after Stalin had ordered the secret police to begin arresting suspects in the entourages of leading party figures. The waves of repression within the inner circles of power commenced in the autumn of 1936, specifically in the aftermath of the first Moscow show trial. Politburo members were now affected, most prominently Sergo Ordzhonikidze, who lost many of his most trusted co-workers in the ministry he chaired, the People's Commissariat for Heavy Industry (NKTP). Repression began to threaten leading party secretaries in the provinces as well. P. P. Postyshev, secretary of the VKP(b) in Kiev, and B. P. Sheboldaev, who held a similar post in the Azov–Black Sea Region, fell victim to growing state terror. These leaders had never participated in the opposition, and although they embodied the power of local party elites, neither could protect their entourage from persecution. Both were publicly libelled, removed from their posts and arrested shortly afterwards. In the press they were charged with a negligent attitude towards "vigilance".

The internal party elections of spring 1937 demonstrated how the VKP(b) *apparat* had lost power to the NKVD. In an atmosphere of "purging" and "unmasking enemies", secret police officers had a decisive say in the election of party officials. Objectively, the mounting repression against regional secretaries and other members of the VKP(b) *nomenklatura* strengthened the position of local NKVD units. This process was also discernible in Moscow, where members of the Politburo and even some of Stalin's most loyal assistants were tyrannised by personal threats to them and their families or subordinates.

The plenum of the Central Committee of the VKP(b) held between 23 and 29 June 1937 deserves special mention in this connection. There is evidence that this assembly marked a caesura in the intensification of repression, with a concomitant weakening in the influence of the party *apparat*. The plenum sanctioned an unprecedented rate of expulsion for members and candidate-members of the Central Committee. In February 1934, 139 persons had been elected to the Central Committee. One year later, Abel Enukidze was expelled because of the "Kremlin Affair", and in 1936 the same fate was ordained for Sokolnikov and Piatakov. A further member, trade union chairman Tomskii, died by his own hand on 22 August 1936. In 1937, a further eleven members were expelled before the Central Committee met in June. This latter figure does not include I. Gamarnik, the head of the Political Administration of the Red Army, who committed suicide on 31 May 1937 to evade arrest. An even higher number were struck off the membership of the Central Committee at the June plenum – thirty-one. Furthermore, on 2 July, shortly after the plenum had ended, the Politburo approved the notorious NKVD operation against "anti-Soviet elements" (Order no. 00447), a decision that marks the beginning of widespread arrests in the native population as a whole. As these events, and the resolutions which preceded them, are chronologically close, they are undeniably part of a wider pattern. We also know that Ezhov spoke at the June 1937 plenum.

A problem for our analysis is that no stenographic record was made of the plenum's proceedings. However, the recollections of those present as told to third parties suggest what happened during the sittings. The first version states that the plenum witnessed the last attempt by a group of Central Committee members to topple Stalin, after they had consulted with one another on the eve of the opening session.[3] Another, better-known, version concerns reports that the Central Committee members Kaminskii and Piatnitskii opposed Ezhov's policies, especially the motion to grant the NKVD extraordinary powers.[4] By contrast, the evidence to support the theory that the plenum attempted to hinder the expansion of the terror, or indeed to oust Stalin, is not convincing. By 1937, a Central Committee plenum had long since lost its role in shaping policy. Various oral reports mention that the assembly granted Ezhov emergency powers. Nikita Petrov and Arsenii Roginskii have found drafts of Ezhov's speech to the June 1937 plenum which include a passage about "exposing" an alleged espionage network set up in the USSR by Polish Intelligence.[5] This discovery indicates that the plenum may have sanctioned mass operations by the secret police, which, as mentioned elsewhere in this volume, began some weeks later. On the other hand, it is not clear why the launching of countrywide arrest sweeps should have needed the approval of the Central Committee.

It seems more probable that the plenum dealt mainly with the repression within the party as it was summoned in order to expel a large number of Central Committee members. Ezhov's speech was, we assume, devoted to this task, including detailed information on how the NKVD had "exposed hostile organisations" in the different regions of the USSR. It is also possible that Ezhov informed the plenum on how the "investigation" against Bukharin and Rykov was progressing. There are two further indications that the plenary sessions were primarily concerned with affairs within the VKP(b). First, the resolutions passed pertained to organisational matters – the expulsion of persons from the Central Committee and the party. Second, as the archival material of local party bodies suggests, the plenum did not pass a general motion on "vigilance" or how the NKVD was to conduct mass repression.

It was customary to summon meetings of the party members at all geographical levels in the wake of a Central Committee plenum. The first secretary of the party in the region or republic would then describe, from personal participation, what the plenum in Moscow had decided. Following the June 1937 plenum, few meetings of this kind were held, and if so, no minutes were taken. Fortunately, documentary evidence is available in two cases. On 10 and 11 July activists of the Kharkov city organisation of the VKP(b) heard M. F. Gikalo, the local first secretary, report on the plenum. The text of his speech is not extant, merely that of the discussion which followed. On 12 July 1937 a similar meeting took place in Omsk, where the local first secretary, D. A. Bulatov, spoke. This session was a closed one, no protocol was taken, but the wording of the resolution has been found. Gikalo and Bulatov were members of the Central Committee and had been present at the June plenum in Moscow.

Those taking part in the discussion at the Kharkov meeting spoke of instructions issued by Stalin at the June plenum and they also mentioned Ezhov's speech there. However, they did not refer to plenum resolutions on an expansion of party "purges", but to decisions of the plenum concerning the need to activate the party rank-and-file:

> The motion of the June plenum continues the line laid down by the February plenum, and it is clear from the facts given by Comrade Gikalo that the members of the Central Committee did not hesitate to expel all those from the Central Committee who cannot be trusted [...] Comrade Stalin said at the recent plenum that all those comrades who had made errors in their work must be permanently monitored.[6]

According to Bulatov, the motion passed by the Omsk Regional Committee of the VKP(b) read as follows:

> The Plenum of the Regional Committee of the VKP(b) considers the findings of Comrade Stalin, namely that remnants of White Guardism and Trotskyist-Bukharinist banditry have not been fully eliminated, to be completely justified. This plenum also accepts that due to the fact that even after the verification of party documents and their exchange, not a few former White Guards and clandestine Trotskyist-Bukharinist bandits remain in the party, all party officials have the duty to destroy once and for all the hidden remnants of the White Guards and the Trotskyist-Bukharinist bandits.

In the Omsk case, the Bureau of the Regional Committee was called on by the local plenum to review the membership of all persons who had served in the White Army but had been re-instated as VKP(b) members.[7]

The aims of the June plenum, in so far as they can be reconstructed or deduced, formed the basis for a weakening of the party and its *apparat*. During the second half of 1937 and throughout 1938, officials and other members of the party were subject to mass repression, as were all sectors of Soviet society. In the first half of 1937, 20,500 persons were expelled from the VKP(b), and in the second half 97,000.[8] Prominent among the latter figure were party functionaries, "Bolshevik cadres" of long standing.

Although no investigation has been carried out to date on how the party *apparat* functioned at lower levels in the years of the Great Terror, several circumstances indicate that the influence of the NKVD grew and that of the party declined. In the first place, VKP(b) luminaries were demoralised by the countless arrests around them, a wave of terror which hit this group more than any other in society. Six percent of all VKP(b) members were expelled during 1937, and many subsequently arrested. The toll of victims was even higher among persons who had been ejected from the Party in the preceding years. In the documents prepared for the February–March 1937 Plenum of the Central Committee, prominent attention was drawn to the fact that over 1.5 million former members or candidate-members had been expelled or automatically struck off the rolls since 1922.[9] Some hundreds of thousands had been ejected from the party's ranks in the years 1935–6. An indication of the accretion of power afforded to the NKVD is the special position Ezhov occupied in 1937 and during the first half of 1938. He was appointed a candidate-member of the Politburo in October 1937, and he and Molotov were those members of the inner circle who visited Stalin's Kremlin office most frequently in the years 1937–8.

We know little about the mutual relations between leading party officials and the heads of NKVD administrations in specific towns or regions. A general and significant trend, however, was the practice of appointing NKVD officers to supervise local committees of the VKP(b). For example, the head of the NKVD administration in the Kirov Region, L. Gasov, was appointed first secretary of the regional committee of the VKP(b) in Krasnodar. Similarly, the NKVD officers Valukhin (Omsk) became first party secretary in Sverdlovsk, Teleshov (Kharkov) took over party affairs in Odessa, and Goncharov (Leningrad) became regional secretary in Ordzhonikidze.

The party regained its traditional supremacy only gradually. The first sign of this turn-around is arguably the Central Committee plenum of January 1938. This assembly has been depicted since Stalin's death as a milestone in the process of reducing the scope and extent of the Great Terror. Khrushchev, in his famous report to the 20th Party Congress (1956), said that the resolutions passed at the January 1938 plenum "gave some measure of improvement to Party organisations. However, widespread repression also existed in 1938".[10] During the January 1938 plenum Khrushchev took Postyshev's place as candidate-member of the Politburo. Khrushchev's positive evaluation of the plenum is borne out by facts. In the first seven months of 1938 37,000 persons were expelled from the VKP(b), i.e. 60,000 less than in the period July–December 1937. This downward trend continued for the remainder of 1938.[11]

Furthermore, a campaign launched at the plenum to examine complaints deposited by expelled party members resulted in the reinstatement of 77,000 communists, 31,000 more than in 1937. Of more import was the fact that new members were now admitted in great numbers once more, a practice that had been restricted in 1937. The party opened its ranks to 148,000 new communists in 1938 (1937: 32,000) and 43,700 candidate-members (1937: 34,000).[12] These developments indicated that the party was functioning in a normal fashion and that its cadres composition was now stable. Consequently, newly-appointed functionaries could feel safer. The Party played a leading role in "re-establishing socialist legality", i.e. scaling down the Great Terror in late 1938 and precipitating a purge of the NKVD officer corps. This sharp turn in the "general line of the party" was executed under the slogan "Re-establishing the control function of the Party over the NKVD". On 22 August 1938 Beria, who carried out this new policy of Stalin's within the NKVD, was appointed Ezhov's first deputy. He was suited to this new field of operations, being a Chekist of long service who had also led a VKP(b) organisation at republic level. On 20 September 1938 the Politburo dealt with the confirmation of officials appointed to high administrative posts in local and central government. It is clear from this document that the intended re-organisation was aimed at NKVD structures. The resolution ordered the examination of leading NKVD officers, especially those in the central *apparat* in the Soviet capital, and in the NKVD administrations in Moscow and Leningrad. The review was to be concluded within three months, and the investigation into NKVD staff at local level was to take one month. A department of the Central Committee supervised these tasks, and a special sector within it was set up for this purpose. It consisted of NKVD officers, court officials and staff from the state prosecutor's office. Twenty persons were employed as permanent sector staff.[13]

The examination of NKVD regional heads took longer than the month proposed. In early winter 1938–9, a significant resolution was passed by the Politburo on this matter: local party leaders were assigned the task of "purging" NKVD cadres. The corresponding directives of the Central Committee, signed by Stalin, were sent to the various regions on 14 November 1938. The new operation consisted of listing, scrutinising and confirming leading NKVD staff – from People's Commissars down to officers who commanded NKVD units in the districts. Files were to be opened on all such persons by 5 December 1938 and deposited in the offices of the Party at the corresponding district, region or republic level. Party leaders, by acquainting themselves with such personnel dossiers, with the results of the *proverka* and by interviewing the NKVD men personally, were expected to purge the secret police service "of all hostile persons [...] of individuals who cannot be trusted politically".[14]

Subsequently, suggestions for filling posts in leading NKVD organs were worked out by commanders of the secret police in the districts, regions and republics. These panels were confirmed by a party committee in the corresponding geographical organisation of the VKP(b). The confirmation of an appointment to head the administration of the NKVD in the cities and outlying districts was therefore now more or less the prerogative of the first secretary of the VKP(b) organisation in question, a decision which was also approved by the local party committee. These decisions were later sent to Moscow for confirmation. The complete re-appointments procedure was to be completed by 1 January 1939.

The pertinent first party secretary (district, region, republic) was also obliged to send reports on the re-structuring of NKVD personnel to ORPO (Department for Leading Party Organs) at the Central Committee of the VKP(b), in particular any information concerning deficiencies in the work of the "higher organs" and how the purging there of "hostile and alien elements" was progressing. A period of three months was set down for the review of subaltern NKVD staff.[15]

The execution of these directives meant that operative NKVD personnel were now more dependent on the goodwill of local party grandees than ever before. There are several reasons why the party leadership in Moscow chose this strategy. First, the ORPO of the Central Committee was not capable of purging the NKVD at local and central level without help from outside. Second, it is possible that

Stalin wanted to placate local VKP(b) secretaries who had often complained of arbitrary and illegal practices on the part of the secret police. One of the main goals of the Great Terror was to install a new generation of leaders who received their offices from Stalin and were therefore unquestionably loyal to him. However, the mass repression unleashed in summer 1937 jeopardised this form of "cadres renewal". Many of the new appointees, who did not question the "guilt" of their predecessors, soon realised that the havoc wrought by an unrestrained state security service could sweep them away in turn. Having acquainted themselves with the state of relations between official Soviet power and an untrammelled NKVD at grass-roots, the newly-appointed party secretaries knew that their own fate hung on a silken thread should the thoroughgoing purging continue without restraint.

Leading party officials, then, struck back in their own interest, mainly by penning lengthy complaints to Moscow. For instance, the first secretary of the Buriat-Mongolian regional committee of the VKP(b), S. P. Ignatiev (Minister of State Security of the USSR, 1951–3), dispatched a report to ORPO on the conduct of state prosecutors in the autonomous republic in September 1938. He stated that the *prokurory* of the region were breaking the law and ignoring the instructions of regional party bodies. He quoted cases of unlawful arrest and demanded that a committee be sent from Moscow to investigate the scandal. The Central Committee sent the report to Vyshinskii, Main State Prosecutor, who replied immediately that he had dispatched an emissary to Buriat-Mongolia and would base his decision on the conclusions of the investigation.[16] In an analogous case, Chuianov, the young party secretary for the Stalingrad region, clashed with NKVD notables. The dispute centred on a denunciation, dated 16 October 1938, on the part of the NKVD chief in Kotelnikovo to the effect that local party and government officials, and some of their subordinates, were involved in counter-revolutionary activities. The regional committee of the VKP(b) defended the accused, and an investigation revealed that the charges were pure invention. Chuianov did not miss the opportunity to exact revenge: in a letter to Stalin (23 October 1938), he accused NKVD personnel of employing torture, systematic beatings and uninterrupted interrogation sessions for days on end, with the accused forced to stand during the entire period. Chuianov requested that a special commission be established to examine the conduct of the secret police in the Stalingrad region. Malenkov, at the time chief of ORPO in the Central Committee in Moscow, sent this complaint to Beria, the new Commissar of the NKVD.[17]

There seem to have been many such depositions against the arbitrary rule of the NKVD. Stalin, for his part, had to take account of the morale of those he had so recently promoted to higher party office. Hence the shift in power-dynamics – the re-establishment of control by the party over the punitive organs of the State. An important decision in this regard was a directive to the NKVD, forbidding it in future to recruit agents from among the staff of executive party offices at all levels. The ban also referred to the recruitment of local government officials or Gosplan employees.[18]

Purged NKVD officers were replaced by cadres made available by the party. Of the 14,500 new employees accepted for NKVD service in 1939, more than 11,000 came from the VKP(b) or the Komsomol. This percentage was even higher in the central *apparat* – 3,242 of 3,460 new officers in the Administration of State Security.[19] At the end of 1938 and into the first months of 1939, those first secretaries of the VKP(b) who had previously served in the NKVD lost their party appointments – Goncharov in the Ordzhonikidze Region, and Valukhin in Sverdlovsk, for example.[20] Others were removed from responsible party posts because they had been reluctant to expose the illegal methods employed by the NKVD in Bashkiria, Irkutsk Region, Dagestan and Altai Region.[21]

Other aspects of the restored equilibrium in VKP(b)–NKVD relations were the public condemnation of "enemies" in the secret police, the rehabilitation of thousands in investigative custody or in the camps, the restoration of party membership to countless victims of the terror and the demands from the latter that the executioners and torturers in NKVD uniform be punished. All these developments produced a weakening in the status of the NKVD, and by the beginning of 1939 the cadres of the secret police were as demoralised as party officials had been in 1937–8. A further result of the shift in power and influence was that state prosecutors could now investigate without fear of reprisal those who had intimidated them in the past – the *kolol'shchiki* ("bone-breakers") of State Security. The fate of these and other NKVD cadres now depended, to a great degree, on the attitude of the local party *nomenklatura*. The new head of the NKVD administration in the Ordzhonikidze Region, for instance, complained in March 1940 that "our staff are unjustly depicted as miscreants." In a speech to a regional VKP(b) conference, he gave some examples: in the Budenovsk area the local Komsomol secretary, when intoxicated, had verbally attacked a policeman: "It isn't 1937 now. Why are you stopping people?" The director of the municipality's economic department replied to a request from prison staff for apartments with the words: "You now have enough empty cells, you can live in them." In the local capital the NKVD summoned an official of the planning board for questioning. He refused to appear, saying: "That time is now gone, we now represent Soviet power."[22] There were also numerous cases of NKVD officers dismissed without the requisite confirmation by the pertinent party organs. The new departure went so far that government authorities had NKVD men assigned to specific tasks in the local economy, often in a *kolkhoz* or factory.[23]

The new NKVD commissar Beria, forced to adapt to the new circumstances, tried to prevent the retreat turning into a rout. He could count on Stalin to protect the interests of the NKVD in the long term. The dictator, to quote the most prominent example, took upon himself the responsibility for the widespread use of torture by NKVD interrogators – one of the main charges levelled at Chekists arrested in 1938–9. The following telegraphic text was sent to all party and NKVD organs from district units upwards on 10 January 1939:

> The Central Committee of the VKP(b) explains that the application of methods of physical pressure in NKVD practice was made permissible in 1937 in accordance with the Central Committee of the VKP(b) [...] It is known that all bourgeois intelligence services use methods of physical influence against the representatives of the socialist proletariat and that they use them in the most scandalous forms. The question arises as to why the socialist intelligence service should be more humane against fanatical agents of the bourgeoisie, against the deadly enemies of the working class and the *kolkhoz* peasants. The Central Committee of the VKP(b) considers that physical pressure should still be used unconditionally, as an appropriate and justifiable method, in exceptional cases against known and obstinate enemies of the people.[24]

As the accusation of torture was frequently the sole charge that could be levelled at disgraced Chekists in court, Stalin's telegram absolved the great majority of them from blame. The purge of the secret police essentially ran along the lines described frankly by Suslov, then first secretary of the VKP(b) in the Ordzhonikidze Region, to a party conference in March 1940: one third of NKVD staff under investigation were dismissed, some dozens convicted. Suslov continued:

> When we were conducting this review we endeavoured to treat each case individually, retaining those comrades, especially lower NKVD

ranks and younger staff, who had been provoked by their hostile superiors into committing acts which sometimes represented breaches of socialist legality. We have purged the NKVD only of those who, in committing such offences, had demonstrated initiative and malice and were motivated by selfish and hostile intentions.[25]

The victims of the purge in the secret police corps were generally "favourites" of Ezhov who had been promoted by him, or simple scapegoats. It should be emphasised, however, that many *chekisty* who participated in the mass repression of 1937–8 stayed in the service and subsequently gained higher rank. Before the Second World War broke out, the traditional balance of forces between the VKP(b) and the NKVD, now under Beria, had been restored. That this relationship had been disturbed in the 1930s is a characteristic example of how the Stalinist dictatorship succeeded in manoeuvring between policy extremes – by Stalin's careful manipulation of the equilibrium in relations between his party and the secret police under his command. In summary, the repression of VKP(b) cadres was entrusted to the NKVD in 1936–8, but the roles were reversed subsequently, when the purging of secret police bodies was entrusted to party office-holders, some of whom then took up positions in Beria's *apparat*. As long as Stalin ruled, these policies of cadres-exchange and power poker were characteristics of the interplay between the ruling party and its "sword and shield", the organs of State Security.

Notes

1. *Voprosy istorii*, no. 10 (1994), p. 14 ('Materialy fevral'skogo-martovskogo plenuma TsK VKP (b) 1937 goda, 2 marta 1937 goda. Vechernee zasedanie').
2. See the complaints on NKVD practices by Vyshinskii and Justice Commissar Krylenko in Peter H. Solomon Jr., *Soviet Criminal Justice under Stalin* (Cambridge, 1996), pp. 232–4.
3. Vadim Z. Rogovin, *1937. Stalin's Year of Terror* (Oak Park, 1998), p. 491.
4. *Oni ne molchali* (Moscow, 1991), pp. 215–25; Vladimir Piatnitskii, *Zagovor protiv Stalina* (Moscow, 1998), pp. 51–70; Boris Starkov, 'The Trial That Was Not Held', *Europe-Asia Studies*, vol. 46 (1994), pp. 1298–300.
5. N. V. Petrov and A. B. Roginskii, '"Pol'skaia operatsiia" NKVD 1937–1938', in L. S. Eremina (ed.), *Repressii protiv poliakov i pol'skikh grazhdan* (Moscow, 1997), pp. 23–5.
6. RGASPI, f. 17, op. 21, d. 5320, ll. 13, 57.
7. RGASPI, f. 17, op. 21, d. 3296, l. 15.
8. RGASPI, f. 17, op. 117, d. 873, l. 23; APRF, f. 3, op. 22, d. 160, l. 135.
9. APRF, f. 3, op. 2, d. 773, l. 115.

10 *Reabilitatsiia. Politicheskie protsessy 30–50 godov* (Moscow, 1991), p. 39. See also the English text in Nikita Khrushchev, *The 'Secret' Speech delivered to the closed session of the Twentieth Congress of the Communist Party of the Soviet Union* (London, 1976), p. 45.
11 APRF, f. 3, op. 22, d. 160, l. 135; RGASPI, f. 17, op. 7, d. 426, l. 69.
12 RGASPI, f. 17, op. 117, d. 873, l. 17.
13 Oleg Khlevniuk et al. (eds), *Stalinskoe Politbiuro v 30-e gody* (Moscow, 1995), pp. 43–4.
14 APRF, f. 3, op. 22, d. 91, ll. 168–70.
15 Ibid.
16 GARF, R-8131, op. 37, d. 116, ll. 1–6.
17 Vladimir Nekrasov, *Trinadtsat' 'zheleznykh' narkomov* (Moscow, 1995), pp. 229–30.
18 GARF, R-9401, op. 2, d. 1, ll. 10–11, NKVD directive of 27 Dec. 1938.
19 A. Kokurin and N. Petrov, 'NKVD: struktura, funktsii, kadry', *Svobodnaia mysl'*, no. 7 (1997), pp. 111–12.
20 RGASPI, f. 17, op. 3, d. 1004, ll. 40–2; f. 17, op. 3, d. 1006, l. 17.
21 RGASPI, f. 17, op. 3, d. 1005, ll. 12–13; f. 17, op. 3, d. 1006, l. 28.
22 RGASPI, f. 17, op. 22, d. 1992, l. 246.
23 Ibid.
24 *Reabilitatsiia. Politicheskie protsessy*, pp. 40–1. For an English text of the telegram see Khrushchev, *The 'Secret' Speech*, p. 47.
25 RGASPI, f. 17, op. 22, d. 1992, l. 83.

3
Ezhov's Scenario for the Great Terror and the Falsified Record of the Third Moscow Show Trial

Wladislaw Hedeler

Introduction

Nikolai Ezhov, head of the NKVD, conferred closely with Stalin in drawing up plans to annihilate the Old Bolshevik elite, not least the former Politburo members executed after the show trials in 1937 and 1938. Documentation recently transferred from the Archive of the President of the Russian Federation (APRF) and the Central Archive of the Federal Security Service of the Russian Federation (TsAFSBRF) to the former Central Party Archive (RGASPI), while still in the process of declassification, allows us to delineate Ezhov's collaboration with the Soviet dictator in order to prepare the indictments, the choice of defendants and the scenario of these major court trials. The papers in question were seized during the house searches after the arrest of the main accused, and were subsequently integrated into Stalin's private archive.[1]

Ezhov's papers contain details of the planning and coordination carried out jointly by the VKP(b) leadership and the Main Administration of State Security (GUGB) of the NKVD in connection with the three great trials, including the steps taken to select the defendants and compile the final indictments. Of great significance in this regard is a text written by Ezhov in the years 1935 to 1937 and edited by Stalin: "From Fractionalism to Open Counter-Revolution and Fascism".[2] Ezhov originally intended to pen an article in the theoretical journal *Bol'shevik*, and in an early draft of the typescript he named "a net of five terrorist groupings" which had been smashed by the NKVD: the staff of the Government library and the special guards unit in the Kremlin, and a military, youth and "White Guardist" conspiracy, 110 prisoners in all. His first chapter was a survey of the struggle waged by the "counter-revolutionary organisation of Zinoviev and Kamenev". Later additions were based mainly on the indictments of the show trials and the confessions extracted during their preparation. Published extracts from other documents which highlight the decision-making process at the highest level during the Great Terror are the so-called "special folders" (*osobye papki*) containing the resolutions of the Politburo and Stalin's decisions,[3] the log-book for visitors to Stalin's Kremlin office[4] and the minutes of the Central Committee plenums held in December 1936,[5] February–March 1937[6] and June 1937.[7] Further publications of interest include letters to and from Nikolai Bukharin while he was in prison[8], the book manuscripts and other texts he wrote in confinement[9] and the well-known correspondence between Stalin and Molotov.[10]

At the very least, these new papers should fill the significant gaps present in the reminiscences of the Politburo members Molotov[11] and Kaganovich[12], specifically their participation in framing the decisions leading to the mass repression of 1937–8. As regards the scenario of the show trials, the only sources hitherto available were the published record[13], Trotsky's writings[14] and Bukharin's "final speech from the dock"[15], all of which indicate or state explicitly that the orchestrated court sessions were directed at Trotsky, Stalin's main enemy. These three printed sources omit essential elements of the Great Terror: for example, the role of the Gulag in economic planning, or the part "scapegoats" played in diverting popular discontent from the Soviet elite. The trials were therefore far more than just a settling of old scores initiated by Stalin in his thirst for vengeance.

Three of the documents already mentioned illuminate the beginning and end of the trials, their genesis and execution: first, Ezhov's manuscript, begun in 1935 and added to by Stalin, Iaroslavskii, Knorin, Malenkov, Mekhlis, Pospelov, Shkiriatov, Stetskii and Tal, contains the charges levelled at the defendants in the show trials and formed the basis for Central Committee directives in the years 1935–8; second, the stenogram or minutes (1,200 pages held in the Central Archive of the FSB) of the third show trial that opened on 2 March 1938 against Bukharin, Iagoda and others ("Right-Trotskyist Bloc"); and third, internal NKVD documents collated before the trial opened, namely the interrogation protocols, the minutes of the confrontations between the defendants and witnesses, the "script" dictated to the defendants by the NKVD, the letters of the accused to their families, and petitions and appeals for clemency. This third source alone encompasses 55 bound volumes.

The fragmentary nature of the reporting on the third trial can now be corrected and enlarged upon in great detail. It is now possible to reconstruct when the arrests took place of those marked down as prospective defendants or court witnesses, how the trial was minutely planned, how the "evidence" was fabricated at Politburo level and exploited as propaganda, especially in regard to other "model" trials in the provinces.

Ezhov and the purges in the VKP(b)

Ezhov had always supported Stalin in the internal Party controversies of the 1920s. In 1927, after the dispersal of the Left Opposition, he was appointed to the staff of the Central Committee and, as Deputy Commissar for Agriculture (1929–30), took part fully in the enforcement of collectivisation. In contrast to other colleagues of Stalin, Ezhov supported the use of violence in implementing the new agrarian policy and fought against its opponents, the "Right deviationists" in the VKP(b).[16] He was appointed head of the prestigious Cadres Department of the Central Committee in 1930, and was a member of the central commission set up to supervise the purging of the VKP(b). At the fateful 17th Party Congress in 1934, Ezhov's career took a new turn: he was elected to the Central Committee and to the Central Commission for Party Control. One year later followed his election to the Organisational Bureau and the Executive Committee of the Communist International (ECCI). He subsequently attained the posts of secretary to the Central Committee, chairman of the Central Commission of Party Control and membership of the commission within the Politburo on criminal cases.[17] Ezhov was also co-responsible, from 1936 onwards, for monitoring the functioning of the NKVD, then still chaired by Genrikh Iagoda.

The increase in the number of arrests from the beginning of the decade had a strong social component – the naming of victim groups as lightning conductors to deflect popular discontent. Stalin directed that newspapers in the provinces carry reports on acts of "sabotage", including details of the trials staged to sentence the "culprits" to death: the "wreckers of Socialist Construction" in the building industry, in the system of food supply and during the harvest campaigns. An impartial investigation into the poor results attained in industrial and agricultural production or into the mishaps and accidents in mining, for example, could have led to a discussion on alternative economic strategies (e.g. a return to NEP) and was therefore ruled out. Whereas the political background to the show trials in the provinces involved production problems of one sort or another, those staged in Moscow served to destroy the so-called "Fifth Column" in the party.[18]

When the first major show trial against Stalin's former colleagues opened in Moscow in August 1936, the most prominent defendants, Zinoviev and Kamenev, were sick and morally broken. They had been in confinement since 1932 and, despite their avowals of loyalty to Stalin, were now accused of being "saboteurs, traitors and spies". Shortly before his transportation from a prison in Cheliabinsk to the Lubianka, Zinoviev wrote to Stalin that he was ill and that he doubted whether he would live much longer. He intervened on behalf of his son, describing him as a "talented Marxist" and recommending that the book he had written himself while living in Uralsk should now be published. Zinoviev signed his letter to Stalin with the formula "now totally yours".[19] Kamenev was likewise concerned with his family's welfare, reassuring his son and advising him to apply for VKP(b) membership. To distract himself from the monotony of prison life, Kamenev studied the writings of the historians Xenophon and Livius Titus – reading Marx gave him no solace, only intensifying his brooding, Kamenev informed his relatives.[20] As with other prominent victims of the terror, Zinoviev and Kamenev had been formed by the Bolshevik canon to which they would remain faithful to the bitter end, victims of a self-imposed discipline.

The contemporaneous expulsion, and later prosecution, of "deviationists" was prepared in detail by the Central Committee. The sector there responsible for "leading organs" (ORPO) drew up, between 1935 and 1937, lists of those members who had been expelled or subjected to lesser party punishments. The lists included those ejected after the Kronstadt uprising,[21] the names of 83 cadres who signed the manifesto of 25 May 1927 and who were subsequently scrutinised during the 1936 *chistka*,[22] and oppositionists expelled from the Institute of Marxism-Leninism and the Central Party Archive in the late 1920s. Others deemed unworthy of trust included those Moscow functionaries who had been expelled between 21 December 1936 and 17 February 1937.[23] Similar lists were compiled on employees of the Central Committee dismissed between January and July 1937 from the departments dealing with the press and publishing, transport and industry, agriculture, finance and trade.[24]

In March 1936 Ezhov ordered that staff in the Academy of Sciences suspected of sympathy with Zinoviev, Kamenev, Bukharin and Radek be examined,[25] thus extending the purge beyond the constituency of Trotsky's supporters to encompass anyone with alleged oppositionist leanings. Concerning the Trotskyists already in prison, the Politburo decided on 20 May 1936 that their cases were to be handed over to the NKVD for the passing of death sentences.[26] "Ezhov, too, is doing a good job, getting down to his task in the Stalin manner", wrote Kaganovich to Ordzhonikidze on 12 October 1936 about the Politburo deliberations of the day before.[27] None the less, Ordzhonikidze continued to stand by his colleagues in the Commissariat of Heavy Industry (NKTP). As of 1 December 1936, a head count of the 743 party members in NKTP revealed that 42 had received various party penalties, twelve because of former adherence to the Trotskyist opposition. A further eighty had belonged to other political groupings before joining the VKP(b), and 160 had been expelled from the party. Concerning the non-party employees, 169 had, at one stage or other, belonged to non-communist parties, 71 were ex-officers of the White Army, 94 were convicted "wreckers", 131 were of aristocratic origin and 287 had served as officers in the Tsarist forces.[28] Moreover, the Cadres Department of the Central Committee compiled extracts from the staff dossiers of functionaries who were responsible for science, culture, propaganda, agitation, the press, publishing houses and party schools and who had been subjected to party disciplinary measures or were suspected of contacts with oppositionists.

Ezhov stated at a plenum of the Moscow party organisation in early February 1936 that "we could have expelled far more", and he demanded that district secretaries exercise more vigilance towards those still in the party.[29] He also signed a circular of the Central Committee in which VKP(b) district officers were directed to hand over lists of members to be expelled to the NKVD. Ezhov also warned party functionaries that they must break the resistance of the staff in state enterprises, just as Kaganovich, who was responsible for the transport system, had done during an inspection of the main rail routes in early 1936.[30] The first reports of Kaganovich to the Politburo in this regard had mentioned the bad technical state of the transport system, but in subsequent missives he blamed the deficiencies and accidents on the work of "wreckers", recommending that such cases be investigated by the secret police.[31]

In a further move against the remnants of the Left Opposition in March 1936, Vyshinskii approved a draft, drawn up by NKVD chief

Iagoda and sanctioned by the Politburo, that all Trotskyists in the Gulag be moved to more distant work camps. This was not enough for Stalin, however, who accused Iagoda of a conciliatory attitude towards the "Right", a phrase later adopted by Ezhov when re-writing the script he had commenced in 1935. Ezhov's typescript now held that "the Right, instead of ceasing hostilities, have established an underground organisation." Agreeing with this formulation, Stalin directed that all "Right deviationists" be treated like Trotskyists and face criminal charges. The NKVD was instructed to organise a show trial against the supporters of Trotsky and Zinoviev,[32] which, in contrast to the political trials of earlier years, was intended to "expose" a gigantic conspiracy against the sitting party leadership. In late June 1936 party organisations were informed by circular of the ongoing investigation into the "terrorist activities of the Trotskyist-Zinovievist Counter-Revolutionary Bloc". Vyshinskii presented Stalin on 7 August 1936 with the initial draft for the indictment in the forthcoming first show trial. Stalin edited the paper and accepted only the third version.

After he had received another report concerning Iagoda's "conciliatory attitude and inconsistent persecution of Trotskyists", Stalin suggested to Kaganovich and Molotov in a telegram on 25 September that the NKVD chief be removed and replaced by Ezhov. Immediately, streets, schools and village settlements carried the name of the new NKVD Commissar. Stalin had also charged in the telegram that the secret police had four years' work to catch up on,[33] and this unequivocal hint was heeded by Ezhov. He summoned all NKVD regional commanders to Moscow for a briefing, and, in order to intimidate his subordinates, accused any who questioned the new course of being "wreckers" and had them arrested on the spot.[34] By March 1937 Ezhov understood the workings of his giant *apparat*, taking care to arrest many of Iagoda's closest colleagues – 238 of the 699 officers in the central NKVD administration in Moscow.[35]

Measured against the Politburo–NKVD coordination axis during the preparations for the 1936 trial, the crude propaganda statements placed in the press, including those made by ex-oppositionists already marked down for liquidation and damning Zinoviev, Kamenev and the other defendants, were merely intended for mass consumption and incitement. Piatakov, the former Deputy Commissar for Heavy Industry, Bukharin and Krylenko, among others, subsequently "welcomed" the verdicts and expressed their satisfaction at the shooting of "these dogs". Similarly, Stalin orchestrated meetings of workers who also demanded the death penalty for the accused.[36]

Preparations for the third show trial

During the investigation of the charges made against those in the dock during the first show trial, a procedure that had lasted from January to August 1936, statements were extracted to incriminate Bukharin as well. Apprised of the accusations made against him by Radek and Tsetlin, Bukharin addressed a letter to Stalin, Ezhov and the Politburo on 11 January 1936, demanding a confrontation with Radek.[37] Although Bukharin had distanced himself from his former "pupils", many of them were arrested in the period December 1936 to February 1937. The "Bukharinists" were forced to sign incriminatory statements against their former ideological "patron" in the following months. Stalin attended one confrontation session staged between Bukharin and his erstwhile "pupils" in a Moscow prison, and did not refrain from participating in the interrogations. Bukharin, however, drew attention to contradictions in this oral "evidence" and demanded a special enquiry to clear his name.

The delegates to the February–March 1937 Central Committee Plenum had the intimidating atmosphere of the second show trial (against Radek, Piatakov, Sokolnikov and others), which ended on 30 January, fresh in their minds. Ezhov made two speeches to the plenum to convince the delegates that the accusations against Bukharin and Rykov warranted an investigation by the NKVD. The secret police officers later assigned to the case were present in the hall, as were Radek and Sokolnikov, who had each been sentenced to ten years one month previously. In his speech on the "Bukharin–Rykov case", which was the first item on the plenum agenda, Ezhov kept to his "From Fractionalism" text. He attacked the so-called Bukharin school[38] and the Riutin platform.[39] In condemning NKVD investigative practices at the plenum, Bukharin was in turn accused of slandering the Cheka.[40] "We are not tormenting the accused [Bukharin and Rykov], but they us" was Iaroslavskii's résumé.[41] In a contribution somewhat later, Ezhov said: "We have been talking now for four days about the Bukharin–Rykov case. It is time to end the discussion".[42] Akmal' Ikramov, the party secretary from Uzbekistan who would share a place in the dock with Bukharin in the coming third show trial, described the latter as a political enemy who vilified the previous trials and had yet to capitulate.[43] At the beginning of the evening session on 27 February, Stalin informed the plenum of the findings of the commission set up to adjudicate on further steps to be taken against Bukharin and Rykov.[44] Both were arrested at the close of the sitting. The arrest-warrant was signed by

Lazar Kogan, the high-ranking NKVD officer who had earlier supervised the slave labour on the White Sea Canal building project. Kurskii, head of the NKVD's Political Department, had acquired permission to issue the warrant from Agranov, Ezhov's deputy, who in turn confirmed the order and sent it to Vyshinskii for counter-signing. When these formalities and the house searches had been completed, the NKVD began to devise the scenario for the third show trial.

The choice of defendants depended on the results of the interrogations. At the outset, so-called "Right double-dealers" were not mentioned in NKVD documentation, just "Trotskyists". The order to arrest Bukharin and the others was partly based on what Radek and Piatakov had "confessed", namely that Bukharin was a leading member of a terrorist, counter-revolutionary "Right" organisation. After supportive calls had been organised on the part of "Soviet workers", the Politburo decided on 5 March to change the titles of all institutes and factories bearing the names of either Bukharin or Rykov. Ezhov began purging Iagoda's leading officers during the same month and replacing them with VKP(b) cadres.

In the ensuing weeks *Pravda* reported regularly on the countless cases of "wreckers and saboteurs" who had been "unmasked by honest citizens", and Vyshinskii was the recipient of similar reports from various regions.[45] Bukharin and Rykov initially refused to admit to the charges but succumbed[46] after the secret trial against Tukhachevskii and other Red Army generals.[47] Bukharin now said that he was prepared to admit his guilt before the party and the working class. He confessed to having established, together with Rykov and Tomskii, a "Right organisation", and to have lead it. On 1 June 1937 he informed Ezhov by letter that he would also speak of his involvement in plans to overthrow the state and carry out terrorist acts. Bukharin handed over a 34-page manuscript the following day, a long explanation about the theoretical origins of his "anti-Leninist views". However, as this tract was confined to the years 1920 to 1932 and barely touched on the 17th Party Congress (1934) or Bukharin's trip abroad in 1936 to purchase part of the Marx–Engels manuscripts, Stalin rejected it *in toto* as "another double-dealing manoeuvre" and forwarded the manuscript, with this evaluation, to other members of the Politburo.

This exercise in breast-beating, and the manuscripts "Socialism and its Culture" and "Philosophical Arabesques",[48] which Bukharin penned in solitary confinement in the Lubianka, were of little interest to his tormentors or Vyshinskii: Bukharin had merely admitted that he had realised and overcome errors made in the theoretical field. At the time of the Tukhachevskii trial in June 1937, nine of the candidate-defendants for the forthcoming third show trial were still at liberty. Following the execution of the leading Red Army men, the NKVD interrogation teams directed their full attention once more to the Bukharin case. Between June and September 1937, the second batch of co-defendants were arrested – Selenskii, Sharangovich, Grinko, Ikramov and Khodzhaev. The prospective defendants from Belorussia were accused of planning a secession of their territory to Poland, and those from the Central Asian republics of offering their lands to British Intelligence. Rykov had incriminated Khodzhaev, Bukharin's statements had led to the arrest of Ikramov, and the other new prisoners were seized on the basis of confessions extracted from persons not involved in the third show trial. Bukharin was interrogated every night from early July to September. Whereas the NKVD teams had charged him in the early stages of his imprisonment with planning to assassinate Lenin, Sverdlov and Stalin, Bukharin's interrogators began, from June 1937, to implicate him in involvement with the Riutin platform. The programme of the latter grouping had included plans to get rid of Stalin, a charge that was also levelled at Tukhachevskii and his colleagues.[49]

Concomitant with the intensified preparations for the third major trial, the level of arrests and executions rose throughout the country, especially during the implementation of NKVD Order no. 00447 against "anti-Soviet elements" and campaigns of mass repression against "national" enemies. Then there were local sideshows, trials staged in accordance with a directive signed by Stalin on 8 August. His letter ordered the VKP(b) in the republics to organise "two to three open show trials in each district [*raion*]" to destroy the "wreckers in the rural economy", and to mobilise the peasantry for the campaign. He specifically mentioned the groups to be targeted: officials in Party, Soviet and agricultural bodies, especially workers at the MTS stations, the chairmen of district executive councils and the Party secretaries in the districts. In reply to a report written two weeks later from Kanst (Krasnoiarsk Region) about a fire in the milk *kombinat* that destroyed all the equipment and wheat and flour stocks, Stalin stated that the catastrophe must have been "organised by enemies" and ordered that all measures were to be taken to find the culprits and to sentence them to death swiftly. Confirmation of the executions was to be published in the local press. His reaction to a similar report from another region about such a trial attended by over 500 chosen peasants was no different. "I advise to sentence the wreckers in the Andreevskii district to death by shooting and to publish the shootings in the local press."[50]

Meanwhile, the NKVD torturers had broken the resistance of Bessonov and Sharangovich by August, and that of Rakovskii the following month. Based on the latter's "confession", a third wave of arrests to supply prospective actors for the third trial took place in September, and a fourth in November and December, which included doctors working in the Kremlin hospital. By the end of 1937 the interrogation of Rykov and Bukharin concentrated on the alleged assassination attempts against Lenin. Informers were placed in the cells of Iagoda, Bessonov, Bukharin and Rakovskii, but, as they could not deliver any new information on the prospective show trial defendants, more "witnesses" for the prosecution were "found" and forced to make false statements. Among the latter was Vasilii Mantsev, already sentenced to death by the Military Collegium of the Supreme Court on 25 December 1937. As he had been convicted according to the law of 1 December 1934, Mantsev should have been shot on the day the verdict was pronounced. However, he was granted a stay of execution, in order to play the role of a useful witness, stating, among other fantasies, that Bukharin had planned the liquidation of Lenin, Stalin and Sverdlov. The scenario for the third show trial was thus complete. Mantsev was shot on 19 August 1938.

Only the main defendants were questioned in early 1938 – Rykov, for example, on 4 and 10 January. In the two months remaining, the 21 defendants and "witnesses" were fully occupied with memorising the roles assigned to them. Some witnesses had died in the meantime, and two, the historian Nevskii and Bukharin's old friend Sokolnikov, refused to make incriminatory depositions and were shot. The *Pravda* leading article of 28 February 1938, announcing the imminent third show trial, surprised many. Careful observers of Russian current affairs, however, could remember that Rykov and Bukharin had been named by Vyshinskii as members of the "Reserve Trotskyist-Zinovievist Centre" at the 21 August sitting of the 1936 show trial. After Stalin, Vyshinskii and Ezhov had completed reading the proofs of the final version of the indictment text on 23 February and presented it to a Central Committee plenum for rubber-stamp approval, TASS issued a short announcement that the trial would commence on 2 March.

The third show trial

At the outset of the courtroom drama, Ulrikh, the chairman of the Military Collegium of the Supreme Court, asked all twenty-one persons in the dock whether they were familiar with the material collated against them during the NKVD investigation. The indictment alleged that the accused had formed a "Right-Trotskyist Centre Bloc" at the behest of several foreign intelligence services. The defendants also planned, the fantastic indictment continued, to overthrow the socialist state, murder its leaders and re-instate capitalism in the USSR. Further charges included systematic espionage activities for Germany, Japan and Britain, the organisation of sabotage and terror and the planned murders of Ezhov, Kirov, and Kuibyshev (d. 1935), of the former OGPU chief Menzhinskii (d. 1934) and of Maxim Gorky's son, Maxim Peshkov.[51]

In the indictment excerpts chosen for publication, the sentences pertaining to the alleged murder conspiracies were given pride of place, and a passage was added which emphasised the "anti-Leninist" basic attitude of the main defendants.[52] Portrayed as "reptiles", "mangy curs" and other unprepossessing representatives of the animal world, the defendants were said to have barked, hissed, squawked and whimpered in the dock. Other epithets chosen by reporters and Soviet writers described the accused as cynical, deceitful, bloodthirsty and criminal, a gang of unprincipled murderers, poisoners, thieves, wreckers and saboteurs.[53]

The core of the prosecution case, penned by Vyshinskii and edited by Stalin,[54] was the attempt to describe a struggle between two theories, two programmes:

> The programme of the Soviet Union has as its goal the victory of socialism in the USSR, the liquidation of capitalist remnants, national independence and the upholding of territorial unity, anti-fascism [...] and peace. The other programme, that of the Trotskyist gang, aims at restoring capitalism in the USSR, subjecting the country to domination by the fascist states and is directed against the interests of the working class and the country's peace policies.[55]

Inherent to this line of argument was the insistence that the programme of the ruling caste was rooted in the revolutionary tradition and supported by the population, whereas the programme of Bukharin and his co-defendants, the indictment went on, was rejected by the masses because it was counter-revolutionary. In one draft of the indictment, Vyshinskii inserted a hand-written addendum that "this Trotskyist gang has become an agency for foreign intelligence services".[56] In his remarks on the drafts of the Main State Prosecutor, Stalin was adamant that specific points be given special prominence:

> 1) That all defendants fought against Lenin before and after the October Revolution.

2) As an explanation for 1) to describe how such former comrades-in-arms of Lenin could have fallen so low. Their deviations had therefore been apparent even during the lifetime of Lenin who, when making the case for the banning of fractions within the party, had argued at the 10th Party Congress that all those who cling to errors after the revolution sooner or later end up in the camp of the enemy, among White Guards and imperialists. And that Lenin had been proved right in this.
3) To answer the question why the "wrecking" carried out by the Trotskyists had not been detected earlier by the party and why it had failed to re-educate the oppositionists. It is now clear [Stalin continued] that the enemies of the party have their own programme. The cornerstone of their politics is a process of re-establishing capitalism and putting policies into effect that would militate against the power of the workers and peasants.
4) The verdict of the court should contribute to the restoration of normal conditions in the country.[57]

Taking Stalin's addenda into account, Vyshinskii wrote an extensive draft for the introductory section of the indictment, an opening piece which consisted of "evidence" indicating that the defendants had had links with the Tsarist secret police (Okhrana) and foreign spying organisations. During the entire trial the real or alleged political views of the defendants were portrayed as criminal ones: Trotsky "supervised" the spies from afar, with Bukharin co-ordinating their operations in Russia. The remarks made subsequently by Vyshinskii and Molotov[58] on the trial hinged on this espionage scenario, while the former was at pains to emphasise that the accused had neither a platform nor a programme.[59]

A comparison between the actual stenogram of the trial with the published – and allegedly complete – court proceedings against "The Right-Trotskyist Bloc" shows that Vyshinskii was ascribed the sole leading role in the bloody farce. During the eighteen sittings (one was held behind closed doors) in the October Hall of Trade Union House, the stenographers recorded the rehearsed statements made by the twenty-one accused, and those uttered by the six witnesses who had been brought from their places of banishment to Moscow. This sextet comprised former members of the Central Committee of the Left Socialist Revolutionaries and three ex-officers of the Okhrana. The speeches of others before the court, namely those made by the two defence lawyers, by five medical experts, by the court's president (Ulrikh) and by the Main State Prosecutor (Vyshinskii), were also recorded for the stenogram. Each time the court recessed, Ulrikh and his staff of military jurists read the stenographers' record. They excised passages which might have cast doubt on the defendants' guilt and ensured that all references made by the accused to the policies of the USSR and the VKP(b) were omitted. Furthermore, all statements to the court based on the "script" dictated to the accused by their NKVD handlers were re-checked.

In like manner, the biographies of the defendants had to conform to the corresponding references in Ezhov's script "From Fractionalism". In the version of the stenogram edited by the military jurists, each defendant now had a biography in line with the general trial scenario. For example, the parents of those in the dock were transformed into capitalists or Orthodox priests. One of the gravest instances of falsification in the stenogram involved the dropping of the fictitious charge that Bukharin had written the tract of the Riutin platform and replacing it with another lie – Bukharin had planned to murder Lenin. As no real evidence of Bukharin's disloyalty could be produced, the murder plot against Lenin was the central charge levelled at this former "favourite of the party". Vyshinskii not only dictated to the defendants how they should "periodise" their confessions before the court, but also determined personally the gravity of the "crimes". To achieve this, remarks or confessions made by the accused had to be given an unequivocal tone, and the military jurists subsequently removed any qualifications in this regard from the trial record. As a result, infrequent meetings noted in the original protocol now became "stable and constant links", the planning of terrorist or sabotage acts was now portrayed as having been attempts near to execution. A "single mission" mentioned during a court session re-surfaced in the published "complete version" as "the constant transmission of information to intelligence services". And it was now held no longer necessary to discriminate between the British Secret Service and the Okhrana.

In addition, all events and contacts that had allegedly taken place abroad were only hinted at or vaguely described. This was to minimise the danger of the kind of mishaps (denials from foreign sources) that marred the "evidence" of the first two trials. The reader of the official published trial record, then, was supposed to believe that Trotsky was in constant touch with all the "conspirator-defendants". Vyshinskii depicted Krestinskii's departure from the prescribed text during a sitting as proof that the accused were still following Trotsky's directives, even from their seats in the dock. The state and party offices previously held by the accused were not mentioned: they were agents of foreign capital and had not influenced Soviet politics since 1917.

Bukharin was portrayed as the "unmasked" leader of an espionage network and as the instigator and organiser of armed uprisings. All such accusations were entered into the court record retrospectively. When Vyshinskii was short of arguments, he mentioned the links, allegedly established as fact during the NKVD pre-trial investigation, between the defendants and those condemned in the previous show trials or in the judicial murder of Tukhachevskii and his comrades in June 1937. The court proceedings later published also contained abridged versions of the pleas made by defence counsel, omitting those passages that the lawyers Nikolai Kommodov and Ilia Braude spoke to exonerate their clients. The printed transcription recorded only their pleas for clemency. In reality, Kommodov and Braude had to proceed under Vyshinskii's direction, and they began their summing-up by expressing agreement with the indictment. They concurred to this blackmail in order to ensure their very presence in court, where they had to take their cues from the prosecuting bench. After their remarks had been "doctored" for the published version of the trial protocol, the contributions from the defence team read like variations of Vyshinskii's main arguments.

Vyshinskii alone had the right to explain and interpret points of law. All passages in the stenogram which showed outlines of the defence strategy or referred to the examination of "evidence", were removed from the published volume: inconsistencies, if not contradictions, in the indictment; statements from the dock about the history of the VKP(b); party groupings became hostile conspiracies; fully lawful discussions between friends in the past were now presented as subversive and conspiratorial. In a word, the published account of the trial turned former opponents of Stalin's course into base criminals.

In memorising what was dictated to them by their NKVD interrogators, the defendants regurgitated the new version of party history, the distortion of historical processes to adjust accounts of the first 20 years of Bolshevik rule to comply with Stalin's megalomania and infallibility. The opposition was thus described as the monolith that the VKP(b) purported to be, as a powerful organisation with no internal disagreements or splits over time, a mighty counter-revolutionary force which threatened Soviet power everywhere. When the accused spoke in court of how the members of the opposition had been arrested, how their links with one another were interrupted so that they had consequently found it well-nigh impossible to agitate in any concerted way against "the general line of the Party", these passages were rigorously struck out.

As regards the alleged sabotage plans, all references undermining these charges were likewise excised, such as the intercession that a defendant, because of his youth, was too politically inexperienced to have been "recruited" by the Okhrana. The interrogation practices and specific diction of the NKVD found mention in the edited protocol only when Iagoda's role was under discussion. Complaints about the treatment handed out by the NKVD interrogators were interpreted by the court as further evidence of the defendants' guilt. Also excluded from the official record were all inferences that the secret police participated in party purges. None the less, there was a considerable NKVD presence in the courtroom: Aleksandr Mironov, director of the Lubianka prison, opened each sitting in his capacity as court commandant, and the NKVD staff who had interrogated the accused sat in the first row of seats.

In guaranteeing that Vyshinskii would be the uncontested star of the judicial farce, the competence of court chairman Ulrikh was reduced to a minimum. The tirades of the Main State Prosecutor sometimes infringed on established court procedure, and Ulrikh cautioned Vyshinskii to address the accused as defendants and not as political enemies. These exchanges were included in the stenographic record, but excluded from the published account. The practice of calling short court recesses deserves further investigation. When Krestinskii, for example, refused to admit his guilt, the sitting was interrupted for twenty minutes. The pause, it is alleged, was used to re-schedule the order of cross-examining defendants. Bessonov was the first to be so questioned by Vyshinskii as he had to play the role of Trotsky's contact with the "bloc" in Russia. When Bukharin asked his co-defendant Ivanov when, as alleged, they had actually met, Ivanov gave an evasive reply. The court then immediately rose hurriedly. After this break Vyshinskii went on the offensive, firing questions at Bukharin about his opposition activities in 1928. But when Vyshinskii quoted from Bukharin's interrogation protocol of 25 December 1937, the accused stated that the file number quoted was different from the one he had been allowed to examine. Ulrikh then cautioned Bukharin. The objections which Bukharin and Krestinskii brought in regard to discrepancies in the state's case by referring to the files they had consulted fell on deaf ears and did not surface in the printed trial record.

"I shall state before the court only what I have stated during the investigation", said Iagoda in an altercation with Ulrikh on 7 March. Vyshinskii then warned him to desist from such tricks. And when Bukharin categorically denied ever being a spy, the court recessed. On resumption of business, he was called upon to be more specific. He then stated that plans to arrest the delegates to the 17th Party Congress (1934) had been the idea of Tomskii, the trade union leader who died by his own hand.

As regards the actual documents compiled while the defendants were in investigative custody, the warrants for the arrests and the house searches were issued after these NKVD operations had taken place. Other papers in the defendants' files, the statements of witnesses for example, were forged by the interrogation team. Contemporary Soviet law was not adhered to in three other aspects: first, applications to have the investigative custody prolonged were not made on a regular basis; second, the right of the defendants to defend themselves was hampered by the fact that the time allowed them to familiarise themselves with the masses of material collated since arrest was far too short; third, the court employed "evidence" that the defendants could not have known about, charges which had never been made during the countless bouts of nocturnal questioning. Not all examples of crass perversions of legal procedure were excised from the stenogram: the actual verdict contains allegations which were not included in the indictment – that Bukharin was behind the *putsch* of the Left SRs in July 1918, or that Rozengolts planned to kill Stalin in August 1937.

The Central Committee Plenum convened in January 1938 shortly before the trial began. Georgii Malenkov admitted to the assembly that errors had been committed in expelling party members. He also criticised the way in which appeals for re-instatement had been handled by the VKP(b) bureaucracy. This was, in effect, a signal like the one Ezhov had given to the Moscow party *aktiv* two years earlier. As Iagoda was to be condemned in the forthcoming third show trial, the party was regaining power at the expense of the secret police. Ezhov's removal to the Ministry for Waterways (8 April 1938) and the appointment of Beria as deputy NKVD commissar (22 August 1938), head of the Main Administration for State Security (29 September 1938) and NKVD chairman (25 November 1938)[60] were logical steps in the process of "normalisation" which Stalin prescribed for the country after the verdicts in the last show trial had been carried out.

Aftermath

After the verdicts in the third show trial had been announced at 4.30 a.m. on 13 March 1938, appeals for clemency to the Supreme Soviet of the USSR were written by Bukharin[61] and Iagoda.[62] Such appeals could be addressed to the highest legislative authority within a seventy-two hour period after sentencing, but this right was ignored and the execution of the "guilty" took place shortly after the court rose. Captain of State Security Petr Maggo shot the prisoners one by one. Bukharin and Iagoda were the last to die and had to witness the execution of their co-defendants. The bodies were cremated.[63]

Few relatives of Bukharin remained unscathed. His father, Ivan Gavrilovich, worked as a teacher, then as a proof-reader in the Krasnaia Pechat printing works and finally as a casual labourer. He died in poverty in 1940. Bukharin's youngest brother Vladimir lived until 1979, after having served over twenty years in the Gulag and in banishment. His wife and children were exiled to Kazakhstan. Nadezhda Lukina, Bukharin's first wife whom he had married in 1911, was arrested on 30 April 1937 and shot three years later. As she was too ill to walk, she was brought on a stretcher to the place of execution.[64] She had written a letter to her party organisation, casting doubt on the decisions of the February–March 1937 plenum of the Central Committee and demanding evidence of the charges levelled at Bukharin. Her brother, the military doctor Mikhail Lukin, was likewise put under pressure to incriminate Bukharin before he died in prison in 1940. Lukin's brother and sister were sentenced to terms in the Gulag.

Esfir Gurvich (1885–1989), Bukharin's second wife (1920–9), was expelled from the VKP(b) after his execution. She was arrested with her daughter Svetlana in 1949 and sentenced to 10 years in the camps. Her daughter was banished for 5 years to the Novosibirsk region. Anna Larina, whom Bukharin had married in 1934, was only 23 and the mother of a baby boy, Iurii, when arrested on 11 June 1937. Iurii was initially looked after by Anna's sister but was later sent to an NKVD orphanage. He was not to see his mother again until 1956.[65]

Concluding remarks

While the links between the major show trials in the capital and their minor counterparts in the provinces are clear since both served as safety valves to deflect blame for economic failure to the scapegoated "wreckers", similarities between the three Moscow court trials and their place in the general scheme of mass repression is a matter of interpretation. The courtroom dramas, like other manifestations of repression in these years, were part of a "conspiracy tapestry" that grew in length over time and was woven by many hands. As regards the August 1936 trial of the "Trotskyist-Zinovievist Terrorist Centre", the prosecution case seems relatively circumscribed in retrospect since the defendants faced, in essence, a single charge – terrorism, that is, murdering Kirov and planning to assassinate members of the Politburo. As in all three trials, Trotsky was the main defendant absent from the dock, but the August proceedings did not mention industrial sabotage or a substantial "foreign" participation in the plot scenario, despite the allegation that roughly one quarter of the defendants were deemed to have entered the Soviet Union on Trotsky's orders and with the assistance of the Gestapo.[66] The internal letter sent to all Party organisations some weeks before the trial commenced adhered to Vyshinskii's strategy in the court: the defendants were terrorists and had escaped detection for years because of the "absence of Bolshevik vigilance".[67]

The court proceedings against the "anti-Soviet Trotskyist Centre" of January 1937, the second great show trial against Stalin's former comrade-in-arms, presented a scenario more akin to what was to become the main script behind the mass operations of the NKVD and resounded in the resolutions of the Central Committee plenum that assembled shortly after that trial ended: the defendants, agents of foreign powers, were intent on destroying the territorial integrity of the Soviet state by undermining its military potential and murdering its leaders; the methods employed consisted mainly of "wrecking and sabotage activities in some factories and on the railways".[68] The wide publicity attending the trial influenced the proceedings in the courtroom, not least the letters addressed to Vyshinskii in *Pravda*. In his speech on 28 January, he made great play of the account by Polia Nagovizina, a switchwoman at the rail halt Chusovskaia who had lost both legs in a rail crash in 1935. Her letter, keeping closely to the prosecution case unfolding in the capital, was a stilted and commissioned text:

> I had no idea at the time that this terrible railway catastrophe was organised by murderers and wreckers. I thought that it was simply an accident. However, now I know whose bloody intentions were behind it. Only with hatred and contempt am I able to utter the disgraceful names of the Trotskyist betrayers of our homeland. [...] The fascist bloodhounds wanted to slip the noose of hunger, unemployment and capitalist oppression around our necks. They are trying to barter our homeland. They did not succeed and nobody else will ever succeed either.[69]

By the time the third show trial opened in March 1938 ("Bloc of Rightists and Trotskyists"), the prosecution text had been "learned" by the Soviet public and the charges were all-encompassing: acting in the remit of foreign powers to contribute to the defeat of the USSR and subsequently apportioning the Ukraine, Belorussia, the Caucasus, Georgia, Armenia, Azerbaijan and Primor'e to hostile states; sabotage in industry, agriculture, the railways, finance and local government; and the murder of Kirov, Menzhinskii, Kuibyshev and Maxim Gorky junior.[70] The "Short Course" of Party history, serialised in *Pravda* from 9 September and issued as hardback in October 1938, while catechising the official show trial texts of 1936 and 1937, gave, by way of contrast, a sober and plausible portrayal of the dangers facing the Soviet Union in the international arena, a situation summarised in the striking sentence: "The second imperialist war has begun."[71] This finding, presaging the Hitler–Stalin Pact of August 1939, can be taken as the conclusion to the "invisible writing" of the Stalin–Ezhov text, that corpus of invented conspiracies which became redundant with the conclusion of the third court farce in Moscow and the curtailment of mass operations eight months later.

Notes

1 The collection consists of the following:

   - deposit Nikolai Bukharin (*fond* 329, 68 dossiers)
   - deposit Lev Kamenev (*fond* 323, 383 dossiers)
   - deposit Grigorii Zinoviev (*fond* 324, 695 dossiers)
   - deposit Karl Radek (*fond* 326, 207 dossiers)
   - papers pertaining to Andrei Vyshinskii's career as Main State Prosecutor (*fond* 588, 'Kollektsiia dokumentov po istorii Rossii 1885–1995')
   - the private archive of Nikolai Ezhov, People's Commissar for Internal Affairs (*fond* 57, 287 dossiers).

2 RGASPI, f. 57, op. 1, d. 274 ('Rukopis knigi N. I. Ezhova: Ot fraksionnosti k otkrytoi konterrevoliutsii, 1–ii variant, okonchatelnaia redaktsiia'). See *Putevoditel' po fondam i kollektsiam lichnogo proiskhozhdeniia RTsKhIDNI* (Moscow, 1996), pp. 302–4. For details of Ezhov's complicity in framing the defendants in the third show trial, see Wladislaw Hedeler, 'Jeshows Szenario. Der Moskauer Schauprozeß 1938', *Mittelweg 36* (Zeitschrift des Hamburger Instituts für Sozialforschung), vol. 7 (April–May 1998), pp. 61–77.

3 See the selection in Oleg Khlevniuk et al. (eds), *Stalinskoe Politbiuro v 30-e gody. Sbornik dokumentov* (Moscow, 1995).

4 'Posititeli kremlevskogo kabineta I. Stalina', *Istoricheskii arkhiv*, no. 6 (1994); nos 2, 3, 4, 5, 6 (1995); nos 2, 3, 4, 5, 6 (1996); no. 1 (1997).

5 *Izvestiia TsK KPSS*, no. 1 (1989).

6 *Voprosy istorii*, nos 2 to 12 (1992); nos 2, 5 to 10 (1993); nos 2, 6, 8, 10, 12 (1994); nos 1 to 8, 10 (1995).

7 See the extracts in Vladimir Piatnitskii, *Zagovor protiv Stalina* (Moscow, 1998), pp. 56–68.

8 *Istochnik*, no. 0 (1993), pp. 23–6; no. 2 (1993), pp. 4–18.
9 Nikolai Bukharin, *Tiuremnye rukopisi v dvukh knigakh* (volume 1: Socialism and its Culture; volume 2: Philosophical Arabesques, Moscow, 1996). Bukharin also wrote a novel in prison that has strong autobiographical characteristics – *Vremena* (Moscow, 1994). For an English translation of the novel, see Nikolai Bukharin, *How It All Began. The Prison Novel with an introduction by Stephen F. Cohen* (New York, 1998).
10 Lars T. Lih, Oleg V. Naumov and Oleg V. Khlevniuk (eds), *Stalin's Letters to Molotov 1925–1936* (New Haven and London, 1995).
11 *Sto sorok besed s Molotovym. Iz dnevnika F. Chueva* (Moscow, 1991).
12 Lazar Kaganovich, *Pamiatnye zapiski* (Moscow, 1996).
13 *Sudebnyi otchet po delu antisovetskogo 'pravo-trotskistskogo bloka'* (Moscow, 1938).
14 *Trotzki. Schriften. Sowjetgesellschaft und Stalinistische Diktatur 1936–1940*, Band 1.2. (Hamburg, 1988).
15 See *Istochnik*, no. 4 (1996), pp. 78–92.
16 See the key documents on these altercations in 'Iz istorii kollektivizatsii 1928 god. Poezdka Stalina v Sibir'', *Izvestiia TsK KPSS*, nos 5, 6, 7 (1991).
17 Khlevniuk, *Stalinskoe Politbiuro*, p. 58.
18 See Molotov's comments in this spirit about the importance of 1937 in Soviet history in *Sto sorok besed*, p. 390.
19 *Izvestiia TsK KPSS*, no. 8 (1989), p. 90.
20 *Izvestiia*, 22–3 March 1990, p. 3.
21 RGASPI, f. 17, op. 71, d. 2, ll. 1–50.
22 RGASPI, f. 17, op. 71, d. 20, ll. 1–22.
23 RGASPI, f. 17, op. 71, d. 117, ll. 1–250.
24 RGASPI, f. 17, op. 71, d. 44, ll. 1–293; f. 17, op. 71, d. 45, ll. 1–272.
25 A. Solov'ev, 'Tetradi krasnogo professora 1912–1941 gg.', in *Neizvestnaia Rossii*, vol. 4 (Moscow, 1993), pp. 184–5.
26 *Izvestiia TsK KPSS*, no. 9 (1989), p. 36.
27 Khlevniuk, *Stalinskoe Politbiuro*, pp. 150–2.
28 Oleg Khlevniuk, *1937-g.: Stalin, NKVD i sovetskoe obshchestvo* (Moscow, 1992), pp. 116–17.
29 RGASPI, f. 17, op. 120, d. 241, l. 3.
30 Kaganovich signed the arrest warrants of, or gave his permission to arrest, 1,587 railwaymen and employees of NKTP in the years 1937–9. These documents fill five bound volumes. See A. Jakowlew, 'Blutige Vergangenheit', in Hermann Weber and Dietrich Staritz (eds), *Jahrbuch für Historische Kommunismusforschung 1993* (Berlin, 1993), p. 235.
31 For details of the mayhem Kaganovich caused in the provinces see Robert C. Tucker, *Stalin In Power. The Revolution from Above, 1928–1941* (New York and London, 1990), p. 449; A. Luk'ianov (ed.), 'Massovye repressii opravdany bit' ne mogut', *Vestnik*, no. 1 (1995), p. 125.
32 *Izvestiia TsK KPSS*, no. 8 (1989), p. 84.
33 *Izvestiia TsK KPSS*, no. 9 (1989), p. 39. The telegram text is also in RGASPI, f. 17, op. 3, d. 981, l. 50. The relevant passage in the telegram is reproduced in Roy Medvedev, *Let History Judge. The Origins and Consequences of Stalinism* (Oxford, 1989), p. 358.
34 For the report of an eyewitness, see the memoirs of a leading NKVD officer: Mikhail Shreider, *NKVD iznutri. Zapiski chekista* (Moscow, 1995), pp. 39–45.

35 *Voprosy istorii*, no. 10 (1994), p. 21. From October 1936 to June 1938 7,298 NKVD employees were arrested. See Luk'ianov, 'Massovye repressii', p. 121.
36 Some party organisations criticised the repression in 1935–6, but later they did not dare. See Khlevniuk, *1937g*, p. 59.
37 RGASPI, f. 329, op. 2, d. 6, l. 91.
38 During the plenum the Komsomol leader Kosarev spoke of the "anti-Leninist" attitude of the "Bukharin school" and described it as a "non-Bolshevik counterpart to the Politburo", all its adherents being "ex-Socialist Revolutionaries or the sons of kulaks with no links to the working class". Beria intervened at this point in the debate, stating he had supplementary information on the school members and that they were conducting a White Guardist, fascist campaign of calumny against the party. See *Voprosy istorii*, nos 8–9 (1992), pp. 15–19.
39 For details of this opposition group see *Izvestiia TsK KPSS*, nos 8, 9, 10, 11, 12 (1990).
40 *Voprosy istorii*, no. 10 (1992), p. 21.
41 RGASPI, f. 17, op. 71, d. 112, l. 10.
42 *Voprosy istorii*, no. 2 (1993), p. 27.
43 *Voprosy istorii*, nos 11–12 (1992), pp. 14–19.
44 *Voprosy istorii*, no. 1 (1994), pp. 3–28.
45 RGASPI, f. 588, op. 2, d. 155, ll. 88–94, reports from Orenburg Region, 18 and 20 August 1937.
46 Rykov was interrogated three times in June and twice in July. There are no further protocolled interrogations in his NKVD file for the period 9 August to 2 December 1937.
47 The case against the military took scarcely a month (13 May to 12 June) to complete. Seventy-six of the 85 members of the Military Advisory Board (*Voennyi sovet pri narkome oborony SSSR*) were arrested, 68 of whom were shot. The board members as of February 1936 are listed (with photographs) in *Izvestiia TsK KPSS*, no. 4 (1989), pp. 74–9.
48 See the commentary on this text in *Voprosy filosofii*, no. 6 (1993), pp. 18–73.
49 It is possible that this point in the Riutin platform was invented by the NKVD. The original text is not extant. See *Izvestiia TsK KPSS*, no. 6 (1989).
50 Originally published in *Rossiiskie vesti*, no. 17, 9 June 1992 and quoted by L. I. Larina (ed.), *Istoriia otechestva v dokumentakh, 1917–1993gg. Chast' vtoraia, 1921–1939gg. Khrestomatiia dlia uchashchikhsia starshikh klassov srednei shkoly* (Moscow, 1994), pp. 154–6. Sheila Fitzpatrick's detailed account of the genesis and course of the local show trials takes a different starting point – not a missive from Stalin, but "letters of complaint and denunciations" from aggrieved peasants. However, as with many aspects of the terror, perhaps here too we are dealing with separate phenomena since Fitzpatrick located the first of such staged assizes much earlier, in the March 1937 columns of *Pravda*. See Sheila Fitzpatrick, *Stalin's Peasants. Resistance and Survival in the Russian Village after Collectivization* (Oxford, 1994), pp. 296–313.
51 Maxim Peshkov died on 11 May 1934, aged 38. On the complicity of the NKVD in his death, see S. Gel'man, 'Zalozhnika OGPU. Snokha Maksima Gor'kogo – poslednaia liubov Genrikha Iagody', *Nezavisimaia gazeta*, 17 January 1997, p. 8. The Peshkov case is also discussed at length in Vitaly Shentalinsky, *Arrested Voices: Resurrecting the Disappeared Writers of the Soviet Regime* (New York, 1996).

52 RGASPI, f. 588, op. 2, d. 155, l. 24.
53 In the "From the Courtroom" column of *Pravda*, reports appeared from the writer and journalist Mikhail Kol'tsov and his colleague N. Krushkov.
54 RGASPI, f. 588, op. 2, d. 155. This archival stock contains those files handed over to RGASPI by the Archive of the Foreign Ministry which are concerned with Vyshinskii's career as Main State Prosecutor.
55 RGASPI, f. 588, op. 2, d. 155, l. 6.
56 RGASPI, f. 588, op. 2, d. 155, l. 16.
57 RGASPI, f. 588, op. 2, d. 155, ll. 17–21.
58 V. M. Molotov, *O vyshei shkole* (Moscow, 1938), p.13. This was the text of Molotov's speech to the First Union Conference for staff in third-level education, 15 May 1938.
59 A. Wyschinskij, 'Die Hauptaufgaben der Wissenschaft vom sozialistischen Sowjetrecht', *Sowjetische Beiträge zur Staats- und Rechtstheorie* (Berlin, 1953), p. 100.
60 *Lubianka. VChk-OGPU-NKVD-NKGB-MGB-MVD-KGB. Spravochnik*. Compiled by A. I. Kokurin and N. V. Petrov (Moscow, 1997), pp. 144, 147.
61 For the text of the appeal see Valentin Kovalov, *Dva stalinskikh narkoma* (Moscow, 1995), pp. 262–3.
62 Ibid., p. 171.
63 Bukharin's NKVD investigation file in TsAFSBRF contains a confirmation of the execution.
64 Aleksandr Borin, 'Listy arkhivnogo dela no. 18856 po obvineniiu N. M. Lukinoi-Bukharinoi', *Literaturnaia gazeta*, 23 November 1988, p. 12.
65 E. Gorelov, *Nikolai Bukharin* (Moscow, 1988), pp. 177–80.
66 *Prozeßbericht über die Strafsache des Trotzkistisch-sinowjewistischen terroristischen Zentrums. Verhandelt vor dem Militärkollegium des Obersten Gerichtshofes der UdSSR, 19.–24. August 1936* (Moscow, 1936), pp. 37–40 (indictment), pp. 179–85 (sentence).
67 *Izvestiia TsK KPSS*, no. 8 (1989), pp. 100–15.
68 *Prozeßbericht über die Strafsache des sowjetfeindlichen trotzkistischen Zentrums. Verhandelt vor dem Militärkollegium des Obersten Gerichteshofes der UdSSR vom 23.–30. Januar 1937* (Moscow, 1937), pp. 19–22 (indictment), pp. 629–36 (verdict). The fictitious charges were specific in respects that were subsequently replicated in mass-operation strategy: firstly, the defendants had "promised" the Ukraine to the German fascists and the Far East territories to the Japanese; secondly, the charged were allotted sole responsibility for industrial accidents and railway collisions, including incidents that had actually occurred with great loss of life.
69 *Nicht ich allein klage an. Berichte von jungen Menschen der Sowjetunion, die den Terror-Anschlägen der trotzkistischen Schädlinge, Spione, Diversanten und Mörder zum Opfer gefallen sind* (Moscow, 1937), pp. 4–7.
70 *Prozeßbericht über die Strafsache des antisowjetischen 'Blocks des Rechten und Trotzkisten'. Verhandelt vor dem Militärkollegium des Obersten Gerichtshofes der UdSSR vom 2.–13. März 1938* (Moscow, 1938), pp. 36–7 (indictment).
71 *Geschichte der Kommunistischen Partei der Sowjetunion (Bolschewiki). Kurzer Lehrgang. Unter Redaktion einer Kommission des Zentralkomitees der KPdSU(B). Gebilligt vom ZK der KPdSU(B)* (Moscow, 1939), p. 400 (first Russian ed., Moscow, 1938, p. 316).

4
Dimitrov, the Comintern and Stalinist Repression

Fridrikh I. Firsov

Before Soviet Communist Party and Comintern archival stocks became accessible to scholars in 1990–1, the standard works on the Stalinist terror between the world wars describing the arrest of Comintern staff and foreign communist cadres living in the USSR had to rely on memoirs and oral evidence.[1] While prominent scholars of inter-war Stalinism described in some detail the fate of members of the Executive Committee of the Communist International (ECCI) and mentioned the most jeopardised national communities of communist exiles in the Soviet Union, they could not have known in any detail of the virulent mass prosecution of foreign revolutionaries, nor of the minute planning behind the purging and cadre reviews imposed on "fraternal" Central Committees exiled in Moscow.

A recently published popular history of the Comintern draws on some pertinent files declassified since 1991,[2] and Russian historians with access to the same sources have offered valuable contributions on the mechanisms of repression within Comintern headquarters.[3] Two important collections of essays reflecting the contemporary state of research and published in German present the most comprehensive overview to date of the decimation of foreign cadres and Comintern staff. The volumes contain papers given at conferences and workshops between 1992 and 1997, which were organised at the initiative of the noted German Comintern expert Hermann Weber.[4] Works written by German-speaking historians on political immigrants in Stalin's USSR also offer valuable insights into how and why exiles with a Party card were "purged" and arrested, mainly in Moscow and Leningrad. This essay examines the role which Georgi Dimitrov, the General Secretary of the Communist International, played during the annihilation of his best cadres in the years 1935 to 1938. Whereas the archival deposits of the Communist International and the Central Committee of the VKP(b) are essential sources in our context, of equal importance are the diary entries of Dimitrov, which are held in the archive of the Bulgarian Socialist Party.[5]

The documentary evidence reveals, above all, that the leading organs of the Comintern, in their official documents, and especially in their directives to the communist parties (CPs), strictly followed Stalin's orders. After the murder of Kirov on 1 December 1934 the NKVD arrested and shot over 100 former "White Guards". In this case the Political Commission of the ECCI sent a coded radio message on 9 January 1935 to the communist parties, demanding that they explain that the violence against the "White terrorists" was undertaken "in the interests of defending millions of toilers from the cruel class enemy and was therefore an act of humanism". The Comintern sections were directed to ensure that "telegrams of approval, resolutions from reformist delegations and revolutionary organisations, from committees and meetings of industrial workers"[6] be dispatched to the Soviet Government.

It is well known that, at Stalin's insistence, the murder of Kirov was later ascribed to the supporters of Lev Trotsky and Grigorii Zinoviev. ECCI called upon its sections to intensify the struggle against the Trotskyists on all fronts, and to present them to public opinion as terrorists and accomplices of fascism struggling against the USSR. The Comintern also issued specific instructions to the communist parties for the organisation of an anti-Trotskyist campaign, and severely criticised any deviations in the foreign communist press from the official Soviet version of "Trotskyist conspirators and terrorists". Within the Comintern material was collected on the Trotskyist movement in different countries. This information was then handed over to the NKVD.

In connection with the show trial against Zinoviev and Kamenev in August 1936, the propaganda onslaught of the Comintern attained a new intensity. It was particularly emphasised that the guilt of Trotsky and Zinoviev was proven, confirmed by the "confessions of the accused".[7] On 21 August articles by Karl Radek, Georgii Piatakov and Christian Rakovskii appeared in the Soviet press. These victims of coming show trials "angrily" condemned their previous comrades-in-arms in the old Left Opposition. The next day, Vyshinskii, the Main State Prosecutor, declared that instructions had been issued to investigate these three ex-oppositionists. This augured badly for Radek and the others, implying that their fate would be the same as those from whom they had just distanced themselves.[8] In the bloody spectacle now unfolding a characteristic ruse was employed – forcing tomorrow's victims to join in the hunt for today's quarry. The Comintern participated in this intrigue. On 25 and 26 August 1936 the Secretariat of ECCI sent all communist parties a radio message from Dimitrov demanding the immediate publication of the above-mentioned articles "in all communist and pro-communist papers".[9] In a special sitting the Presidium of ECCI listened to Ercoli (Palmiro Togliatti) lecture on the "lessons from the trial of the Trotskyist-Zinovievist terrorist centre". In his talk Togliatti, by referring to the "confessions" and statements by Stalin, portrayed the "guilt" of the defendants as proven. Togliatti stated that "all evidence which could be reasonably expected from the court was heard in the courtroom."[10] Stalin's reckoning with those who had opposed him in the past was an opportunity to extend the terror, but it was described by Togliatti as "an act to defend democracy, peace, socialism and the revolution".[11]

ECCI organised the dissemination of material on the show trial, issuing various brochures devoted to the sham court proceedings. The appeal issued by ECCI to its sections read:

> The international working class must stand together like an iron wall around the USSR, guarding with its breast our great leader from the despicable machinations of the class enemy and surrounding our Stalin with an impermeable wall of love and self-sacrifice.[12]

The Comintern directed that Maurice Thorez and Harry Pollitt be responsible for the running of this campaign of "enlightenment", exploiting the presence of communists from many countries attending the Brussels Peace Conference. However, the Comintern leadership was not satisfied with the conduct of the propaganda campaign. The ECCI Secretariat sent a radio-telegram to the communist parties of France, Great Britain, the USA, Holland, Sweden, Norway, Switzerland and Belgium with the following text:

> The campaign around the trial against the Trotskyist-Zinovievist terrorist gang is developing extremely weakly ... We repeat once more that it is necessary for the Parties' Central Committees, revolutionary organisations, mass meetings, and especially social democratic workers, to express their fraternal solidarity with the toilers of the USSR, with the leadership of the VKP(b) and the leader of the international proletariat, Comrade Stalin.[13]

Dimitrov stated that it was imperative to conduct polemics against those who cast doubt on the correctness of the court verdicts. He defined the proper approach to the question of the defendants' guilt in the headline to this article: "To Defend Vile Terrorists is to Help Fascism". Dimitrov knew full well the significance of establishing true facts in the courtroom – his strategy during the Leipzig trial – but he now asserted that the guilt of those charged in the Moscow show trial was proven by "documents, facts and substantial [other] evidence".[14] The article ended with a call, typical for the time, to exercise vigilance and expose "two-faced types who are class enemies."[15]

The notes in Dimitrov's diary on the August 1936 show trial are extremely brief. His entry of 19 August, for example, reads: "Trial Zin., Kam. and others (begin)."[16] On 24 August he noted: "The verdict was carried out."[17] These notes were made for the preparation of the above-mentioned article in *Communist International* and for the translations of the trial proceedings. Dimitrov could see that the charges were based solely on the confessions of the defendants. Lion Feuchtwanger, the German author, drew his attention to this point, as shown in the diary entry of 18 December:

Feuchtwanger and Maria Osten[18] [visited] us. About the trial:
1) Cannot understand how the charged could have committed such crimes.
2) Cannot understand why all defendants confessed to everything, knowing that this would cost them their lives.
3) Cannot understand why no evidence was produced other than the defendants' confessions.
4) Cannot understand why such severe punishment was meted out to political opponents, when a regime as mighty as the Soviet one cannot be threatened by persons already in prison. Court proceedings prepared for publication carelessly, full of contradictions and implausibilities. Trial conducted in a scandalous manner.[19]

The contents of this conversation are confirmed by the account of (Mrs) D. Karavkina, an employee of VOKS (All-Union Society for Cultural Relations with Foreign Countries), who worked with Feuchtwanger and took down what he said:

19.12.1936. He told me of his visit to Dimitrov. He had gone there specially to discuss the Trotskyist trial. Said that Dimitrov was very agitated when speaking on this subject, explaining for half an hour, but not convincingly. Feuchtwanger told me that a very hostile attitude was taken to the trial abroad and that nobody believed that fifteen highly-principled revolutionaries who had risked their lives by participating in conspiracies, would all suddenly and of one accord confess and voluntarily do penance.[20]

It is possible that Dimitrov's account reflected not only what Feuchtwanger said in connection with the trials, but also his own doubts on the matter. However, it seems more probable that Dimitrov recorded Feuchtwanger's words in order to emphasise his own fully loyal position. In his conversation with Feuchtwanger and in his publications, Dimitrov continued to demonstrate absolute support for the official Soviet version of the trial. The Secretariat of ECCI sent a directive of Dimitrov by radio to the communist parties on 30 December. The Comintern sections were ordered to carry out a systematic struggle against Trotskyists, to describe them as counter-revolutionary terrorists and agents of the Gestapo. Specially underlined was the necessity "to refute the slanders directed at Comrade Stalin by contrasting such slurs with the high popularity he enjoys because of his gigantic revolutionary activities and by explaining his role as leader of the international proletariat and of all toilers all over the world."[21]

The reaction to the first show trial had not satisfied the Comintern leaders and they notified the communist parties of this when sending instructions about the second show trial (January 1937), soon to begin against the defendants Radek, Piatakov and others. Once again Comintern headquarters endeavoured to prove the hostile activities of the accused, charges that were "confirmed" solely on the basis of personal confessions. On 15 January, as the trial was beginning, the ECCI Secretariat wrote to foreign communist leaders "that is necessary to organise [a campaign] to refute the arguments of the bourgeois and social democratic press, who will attempt to discredit the trial. You are to start immediately, in the press and among the masses, a campaign against Trotsky and Trotskyism, [depicting] them as terrorist agents, gangs of wreckers, saboteurs, spies and accomplices of the Gestapo."[22] Chosen to work as correspondents of communist newspapers for the duration of the trial were a large number of communists whose parties had permanent representatives at ECCI. Leading officials of the Comintern *apparat* were also employed as trial observers and journalists. Togliatti led this group and the NKVD was informed accordingly.

In regard to the second show trial, the ECCI Secretariat issued instructions to the leadership of the Spanish Communist Party to carry out "a

Piatakov & co. trial in order to liquidate POUM [an anti-Stalinist Marxist party with strong support in Catalonia] politically".[23] In October 1938, not long before the Spanish Republic fell, a trial was held there against POUM members, under the appearance of legality. During the second Moscow show trial examples came to light of how events had been falsified or invented in the confessions of the accused. Piatakov, asked by the State Prosecutor about his contacts with Trotsky, stated that he had flown to Oslo from Berlin in December 1935 for talks with Trotsky. On that occasion, Piatakov continued, Trotsky had told him of talks which he, Trotsky, had conducted with Rudolf Hess, Hitler's deputy. Trotsky then gave concrete instructions to his fellow-conspirators. The exposure in the Norwegian press of this fantasy, namely that no German aircraft had landed on the alleged date at Heller aerodrome near Oslo, caused embarrassment in court. This rebuttal compromised the entire line of Comintern propaganda. The Norwegian CP leaders appealed to the Comintern leadership for instructions. Helena Walter, Dimitrov's secretary, wrote the following note on the radiogram received from Norway:

> Statement from Com. Ercoli. No answer is to be given to this telegram because they already received directives re the trial. There [Norway], press opinion is divided, some [papers] confirm the fact with the aeroplane.[24]

As it proved impossible to contest the charge of falsification, Moscow could only pretend that nothing had happened. This attitude did not change, even when the Norwegian and other communist parties sent further enquiries to Moscow.

A note in Dimitrov's diary about the second show trial was significant. On 4 December 1936 he wrote about the current Plenum of the Central Committee of the VKP(b):

> Ezhov's speech on the counter-revolutionary activities of the Trotskyists and the Right org[anisations] – Piatakov, Sokolnikov, Serebriakov and others, Uglanov, Tsulimov, Kruglikov, Kotov. (400 arrests in the Ukraine, 400 in Leningrad, 150 in the Urals etc.).
> – The speeches of Bukharin and Rykov (tears and avowals of innocence). Stalin's speech
> – "We cannot take the former opposition at their word": the suicide of Tomskii and others is the last desperate throw in the struggle against the Party ...
> – Speeches of Molotov and Kaganovich (Molotov quoted from a letter from Bukharin to Voroshilov, "polit[ical] cowards").[25]

On 7 December Dimitrov noted:

> Sitting of Plenum. Stalin's motion was not to decide finally on the Bukharin–Rykov affair, but to continue the investigations because the confrontation of Piatakov and others with Bukharin and Rykov will demonstrate the necessity of investigating this affair to the end.[26]

The diary entry of 16 December 1936 contains a long quotation from the confession Sokolnikov had made four days earlier. The statements therein confirmed the "conclusion" of the NKVD about Trotsky's "negotiations" with the accused and of "the existence of a conspiratorial centre" acting together with the German and Japanese governments to prepare a war against the USSR with the aim of defeating it and seizing power.[27]

This entry testifies that Dimitrov belonged to that elite group which received copies of the prisoners' confessions from the Soviet secret police. Dimitrov noted on 11 January 1937: "Read the confession of Radek and Ust.[?] Bukharin's guilt is definite."[28] Before the official statement on the trial was issued, Dimitrov penned a draft for instructions to the CPs on the court drama. On 21 January he wrote a note on a statement by Vyshinskii during the trial against Piatakov, Radek and others. Dimitrov subsequently reported on the proceedings and also, briefly, on the measures to be taken by ECCI in this connection. His entry on the court verdicts reads: "Radek, Sokolnikov, Arnold, Stroilov – prison sentences. The rest – death penalty."[29]

In another meeting with Feuchtwanger, on 2 February, the German novelist again uttered grave doubts:

> On the trial:
> 1) Sabotage acts, spying, terror – proven.
> 2) Also proven that Trotsky inspired and directed [the crimes].
> 3) The agreement between Trotsky and Hess based merely on the confessions of the accused – no further proof at all?
> 4) The fact that Radek and Sokolnikov were not sentenced to death will be exploited abroad as proof that they made such confessions in order to save their lives.
> 5) The abusing of the defendants [by Vyshinskii] made a bad impression. If they are enemies, they deserve to be destroyed. But if they did not act from personal motives, was it necessary to call them scoundrels, reptiles etc.?[30]

6) Does not understand the whole uproar about the trial. It created an atmosphere of extreme agitation among the people, mutual suspicion, denunciations etc. Trotskyism has been killed off, why this campaign?[31]

On 5 February the Presidium of ECCI passed the motion "Results of the Trial against the Trotskyists". The long document was based on the lines of the investigation that had been dictated by the NKVD to the defendants. If the defendant did not confess, this was considered to be proof of his guilt. All the more so, it was alleged, as the trial was conducted "by adhering to proper standards in order to guarantee objectivity."[32] The motion stated categorically that Trotskyism had transformed itself into "an international agency of fascism."[33] Stalin, however, remained dissatisfied with this motion. On 11 February, in a conversation with Dimitrov, he stated: "The motion is rubbish. All you people in the Comintern are playing into the hands of our enemies [...] It's not worth passing motions, they are obligatory things. Better to send a letter to the parties."[34] He then explained what such a document should contain:

1) Discount what the European workers think, that it has all happened because of a fight between myself and Trotsky, because of St[alin's] bad character.
2) Necessary to show that these people fought against Lenin and against the Party when he was alive.
3) Use Lenin quotations on the opposition: all kinds of opposition under conditions of Soviet power, while adhering to their errors, slide into White Guardism.
4) Make reference to the stenogram [minutes] of the trial, quoting from the confessions of the accused.
5) Show up their politics and how they conspire for the defeat of the Soviet Union.[35]

In reality, Stalin acted as the director of the campaign carried out by the Comintern. He showed his dissatisfaction at the way ECCI leaders were conducting it and his words "playing into the hands of our enemies" sounded decidedly ominous. Stalin's demand was soon realised. On 17 February Dimitrov asked him humbly to give "your remarks and instructions" regarding the text of an altered letter to be sent to the CPs. The letter was full of long quotations from the confessions made during the second Moscow show trial, purporting to demonstrate that the defendants "were ensured full freedom to defend themselves" and had been:

> given the unrestricted right to contest, before the whole world, what had been established during the preliminary investigation of the charges. When incontestable evidence was presented, however, all defendants, many of whom had persisted in denying the charges over some months, could not now deny their crimes against Soviet power, the country and the people.[36]

In carrying out Stalin's order, the leading figures in the Comintern made use of the court confessions, giving credence to the pure fantasy of a Trotskyist conspiracy to provoke a war between the fascist countries and the USSR, leading, after the defeat of Soviet power, to the re-establishment of bourgeois rule. In this, too, Stalin's line of "argument" was strictly adhered to – to portray the defendants as enemies of Lenin. The letter issued to the communist parties therefore contained a long extract from Piatakov's confession concerning his alleged meeting with Trotsky in Oslo. This NKVD invention, as noted above, was the subject of adverse comment in the foreign press, with implications for the plausibility of the charges proffered. Of more importance for the Comintern leadership, however, was the exact execution of Stalin's directive.

At the February–March 1937 Plenum of the Central Committee of the VKP(b), growing persecution, the predominant theme, was given a theoretical underpinning by Stalin's statement that the class struggle sharpens the closer the Soviet Union approaches socialism.[37] Dimitrov wrote about the Plenum in his diary: "The Plenum is indeed historical".[38] Considering the investigation of the "Bukharin–Rykov" case, Dimitrov wrote on 23 February: "Bukharin's speech (a repulsive and pitiful picture!)". Four days later in the diary are the words: "Resolution on case of Bukh[arin] and Ryk[ov], expulsion from the Party, the matter is to be handed over to the NKVD."[39] Dimitrov did not mention Bukharin's fate in subsequent entries.

The 5 April sitting of the ECCI Presidium discussed anew the struggle against Trotskyism. The motion passed, while repeating traditional appraisals, contained a passage which suggested that the Communist International and the CPs had underestimated the dangers of Trotskyism:

> The Presidium of ECCI emphasises that many functionaries in the Communist parties of the capitalist countries, and Comintern employees, have not shown the obligatory vigilance towards

Trotskyism, have not warned in good time of the fusion process between Trotskyism and fascism, even when all the deeds of the Trotskyists demonstrate that a basic political agreement exists between the goals of Trotskyism and fascism.[40]

Similar resolutions of the ECCI Presidium, directed at ridding the communist parties of "two-faced Trotskyist elements",[41] were, in essence, identical with the "purge language" employed in the VKP(b). The text of the resolution was published in a detailed article in the journal *Communist International*.[42] On 11 November 1937 Dimitrov sent Stalin the text of this resolution. On this occasion what he heard was far from approving. According to his diary entry of 11 November, Stalin said to him:

> The resolution of the Secretariat is out of date. That's what comes from people sitting in their offices and inventing things! Intensify all modes of struggle against the Trotskyists [in the motion], it's inadequate. It is necessary to hunt down the Trotskyists, to shoot them, to destroy them. They are provocateurs, all over the world, deadly agents of fascism.[43]

Dimitrov received the direct order from Stalin to summon the prominent German communist Willi Münzenberg from Paris to Moscow: "Münzenberg is a Trotskyist. When he arrives we'll arrest him without fail. Try to entice him to come here."[44] In the course of this talk with the dictator, Dimitrov heard Stalin's version of the causes for the terror:

> The turning points: 1) 1905. 2) 1917. 3) Brest-Litovsk Peace. 4) Civil War. 5) Particularly collectivisation, something completely novel and unprecedented in history. Several weak elements fell away from the Party then. Retreating before the Party's strength, they did not agree, in their hearts, with the Party line, did not grasp the significance of collectivisation (when we wished to cut into the living body of the kulak), and then they went underground. Being powerless themselves, they linked up with our external enemies, promising the Germans the Ukraine, the Poles Belorussia, the Japanese our Far East. They were waiting for a war, and hoped specifically that the German fascists would soon start a war against the USSR. We knew [about their activities] in the past year, set about to make short work of them, but waited until we had proof. At the beginning of the year they intended to carry out something big, but

did not decide definitely. In July they wanted to launch an attack on the Politburo in the Kremlin saying "Stalin will start to shoot and there will be hell to pay". I said to our men that they [the enemies] could not make up their minds to strike or not, and laughed at their plans. In regard to some in our circle we really were negligent. This is a big lesson for us and for all Communist parties.[45]

Dimitrov did not dare to comment on this outburst when writing his diary entry. Somewhat earlier, on 7 November 1937 during the parade and demonstration on the occasion of the 20th anniversary of the Bolshevik Revolution, Dimitrov, standing beside the Soviet leaders on the tribune of the Lenin Mausoleum, received from Stalin directly the order not to be in any particular hurry to inform the Comintern sections about the arrests:

> We will have to wait before dispatching a statement disclosing the facts of counter-revolutionary activities in the VKP(b) and the Comintern. At the moment it is important to compile the material. It is not worthwhile sending just snippets of information.[46]

Stalin added that the Trotskyists had turned into spies and provocateurs, as had the former Comintern officials Osip Piatnitskii, Waldemar Knorin, Béla Kun and others, including Trotsky. The latter had all joined the "Tsarist counter-intelligence service in 1904 or 1905".[47] In the last instance, any version of events uttered by Stalin was true for the General Secretary of the Comintern. Dimitrov diligently wrote down his leader's words, including what Stalin said at the banquet after the festivities on Red Square. According to the diary, Stalin stood up and gave the following toast:

> I'd like to say a few words, which perhaps are not very positive. The Russian Tsars did a lot of bad things. They robbed and enslaved the people. They conducted wars and annexed territories in the interests of the landowners. But they did one great thing – they built a huge state as far as Kamchatka. We subsequently inherited this state. And we, the Bolsheviks, for the first time united and strengthened this state, making it one and indivisible, but not in the interests of the landowners and capitalists, but for the benefit of all workers and all people who make up this state. We united the state in such a way that any part that might be torn away from the common socialist state, while a loss in itself, could not exist independently and would

inevitably fall under foreign domination. Anyone, therefore, who attempts to destroy this united socialist state, who strives to separate it from its single parts and nationalities, is an enemy, a sworn enemy of the state, and of the peoples of the USSR. And we shall annihilate every one of these enemies, even if he is an old Bolshevik. We shall annihilate him and his relatives, his family. Anyone who in deed or in thought, yes, in thought, attacks the unity of the socialist state will be mercilessly crushed by us. We shall exterminate all enemies to the very last man, and also their families and relatives![48]

Dimitrov wrote in a supplementary entry that Stalin had the support of the "secondary" cadres, who ensured his victory in the struggle against "enemies". Following Stalin's toast Dimitrov proclaimed:

I cannot add anything to what Comrade Stalin has said in regard to the merciless struggle against enemies and the question of secondary cadres. That will be taught in the Party, and I shall do everything in my power to ensure that it is taught also in the ranks of the Comintern. But I must say that it is not only my deep conviction but I experienced it myself during my painful prison ordeal, namely that it was the good fortune of the socialist revolution and the international proletariat that Comrade Stalin, after Lenin's death, carried on his legacy with tenacity and genius, and that Comrade Stalin, despite all turning points, has secured the victory of our cause. It is impossible to talk of Lenin without linking his name to Stalin.[49]

The Comintern adopted the murderous vocabulary of Stalin, terming, for example, the judicial massacre of the elite of the Soviet officer corps (June 1937) "a Bolshevik blow against fascist war-mongers."[50] ECCI's stance was similar on the occasion of the third great Moscow show trial (2–13 March 1938), that against the so-called "anti-Soviet, Right-Trotskyist Bloc" of Bukharin, Rykov and others. The verdicts were published in *Communist International* and the Secretariat of ECCI characterised the bloody courtroom farce as being "of great service to all of peace-loving mankind."[51] Once more the communist parties were instructed to carry to the masses "the truth about the trial and its significance".[52]

The Communist International, however, did not restrict itself to the role of apologist for Stalin's monstrous crimes but made itself his accomplice in a more direct manner: by exerting "cadre control" over the thousands of political immigrants who had come to the Soviet

Union for a variety of reasons. Information emanating from the Comintern was used by the NKVD to repress these foreigners, including the official representatives of the fraternal communist parties and their rank-and-file. The staff in the ECCI *apparat*, too, were subjected to the terror. The NKVD, in Comintern parlance, were "the neighbours". The Cadres Department of ECCI collated material on the political immigrants and participated in the reviews of their Party records. This check was conducted by VKP(b) bodies at the different geographical levels and in co-operation with the ECCI representative of the CP in question. Officials of the Cadres Department took special note of foreigners whom they termed provocateurs, renegades, thieves, crooks, drunkards and other suspicious "elements". This information was subsequently related to the NKVD.

On one such list, compiled in 1936, 38 persons from Germany were noted, about whom information had been sent in the first half of 1933 to "S", that is to NKVD officer Ignats Sosnovskii. The list contains brief, denunciatory remarks. For example: "Hengst Paul is in Nizhnii Novgorod. Spent his holidays in Germany. Slanders the USSR, that there is hunger and surveillance here, that the Russian proletariat is forced to work at the point of a bayonet." Data on Hengst was sent to Sosnovskii on 2 February 1933.[53] Another note read: "Reck Julie, Dneprostroi; makes anti-Soviet comments to work-mates. We request that suitable measures be taken in respect of R." This denunciation was sent by the Comintern to the secret police on 5 March 1933.[54] Under the conditions of the intensified hunt for "wreckers and spies", the immigrants found themselves in a particularly perilous situation. Leading Communist functionaries contributed to the fiction that there were a great number of "camouflaged" police agents, spies and provocateurs among the political refugees. During a sitting in Dimitrov's secretariat on 25 October 1934, Anton Kraevskii, the head of the Cadres Department in ECCI, spoke about his work. Underlining the necessity of "unmasking" provocateurs, he stated:

> Under the guise of emigrants, spies are being dispatched here who carry out their work very well and very easily, alleging that they had fled from [fascist] terror. Later they became provocateurs. This is a channel for espionage against the USSR and represents an organisation of systematic spying and provocation on an international scale.[55]

Kraevskii also maintained that the fractional struggles in the communist parties were being kindled by the police abroad. In his eyes, then, any participant in (past) fractional struggles and now resident in Russia could be charged with being a police agent.

A general verification of the emigrants' *bona fides* started anew after the December 1935 Plenum of the Central Committee of the VKP(b) had passed a resolution which stated that members of fraternal parties who had emigrated to the Soviet Union under the guise of political refugees were agents of foreign intelligence services and had by now even penetrated the ranks of the Soviet party.[56] At a sitting held in the Cadres Department on 19 January 1936, the Secretary of ECCI Dmitrii Manuilskii censured the department's record, and, citing the resolution of the plenum of the VKP(b), said that the ECCI and the representatives of the fraternal parties had to "work out, jointly with us, a series of measures which should prevent in future the infiltration of our country and of the Party on the part of suspicious, undesirable elements, agents of the class enemy."[57] In a letter to Nikolai Ezhov, who was secretary of the Central Committee of the VKP(b) at that time, Manuilskii reported that the verification would be completed by 8 March and that 8,000 to 10,000 persons had been checked to date; however, he continued, there remained many persons about whom neither the Cadres Department nor MOPR (International Red Aid) knew anything.[58]

The Soviet party leadership urged the Comintern to speed up the verification process. A motion of the Central Committee of the VKP(b) passed on 28 February 1936 on "Measures to protect the USSR from the infiltration of spies, terrorists and saboteur elements" reads:

> In view of the fact that a great number of political emigrants are present in the USSR, some of whom are direct agents of espionage and police organs of capitalist countries, the Comintern has been assigned the task of carrying out a review, jointly with the NKVD, within three months, and to produce an inventory of political emigrants who arrived in the USSR at the invitation of MOPR, ECCI and the Profintern.[59]

The Comintern leadership directed the representatives of the fraternal communist parties at ECCI to check once more on all political immigrants, to pass a decision on each refugee and hand over data on suspicious cases. A summary of reports compiled in May 1936 about "doubtful elements" from Germany contained the date of the denunciation and a précis of its contents.[60] Accordingly, information reached the NKVD on 44 such "suspicious cases" in 1933, 55 in 1934, 59 in 1935 and 27 in the first months of 1936. In some cases the data had been collated at the request of the secret police; usually, however, the Cadres Department had sent the material to the NKVD on its own initiative. As a rule, persons thereby depicted in negative terms were later arrested.

The results of the review (*proverka*) were presented by the Cadres Department to Dimitrov in late August 1936. The report stated:

> The Cadres Department of ECCI has given the NKVD data on 3,000 persons who are under suspicion of being spies, provocateurs, saboteurs etc. It is a fact that the Cadres Department carried out an extensive review during the verification of Party documents in order to expose a significant number of enemies who had infiltrated the VKP(b). It is likewise a fact that many major cases concerning the most frequent provocations and the presence of alien, anti-Party elements in the Polish, Romanian, Hungarian and other Comintern sections were dispatched by the Cadres Department on time. Alien elements and agents of the class enemy were discovered in the Central Committees of several communist parties as well, again because of the assistance rendered by the Cadres Department.[61]

The rapid escalation of the witch-hunt began to threaten the Comintern *apparat* itself. In a report of the Cadres Department on 29 August, Moisei Chernomordik, departmental deputy-director, summed up the examination of the political immigrants and made the urgent demand that "lists of old Trotskyists and doubtful emigrants are to be prepared."[62] One week later the Secretariat of ECCI received "an information sheet on Trotskyists and other hostile elements among the immigrants of the KPD." This document included 32 names of "active Trotskyists and fractionalists", of eight persons "who are under suspicion because of their links to individuals already arrested, to defendants in the [show] trial or who are suspected of working for the Gestapo or being provocateurs."[63] Dimitrov's decision on the contents of the sheet is revealing: "Press on with the review of German immigrants."[64]

It was characteristic of this document that not only were those listed on it termed open or closet Trotskyists, or infiltrators with hostile intentions in the USSR, but that they were also earmarked for arrest as "enemies of the Party and of the people". According to the officials of the Cadres Department, such groups acted like agents in networks established by foreign espionage agencies. Similar "cadre reviews" were conducted within those exiled communist parties that had a permanent representative at ECCI.

A commission set up by the Italian Communist Party (PCI), for instance, examined the personal dossiers of 307 immigrants. It subsequently registered 98 persons who had been "removed" (i.e. arrested) by the NKVD in the years 1936–8.[65] On another list, with the title "Italians arrested by the NKVD, 1935–1938", 108 persons were named. Fifty-eight surnames were typed, the remainder hand-written by the Italian official of the Cadres Department, Antonio Roasio. The list had columns for place of residence (Moscow, Odessa, Gorkii etc.) and for the year of arrest. Against some surnames was written "Trotskyist", "provocateur", or in one case, "anarchist". In three cases the individual was expelled from the USSR, and one release from custody was also noted.[66] The consequences were also tragic for the compilers of such lists. The authors of the information sheets on German communists mentioned earlier, for example, Albert Müller (i.e. Georg Brückmann) and Edna Martens (i.e. Greta Wilde), were eventually destroyed by the regime they had served so diligently.

The mass repression was directed from the highest echelons of power, by the Politburo. The motions it passed on repressive measures grew from 40 in 1936, to 123 in 1937 and 72 in 1938.[67] A leading KGB officer stated in 1990 that members of 31 foreign communist parties were among the victims of the Great Terror.[68] This avalanche of repression prompted many, themselves fearful of arrest, to write true or libellous reports to the secret police. A letter of 18 May 1937, for example, was written by Henryk Walecki and intended for Ezhov. It contained incriminatory material on eight persons, including Fedor Raskolnikov, Willi Münzenberg, Jakob Hanecki and Boris Melnikov (Müller). Within one month the instigator of this denunciation was himself one of Ezhov's "guests", but Belov (i.e. Georgii Damianov), the deputy-head of the Cadres Department of ECCI, sent the letter to Ezhov on 26 July. Copies of his accompanying letter were deposited in the cadre-files of the denounced, all of whom suffered tragic fates.[69]

The Comintern's full complicity in the slaughter of its best cadres is well illustrated by its attitude to the extermination of Polish communists. The arrest of KPP members in the USSR began in the early 1930s. NKVD investigators forced the prisoners to confess to the slander that the KPP had been "contaminated" by the agents of Polish counter-intelligence (*defensivy*), persons purported to be members of Pilsudski's POV (Polish Military Organisation). Dimitrov's secretariat received in February 1936 a letter from Bronislaw Berg (Witold Salzberg), then a prisoner in Medvezhia-Gora

NKVD camp in Karelia. He had been arrested in December 1934 and sentenced to five years. Berg wrote:

> As you know, in the last two years several hundred communist and non-communist Poles, many of whom are political immigrants from Poland, were arrested in the Ukraine. They were accused, as I was, of membership in the Polish counter-revolutionary organisation POV.[70]

Berg also disclosed details of the methods and ruses employed by NKVD interrogators to extract confessions – 24 hours in a bath filled with cold water, continuous questioning over a period of three days, mock executions, threats to the prisoners' families etc. He emphasised that the secret police forced the prisoners to make compromising statements about the KPP leadership, including its General Secretary Julian Lenski. On Dimitrov's instructions the letter was shown to Manuilskii. He made a copy before sending the missive to the NKVD. Dimitrov does not mention Berg's letter in his diary, but he does refer to the fact that the Polish communist leaders were summoned to Moscow:

> 17.6.1937. Lenski has arrived. Rylsky, Skulski and Próchniak have also been summoned.
> 20.6.1937. L[enski] at "Ezhov's".
> 21.6.1937. Walecki as well ...
> 7.7.1937. Próchniak also here, at Ezh[ov's].[71]

Even after his arrest, radio cables were sent in Lenski's name to other KPP leaders ordering them to come to Moscow. The cable of 8 July read: "Sewer has arrived. When is Stefan coming? Robert."[72] (Robert was Lenski's pseudonym, Sewer was the Party name of Edward Próchniak, Stefan Skulski that of Stanislaw Mertens.) Similar cables were sent in Lenski's name to Spain, to the Cadres Department of the International Brigades in Albacete, for instance. The department was managed by Kazimierz Cichowski. One of his commissars was Gustav Reicher (Rwal'). One such extract had the following text:

> 10 July. To Kautsky[73]. I request you to send Cichowski here for him to report on his work. Citrine." [the text of the telegram was drafted by Dimitrov]
> 17 September. To Kautsky. Send here the representative of the Polish party Rwal'.[74]

Both Poles shared Lenski's tragic end. By the autumn of 1937 the KPP was bereft of its leaders. On 9 August 1937 the Soviet Politburo decided to "confirm the order of the NKVD on the liquidation of the Polish spying and sabotage ring POV."[75] Dimitrov was presented with material compiled by NKVD interrogators, including confessions, on eight persons belonging to the KPP leadership. According to the "confessions", all of them had admitted their guilt and confirmed that they had infiltrated the KPP with the purpose of "crippling" it and subordinating it to Pilsudski's agents. These admissions also stated that an espionage organisation existed within the Comintern. Dimitrov made excerpts from these files in his own hand, filling over 60 pages. Much of what he copied is simply absurd. In Lenski's NKVD deposition, for instance, it was alleged that he was a POV agent since 1917 and as such had joined the Bolsheviks "with the aim of supporting the Bolshevik upheaval so that he could later attain a leading position in the Soviet government."[76] Equally monstrous was the assertion ascribed to Lenski that 90 per cent of the delegates to the 6th Congress of the KPP in 1932 were also POV members. The "confessions" of other prominent Polish communists are just as ridiculous.

Did Dimitrov believe that the charges were authentic? Hardly. From the confession of Rylsky (Jan Lubiniecki) Dimitrov copied the allegation that Burkhardt, the Commissar of Polish State Intelligence, had said to Rylsky "that Popov [a co-defendant of Dimitrov's in the Leipzig Trial] had links to the Bulgarian police and is supposed to have betrayed Dimitrov."[77] After Popov was subsequently arrested and sentenced by the NKVD, Dimitrov applied for his release on several occasions, but to no avail.[78] Apart from his underlining of certain passages, Dimitrov did not confide to his diary what he thought of such "confessions". This was a sensible prophylactic. His last note on this subject (23 November 1937) was laconic: "Man[uilsky], Kuus[innen], Mosk[vin], Pieck. Motion to dissolve the KPP."[79] Shortly afterwards Dimitrov sent the draft resolution to Stalin. Suggesting that the decision should be published, Dimitrov asked when the best opportunity for such a press statement could be.[80] Stalin's answer was brief: "The dissolution [of the KPP] is one or two years late. It must be wound up, but this decision, in my opinion, need not be published in the press."[81]

The motion dissolving the KPP was passed by the ECCI Presidium on 16 August 1938. In connection with the persecution of Comintern employees, the ECCI functionaries, and the officials of the pertinent VKP(b) cell of the Moscow party organisation, used the material held in the Cadres Department to target subordinates they thought were suspicious or questionable "elements". Dismissal from Comintern employment was usually followed by arrest.[82] The Secretariat of ECCI had set up a commission in January 1936 to review its *apparat*. The body was chaired by the Secretariat's candidate-member Moskvin (the pseudonym of Meer Trilisser, the former head of the foreign department of OGPU). The protocols of the commission's sittings record minutely all the data of those under scrutiny and frequently end with the phrase: "dismiss from work in the ECCI *apparat*."[83] The findings were examined and confirmed by Dimitrov. Up to 5 February 1937 the cadre records of 387 ECCI employees and international organisations had been examined. The commission thought it necessary to "dismiss" 58 persons, the majority of them for "political motives".[84] A dismissal recommendation thus phrased was, as a rule, an arrest warrant for the NKVD.

Moskvin, as the representative of ECCI, also took part in a purge of the Comintern school KUNMZ (Communist University of Western National Minorities), which was directed against political immigrants and carried out in the summer of 1936. The commission either recommended expulsion from the USSR, an extension of the residential permit or arrest. In the case of Alexander Kravchuk, a member of the Belorussian party suspected of police contacts abroad and having crossed the border into the USSR illegally, the commission in KUNMZ decided to have him arrested and his case investigated in depth.[85] A similar motion was passed concerning "Erich Eisen" (i.e. Weinberg), a member of the German Communist Party (KPD) since 1930. The decision in his case was based on the following:

> Up to his arrival in the USSR Eisen led a district organisation of the Party in Hamburg. He was arrested in December 1933, but later released, despite the evidence that he was involved in the Party. This circumstance gives grounds to suspect that he was recruited by the Gestapo. He himself has said that the Gestapo suggested that he become a secret informant, and despite his refusal, he was released. After his release he fled from Germany to the Soviet Union.[86]

The decision on "Alfred Rohde" (i.e. Wilhelm Theo Marker) was based on similar suspicions:

> According to our data, he worked for the Rotfrontkämpferbund [KPD paramilitary organisation] in Berlin and was arrested there by the Gestapo. He betrayed two Party members who were later arrested. He has also confessed that he was the person responsible

for illegal military activities in the Berlin organisation of the Party. The circumstances of his escape were, according to his own words, that he jumped out of a police car. This gives grounds for suspecting that he took part in provocative activities.[87]

Marker was arrested in August 1937.[88] Two years later, his wife sent a letter to Dimitrov requesting information on the fate of her husband. Having forwarded the letter to the secret police, Dimitrov duly received a reply from NKVD Deputy-Commissar Merkulov to the effect that Marker had been sentenced on 30 November 1937. It was recommended that the supplicant be informed that her "husband has been sent to a distant Gulag without the right to correspond."[89] This was NKVD shorthand for a death sentence – Alfred Marker was shot in Butovo near Moscow on 8 December 1937.[90] Similar purges were carried out in the Comintern's other schools.

The purge of ECCI staff was renewed after the February–March 1937 Plenum of the VKP(b). A special commission was established, consisting of Dimitrov, Manuilskii and Moskvin. Before the commission had begun to operate, Dimitrov had noted in his diary the arrest of prominent functionaries: "Up to 25.5.37," he wrote, "arrest of Müller, Alikhanov, Dobrich."[91] "Müller" was Boris Melnikov, head of OMS, the courier and communications service of ECCI; Gevork Alikhanov was the head of ECCI's Cadres Department. Both were key figures in the Comintern hierarchy. Their arrest shocked Dimitrov. On 26 May he confided in his diary: "At Ezhov (1am). 'Powerful spies were working in the Comintern'."[92]

The commission on ECCI employees began its work in May and had it completed by July. As a result, 65 persons were dismissed, among them foreign party representatives at ECCI. The standard phrase was "replace them".[93] These words subsequently led to the arrest and execution of the following ECCI representatives: Mathias Stein [i.e. Hannes Mekkinen] (Finland), Zigmas Angaretis (Lithuania), Maria Chobianu [i.e. Helena Filipovic] (Romania), Arne Munk-Petersen (Denmark), Richard Mehring (Estonia), Stefan Fleischer [i.e. Ivan Grzetic] (Yugoslavia), Janis Kruminš-Pilat (Latvia). As a result, the ECCI *apparat* was more or less paralysed, and many of its sub-units, especially the communications service OMS, ceased to function. Those arrested were later expelled from the VKP(b) party cell within ECCI "as an enemy of the Party and of the people". Moskvin admitted in a party assembly on 22 June 1937 that the worst disasters had befallen the "important departments of communications and cadres."[94] He also said that the leadership of ECCI had taken the decision to "rid our *apparat* of persons of whom it cannot be said whether they are enemies or not."[95] This reflected the atmosphere of panic prevalent not only in the *apparat*, but within ECCI's leading circle as well. Moskvin admitted as much in his concluding remarks: "One can observe how dismayed the staff of ECCI is. This is intolerable because it could play into the hands of our enemies."[96]

Moskvin's turn came soon afterwards, as Dimitrov duly noted in his diary (23 November 1938): "M. was summoned to the NKVD. He has not returned."[97] On the following day Dimitrov noted:

> Was at Ezhov's dacha. He said: 'M. was closely linked to all those types. To what extent he had these links in recent times – that will have to be established, as will whether he fell into some kind of trap laid by a foreign intelligence service which was pressurising him. We'll find out.'[98]

On the evening of the following day, Dimitrov obeyed the summons to meet Ezhov's new deputy, Lavrentii Beria. The latter said to the Comintern man: "A series of cases will have to be looked at again. There is a new assignment from Stalin, to work out an instruction pertaining to arrests."[99]

After this conversation Dimitrov sent the following letter (25 November 1938) to Stalin:

> I have temporarily taken over, from yesterday, all functions that had been carried out by the arrested Moskvin in his capacity as a member of the ECCI Secretariat (leading the communications service, being responsible for the supervision and regulation of financial questions). It is beyond my powers, however, to execute these functions for a prolonged period. It is necessary to assign a suitable comrade to the VKP(b) delegation at ECCI who could be designated for this work. All the more, as the arrested enemy of the people has undoubtedly caused so much harm to the *apparat* of ECCI that it must now be remedied and the work re-organised. I urgently request your assistance in appointing such a comrade soon.[100]

Dimitrov did not receive a reply. Letters of another kind flooded his desk – requests for help and information from the relatives of arrested political immigrants who hoped that the Communist International could right obvious cases of injustice and save the lives of innocent people. Despite the fact that such supplications had little chance of success, Dimitrov and several Comintern leaders – Pieck, Koplenig, Togliatti, Florin – made applications on the prisoners' behalf. In the majority of cases the Comintern used its good offices only for persons whom foreign party leaders knew well or who were in receipt of a good recommendation from the ECCI representative of the communist party in question. As a rule, the letters to the NKVD or the State Prosecutor requesting a review of the case or the prisoner's release were followed by a laconic reply that the person involved had been justly sentenced. In some cases, however, Comintern intervention did lead to releases from custody. The lists Dimitrov sent in this connection often contained more than 100 names. The majority were fellow-countrymen – Bulgarians – some Germans, Hungarians and Austrians. The final results, as mentioned, were meagre.

The close interaction between the ruling VKP(b) and the punitive organs of the NKVD gave Stalin's entourage untrammelled powers to deal with "enemies" at will. Party organisations were thus reduced to active accomplices of state terror policies, and fell victim to this relationship in many cases. The tragedy befalling many Comintern workers and political refugees when engulfed in the repression process was a harsh reward for the service they had given to the Stalinist system.

Notes

1 Robert Tucker, *Stalin in Power: The Revolution from Above, 1928–1941* (New York and London, 1990), pp. 504–13; Robert Conquest, *The Great Terror. A Reassessment* (London, 1990), pp. 399–408; Roy Medvedev, *Let History Judge: The Origins and Consequences of Stalinism* (Oxford, 1989), pp. 430–6. Dmitrii Volkogonov's volume on the Soviet dictator, *Stalin: Triumph and Tragedy* (London, 1991) does not mention the massacre of foreign communists, and E. H. Carr's monograph on the history of the Communist International between the "Third Period" and the acceptance of the "Popular Front" (E. H. Carr, *Twilight of the Comintern 1930–1935*, London, 1982), based exclusively on printed sources, does not specifically discuss purge procedures for the period up to 1935.
2 Kevin McDermott and Jeremy Agnew, *The Comintern. A History of International Communism from Lenin to Stalin* (Basingstoke, 1996).
3 M. M. Panteleev, 'Repressii v Kominterne (1937–1938 gg.)', *Otechestvennaia istoriia*, no. 6 (1996), pp. 161–8; Leonid Babichenko, 'Die Moskvin-Kommission. Neue Einzelheiten zur politisch-organisatorischen Struktur der Komintern in der Repressionsphase', *The International Newsletter of Historical Studies on Comintern, Communism and Stalinism*, vol. 2 (1994–5), pp. 35–9.
4 Hermann Weber and Dietrich Staritz (eds), *Kommunisten verfolgen Kommunisten. Stalinistischer Terror und 'Saüberungen' in den kommunistischen*

Parteien Europas seit den dreißiger Jahren (Berlin, 1993); Hermann Weber and Ulrich Mählert (eds), *Terror. Stalinistische Säuberungen 1936–1953* (Paderborn, 1999).
5 A typewritten copy of Dimitrov's diary for the years 1935 to 1945 is held in the Moscow Archive RGASPI, but the manuscript is not the property of the archive and is not accessible to scholars. The diary will be published in the Yale University Press *Annals of Communism* series. For the Bulgarian language version, see Dimitir Sirkov, Petko Boev and Nikola Avreiski (eds), *Georgi Dimitrov, Dnevnik (9 mart 1933–6 fevruary 1949)* (Sofia, 1997). The references to diary entries in the following footnotes are taken from the first volume of the German edition and prefixed by the letters DTI: Bernhard H. Bayerlein (ed.), *Georgii Dimitroff. Tagebücher 1933–1943* (Berlin, 2000), 2 vols: vol. 1, diary; vol. 2, commentary, bibliography, speeches and articles by Dimitrov.
6 RGASPI, f. 495, op. 184, d. 55, general directives 1935.
7 RGASPI, f. 495, op. 184, d. 15, special radio telegram, 29 August 1936.
8 Piatakov was arrested on the night of 11–12 September, Radek on 16 September, and Rakovskii on 27 January 1937.
9 RGASPI, f. 495, op. 184, d. 22, directives to Spain 1936.
10 *Kommunisticheskii internatsional*, no. 15 (1936), p. 37.
11 Ibid., p. 33.
12 RGASPI, f. 495, op. 184, d. 15, special radio telegram, 29 August 1936.
13 RGASPI, f. 495, op. 184, d. 73, general directives 1936.
14 *Kommunisticheskii internatsional*, no. 14 (1936), p. 4.
15 Ibid., p. 6.
16 DTI, p. 125. The original manuscript of the diary is held in the former Bulgarian party archive: CPABSP, f. 146, op. 2, d. 34.
17 DTI, p. 126.
18 Real name Maria Greßhöner, born 1908 in Germany, member of the KPD, intellectual and journalist. Wife of the famous Soviet journalist Mikhail Kol'tsov. She returned to Moscow in 1939 to find out what had happened to her husband who had been arrested in December 1938. Maria Osten was arrested on 26 July 1941 in Saratov and shot on 8 August 1942. See V. F. Koliazin and V. A. Goncharov (eds), *Vernite mne svobody. Memorialnyi sbornik dokumentov iz arkhivov byvshego KGB. Deiateli literatury i iskusstva Rossii i Germanii – zhertvy stalinskogo terrora* (Moscow, 1997), pp. 284–302.
19 DTI, p. 140. This note was written in Russian, the only German word is the second last one "ungeheuert" (recte: ungeheuerlich), i.e. "scandalous".
20 Quoted from Edvard Radzinskii, *Stalin* (Moscow, 1997), pp. 376–7. See the English edition *Stalin* (New York, 1998), p. 352.
21 RGASPI, f. 495, op. 184, d. 73, general directives 1936.
22 RGASPI, f. 495, op. 184, d. 19, general directives 1937.
23 RGASPI, f. 495, op. 18, d. 12, directive to Spain, radio telegram, 21 January 1937.
24 RGASPI, f. 495, op. 184, d. 24, directives 1937: radio telegram from Stockholm, 29 January 1937.
25 DTI, p. 136.
26 Ibid., p. 127.
27 Ibid., p. 140.
28 Ibid., p. 145.

29 Ibid., p. 148.
30 The Germans words "Schüfte" and "Reptilien" are in the original text.
31 See Feuchtwanger's generally apologetic account of Stalin's politics: Lion Feuchtwanger, *Moskau 1937. Ein Reisebericht für meine Freunde* (Berlin, 1993).
32 RGASPI, f. 495, op. 2, d. 246, l. 8.
33 RGASPI, f. 495, op. 2, d. 246, l. 11.
34 DTI, p. 149.
35 Ibid.
36 RGASPI, f. 495, op. 2, d. 245, ll. 53–4.
37 For extracts from Stalin's speech and summing-up to the plenum, see *Partizdat* (Moscow, 1937), p. 22.
38 DTI, p. 152.
39 Ibid., pp. 151–2. This entry and others suggest that Dimitrov wrote his diary notes conscious of the eventuality that the manuscript might fall into the hands of third parties.
40 RGASPI, f. 495, op. 73, d. 48, l. 90.
41 RGASPI, f. 495, op. 73, d. 48, l. 92.
42 'Izgnat' trotskistkikh vreditelei iz rabochego dvizheniia', *Kommunisticheskii internatsional*, no. 6 (1937), pp. 99–102.
43 DTI, pp. 163–4.
44 Ibid., p. 165. Dimitrov, after sending several such summonses, dispatched an ultimatum to Münzenberg on 7 August 1937: "Herfurt [Münzenberg] has to arrive before 22 August. If he does not come, the question of his expulsion will have to be decided" (RGASPI, f. 495, op. 184, d. 15, special directives 1937). Despite the repeated calls, however, Münzenberg refused, knowing what awaited him in the Soviet capital. On 3 March 1938 Dimitrov signed a radio telegram, issued in the name of the ECCI Secretariat, and dispatched it to Maurice Thorez: "Inform Münzenberg and the appropriate persons that he is no longer entitled to sign documents in his capacity as member of the ECCI Secretariat because he has long ceased to be such a member and systematically avoided coming to Moscow, although he was directed by the Secretariat to do so" (RGASPI, f. 495, op. 184, d. 1, directives 1937).
45 DTI, pp. 165–6.
46 Ibid., p. 161.
47 Ibid.
48 Ibid., p. 162.
49 Ibid., p. 163.
50 *Kommunisticheskii internatsional*, no. 6 (1937), p. 8.
51 RGASPI, f. 495, op. 18, d. 1238, l. 29, resolution of ECCI Secretariat, 22 March 1938.
52 RGASPI, f. 495, op. 18, d. 1238, l. 30.
53 RGASPI, f. 495, op. 175, d. 101, l. 105.
54 RGASPI, f. 495, op. 175, d. 101, l. 107.
55 RGASPI, f. 495, op. 21, d. 6, l. 23.
56 See 'Itogi proverki partiinykh dokumentov (Rezoliutsiia plenuma TsK VKP(b), 21–25 dekabria 1935 g.', in the collection *KPSS v rezoliutsiiakh s"ezdov, konferentsii i plenumov TsK*, vol. 6 (Moscow, 1985), pp. 295–304.
57 RGASPI, f. 495, op. 21, d. 34, l. 2.
58 RGASPI, f. 495, op. 21, d. 21, l. 20.

59 RGASPI, f. 17, op. 162, d. 19, l. 99.
60 RGASPI, f. 495, op. 175, d. 105, ll. 5–9.
61 RGASPI, f. 495, op. 10a, d. 391, l. 49.
62 RGASPI, f. 495, op. 21, d. 34, l. 210.
63 RGASPI, f. 495, op. 74, d. 124, l. 27.
64 RGASPI, f. 495, op. 74, d. 124, l. 11.
65 RGASPI, f. 495, op. 21, d. 125, l. 126.
66 RGASPI, f. 513, op. 2, d. 69, "Italiani arrastati dall´NKVD, 1935–1938".
67 Calculated on the basis of the Politburo resolutions in RGASPI, f. 17, op. 3, d. 974–1004.
68 *Nedelia*, no. 20 (1990), p. 11.
69 RGASPI, f. 495, op. 252, d. 519, ll. 1–10.
70 RGASPI, f. 495, op. 73, d. 212, l. 7, as quoted in *Istoricheskii arkhiv*, no. 1 (1992), p. 115.
71 DTI, pp. 159–60.
72 RGASPI, f. 495, op. 184, d. 11, directives 1937.
73 "Kautsky" was the pseudonym of Stoian Minev (1891–1959) in Spain. He was a member of the Bulgarian Socialist Party in the pre-1914 era, and later a Comintern functionary who also used the pseudonyms Vanini and Stepanov. Minev was Dimitrii Manuilskii's political assistant in the Comintern after 1935 and worked in the economics institute of the Soviet Academy of Sciences in the years 1941–5. He was the author of many lengthy telegrams from Spain to Dimitrov, who later passed on the missives to Stalin. The Comintern leaders of the time apparently took delight in giving themselves pseudonyms which were the real names of their enemies in the Socialist International: Dimitrov (Citrine, the British TUC leader), José Diaz (Fritz Adler or (Henry?) Ford), Dolores Ibarurri (Otto Wels of the SPD), Comorera (Otto Bauer of the Austrian SP), Hernandez (Breitscheid of the SPD) etc.
74 RGASPI, f. 495, op. 184, d. 4.
75 RGASPI, f. 17, op. 162, d. 21, l. 142.
76 RGASPI, f. 495, op. 74, d. 411, l. 3.
77 RGASPI, f. 495, op. 74, d. 411, l. 30.
78 RGASPI, f. 495, op. 74, d. 81 , l. 41; f. 495, op. 74, d. 92, l. 69.
79 DTI, p. 167.
80 RGASPI, f. 495, op. 84, d. 402 , l. 6.
81 Ibid.
82 For further details, see F. I. Firsov, 'Die Säuberungen in der Komintern', in Weber and Staritz (eds), *Kommunisten verfolgen Kommunisten*, pp. 37–51.
83 RGASPI, f. 495, op. 21, d. 52, l. 4.
84 RGASPI, f. 495, op. 21, d. 52, ll. 24–5.
85 RGASPI, f. 495, op. 21, d. 166, l. 31.
86 RGASPI, f. 495, op. 21, d. 166, ll. 38–9.
87 RGASPI, f. 495, op. 21, d. 166, l. 38.
88 See his biographical data in Institut für Geschichte der Arbeiterbewegung, Berlin (eds), *In den Fängen des NKWD. Deutsche Opfer des stalinistischen Terrors in der UdSSR* (Berlin, 1991), p. 147.
89 RGASPI, f. 495, op. 73, d. 69, l. 36.

90 *Martirolog rasstreliannykh i zakhoronennykh na poligone Ob"ekt Butovo* (Moscow, 1997), p. 290.
91 DTI, p. 158.
92 Ibid.
93 RGASPI, f. 495, op. 21, d. 52, ll. 63–4.
94 RGASPI, f. 546, op. 1, d. 388, l. 50.
95 RGASPI, f. 546, op. 1, d. 388, l. 51.
96 RGASPI, f. 546, op. 1, d. 388, l. 82.
97 DTI, p. 225.
98 Ibid.
99 Ibid., p. 226.
100 Ibid.

Part II
The Police and Mass Repression

5
Social Disorder, Mass Repression and the NKVD during the 1930s
David Shearer

Introduction

This chapter examines the character of mass repression during the 1930s by focusing on the evolving policies of the People's Commissariat of Internal Affairs, the NKVD (*Narodnyi komissariat vnutrennykh del*). The NKVD included both the regular police (*militsiia*) and the organs of state security, the GUGB (*Glavnoe upravlenie gosudarstvennoi bezopasnosti*). The predecessor to the GUGB was the Unified State Political Administration, the OGPU (*Ob'edinennoe gosudarstvennoe politicheskoe upravlenie*). Although administratively linked throughout the 1930s, the police and the OGPU/GUGB were supposed to have different functions. The regular police were charged to fight crime and to maintain social order. The OGPU/GUGB was charged to protect the Soviet state and its leaders from the country's political enemies. In fact, as I will show, early in the 1930s these two functions merged in the policies of the police and the OGPU. Solving problems of mass social disorder became synonymous with the political protection of the state and defined a major priority for political leaders and high officials of the OGPU/NKVD. That priority was reflected in the primacy given to operational policies of "social cleansing" and mass social reorganisation. Throughout the middle 1930s especially, wide-scale police operations targeted criminals and other marginal social groups. Officials perceived these populations not just as socially harmful but as a threat to the Soviet state and to the construction of socialism in the USSR. I will examine the reasons why the functions of social order and state security became linked in the 1930s and I will explore the consequences of this linkage in the changing character of the state's policies of repression.

Campaigns of mass repression targeted different groups at different times and were not all directed against criminal or socially marginal populations. The largest mass operations, of course, were those associated with de-kulakisation in the early 1930s, the state's attempt to destroy organised class resistance in the countryside. Party and police officials focused de-kulakisation campaigns on property confiscation, imprisonment, exile, and even execution of supposedly rich peasants – *kulaks* – and other rural anti-Soviet elements. After 1933, the police shifted attention away from class war in the rural areas to cleanse the country's major cities, as well as other strategic regions – borderlands, new industrial centres, and even resort areas of the political elite. Yet as the criterion of class became less prominent in the state's campaigns of social repression, the range of groups which police and security organs regarded as potentially dangerous broadened. During the course of the decade, the police applied methods of mass repression against an increasing number of ethnic and national minorities, as well as against criminal and other socially marginal categories. The state's policies of mass repression reached their apogee in 1937 and 1938. Operations associated with the Great Purges of those years encompassed nearly every group that had, at one time or another, become marginalised or politically suspect during the 1930s: so-called kulaks, criminals and socially marginal populations, and national minorities, including large numbers of political refugees. I will focus attention primarily on the background to the 1937 and 1938 repressions, but it should be noted that mass operations did not end with the repressions of those years. Campaigns, especially against certain national minorities and ethnic populations, continued well into the 1940s.[1]

I believe that resolving problems of social order provided a major motivation for the mass repressions at the end of the decade, but so was the increasing threat of war during the late 1930s. I will explore how the threat of war shaped leaders' perception of politically suspect populations as the social basis for a potential uprising in case of invasion. I agree with those who argue that the mass repressions of the late 1930s were a prophylactic response to this potential threat rather than the reaction of the regime to ongoing social chaos. In making this argument, I am revising my own earlier assessment of the mass repressions as a response to a recurrent crisis of social order.[2]

Throughout this paper, I will examine the politics of policy formation at high levels of the NKVD, the party, and the Soviet state, but I will also explore the problems of implementing policies at local levels and the social consequences of state policies. While I rely largely on information from central state and party archives, I will focus parts of my article on the Western Siberia district, or *krai*. I have chosen Western Siberia because that area exemplified, in some ways in the extreme, many of the trends that occurred in other parts of the country. Records from the administrative centre of the district in Novosibirsk reflect well how central policies worked, or did not work, in practice. I will argue that, by the late 1930s, party and state leaders believed that policies of mass repression and re-organisation of the country's population had resolved many of the problems of social disorder, which they had perceived as so threatening. The increasing possibility of war, however, aroused fears, not of social disorder, but of organised uprisings by disaffected and marginal segments of the population. Party and NKVD records reveal the mechanism, social context, and motivation for the mass repression of 1937 and 1938.

The February–March 1937 plenary sessions

In late February and early March 1937, several hundred leading functionaries of the ruling Communist Party of the Soviet Union gathered in Moscow for a plenary session of the party's executive body, the Central Committee. N. I. Ezhov, a leading party secretary and head of the NKVD, delivered one of the major speeches at the session and his remarks are worth recalling in some detail. Although highly politicised, Ezhov's speech provides one of the few candid overviews of the NKVD's work for the previous years of the 1930s.[3]

Ezhov's remarks amounted to a harsh indictment of NKVD policies and a damning criticism of the previous head of the Commissariat, Genrikh Iagoda. Ezhov charged Iagoda and the NKVD with having failed to protect the party and the country from the threat of political sabotage by opposition organisations inside the country and enemy intelligence services working from outside the Soviet Union. Instead of using its resources to expose underground political organisations and agents of foreign governments, the GUGB, charged Ezhov, had dissipated its energies in chasing criminals and fighting social disorder. This was the business of the regular police, the *militsiia*, chided Ezhov, not the work of the organs of state security. Ezhov cited figures from 1935 and 1936, acknowledging that the NKVD, in particular the GUGB, had arrested a "significant number" of people, "but when we analyse the crimes for which these people were arrested," he continued, "it turns out that eighty per cent [of those crimes] had no connection to [the function of] the UGB." According to Ezhov, the great majority of people arrested by the UGB were apprehended for offenses such as "professional white-collar crimes, for petty crimes, for hooliganism, petty theft, etc.; that is, people who should have been arrested by the civil police or the procuracy organs, but who were arrested by the UGB." By paying so much attention to fighting ordinary crime, the UGB had "fettered" itself; the state security organs had neglected their agent work and investigations of serious political crimes.[4]

If the overall direction of NKVD policies was wrong, so were its methods of work. Ezhov summarised the campaigns of mass repression against anti-Soviet kulak peasants in the early 1930s as a peculiarity of that period of large-scale, open class war. Such methods were justified then, according to Ezhov, when the party fought an all-out struggle for the collectivisation of agriculture. By 1933, however, the major struggle for collectivisation had been won. The kulaks had been defeated as a class. As Ezhov reminded his audience, however, the victory of socialism in the USSR did not mean the end of class war. Class enemies were no longer able to defeat Soviet power through direct confrontation, and so the party's enemies changed tactics to wage a war of underground sabotage. This change in tactics by the enemies of socialism required, in turn, a change in tactics by the party, by Soviet institutions, and most of all by the organs of state security, the UGB. Ezhov recalled the directives of the party and the government, and speeches by party leaders, including Stalin, about the sharpening of class war, about the "quiet sabotage" (*tikhoi sapoi*) of enemies, and about how to meet this new challenge. New methods of class war required new methods of operation, Ezhov said, but the NKVD had failed to reorient itself. "It is one thing," Ezhov declared, "to rout mass kulak organisations in the earlier period, but another to uncover diversionaries and spies who hide behind the mask of loyalty to Soviet power."[5] Ezhov charged that the UGB had failed to give priority to development of an effective agent and investigative apparatus. Instead, the organs of state security continued "automaton-like" to employ the "mass work" and "campaign-style methods" of the past.[6]

Ezhov tailored his speech to discredit Iagoda and to justify the purge of the NKVD, which had already started in late 1936.[7] Yet if Ezhov tailored his facts to fit his political ends, he none the less gave to plenary delegates a roughly accurate account of NKVD policies and methods during the previous years. Throughout much of the 1930s, police, party and state agencies struggled to cope with the massive social and economic dislocation caused by the state's crash industrialisation programme and by the social war of collectivisation in the countryside. As a result, much of the OGPU and then NKVD operational policies were directed toward combating crime and social disorder and given the inadequacies of regular policing methods in the country, OGPU and NKVD officials resorted to large-scale campaigns to arrest, remove or otherwise contain what leaders regarded as socially harmful or politically suspect populations. Ezhov denounced these policies and methods in 1937 as a grievous political mistake, and even worse as part of a plan of counter-revolutionary sabotage. Yet what Ezhov described as political error in 1937 was party and state policy during much of the decade.

Social order and state security

The merging of social control and political defence of the state came about in the early years of the 1930s, in part from the administrative intermingling of the civil and political police. Administrative coordination of the two organs first occurred as the result of reforms in 1930 and 1931 of the Worker-Peasant Militia, the RKM (*Raboche-krest'ianskaia militsiia*). In order to centralise state administration and to raise professional standards within the civil police, Iagoda, with the backing of the Politburo (the Party's highest executive body) and Sovnarkom (the Council of People's Commissars), placed the *militsiia* under effective if not complete administrative control of the OGPU.[8] As a result of the reforms, administrative integration or at least coordination was to occur at all levels. Officials working in the high police apparatus, for example, were to be OGPU officers appointed either by or through Iagoda. At the county level (*oblast'*) and below, the RKM continued to operate as a partially independent organisation subordinate to local soviet councils. In fact, OGPU plenipotentiaries and inspectors oversaw cadre selection, accounting, and other administrative functions. As the police began to expand the number of precincts in cities and regions, the head of each *uchastkovoi* (precinct) was supposed to be both an RKM and an OGPU officer. Formation of a central all-union police administration in 1932 further increased central state and OGPU authority over the RKM. The formation of the NKVD in the summer of 1934 brought the RKM under Iagoda's formal and complete control within the same commissariat as the organs of state security.[9]

Instructions to the police in the early 1930s defined their new roles, which differed significantly from their previous functions. Hitherto, the police were subordinate to local Soviet authorities and acted as a constabulary force. They had many duties, vaguely defined, and all concerned the keeping of public order, but the police had limited investigative and arrest powers, and in the area of crime fighting acted primarily to make initial inquiries. Criminal investigations were conducted by procuracy officials or, in the case of more serious and especially organised crimes, by the branches of the state's *ugolovnyi rozysk*, or special criminal investigation units. Police subordination to the OGPU required them now to take a more active role in the fight against crime, social disorder and anti-Soviet activities. With the promulgation of a new Statute (*polozhenie*) in 1931, the police were to have greatly expanded investigative and arrest powers. In addition to these new powers, they were also supposed to become an active part of the state's system of social surveillance. Local precinct officers, for example, were required to establish a surveillance system of their neighbourhoods that relied on regular information gathering from doormen, shopkeepers, shoe-shine men, waiters and other service personnel. Using the passport card index that was supposed to be kept in every precinct, the *uchastkovoi* inspector was responsible for keeping track of all people coming in and out of the areas under his authority.[10]

The reforms of the RKM made clear Iagoda's intention to turn the police into an organ of social control subordinate and equal in preparedness to the organs of state security. By placing the police under the administrative control of the OGPU, Iagoda intended to "militarise" or to "cheka-ise" (*chekaizatsiia*) the police, but he did not intend for administrative merger to lead to operational merger. Officials attempted to keep police and OGPU activities separate since they believed, at least still in the early 1930s, that there was an ideological as well as an operational difference between the functions of social control and state security. The police were to work as an auxiliary force to the OGPU in the establishment of social discipline and the protection of state interests and property, but the fight against counter-revolutionary activities was to remain a prerogative of the OGPU, the organs of state security.

However, the distinction between social control and state security soon broke down. The most significant overlap occurred at first between operational sectors of the OGPU and the police criminal investigative forces, the *ugolovnyi rozysk*. At times these groups either overlapped in their work or even stumbled into each other's operations, since both organs ran agent and informant networks and conducted special operations against organised crime. The OGPU, and Soviet officials in general, regarded organised criminal activity as more than a problem of social deviancy or even as an economic threat to the state. As one OGPU official declared, agents saw the hand of counter-revolution behind all forms of organised criminal activity.[11] As a result, officials regarded organised economic crime – banditry, for example, and even some forms of group hooliganism – to be anti-state as well as socially harmful crimes. The definition of these types of crimes as both politically and socially dangerous led to operational overlap between the OGPU and the forces of the *ugolovnyi rozysk*, and this operational overlap led some officials to recommend a formal merging of the *ugolovnyi rozysk* and the OGPU.[12] The two organs never formally merged, and neither did the regular police and the OGPU. However, the operational and "ideological" distinction between the police and OGPU broke down almost from the beginning of the 1930s as officials conflated economic and social control with state security.

If civil police investigators encroached on the operational territory of the political police, OGPU officers in turn soon found themselves unexpectedly involved in the business of social control and the maintenance of public order. Political police involvement on the railroads provides a good example of how this process occurred. Ostensibly, the OGPU's transport forces were charged to "defend" the railroads against counter-revolutionary sabotage, that is, against the enemies of the state. In practice, OGPU officers brought order to the railroads by providing protection to passenger trains from robbery and gang violence. In the absence of regular police, OGPU operational groups routinely cleared yards, depots, stations, and facilities of gangs and drifters. OGPU units spent much of their time engaged in operations against the organised transportation of stolen or contraband goods and the organisations that used the railroads for criminal purposes. At times, OGPU officers even checked passenger tickets and commercial train manifests. During periods of severe breakdown, OGPU forces were given authority to place certain lines under OGPU martial law, taking over the actual administration of the road. Such was the case on the Omsk and Tomsk lines in Western Siberia in 1935 and 1936. For a period of six months spanning those two years, Lazar Kaganovich, then transport commissar, requested the OGPU to oversee the administration and operation of the road.[13] OGPU forces did much to bring discipline to the railroad system, but their efforts resulted in a militarisation of social order and a conflation of social discipline with political defence of the state.

The conflation of state security and social control functions was not just the result of organisational "drift" or colonisation of authority by the political police. Stalin set the tone for this shift in policy as early as

January 1933 in his remarks to the party's Central Committee plenary meetings. In his speech, Stalin emphasised that open class war had ended with the victory of collectivisation and the successful de-kulakisation of the countryside. Stalin cautioned, however, that enemies of the Soviet state would continue their opposition to Soviet power. They would do so not through open organised opposition, but through more subtle forms of sabotage and subversion – the infamous *tikhoi sapoi* – and, because of their weakness as a social force, would seek alliance with other socially alien populations, such as criminals and other marginals. Criminality and lack of social discipline, said Stalin, now posed the greatest single danger to the construction of socialism in the USSR. The state needed to use all its measures of repression against laxness and this new kind of class war.[14]

This new understanding deeply influenced police and OGPU policies in the mid-1930s and turned the fight against crime and social deviancy – indeed, any kind of social disorder – from a matter of social control into a political priority in defence of the state. Socially harmful elements (*sotsial'no-vrednye elementy*) were now to be regarded as also politically dangerous. With this pronouncement, OGPU officials saw their suspicions confirmed by the country's political leaders. Behind any criminal activity lay the hand of counter-revolution. Now, suddenly, petty and big criminals alike, hooligans, and other socially marginal groups became the business not just of the civil authorities, but of the OGPU.

Following Stalin's lead, high officials in all branches of the state's punitive and judicial organs adopted the argument that social deviance was a major, perhaps the primary threat to the existence of the state.[15] Iagoda, the head of the OGPU/NKVD, gave one of the clearest statements about the political danger of social disorder in an April 1935 speech to a gathering of senior police officials. "For us," declared Iagoda, "the highest honour is in the struggle against counter-revolution. But in the current situation, a hooligan, a robber, a bandit – is he not the real counter-revolutionary? ... In our country ... where the construction of socialism has been victorious ... any criminal act, by its nature, is nothing other than an expression of class struggle."[16] We might assume that Iagoda exaggerated the significance of policing functions in order to inflate the morale of his audience of policemen. Yet Iagoda emphasised the same priorities in his regular reports to Sovnarkom and, in the view of his critics, the NKVD chief reiterated similar priorities even in his communications with the GUGB. According to Leonid Zakovskii, a senior OGPU/GUGB official under

Iagoda, the latter stressed protection of state property as the foremost concern for OGPU operational and territorial organs in the struggle against counter-revolution. According to Zakovskii, Iagoda laid out this priority in one of his first directives as head of the NKVD in August 1934. Zakovskii, as well as other critics such as Iakov Agranov, Iagoda's assistant chief, claimed that Iagoda maintained this emphasis in his operational administration of the GUGB, even after the murder of Leningrad party head, Sergei Kirov, in December 1934.[17] By and large, Iagoda's critics were correct about his policy priorities. Throughout the 1930s, Iagoda understood that the maintenance of social and economic order was the primary task of the NKVD in defending the political interests of the Soviet state.

Passportisation and mass repression

The internal passport and registration system, initiated in early 1933, became the primary instrument that police and the OGPU/NKVD used to protect the country against what were considered criminal and socially harmful elements. Initiation of the passport system was also the occasion for the first real administrative and operational meshing of the police and state security organs. Initially, the passport system was designed to deal with the consequences of mass dispossession and forced migration out of the countryside during de-kulakisation and collectivisation. It was established specifically to seal off major "socialist" spaces (main cities, industrial zones, and border areas) from contamination by "superfluous people, those not tied to productive labour, kulaks fleeing to cities, criminals, and other anti-social elements." In other and later variations, anti-social became interchangeable with anti-Soviet.[18] By August 1934, initial passportisation of major cities in the Russian republic, including the Moscow and Leningrad *oblast*s, resulted in the issuing of 27,009,559 passports. The police issued about twelve million passports to citizens living in so-called "regime" cities, that is, cities on privileged supply lists and of special significance, either political or economic. Nearly fifteen million passports were issued to citizens living in non-regime cities.[19]

Passportisation allowed police officials to quantify what they believed were the number of socially alien elements in the country. Passportisation also allowed the regime to locate, at least initially, the areas of the country most saturated with marginal and dangerous populations. In an August 1934 report to the Russian Federation Soviet Executive Council, Fokin, the head of the police passport department, counted 384,922 individuals who had been refused passports. This figure amounted to slightly more than three per cent of the overall number of citizens who had been granted passports. In the border regions of Eastern Siberia, nearly 11 per cent of the population had been denied passports, while 1.5 per cent of the population of Leningrad *oblast'* and the western border areas of the country were denied passports.[20] After initial passportisation of Moscow, Leningrad, Khar'kov, Magnitogorsk and several other cities, authorities could count about 70,000 "alien elements" – fleeing kulaks, individuals under judicial conviction, escaped convicts, individuals deprived of voting rights (*lishentsy*), and those with no socially useful employment. This number amounted to 3.4 per cent out of a population of 2,088,422 who received passports.[21]

The process of passportisation set the country's marginal populations in motion. Hundreds of thousands of people fled the regime cities and industrial areas, either as a consequence of being denied a passport or in advance of the passport campaign. Officials estimated that, in the course of the two to three months of the passport campaign, about 60,000 individuals migrated out of Moscow, 54,000 fled Leningrad, and 35,000 left Magnitogorsk.[22] Overall, during the first half of 1933, Soviet cities experienced a total out-migration of nearly 400,000 people. This was the only period since the Civil War years in which the population of cities actually declined, and it was exceptional for the period of rapid industrialisation and urbanisation during the 1930s.[23]

Anticipating a large demographic movement, police and OGPU officials set in motion their own populations, not only to count but to round up the country's alien and dangerous peoples during the period of passportisation. Throughout 1933 and 1934, the OGPU mounted a number of operations in various cities and in particular border and industrial areas. Some of these operations, while they coincided with passportisation, seemed not to be connected directly to it and required Politburo approval.[24] Most operations, however, were related to the passportisation campaign and were conducted on the basis of specific OGPU operational orders. In preparation for these operations, OGPU leaders ordered police and OGPU units to compile lists of undesirables in their districts, even before the issuing of passports. These lists were to be based on many sources of "compromising" information, but in particular on the basis of agent and informant operational work. This work was to be conducted by both police and OGPU operational groups.[25] The police completed the initial passportisation of Moscow, Leningrad, Khar'kov, Magnitogorsk and several other cities by the end of March 1933, and the OGPU launched individual campaigns to sweep these cities of particular groups.[26] Special operations followed in other cities, but by late summer of 1933 the OGPU attempted to organise a systematic set of procedures to process the repression of undesirables. This was in keeping with the Central Committee's 8 May 1933 directive to cease campaign-style measures of repression and Iagoda's instructions to use the passport and registration system as a regular method of protecting cities.

On 13 August, Iagoda issued a circular, number 96, outlining the rules for the "non-judicial repression of citizens violating laws relating to the passportisation of the population." This order established special passport *troiki* at the republic, *krai*, and *oblast'* levels to review and sentence violators of passport laws. The *troiki* were to be chaired by the OGPU plenipotentiary who exercised control over the police, and its members were to include the head of the police passport department and the OGPU operational department, with the participation of the local procuror. These *troiki* reviewed the cases of passport violators according to the lists sent to them from localities in their jurisdictions. They were empowered to pass sentence on violators, subject to review by the OGPU *Osoboe Soveshchanie*, the Special Board in Moscow that adjudicated cases of counter-revolution and state crimes. In his circular, Iagoda specified the kinds of sentences to be given for four categories of individuals: those with no useful employment and disorganisers of industry; *lishentsy* and kulaks; people who had been released from prison or sentences of exile (but who did not have the right to live in the city from which they had been exiled); and "criminals and other anti-social elements." The latter were to be sent to labour camps for up to three years, while those in the other categories were to be sent to penal resettlement colonies (*spetsposelki*), or exiled to live outside a 30-kilometre circumference from a passportised city. The order was especially hard on repeat violators (recidivists) in any category, who were to be sent to camps for up to three years.[27]

The work of the passport *troiki* yielded considerable results which, in turn, reflected the extensive work of police and OGPU operational groups. In the last five months of 1933, the *troiki* for the RSFSR adjudicated the cases of 24,369 individuals who had been arrested under one of the above categories. Interestingly, nearly 17,000 of those arrested were freed, apparently convincing police that they were, indeed, upstanding citizens. In all, passport *troiki* convicted approximately 7,000 individuals, about 1,300 of whom were sentenced to the camps (*kontslager'*), 3,300 to labour or other "special" colonies, and another 2,000 to "near" exile under the category "minus 30".[28]

High police and state authorities intended the passport system to provide a daily means by which police could protect cities and other vital areas from penetration by socially harmful and anti-Soviet elements. Yet local police and OGPU officials continued to operate in the old ways, using campaign-style methods to clear their cities of undesirable and marginal populations. They did so very likely for several reasons. As Iagoda noted in his numerous reprimands of local organs, police did not appreciate the importance of daily maintenance of their passport offices as a way to combat the in-migration of undesirable populations. Moreover, most local authorities did not have the material resources and manpower to keep a constant registry of who was coming and going in their precincts. And in the absence of these kinds of resources, police, especially under the influence of the OGPU/UGB, reverted to the methods of periodic campaigns or sweeps of their cities. Most OGPU/UGB operatives in the 1930s were veterans of the old Cheka of the 1920s and early 1930s and were used to traditional *chekist* ways. Thus, Iagoda found himself constantly chiding local organs for neglecting daily passport control and then resorting to campaign-style methods, clearing cities of socially dangerous elements "in fits and starts."[29]

The special powers of all OGPU *troiki* ended in the summer of 1934 with the reorganisation of the OGPU and the police into the NKVD USSR. With this reorganisation, all cases that had been adjudicated in non-judicial or administrative fashion were transferred for review within the country's restructured court system. This included all cases that had passed through the passport *troiki* as well cases of counter-revolutionary and other state crimes that had been under the jurisdiction of other OGPU *troiki*. The only non-judicial body that was supposed to remain in operation after the 1934 reforms was the NKVD's Special Board. Yet, the country's fledgling court system could not handle the crush of cases that passed through it, and soon the attempt to pass from administrative to judicial repression broke down.

Already in early January 1935, Iagoda and A. Vyshinskii, the Procurator General of the USSR, gave instructions to re-establish special *troiki* to handle cases of passport violations by "criminal and déclassé elements." These special "police" (*militseiskie*) *troiki* were similar in make-up and function to the recently disbanded OGPU passport *troiki*. They were to operate at the republic, *krai*, or *oblast'* level, and included the appropriate head of the UNKVD (who was the administrative head of the UGB), the head of the corresponding level URKM, and the corresponding procurator. In a letter to Stalin from 20 April, Vyshinskii explained that the formation of these *troiki* had been necessary due to the significantly large number of passport cases of socially harmful elements. These cases had clogged the judicial system and the *Osoboe Soveshchanie*. They had led to overcrowding of preliminary holding cells and the consequent violation of Soviet law for detaining individuals without indictment. Vyshinskii was writing to Stalin for approval of a draft Central Committee directive agreeing to the continuation of these *troiki* for operations that would "achieve the quickest clearing (*bystreishaia ochistka*) of cities of criminal and déclassé elements."[30]

Vyshinskii's draft was short, but in it he stated interestingly that one of the primary functions of the *troiki* was to hear cases of criminal and déclassé elements "for which there is no foundation for transfer to a court." In other words, the *troiki* were designed to simplify the process of repression of undesirable populations by bypassing the judicial system's normal requirements for submission of evidence. Thus, the *troiki* could convict and pass sentence on an individual whose case might be quashed (*prekrashcheno*) by a regular court for lack of evidence. In order to preserve legal sanction, according to Vyshinskii, sentences for these types of cases were to be confirmed by the *Osoboe Soveshchanie* on condition that there was no objection from the procuracy at any level.[31] In a note at the top of Vyshinskii's letter, Stalin replied that a "quick clearing is dangerous." Stalin recommended that clearing the cities should be accomplished "gradually, without jolts and shocks [*bez tolchkov*]" and "without superfluous administrative enthusiasm [*bez … izlishnego administrativnogo vostorga*]"; that is, without administrative excesses. Stalin recommended that operations based on the directive last one year. With the rest of the draft, Stalin agreed.[32]

Order 00192 and other operations

The actual Central Committee directive, based on Vyshinskii's proposal, is not yet available in declassified archive materials, but it became the basis for some of the largest NKVD campaigns of mass repression during the mid-1930s. On 9 May 1935, Iagoda and Vyshinskii sent a joint set of operational instructions, Order no. 00192, to all republic, *oblast'* and *krai* level NKVD administrations detailing the work of the new *troiki*. The substance of these instructions is worth noting since they show the extent to which the definition of socially harmful elements had broadened. In the 1920s, the police defined socially dangerous elements narrowly as people with a criminal record. While they were suspect, they were generally not subject to summary arrest simply because of their socially deviant or marginal background.

According to the new decree, however, socially harmful elements fell into one of several categories: persons with previous criminal convictions *and* (author's italics) "continuing uncorrected ties" to the criminal world, and persons with no criminal convictions, but with no definite place of work and ties with the criminal world. The category also included "professional" beggars, persons caught repeatedly in urban areas without proper residence permits, persons who returned to places where they were forbidden to live, and children over the age of twelve caught in a criminal act. All of these types of people were to be regarded as socially harmful. They were now subject to summary arrest and sentencing by the extra-judicial *troiki* of the NKVD for up to 5 years in corrective labour camps.[33]

Operations based on the directive of 9 May 1935 continued at least through the early months of 1936. Sweeps by police and UGB units targeted particular city areas, especially flop-house districts where large numbers of itinerant workers and vagabonds slept; they focused on shanty towns in industrial districts, market places, train stations and other urban public spaces, and on particular farms and villages. By the end of the year, operations by the police alone netted close to 266,000 people classified under the rubric "socially harmful elements". Approximately 85,000 of these individuals came under the jurisdiction of NKVD *troiki*, while the cases of another 98,000 were sent for hearing within the regular court system. In the single month of October, police in the capital and in the Moscow *oblast'*, detained nearly 6,300 people for not having proper residence and work documents, or for other reasons that defined them as socially dangerous types. By November, the police had brought in 26,530 people in Leningrad, and in Moscow city by the same month, 38,356.[34]

Operations against socially dangerous elements in Western Siberia mirrored trends in the rest of the country. The numbers of people swept up in these operations in that district were not as high as in *oblast*s of major cities such as Moscow, Leningrad, or Sverdlovsk, nor as high as the numbers in the Far Eastern province and in the always troublesome Black Sea region, but operations in Western Siberia ranked among the most extensive. The police pulled in close to 9,000 individuals by November 1935. NKVD *troiki* convicted about half that number, while the cases of the rest were sent through regular courts. Close to 1,800 individuals were eventually freed.[35]

The chief prosecutor of Western Siberia, I. I. Barkov, followed the general line laid down by Vyshinskii. As interpreted by Barkov, the decree on socially dangerous elements provided the NKVD with a powerful weapon in the fight against criminals and other enemies of Soviet order. He declared that the new authority given officials under this decree allowed "a maximisation of effort to sweep away criminal-déclassé and itinerant (*brodiachego*) elements, to reduce crime significantly, and to liquidate especially aggravated assault and armed robbery."[36] Regardless of what he may have thought privately, Barkov publicly saw no contradiction between the principles of socialist legality and the use of such extra-judicial police methods against harmful populations. When it came to cases processed through the judicial system under statutes of the criminal code, Barkov hounded *militsiia* and UGB officials constantly for their investigative sloppiness, violations of procedure, and abuse of rights. Yet he only rarely criticised police activities related to these administrative forms of repression.[37] In keeping with the language of 9 May instructions, Barkov recommended that the police avoid "campaign-like mass operations", but in the same sentence he urged an increase in "daily sweeps of criminal-déclassé elements."[38]

Police and UGB groups mounted other operations against populations the regime perceived as harmful or politically dangerous. By May 1935, even before the formal establishment of the police *troiki*, NKVD sweeps of Leningrad *oblast'* and the Karelia border regions led to the deportation of 23,217 "kulak and anti-Soviet elements" to special labour colonies in Western Siberia and Uzbekistan.[39] UGB units, using police and local party activists, also began large-scale deportations of suspect national minorities to Siberia and Central Asia, especially from the Western and Far Eastern border zones. In the two years 1935 and 1936, UGB operations targeted tens of thousands of Finnish, Polish, German, Korean, and Ukrainian populations living in border areas whom the regime suspected of cross-border loyalties.[40] In 1935, Iagoda also recommended the removal of several thousand Soviet citizens of Greek origin living in the Black Sea border regions.[41]

The regime regarded these populations with suspicion, especially in the context of rising international tensions during the mid-1930s, and party and state leaders regarded it as entirely within the authority of the state to remove these peoples as a precautionary measure. Yet officials did not regard them as *ipso facto* anti-Soviet. Even the populations that were to be resettled were not supposed to be deprived of their rights as Soviet citizens. Vyshinskii insisted, for example, that the "Greeks" to be moved from the Black Sea areas were to be compensated for their dislocation. Party, police and UGB officials were supposed to distinguish carefully between those who were to retain their rights and those who should be categorised as socially dangerous or anti-Soviet. The latter were to be arrested, or if not arrested, processed and sentenced through special *troiki* to camps or labour colonies. In some instances, high GUGB officials provided operational officers with approximate figures of how many individuals to arrest or detain as dangerous.[42]

The mass operations against *sotsvredelementy* and national minorities worked so well that the regime applied the same methods to resolve a number of other major problems. Sweeps of orphan children became the primary method, for example, to resolve the problem of juvenile homelessness and gang crime. Over the course of the two years 1934 and 1935, Iagoda and the NKVD won out over more moderate solutions to these problems, and by spring 1935 the police were engaged in mass round-ups of street children, who were then sent to NKVD labour colonies. In effect, the takeover of the orphan problem by the NKVD criminalised this group in the same way that passportisation and the law on harmful elements criminalised the unemployed and other socially marginal populations.[43] Likewise, in July 1936 the Central Committee and Sovnarkom responded to problems of deficit goods and long lines by ordering police and UGB units to organise a campaign of sweeps against small-time speculators. The joint government-party order took the form of a directive, dated 19 July 1936, signed by Molotov and Stalin. This directive ordered the police and UGB to submit a plan for a one-time sweeping operation, "using administrative procedures" in Moscow, Leningrad, Kiev and Minsk. The directive provided a guide figure of 5,000 speculators to be arrested and processed through specially authorised *troiki*.[44] By the end of August, according to Vyshinskii, *troiki* had convicted 4,000 individuals in the cities marked for special operations, while regular courts had convicted 1,635 individuals as part of the anti-speculators' campaign. The latter, however, represented figures from only 25 reporting districts and regions from around the country.[45]

In the absence of a regular policing system, the clearing (*iz"iatie*) campaigns became the primary method for the regime to fight criminality and other forms of social disorder, and to protect cities and other vital spaces, such as border regions and state resorts. Iagoda stressed how well these methods had worked by noting in his March 1936 report to Sovnarkom that crime rates in the rural areas were not declining as rapidly as in urban areas. One of the main reasons, apart from fewer numbers of police, Iagoda emphasised, was that the government and party directives to clear cities of "parasitic and itinerant elements" had not been extended to cover operations in rural areas.[46] In fact, because of the success of sweep operations, Iagoda recommended in his March report that Sovnarkom grant continuation of the work of the NKVD *troiki* to sweep déclassé elements from cities and workers' settlements. When queried for his reaction to this request, Vyshinskii replied that he had no objections in principle. He noted only that the matter needed to be discussed in a special commission, since there existed "special directives" governing the work of these *troiki*.[47]

Sovnarkom approved Iagoda's request. Lists compiled in 1953 by the Soviet Interior Ministry showed a total of 119,159 individuals sentenced by *troiki* in 1935 and 141,318 individuals in 1936.[48] Nearly three quarters of those sentenced by *troiki* in 1935 had been caught up in sweeps as *sotsvredelementy* under the NKVD Order 00192. The next most significant category was very likely that of national minorities, followed by groups caught up in smaller operations – speculators, thieves, agricultural disorganisers and other criminal elements. No breakdowns of sweeps exist for 1936 in open archives, but the relative weights of categories probably remained about the same as in 1935. Interestingly, these numbers far outweigh the numbers of individuals who were sentenced specifically for counter-revolutionary crimes through the NKVD's Osoboe Soveshchanie (29,452 in 1935 and 18,969 in 1936).[49] About the same number of individuals were sentenced for major state crimes in 1935 as were sentenced by *troiki* (118,465 and 119,159 respectively). Yet, while the number of those convicted for high state crimes declined in 1936 to 114,383, the number of individuals sentenced through *troiki* rose sharply in that year to 141,318.

Much has been written about numbers. They are the source of much historical contention. Figures for any category of arrest or repression can vary by the thousands, depending on which source one uses. Yet the figures above, combined with a close reading of operational orders and policy directives, show a clear trend. The Stalinist regime, the NKVD in particular, continued the policies of mass social repression, using administrative means, throughout the 1930s. The regime moderated policies of repression only in the sense that it curtailed the political repression of individuals under specific legal statutes of counter-revolution. Iagoda fell into line with the moderating tendencies of the mid-1930s over use of political terror against the party and state apparatus.[50] Yet the NKVD under Iagoda, including the GUGB as well as the police, continued to use administrative methods of mass repression to establish social order. In the middle years of the decade, the NKVD did not direct its campaigns of mass repression against peasants, but against a range of different and undesirable populations. Indeed, for Iagoda and for the NKVD, the struggle against social disorder was not only a social priority but also a political one. Iagoda, like many leaders, believed that, after the victories of de-kulakisation and collectivisation, social disorder posed the greatest political danger to the state. Thus, the struggle against social disorder became, for him, the equivalent of political struggle against counter-revolution. While Stalin and other leaders supported this policy line at first, it became problematic after the murder of Kirov and by late 1936 Stalin was ready to oust Iagoda for continuing this line in the operational policies of the NKVD.

Ezhov's criticisms of the NKVD at the February–March 1937 Central Committee Plenum were in keeping with this turnabout and his reforms of the NKVD after this meeting reflected his attempt to separate the social order functions of the police from the functions of state security, which were supposed to belong to the GUGB. Administratively and operationally, Ezhov sought to re-orient the GUGB toward the fight against political opposition, understood not as social disorder but as direct organised political subversion and spying. Thus, Ezhov jettisoned the economic crimes sector of the GUGB, which had drained so much operational time and energy. He placed responsibility for the fight against organised crime in the hands of a newly created and strengthened police body, the Department for the Struggle against the Misappropriation of State Property, the OBKhSS (Otdel bor'by s khishcheniem sotsialisticheskoi sobstvennosti). In a major reorganisation, and as a direct result of the February–March plenum, Ezhov also established a new railroad police department within the structure of the GURKM. He clearly distinguished its functions from those of the newly reformed transport department of the GUGB. In a draft directive for the Central Committee, Ezhov outlined the functions of the new eleventh department of the GUGB. "The transport department of the GUGB", wrote Ezhov, "will be freed from functions of securing social order on railroad lines, maintaining public order in train stations, fighting against theft of socialist property, hooliganism and child homelessness. These functions are to be transferred to the newly formed railroad police, which will be subordinated to the GURKM NKVD." According to Ezhov, officers of the railroad department of the GUGB were to engage themselves exclusively in the fight against counter-revolutionary sabotage of the country's vital rail systems. What this meant in practice is not entirely clear, but whatever Ezhov intended, it is evident that he wanted to get the GUGB – the organ of state security – out of the business of guarding mail cars, rounding up hooligans from train yards, chasing itinerant kids, robbers and hobos riding on trains, patrolling train stations and checking for ticket violations.[51]

Whatever other reorganisations Ezhov carried out is a matter of speculation. It is not known whether he streamlined and reoriented the work of the NKVD's agent informant networks, which he claimed needed to be done. Neither is it clear to what extent he purged the NKVD apparatus and fundamentally reorganised it. Despite his initial reforms, Ezhov never entirely separated the police from the GUGB. The government separated the two organs only in 1940, after Ezhov's brief but bloody tenure, and after the leadership of the NKVD passed to Lavrentii Beria. Yet, the separation of internal policing functions from the functions of state security began under Ezhov, immediately following the February–March 1937 Central Committee Plenum.

Immediate origins of the Great Purge

Ezhov's criticism of Iagoda and NKVD policies was sharp and unequivocal. No one could have misunderstood his intent to change the previous policies of the NKVD. However, just five months after the February–March plenum, in late July 1937, Ezhov issued the now infamous operational Order 00447. That order began the mass operations of 1937 and 1938. By decree of the Politburo, the NKVD was charged to begin mass shooting or imprisonment of several categories of socially harmful elements. Leaders regarded former kulaks, bandits and recidivist criminals among the most dangerous of these groups, alongside members of anti-Soviet parties, White Guardists, returned émigrés, churchmen and sectarians, and gendarmes and former officials of the Tsarist government.[52] By the end of November 1938, when leaders stopped the operations, nearly 766,000 individuals had been caught up in the police and GUGB sweeps. Almost 385,000 of those individuals had been arrested as category I enemies. Those who fell into this category were scheduled to be shot, while the remaining arrestees, in category II, were to receive labour camp sentences from 5 to 10 years.[53]

How are we to understand these operations and the order that initiated them? The mass operations of 1937–8 seem to have been a direct contradiction of Ezhov's new turn in the NKVD. Except for the scale and the level of violence, the mass operations of 1937–8 were similar in many details to the kinds of campaigns that Iagoda had conducted against marginal populations and criminal elements. The mass repressions involved the same kind of operational procedures – procedures that Ezhov had condemned – and were directed against similar kinds of social groups – groups that Ezhov had declared were not the business of the organs of state security. Once again, GUGB officers and units, in addition to the police, found themselves in the business of large-scale social purging. In campaign style, they rounded up criminals, itinerants, beggars, gypsies, so-called kulaks, and a host of other categories of suspect people.

The return to mass social repression also seemed to belie the success of Iagoda's policies. In his March 1936 report on crime, Iagoda informed Sovnarkom that, with a few exceptions, the problem of social disorder had been resolved. Rates for nearly every major crime had declined, and although he recommended extension of campaigns against socially harmful elements, Iagoda looked forward to an increasingly stable social situation.[54] Finally, there seems to have been no warning or discussion within the ranks of the party elites about the need for mass purging. In previous campaigns, whether against kulaks, national minorities, or deviant populations, party leaders had prepared the groundwork with widespread propaganda campaigns. No such groundwork was laid for the mass operations of 1937 and 1938. The Politburo resolution of 2 July, on which Order 00447 was based, seemed to arise out of nowhere. Certainly, mid-level party officials, such as Robert Eikhe in Western Siberia, were aware of the continuing problems in their districts, and Eikhe, for example, communicated those difficulties to higher party authorities. Discussions at the level of the Central Committee and in the Politburo show that concern existed at the top of the party hierarchy about continuing problems of social and economic disorder. Yet there is nothing to indicate that officials perceived a growing threat from social disorder, or a threat in any significant way greater than in previous years. Neither does there appear to have been any discussion at higher party levels that would have led to the decision to engage in mass operations against such large numbers of people.

Still, the language that officials used in describing marginal and undesirable populations changed suddenly in the summer of 1937, and the change in language is indicative of the origins of the mass operations. NKVD and party authorities had long seen a link between criminal and other marginal populations on the one hand, and anti-Soviet, even counter-revolutionary elements, on the other. In the early summer of 1937, however, NKVD and party authorities began to perceive what they believed were active organising efforts for "fifth column" activities in case of war with Japan and Germany. I believe Oleg Khlevniuk is correct in his argument that the decision to engage in mass operations against suspect populations was tied to Stalin's reading in early 1937 of rear-guard uprisings against the Republican regime in Spain during that country's civil war. As Khlevniuk argues,

Stalin feared that enemy states might attempt to organise the same kind of rear-guard uprisings, which would threaten the country should war break out and hostile powers such as Germany and Japan invade.[55] In fact, this is the language that appeared in NKVD reports about suspect populations in Western Siberia in the early summer of 1937. It is the language of "rebellious moods" and fifth-column activities by foreign-directed agents and organisations. Thus, in a report to Eikhe from June 1937 Sergei Mironov, head of the Western Siberian UNKVD, described operations to root out "kadet-monarchist and SR organisations." These underground organisations, according to Mironov, had united under orders from the Japanese intelligence service into an overall organisational front called the "Russian General Military Union" (ROVS). The organisations in this union were preparing a "revolt and a seizure of power" in Siberia to coincide with an invasion by the Japanese army. Mironov described the various branches of this union, which the NKVD had uncovered through its investigative operational work, and then he made the connection between the work of these groups and the problem of marginal and other suspect populations.

> Consider [wrote Mironov] that in the Narym and Kuzbass areas there are 208,400 exiled kulaks; another 5,350 live under administrative exile and include white officers, active bandits and convicts, and former [Tsarist] police officials ... This is the social base for their [ROVS] organising work – kulaks and penal settlers scattered across the Narym and in the cities of the Kuzbass ... It is clear, then, the kind of a broad base that exists on which to build an insurgent rebellion.[56]

This kind of language was different from the language of the mass operations to clear cities of harmful elements during the mid-1930s. It is a language that tied socially suspect populations to active military uprisings. This was a threat more dangerous than that of social disorder. Mironov's warning was not about the threat of social chaos, but about the formation of organised opposition. Mironov's language was a language consistent with Stalin's rising concern about the prospects of war, and the domestic consequences of war. Mironov's assessment of the danger to the country from harmful populations also applied to rural as well as to urban areas. This rural aspect also distinguished the discussion about harmful elements in 1937 from previous assessments. The discussion about anti-Soviet elements in early summer of 1937 was not just about making cities safe for socialism; it was about the organised military threat that marginal populations posed throughout the entire country, and specifically in rural areas. In fact, Ezhov began Order 00447 with reference to the countryside. He noted that "a significant number of former kulaks, those previously repressed, those hiding from repression, and escapees from camps, exile, and labour colonies have settled in rural areas." He wrote further that significant numbers of anti-Soviet elements – including sectarians, members of previous anti-Soviet parties, bandits, repatriated white officers, and others – "have remained abroad in rural areas, nearly untouched." These, along with a "significant cadre of criminals" – including livestock rustlers, recidivist thieves, armed robbers, escapees and others – posed a significant danger to the country as the source of "all sorts of anti-Soviet and diversionary crimes".[57]

Ezhov's assessment of the situation in the country reflected the paranoia of the day, but his description of the social dynamics of Soviet repressive policies during the 1930s was, for the most part, accurate. Previous mass operations had cleared the cities of suspect populations. Through passportisation and clearing operations in the mid-1930s, groups which the regime deemed anti-Soviet had been sent into exile or had been driven out of regime cities and border areas and had taken refuge in non-regime towns and in the countryside. There they had stayed, while many others had fled exile and camps, or had been released. The latter contingent was a sizable one, and included a significant proportion of those who had been de-kulakised in the early 1930s and had served their 5-year exile terms or had been released under the amnesty campaigns of 1934 and 1935. These groups were not allowed legally to return to their cities or regions of origin, and so many were, by the late 1930s, also living in rural areas and "unprotected" towns and cities. Thus, while the NKVD had secured the cities as "model socialist places" they had lacked the resources and, as Iagoda noted in March 1936, the authority to extend that control to rural areas of the country. According to Ezhov, insufficient policing measures against these groups had, by 1937, permitted anti-Soviet elements that populated rural areas to begin to filter back into regime cities, industrial sites, into the transport and trade system, and into collective and state farms. Order 00447, then, can be seen as an attempt to extend and finish the job begun with the campaigns against harmful elements in cities from 1933 through 1936. The difference, of course, was that mass operations under Order 00447 were to be mounted in rural areas as well as in towns and cities. Another major difference was the context of imminent war in which Order 00447 was to be carried out. That context was missing in previous campaigns, and it gave to the mass operations of 1937 and 1938 their particular ruthlessness.

The mass operations of 1937–8

To date, little is known about how, exactly, police conducted the mass operations of 1937 and 1938, although they differed from the political purge process that was simultaneously sweeping the party and Soviet bureaucracies. The latter, as many histories and memoirs have shown, struck hardest at elites within Soviet and party officialdom. The purge campaign relied heavily on a bureaucratised process of denunciation, arrest, and interrogation. The party purge, especially, involved a laborious process of document review and appeal. Individual arrests could generate thick case files. In contrast, the operations mounted under authority of the July 1937 order encompassed a much broader spectrum of criminal and socially marginal groups than did the political purges directed against the party and state elites. Denunciations played a part in some aspects of the mass operations, but most who fell victim to this process were targeted not because of any specific criminal or political act which they supposedly had committed, but because they belonged to a suspect social category. In other words, the purge process focused on individuals, the mass operations on social groups. In the Western Siberian *krai*, local NKVD residents compiled lists of socially dangerous individuals in their region (*raion*), based on the criteria outlined in the now infamous 2 July 1937 Politburo directive. In turn, NKVD authorities in Novosibirsk used these lists to select geographic areas for special operations. Mironov, still head of the district's NKVD in early summer 1937, brought in special units of NKVD cadets to process the increased paperwork flowing in from regional offices.[58] Police and UGB officers also used work rolls and passport information to investigate the social background of rank-and-file workers in local state administrative bureaucracies. These, too, became a focus of mass operations.

It did not take long for the police in Western Siberia to respond to the July 1937 order and to work up their forces for the kind of sweeping operations demanded by the party's leaders. Under authority of Ezhov's directive 00447, *militsiia* and units of the UGB set in motion "mass operations ... to repress kulaks" and "to expose and rout criminal elements" (*ugolovnykh elementov*) that they had already been using to deal with socially dangerous populations. These operations could last for months at a time, and special NKVD courts, or *troiki*, were given authority to arrest and sentence individuals.[59]

In the early stages of the Great Purges, "kulaks" bore the brunt of the police's repressive campaigns, as they had in the early 1930s, and by the summer of 1937 kulaks were more "visible" than they had been previously. This was so because the state's collective and state farm workers had been demoted, in a sense, for the purpose of repression. The instructions that party plenipotentiaries gave to local officials during the campaigns of repression no longer referred to residents of collective and state farms as *kolkhozniki* and *sovkhozniki*, a practice that reflected the official sovietisation of the countryside during the early 1930s. Beginning in 1937, officials reverted to the use of pre-collectivisation terms. Now, they referred to rural inhabitants of the country once again as peasants (*krest'iane*). This change in name opened the door to de-sovietise farm workers and reclassify them as kulaks. In June 1937, for example, a Party plenipotentiary, touring the Western Siberian district, chastised local officials in several regions for adhering to the "attitude" that the class enemy had been defeated. As in previous tours, the plenipotentiary, a man named Pozdniakov, exhorted local officials to remain ever vigilant against the Party's enemies. In June 1937, however, Pozdniakov spoke in specific terms about the threat to the socialist countryside. No longer did he make vague references to ubiquitous "anti-Soviet elements" still abroad in the countryside. "It is anti-Soviet", he said bluntly, "to believe that peasants cannot be wreckers." In reporting the results of his tour to Robert Eikhe, the Western Siberian Party head, Pozdniakov recounted the numerous examples of "peasant-kulaks" he had encountered who engaged in anti-Soviet agitation or outright sabotage. To Pozdniakov and other high party leaders in Western Siberia, rural inhabitants were no longer protected by their socialist identities as collective or state farm workers.[60]

By October 1937, 14,886 kulaks and 5,009 individuals with criminal records had been arrested and sentenced by special NKVD *troiki* in the Western Siberian *krai*. As of the above date, authorities had sentenced 9,843 of this number to be shot and 5,568 to terms of eight to ten years in labour camps.[61] An additional 3,480 individuals had also been swept up in the hunt for criminals and kulaks that summer. Fitting into neither category, police listed these individuals simply as "other counter-revolutionary elements". In related operations, police (including the *militsiia* and UGB units) netted an additional 3,702 individuals with suspect backgrounds. The latter included several former Russian princes, counts and landowners – 74 in all – 646 former White Army officers, 400 former "bandits" and Tsarist police officials, 236 former commercial trade agents, 450 priests or believers, and 149 former members of the Socialist Revolutionary Party. In all, police sweeps in the summer and autumn of 1937 led to the arrest of 25,413 kulaks, criminals or former criminals, and other socially dangerous elements in Western Siberia. By 5 October, NKVD special *troiki* had passed sentences on 19,421 of all those arrested; 12,876 had been sentenced to execution and 6,093 had received sentences of 8 to 10 years in labour camps. Only 452 individuals received the lightest sentence recorded – 5 years in a camp. Of those arrested, 134 had been released, and the cases of only 31 individuals had been transferred to the regular court system. By early October, authorities had carried out sentences on 9,525 individuals.

The figures cited above were included in two separate reports, or *svodki*, prepared by the operational secretariat of the Western Siberian NKVD for the bureau of the district party's Central Committee. One of the *svodki*, a summary report of all mass operations to date, broke down the arrest and sentencing figures by region, fifteen in all, and included the original target figures for arrest in each *raion*.[62] Target figures were given for each of the social groups of kulaks and criminals to be arrested, and these target figures were further divided into category I or II for each social group. Category I were considered especially dangerous types to be executed or given maximum sentences in confinement. Category II included those to be sentenced to varying periods in labour camps. Target limits for kulaks and criminals were listed in the first vertical columns of the table. Actual arrest figures, broken down in the same manner, were listed in the second set of vertical rows. The columns that followed included the numbers in each social grouping sentenced to shooting, or to labour camps for 10, 8, or 5 years. The final page of the table provided a summary for the whole of the *krai*.

From these tables, it is clear that the NKVD in Western Siberia concentrated their first series of mass operations in the summer of 1937 on the traditionally unruly areas of the south and west: Biisk *raion*, Barnaul, Tomsk, Stalinsk region, the mining region of Kemerovo, and the Marinsk, Kamensk and Cherepanov regions. These had been centres of strong peasant resistance to collectivisation in the early 1930s, and areas to which many exiles and former "kulaks" had returned during the course of the decade.[63] In addition, these regions had all experienced large-scale immigration during the decade of the 1930s of workers seeking employment in the new industrial towns, and of large numbers of marginal populations pushed east by the imposition of passport and rationing restrictions in Western cities of the Union. From similar reports in early autumn, it is clear that police also targeted the mostly non-Russian Altai and Narym areas, and the cities of the Kuzbass. The latter, too, had seen strong resistance to Stalinist policies, both agrarian and industrial, and had undergone a large influx of new populations during the industrialisation period of the early 1930s. As a result, police regarded the populations in the Western Siberian areas as especially dangerous.[64]

One of the major police operations in Western Siberia in the summer of 1937 targeted the system of grain procurement centres throughout the district. Already by 8 July of that year, Mironov had submitted a report to the party's secretariat, based on information gathered by *raion*-level police, that detailed the "extreme contamination" of the procurement system by "class-harmful and criminal elements."[65] Based on a review of the thirty largest centres, Mironov estimated that 400–500 such individuals were working in responsible positions, and these did not include another 259 who had already been removed and arrested. In addition to the dreaded and ubiquitous kulaks, Mironov listed other dangerous groups: white officers, former *lishentsy*, former small-time traders and commercial agents and ex-convicts. Interestingly, Mironov also named groups of political refugees working in procurement centres as suspect populations. The latter included people who had fled from Germany, Poland, the Baltic states, Romania, and finally from the Far East – the *dal'nevostochniki*.[66]

At the end of his report, the chief of the Western Siberian NKVD included a list of 218 names. Each name was followed by a brief designation of the individual's job and what made that person suspect as a member of a harmful social category. At the Barnaul procurement centre, for example, the driver Kamenets was suspect as a refugee from Romania. The assistant manager of the same centre, Kurzhamov, was related to a kulak family and was, himself, an "unstable element." The typist Tamara Koroleva was the wife of a former white officer; L. V. Livshits, who worked as a clerk at the Zyriansk centre, was serving a 5-year sentence of administrative exile from Leningrad; and Mikhail Polkovnikov, a mechanic at the Biisk centre, was suspect because he had been stripped of his voting rights in 1929. The report gave no information why Polkovnikov had been stripped of his voting rights or whether, according to the new Constitution, he had, in fact, regained his rights. Many of those included on the list were *lishentsy* or former *lishentsy*. Many were on the list because of a past criminal conviction or because of kulak connections. Thus, Vasilii Kliushkov, an agronomist, was there because his father had been a kulak exiled to the Narym region. Others were either married to a kulak or in some other way related to a kulak family.

These individuals were typical of those caught up in the mass operations carried out under Order 00447. Their identities support, in part, the argument that it was ordinary people who suffered the most from the Great Purge of 1937 and 1938.[67] Yet, these ordinary people were also members of socially marginal populations. They had been marginalised either by choice (as criminals or voluntary outcasts) or by definition of the state (as kulaks, refugees, intellectuals, etc.). State officials had always seen these groups as socially harmful and in 1937 and 1938 as particularly dangerous. Mass operations under Order 00447 were to rid the entire country "once and for all," in Ezhov's words, of these supposedly anti-Soviet and potentially rebellious elements.

Conclusions

The Soviet state's response to social disorder during the early and middle years of the 1930s provided the infrastructure that was eventually used for mass repression and surveillance of the population in the latter part of the decade. The dramatic increase in NKVD numbers and activities during the course of the 1930s, the establishment of widespread informant and agent networks and the change in police functions and methods from crime solving to social repression, the growing operational and administrative interaction between the *militsiia* and the OGPU/GUGB, the social purging of cities and formation of the internal passport system – all this was created by the state in order to deal with the perceived threat of social disorder. Certainly, many officials hesitated to carry out political repression. Oleg Khlevniuk and others have documented this reluctance, even within the party structure, to use repressive measures during the mid-1930s, and as Khlevniuk has demonstrated Genrikh Iagoda was very likely removed from his position in late 1936 for his slowness to respond to Stalin's perceived political enemies. Yet, whatever his faults in the sphere of *party* politics, Iagoda created the infrastructure of *social* repression that was used to its fullest in 1937 and 1938.

As in the early 1930s, the regime turned on peasants during the Ezhovshchina, at least in Western Siberia. Collective and state farmers, as well as individual farmers (*kolkhozniki, sovkhozniki* and *edinolichniki*) were "de-sovietised", which opened the way for their arrest in the tens of thousands. Yet, the mass repressions of the late 1930s were more than a second de-kulakisation. Criminal elements, former convicts, sectarians, and a host of other marginal populations, along with farm workers, local Soviet officials, and free-holder peasants, became targets of the state's campaigns of mass repression. As Terry Martin and several authors in this volume have shown, the repressions of 1937 and 1938 also encompassed significant numbers of national minorities. If the campaigns of mass repression began as a purge of socially suspect groups, they turned into a campaign of ethnic cleansing against "enemy" nations.[68]

Indeed, the threat of war introduced a national and ethnic element into Soviet policies of repression and gave to those policies a sense of political urgency. Soviet leaders had, for some years, feared the potential danger posed by populations that had national or ethnic ties beyond the borders of the Soviet Union. Large-scale deportation of certain ethnic populations started in 1935 and 1936 and coincided with the campaigns to clear cities of anti-Soviet and socially harmful elements. Deportations of national minorities continued under special orders throughout the late 1930s, but these operations also merged with mass repressions under Order 00447. The repressions of the late 1930s combined an emerging xenophobia among Soviet leaders with traditional fears of political opposition and social disorder.

Here, then, were the elements that gave the Great Purge its particular characteristics and virulence. The de-kulakisation and social order campaigns of the early part of the decade formed the background for the mass repressions of the late 1930s. The conflation of social disorder with counter-revolution, especially, influenced state and NKVD policies and methods: the mechanisms employed during the repressions of 1937 and 1938 were similar to those used earlier to dispose of undesirable populations and, in 1937 and 1938, the NKVD targeted many of the same social groups. Yet it was not the threat of social disorder, alone, that generated the mass repressions of the late 1930s. The fear of opposition political organisations – Trotskyists, Zinovievists, et al. – arose after the murder of Sergei Kirov and merged with leaders' concern over control of marginal and other undesirable social elements. By 1937, leaders were convinced that oppositionists, working with foreign agents, were actively organising socially disaffected populations into a fifth-column force. In fact, official xenophobia reached such a level in 1937 that the Soviet head of the police warned all his officials to regard every foreigner with suspicion. "It has been established," wrote L. N. Bel'skii in an astonishing secret memorandum, "that the overwhelming majority of foreigners living in the Soviet Union provide the organising basis for spying and diversionary activities."[69] The authorities feared that invasion, which seemed increasingly likely in the late 1930s, would be the signal for armed uprisings by disaffected groups, led by these supposed foreign agents and oppositionists. Each of these concerns – over social disorder, political opposition, and national contamination – had generated separate political responses and operational policies throughout the previous years, but they coalesced in 1937. The various fears of Soviet leaders combined in a deadly way within the context of imminent war and invasion. The police launched the massive purge of Soviet society in 1937 and 1938 in order to destroy what Stalinist leaders believed was the social base for armed overthrow of the Soviet government.

The changing character of repression during the 1930s reflected the changing character of the Soviet state. In the early 1930s, party and OGPU officials directed campaigns of mass repression against what were considered hostile social classes, especially small-holding rural inhabitants. During collectivisation and de-kulakisation, mass repression was employed as part of a class war to establish Soviet power and the dictatorship of the proletariat. Ironically, the "victory" of socialism in 1933 and 1934 not only marked the end of class war; it also ended any pretense to class-specific forms of repression. Increasingly, officials justified repression in defence of the state, the *gosudarstvo*. With class no longer a primary criterion, repression encompassed an increasingly broad range of social and then ethnic groups. Soviet leaders believed that, in one way or another, these groups threatened social and political stability or the territorial integrity of the state. Having developed methods of mass repression early in the decade, the regime continued to employ and to systematise the use of these methods. Mass repression became the primary way authorities dealt with social disorder. In the process, mass repression became one of the main ways the regime redistributed the Soviet population, constructed politically acceptable national identities, protected the country's borders, and imposed social and economic discipline on Soviet society. Mass repression was more than a means to fight the state's enemies. Under Stalin, it became a constitutive part of Soviet state policy.

Notes

Research for this paper was made possible by grants from the International Research and Exchanges Board, the National Council for Eurasian and East European Research, the National Endowment for the Humanities, and the University of Delaware. I am grateful for the support of these organisations. Parts of this essay have been previously published in David Shearer, 'Social

114 Stalin's Terror

Disorder, Mass Repression, and the NKVD during the 1930s', in *Cahiers du Monde russe*, vol. 42, nos 2–4 (2001), pp. 505–34. I am grateful for permission to republish these parts.

1. See, for example, L. S. Eremina (ed.), *Repressii protiv poliakov i pol'skikh grazhdan* (Moscow, 1997); Terry Martin, 'The Origins of Soviet Ethnic Cleansing', *Journal of Modern History*, vol. 70 (1998), pp. 813–61, especially 847–50; Aleksandr Nekrich, *The Punished Peoples: The Deportation and Fate of Soviet Minorities at the End of the Second World War* (New York, 1978); I. L. Shcherbakova (ed.), *Nakazannyi narod: repressii protiv rossiiskikh nemtsev* (Moscow, 1999); V. N. Zemskov, 'Prinuditel'nye migratsii iz Pribaltiki v 1940–1950-kh godakh', *Otechestvennaia istoriia*, no. 1 (1993), pp. 4–19.
2. David Shearer, 'Crime and Social Disorder in Stalin's Russia: A Reassessment of the Great Retreat and the Origins of Mass Repression', *Cahiers du Monde russe*, vol. 39 (1998), pp. 119–48.
3. RGASPI, f. 17, op. 2, d. 597, ll. 1–68.
4. RGASPI, f. 17, op. 2, d. 597, l. 10. The UGB was the regional administrative system of the Chief Administration of State Security, the GUGB.
5. RGASPI, f. 17, op. 2, d. 597, l. 15.
6. RGASPI, f. 17, op. 2, d. 597, ll. 8–9.
7. In September 1936, Ezhov, on Stalin's recommendation, replaced Iagoda as chief of the NKVD. Iagoda was not yet under arrest. At the time of the plenary session, he was head of the communications commissariat. Iagoda took part in the plenary session, acknowledging his failure to understand and follow the proper political line in directing the work of the GUGB. He claimed that if he had not been so preoccupied with administrations of the NKVD as a whole, he could have given more attention to the GUGB, in particular. RGASPI, f. 17, op. 2, d. 596, l. 40.
8. In fact, administrative reform of the police resulted from a bitter political struggle in 1928 and 1929 between Stalinist centralisers and leaders of the Russian Federation Commissariat of Internal Affairs, then under V. N. Tolmachev. The most thorough account is George Lin, *Fighting in Vain: The NKVD RSFSR in the 1920s*, Ph.D. dissertation, Stanford University, 1997.
9. A similar process of subordination occurred with the state's border forces, internal security forces, and forces for convoying prisoners. See A. V. Borisov et al., *Politsiia i militsiia Rossii: stranitsy istorii* (Moscow, 1995), pp. 142–3 and L. P. Rasskazov, *Karatel'nye organy v protsesse formirovaniia i funktsionirovaniia administrativno-komandnoi sistemy v sovetskom gosudarstve, 1917–1941* (Ufa, 1994), pp. 231–306.
10. See Iagoda's instructions to police in GARF, f. 5446, op. 15a, d. 1130, l. 2.
11. GARF, f. 9415, op. 5, d. 475, ll. 6–7.
12. GARF, f. 9415, op. 5, d. 475, l. 12.
13. On the Tomsk line, for example, during 10 months of 1935, there were 5,972 "incidents" (*proisshestviia*) which resulted in the breakdown of 166 locomotives, 38 passenger cars, and 1,256 freight cars. These crashes resulted in 59 deaths and 119 injuries, 62 kilometers of rail lines were torn up and movement was halted for a total of 686 hours. RGASPI, f. 17, op. 120, d. 158, ll. 232–8. For reports by the OGPU plenipotentiary in temporary charge of the line, see ibid, ll. 154–87.

14 RGASPI, f. 17, op. 2, d. 514, ll. 14–16.
15 See, for example, N. Krylenko, 'Proekt ugolovnogo kodeksa Soiuza SSR', in *Problemy ugolovnoi politiki, kniga 1* (Moscow, 1935), pp. 21, 23; G. Volkov, 'Nakazanie v Sovetskom ugolovnom prave', in *Problemy ugolovnoi politiki*, p. 74; A. Vyshinskii, 'K reforme ugolovno-protsessual'nogo kodeksa', in *Problemy ugolovnoi politiki*, p. 35.
16 GARF, f. 9401, op. 12, d. 135, document 119, l. 2. I am grateful to Paul Hagenloh for help in reconstructing Iagoda's speech. For a more complete description of this speech, see Paul Hagenloh, '"Socially harmful elements" and the Great Terror', in Sheila Fitzpatrick (ed.), *Stalinism: New Directions* (New York, 2000), pp. 286–308.
17 RGASPI, f. 17, op. 2, d. 598, ll. 12 and 41–3, respectively. These remarks were made at the February–March 1937 plenum. Again, given the highly politicised and scripted nature of that session, we should approach these comments with caution. Still, in substance, they seem to be an apt description of political police policy during the mid-1930s. See also Iagoda's directive to operational departments of the UGB, as well as the police, in March 1936 to free themselves from unnecessary tasks and to "focus on priorities of aggravated robbery, murder, and theft of socialist property." GARF, f. 9401, op. 12, d. 135, l. 4.
18 RGASPI, f. 17, op. 3, d. 907, l. 10.
19 GARF, f. 1235, op. 141, d. 1650, l. 31.
20 GARF, f. 1235, op. 141, d. 1650, l. 30.
21 GARF, f. 5446, op. 71, d. 154, l. 78.
22 GARF, f. 1235, op. 141, d. 1650, l. 30.
23 RGAE, f. 1562, op. 329, d. 131, l. 3.
24 See, for example, Politburo approval in February 1933 of an OGPU operation to sweep Magnitogorsk of criminal elements, and approval in January 1934 of an OGPU operation, to last three months, to sweep Khar'kov of déclassé elements. RGASPI, f. 17, op. 3, d. 914, l. 3 and RGASPI, f. 17, op. 162, d. 15, l. 164.
25 See, for example, the order for collecting information for sweeps of Moscow in GARF, f. 9401, op. 12, d. 137, doc. 1, l. 1.
26 See reports on operations in June and July to clear Moscow of gypsies, and in the same summer to clear the city of déclassé elements. GARF, f. 9479, op. 1, d. 19, ll. 7, 9.
27 GARF, f. 9401, op. 12, d. 137, doc. 48, ll. 202–4.
28 GARF, f. 1235, op. 141, d. 1650, l. 19.
29 GARF, f. 9401, op. 12, d. 135, doc. 14, l. 2. Iagoda singled out Western Siberian officials for particular though by no means unique criticism, noting that police in March 1934 had launched operations that led to the arrest of 4,000 undesirables, but had only arrested 300 the following month. In December of the same year, the district's party secretariat reprimanded M. Domarev, head of the district's *militsiia*, for failing to step up passport sweeps in the district. The party's reprimand instructed the police chief to intensify his efforts and to present a plan for 1935 "to purge the most important cities of Western Siberia of déclassé elements." GANO II, f. 3, op. 1, d. 550, l. 18. See also GARF, f. 5446, op. 16a, d. 1270; GARF, f. 9401, op. 12, d. 137, l. 24.
30 RGASPI, f. 588, op. 2, d. 155, ll. 66–7.

31 RGASPI, f. 588, op. 2, d. 155, l. 67.
32 RGASPI, f. 588, op. 2, d. 155, l. 66.
33 GARF, f. 8131, op. 38, d. 6, l. 61. See also the summary of the decree contained in the records of the Western Siberian Procurator's office. GANO I, f. 20, op. 1, d. 220, ll. 32–3. For further work on passportisation and socially dangerous elements, see Hagenloh, '"Socially harmful elements"', op. cit.; Nathalie Moine, 'Passeportisation, statistique des migrations et contrôle de l'identité sociale', *Cahiers du Monde russe*, vol. 38 (1997), pp. 587–600; Gábor Rittersporn, 'The Impossible Change: Soviet Legal Practice and Extra-Legal Jurisdiction in the Pre-War Years', paper given at the University of Toronto, March 1995; Shearer, 'Crime and Social Disorder'.
34 GARF, f. 9401, op. 12, d. 135, l. 148.
35 GARF, f. 9401, op. 12, d. 135, l. 148.
36 GANO I, f. 20, op. 1, d. 220, l. 32.
37 See, for example, GANO I, f. 20, op. 1, d. 220, ll. 1–1ob.
38 GANO I, f. 20, op. 1, d. 220, l. 32.
39 GARF, f. 9479, op. 1s, d. 30, ll. 13–14b. I am grateful to Lynne Viola for this and other references to *fond* 9479.
40 Martin, 'Origins', especially pp. 847–50.
41 See the exchange of opinion about this proposal in GARF, f. 8131, op. 37, d. 59, ll. 183–98.
42 GARF, f. 8131, op. 37, d. 59, l. 98.
43 Shearer, 'Crime and Social Disorder', pp. 128–30. See, for example, the police summary of expenses and other resources needed for mass operations against homeless and unsupervised children from July 1934 in GARF, f. 5446, op. 26, d. 18, ll. 256–8. See also the Politburo-Sovnarkom commission recommendation for mass operations in summer 1934 in GARF, f. 5446, op. 71, d. 176, l. 23. According to Iagoda, territorial and railroad police detained (*zaderzhano*) nearly 160,000 juveniles in 1935 as a result of sweeps. Of these, 62,000 were sent to NKVD camps or colonies. GARF, f. 5446, op. 18a, d. 904, l. 6. According to VTsIK reports, police and UGB operations rounded up close to 62,000 children in the last half of 1935 and slightly over 92,000 children during 1936. Close to 14,000 of these children were deported to NKVD youth labour colonies in 1935 and about 17,000 in 1936. GARF, f. 1235, op. 2, d. 2032, ll. 21–2.
44 GARF, f. 5446, op. 57, doc. 1285, ll. 124–8, 164.
45 GARF, f. 8131, op. 37, d. 73, l. 19. In all of 1935, according to Iagoda, 104,645 individuals had been apprehended on charges or suspicion of speculation. GARF, f. 5446, op. 18a, d. 904, l. 4.
46 GARF, f. 5446, op. 18a, d. 904, l. 3.
47 GARF, f. 5446, op. 18a, d. 904, l. 16.
48 GARF, f. 9401, op. 1, d. 4157, l. 203.
49 GARF, f. 9401, op. 1, d. 4157, l. 203. In a letter to Stalin in March 1936, Krylenko cited a total of 24,737 individuals convicted for counter-revolutionary crimes in 1935, about 4,000 less than the figures compiled in 1953. GARF, f. 8131 op. 37, d. 73, l. 228.
50 On trends to reduce political terror against party and state officials, see Oleg Khlevniuk, *Politbiuro: mekhanizmy politicheskoi vlasti v 1930-e gody* (Moscow, 1996), pp. 127–34.

51 GARF, f. 5446, op. 20a, d. 479, l. 36.
52 *Izvestiia TsK KPSS*, no. 10 (1989), pp. 81–2; *Trud*, 4 June 1992, p. 4.
53 Marc Junge and Rolf Binner, 'Tabelle zum Befehl 00447', forthcoming in *Cahiers du Monde russe*.
54 GARF, f. 5446, op. 15a, d. 1130, ll. 2–10; GARF, f. 9401, op. 12, d. 135, doc. 31, ll. 1–5.
55 Oleg Khlevniuk, 'The Reasons for the "Great Terror": The Foreign-Political Aspect', in S. Pons and A. Romano (eds), *Russia in the Age of Wars, 1914–1945* (Milan, 2000), pp. 159–69.
56 GANO II, f. 4, op. 34, d. 26, l. 2.
57 See republication of this order in Iu. M. Zolotov (ed.), *Kniga pamiati zhertv politicheskikh repressii* (Ulianovsk, 1996), pp. 766–80. References are to p. 766.
58 Sergei Papkov, 'Massovye operatsii v zapadnoi sibirii', unpublished paper, Sibirskoe otdelenie, Institut istorii, Akademii Nauk, 1996, p. 12.
59 See the reference to these operations in Western Siberia in GANO I, f. 20, op. 1, d. 239, l. 1.
60 For Pozdniakov's comments, see GANO I, f. 47, op. 1, d. 233, ll. 16–17.
61 Calculated from charts, GANO II, f. 4, op. 34, d. 26, ll. 4 and 14.
62 GANO II, f. 4, op. 34, d. 26, ll. 10–14. The target figures were most likely taken from estimates provided by local NKVD offices.
63 For a discussion of peasant resistance to collectivisation in Siberia, see James Hughes, *Stalinism in a Russian Province: Collectivisation and Dekulakisation in Siberia* (Basingstoke, 1996).
64 See the report, above, from Mironov to Eikhe.
65 GANO II, f. 4, op. 34. d. 4, ll. 51–64.
66 GANO II, f. 4, op. 34, d. 4, l. 51.
67 Rolf Binner and Marc Junger summarise the various arguments about the "ordinary" character of the so-called Great Terror in 'Wie der Terror "Groß" wurde: Massenmord und Lagerhaft nach Befehl 00447', forthcoming in *Cahiers du Monde russe*.
68 Martin, 'Origins'.
69 GARF, f. 9401, op. 12, d. 135, doc. 139.

6
Mass Operations of the NKVD, 1937–8: A Survey

Barry McLoughlin

Introduction

The "embarrassment of riches" observed by John Arch Getty in respect of the archival material made accessible in Russia since 1991[1] can also be applied to new insights into the mechanisms of the "new Red terror of 1937"[2] on an operational scale: the so-called *massoperatsii* (mass operations) of the Ezhovite secret police targeting putative enemies throughout the population on the basis of crude social or national criteria. This tidal wave of terror, unannounced and unprecedented in its scope when it broke, should be seen as a specific form of mass repression distinct from the arrest and annihilation campaigns against the *nomenklatura* at the fulcra of central and local state power. Investigations into the mass terror in the localities in 1937–8, largely an initiative of native scholars and public bodies in the former USSR, have not found their rightful place among Soviet studies in the English language, mainly because the archival sources are closed to foreigners or due to the fact that the publications appear in low editions, often in regions far from Moscow. Even harder to obtain are local studies on the Great Terror in the form of remembrance books (*knigi pamiati*), which are not sold but distributed to the families of the victims.[3] Taking account of this new literature may induce scholars to re-think their theses on how the mass repression of the late 1930s originated, how the arrest sweeps proceeded, why some ethnic or social segments suffered more than others and, finally, why the bloodbath was curtailed. The preliminary results presented here also allow us to set the temporal framework of the terror against the general populace (July 1937 to November 1938), to locate the fluctuations in the intensification and deceleration of mass executions and, finally and more tentatively, to expound on the composition of the victim mass. Given the fairly elementary state of our knowledge on mass operations, my account is therefore as much "work in progress" as a synthesis of the latest findings in Russian, supplemented by my own researches in Moscow. The material in the following pages "takes the story further" from standard English language works on the pre-history of 1930s mass repression. Sarah Davies charted the development of increasingly harsh sentencing parameters for "anti-Soviet agitation", which transformed "every day grumbling" into counter-revolutionary indictments – a conclusion which fits the targeting and sentencing policies in place during mass operations.[4] Similarly, the analysis presented in the following pages, and in the chapter by David Shearer, underlines the argument of Paul Hagenloh that the Great Terror was the "culmination of a decade-long radicalisation of policing practice against 'recidivist' criminals, social marginals, and all manner of lower-class individuals who did not or could not fit into the emerging Stalinist system."[5] And in respect of ethnically based repression, Terry Martin has delineated the deterioration in relations between the Soviet state and non-Russian minorities, and the death toll exacted on them in 1937–8.[6]

Origins and "operative orders" of mass operations

Massoperatsii was the internal cipher used by the Administration of State Security (UGB) units of the NKVD to denote major and ubiquitous offensives against certain groups in society. The requisite operational orders, prefixed by double noughts to denote "top secret", were issued between July 1937 and November 1938. The victims were convicted *in absentia* and *in camera* by extra-judicial organs – the *troiki* sentenced indigenous "enemies" (Operation 00447), the two-man *dvoiki* (NKVD Commissar Ezhov and Main State Prosecutor Vyshinskii, or their deputies) those arrested along "national" lines. This strict division of labour in implementing state terror was also adhered to at the highest echelons of power. The Commission for Political (Legal) Matters, established by the Politburo in 1928,[7] decided on the fates ("1" – shooting; "2" – Gulag) of leading cadres to be condemned by the Military Collegium of the Supreme Court: ex-members of the Central Committee and other higher Party bodies, top ministerial staff, Party leaders or administrators from the provinces, military and NKVD commanders. Such lists were presented by Ezhov and counter-signed (approved) by Stalin, Molotov, Kaganovich and Voroshilov – the quintet (*piatërka*) governing the country during the Great Terror.[8]

Overall repression strategy, in particular the course of mass operations and the composition of NKVD command structures, was directed by the *piatërka*, apparently in the Permanent Commission of the Politburo set up in April 1937.[9]

However, it was forbidden as early as April 1923 to put anything in writing in preparing matters of state security for deliberation in the Politburo: the questions were to be discussed beforehand in the Secretariat of the Central Committee, that is, with Stalin.[10] Repression policy, then, was determined by a closed circle, or by Stalin personally, long before the *ad hoc* nature of decision-making in the Politburo became the rule in the 1930s.[11] The recently published Politburo agenda (1930–9) suggest that the majority of such decisions made in the years 1937 and 1938 referred to the planning and implementation of the "anti-kulak" campaign (Operation 00447) – the rubber-stamping of petitions from NKVD and VKP(b) administrations in the provinces for additional arrest quotas (*limity*) or changes in the composition of the local *troiki*, both under the rubric "about anti-Soviet elements".[12] The resolutions passed in respect of "national" operations were relatively few, primarily because their scope was not limited by quotas; no repression totals were ordained at the beginning of such arrest campaigns so that applications to Moscow for supplementary *limity* were not necessary. While such orders were issued in the name of the Politburo, our present state of knowledge does not allow us to state definitely which members were personally involved, apart, of course, from Stalin and Ezhov.

The countrywide campaigns of arrest and annihilation unleashed by the Politburo in late summer 1937 signified – as noted above in respect of dissent, social deviancy and national affiliation – a bloody final reckoning. The mass terror of 1937–8 in rural regions was a re-run of 1930–1 because it concentrated once more on "kulak elements" and aimed to "disestablish the parish church and repress lay activists".[13] Arrests affecting Germans and Finns had grown steadily since the early 1930s. Prosperous German farmers had resisted collectivisation and attempted to emigrate in 1929–30, but the movement was stifled by special police operations.[14] Subsequent events seemed to justify the authorities' labelling of Germans as a suspect minority because of the aid granted to famine victims in the USSR by the German Government and German charitable organisations. Numerous "fascist conspiracies" were construed by the Soviet secret police from 1932 onwards (concomitant with the rise of Hitler). The number of indictments on "spying for Germany" grew from 119 in 1932 to 1,315 in 1937.[15]

The persecution of Finns, too, predated the *ante bellum* scenario of 1937. The establishment of the Karelian ASSR in 1923 was a unique experiment – the only example of a region ruled by foreigners, the defeated Reds of the Finnish Civil War. The persecution of the Karelian Finnish minority began with an assault on "Finnish nationalism", part of the general reversal of indigenisation policies which meant that the Finns had to hand over power to the Leningrad Party Secretariat as early as 1929.[16] In a report to Stalin in 1933, Iagoda stated that "the third most dangerous counterrevolutionary organisation in the USSR" comprised espionage groups purportedly established in Karelia and the Leningrad Region by the Finnish General Staff.[17]

As regards the texts of the NKVD operational orders issued in 1937–8, they followed the phantasmagoric scenarios presented during the great show trials or expressed during the February–March 1937 plenum of the Central Committee: "Trotskyist agents of the German-Japanese counterintelligence services"[18] had penetrated (*pronikli*) the Party, the NKVD and industry. In a passage of his speech to the plenum on 3 March 1937, Stalin revealed his homicidal distrust of foreigners, alleging that "the comrades had forgotten" that the USSR was surrounded by capitalist countries, states which were combating one another by sending spies, murderers and saboteurs to cause havoc in bourgeois countries. The rhetorical question that followed was both a threat and an insight into the thinking of the ruling Party group:

> Is it not clear that as long as the capitalist encirclement [of the USSR] exists there will continue to be present among us wreckers, spies, saboteurs and murderers, sent into our hinterland by the agents of foreign states?[19]

His speech of 3 March was published in the press on 29 March, and his concluding words to the plenum (5 March) on 1 April. Both programmatic statements were issued as a brochure later in the year[20] so that Party members, and NKVD staff, were very familiar with the "encirclement" mentality of the country's leaders. Another, but less well-known, publicity offensive to foster vigilance was the publication, starting in *Pravda* on 4 May 1937, of the long article "Some insidious methods of recruitment by foreign intelligence services". Stalin personally edited the *Pravda* feuilleton serial, changing the heading and the text. This tract and others were re-printed in the central and provincial press during summer and autumn 1937.[21] Leonid Zakovskii, NKVD chairman in Leningrad, was Stalin's ghostwriter. The prominent

Chekist supplied an ideological justification for the onslaught on foreigners by publishing, under his own name, the second brochure "We Shall Completely Destroy the Spies, Saboteurs and Wreckers".[22]

In expounding this "severe appraisal" by Stalin at a meeting of leading NKVD cadres on 19 March, Ezhov repeated the thesis which had led to his appointment six months earlier, namely that the "organs" were four years behind schedule in rooting out the enemy. The core of his message, while signalling continuity in repressive strategy, prefigured the exterminatory nature of the tasks ahead:

> It is important to overcome the various deficiencies we have, we can't tolerate them any longer as so much time has passed [...] our main task [...] therefore consists of making good the delay [...] in smashing the enemy. We are smashing the enemy, smashing him hard. We smashed the Trotskyists, smashed them hard. I shall not name any figures, but they are striking enough, we have annihilated not a few. We are smashing the SRs, we are smashing the German, Polish and Japanese secret agents [*spikov*]. That is not all but rather, as the saying has it, the first assault, as there are more of them.[23]

The "lessons" of the Plenum – conspiratorial links between foreign spy-rings and Trotskyists on the one hand, and espionage and industrial sabotage on the other – was clearly spelt out in the "operative orders". In the case of the Harbin re-emigrants (Kharbintsy), Ezhov prefaced the 13-point catalogue of immediate measures by stating that "the overwhelming majority belong to the Japanese secret service, which sent them to the Soviet Union over the last few years" so that they could be activated "as spies, terrorists and saboteurs" in the transport system and industry.[24] Similarly, the "German" Order no. 00439 began with the allegation that the German General Staff and the Gestapo were infiltrating German citizens to organise spying and wrecking in important factories, especially those producing for the war effort.[25] A comparable passage in the draft of the "Finnish" order read: to liquidate the activities of "Finnish intelligence agencies [...] in industry, transport, state and collective farms".[26] Finally, coded telegram no. 4990, sent by Ezhov to his units on 30 November 1937 to launch the "Latvian" operation, emphasised the imminent danger posed by "Latvian counterrevolutionary organisations established by the Latvian secret service and linked to the intelligence services of other [unnamed] countries."[27]

The "Harbin" order was prompted by circumstantial evidence of "infiltration", as many of the repatriates were opponents of Soviet rule since the Civil War or were persons compelled to collaborate with the Japanese forces that occupied Manchuria since 1931. Following the sale of the Russian-built Chinese Eastern Railway (KVZhD) to the Manchukuo (Japanese) authorities in 1935, approximately 25,000 ethnic Russians (including 20,000 railway staff) were repatriated.[28]

The "German" operation of the NKVD began in late July, the "anti-kulak" campaign in the first week of August, and the mass arrest of Poles six days later. Mass arrests of Kharbintsy commenced in late September, those against Latvians in early December.[29] Twelve such orders are said to have been issued,[30] but some operations developed "on the ground" in the general course of the terror. Specific "national" orders targeting Germans, Poles, Kharbintsy, Latvians, Greeks and Afghans were issued to UGB units, but "Romanian" operations started as a "local initiative" in the Ukraine in August 1937, and mass arrests of Finns in similar fashion one month later in Karelia and the Leningrad region. The round-up of suspect Iranians and Afghans did not reach operational proportions until February 1938.[31] The orientation in "national" arrest campaigns was to concentrate initially on foreigners working in factories or on the railways. A further common feature of "foreigner" mass operations was their flexible duration, prolonged three times to cover 16 months in all. Originally, they were supposed to be wound up in a relatively short period: the Polish, Harbin and Finnish sweeps within three months, and the arrest of Germans and Latvians in a matter of days. Deportations of minorities took place shortly before and during mass operations, in order to clear border areas of "unreliable" peoples and send them to Kazakhstan and Kirghizia: 70,000 Poles and Germans from the Ukraine in 1936, Kurds and Iranians from Azerbaijan and Armenia in July 1937, and Koreans in early autumn 1937.[32]

Operation 00447, being aimed at "endemic" enemies (kulaks, clergy and believers, criminals and ex-Socialist Revolutionaries), was a joint Party-NKVD undertaking that "came from below" to a certain extent, and definitely went beyond the Stalin-Ezhov axis behind the planning of "foreigner" mass operations. Several VKP(b) leaders spoke at the February-March plenum of the imminent danger posed by returned kulaks, who, it was alleged, were demanding their property back or had gone to ground and were continuing their "anti-Soviet activities" under assumed social identities in the big cities and industrial plants.[33] According to Zhdanov, the newly enfranchised village clergy were assembling an electoral following to contest the Communist hegemony at the December 1937 Supreme Soviet polls.[34] Iaroslavskii, the chairman of the atheist movement, stated that there were over one million registered believers, not least religious activists who frequently chaired the local *kolkhoz*.[35] The Politburo knew from the census returns completed in January (but promptly suppressed) that 60 per cent of the population over 16 years had declared themselves "believers".[36]

On 3 July the Politburo directed Party organisations to register, in cooperation with the secret police, the returned kulaks and criminals. The "most hostile" were now subject to immediate arrest and death by shooting on the basis of verdicts to be passed by new *troiki*; the "less active" were destined for a place of exile chosen by the local police chief.[37] In most cases the Politburo accepted the repression totals, and the *troika* composition (NKVD commander, state prosecutor, local Party secretary) suggested by provincial centres. The final text of Order No. 00447, which was sanctioned by the Kremlin on 31 July, contained totals for immediate repression generally close to those compiled in early July – 268,950 verdicts, including 75,950 executions ("first category").[38] One major difference between the drafts of July and the final product was that the exile option was dropped, which meant that "second category" prisoners were to be sentenced to 8-10 years in the Gulag. As in all mass operations, the purpose of the 00447 campaign was of more import than the wording of the operational order, which, as was intended, induced many provincial NKVD commanders to enlarge the victim spectrum beyond the kulak and criminal constituency even before the operation began. In Leningrad the targeted groups included from 16 July "other hostile elements carrying out subversion and anti-Soviet activities"[39] – in Chekist jargon *antisovetchiki*. Ezhov's deputy Frinovskii was responsible for the execution of the Order 00447. He set his stamp on operational priorities, by issuing, two days after the commencement of the "anti-kulak" offensive, a detailed directive that listed the most dangerous types of recidivist criminals, including those "who have not broken with the criminal world, have no permanent place of residence and do not carry out socially useful work, even if they have not committed a definite criminal offence immediately prior to arrest". That meant open season on all kinds of social outcasts, not least the homeless and beggars. Frinovskii instructed the street patrols of the normal police to stop suspects on sight and check their particulars carefully "so that not one criminal-recidivist might slip through". He also intimated that social outlaws would be the first to be exterminated: "All cases brought before the special *troika* will be processed in the shortest time possible [*samye szhatye sroki*]".[40]

The technology of mass operations

A characteristic of all mass operations was flexibility: first, the numbers – the so-called *limity* – to be convicted in the "anti-kulak" operation could be easily increased; second, it was left entirely to the UGB officers (department and group leaders) whether the prisoner was to be shot or sent to the camps; third, the time-limits set for the completion of single operations were extended time and again; fourth, operations against foreigners were not subject to *limity* and the convicted were usually executed; finally, simplified investigation procedures were adopted to convict suspects.

Regulations governing the powers to arrest, or to restrict the length of investigative custody, decided by the Politburo in July 1931[41] and confirmed by government decree in May 1933[42] and June 1935[43] proved meaningless as long as mass operations were in force. Suspended for that duration was also the resolution of the Politburo of 5 January 1936 governing the arrest of foreign citizens. The arrest of persons with a foreign passport, the resolution stated, had to be accorded with Stalin and Molotov; the police had to defer to the wishes of the Commissariat for Foreign Affairs in unimportant cases and the accused was to be expelled from the Soviet Union; serious indictments, on the other hand, were held behind the closed doors of the Military Collegium.[44]

Addressing Party activists of the procuracy in mid-March 1937 on the "lessons" of the recently held Central Committee plenum, Vyshinskii justified the instrumentalisation of justice to suit the new political situation:

> Our laws differ in that the factual aspect prevails [...] Mastering the application of the principles of Soviet law means defining one's line of work so that it conforms to the tasks, interests and cause of constructing socialism.[45]

In a circular to enlighten procurators of their responsibilities in connection with Order 00447, he stated that they were not required to sanction such arrests or to observe whether investigative procedures were being adhered to, by being present during interrogations. A further directive to procurators in December ordered the use of the *troika* instead of local courts in cases where evidence, for security reasons, could not be presented.[46] Similarly, the military procurors were "relieved" one month earlier of their duty to be present at the questioning of "counter-revolutionaries".[47] The NKVD operatives were therefore not hampered by outside interference for the foreseeable future and could force the civil and military procurators to assent to a sentencing policy in which they had no real input: to put their signatures to sentencing protocols and to countersign arrest-warrants.

In the course of carrying out arrests and interrogations on such a vast scale, UGB units were supplemented by a variety of Soviet institutions. In Tomsk this assistance comprised, among others, ordinary policemen (*militsionery*), middle and higher ranks serving with internal and border troops of the NKVD, members of the Komsomol and the directors of "secret sectors" in factories and scientific institutes.[48] In Karelia, Party activists and local government officials carried out arrests.[49] When listing those to be collected in nocturnal raids, the NKVD could draw on catalogues of suspects[50] assembled by their colleagues from the early twenties:

a) Former Tsarist civil servants.
b) Participants in peasant rebellions.
c) Re-emigrants.
d) Former White Guards.
e) Political immigrants.
f) Former POWs held by the German and Austro-Hungarian armies during World War I.
g) "De-kulakised" peasants previously convicted.
h) Members of the clergy previously convicted.[51]

These index-cards systems grew as hostile categories were brought up-to-date in the preparatory phase of Operation 00447.[52] A district unit of the UGB-NKVD in the Kuibyshev Region subsequently used the following additional lists:

i) Polish immigrants ("defectors").
j) Prisoners taken by the Red Army during the Civil War.
k) White officers, including those who had lived abroad.
l) Persons exiled to the district.
m) Persons deprived of voting rights.
n) "Kulaks" who had escaped from their place of exile or detention.
o) Persons expelled from the regional organisation of the VKP(b).[53]

Operational problems arose everywhere at a later date, after the original allotment had been exhausted and new arrest contingents had the force of law for the overworked sectors of the UGB administrations. One of the greatest difficulties stemmed from the fact that the index-card system had been so thoroughly filleted for suspects that few were still at large. From November to December 1937 the terror entered its most arbitrary phase. UGB units, now subject to reaching arrest norms and a "casework minimum" (*kontrolnye tsifry*), sketched out their operational schedule by simply writing on pre-printed forms how many persons from each sociological group or industrial sector were to be seized and sentenced. In the Tomsk and Khakassian regions, for example, entries were made in the following columns:

Workers: transport, industry, building.

White-collar employees; lawyers; doctors; agricultural experts; engineers; university teachers; peasants ("kulaks", "middling" and "poor"); Red Army officers and other ranks; policemen; clergy etc.[54]

The records of the interrogation were not verbatim minutes, rather the transcription of stereotype question and answer sessions which pivoted on key phrases such as "Who recruited you for this espionage work and when?" and "Whom did you recruit for this espionage work?" Each response was signed by the accused.[55] Sometimes, in order to save time, the prisoners were forced to sign blank pages of the pre-printed interrogation folios on which the interrogator later typed up the confession, the contents of which were scrutinised by the UGB commanding officer. If the prisoner's statement did not adhere to the "general line" of the prosecution scenario, the head of the UGB department inserted his own fantastic screenplay, and had the forgery re-typed for signature by the defendant.[56] NKVD groups in the city of Cheliabinsk brought this rationalisation to a fine art, setting up what they themselves called a sector for "spare parts" (*zapasnykh chastei*): a "model" protocol was copied by eleven typists; the interrogating officer then filled in the prisoner's data and, from case to case, changed marginally the circumstances of the "spying" activities and their "instigators".[57]

The methods used in 1937-8 to extract the requisite confession were likewise at variance with existing legal norms. Whereas uninterrupted interrogation for days on end (*konveier*), or making the prisoner stand (*stoika*) for just as long seem to have been standard Chekist methods, the use of torture on such a vast scale, in particular merciless beatings (*izbienie*), seems to have been applied in 1937-8 for the first time.

Whether the Party leadership did in fact issue a decree allowing the use of "physical influence" (torture) is still an open question.[58] Ezhov's insistence that "all criminal connections of arrested persons" were to be "uncovered" was an exhortation in this direction, if not direct assent.[59]

Supplementary definitions of targeted groups swelled the victim spectrum considerably. In the early stages of the "national" raids, Ezhov justified his demand for the immediate arrest of all "defectors" by stating that all who had entered the Soviet Union from abroad in recent times were "foreign agents" and "saboteurs", especially the re-emigrants from Harbin, and Poles or Germans who had applied for political asylum.[60] An intensification, or prolongation, of mass operations also came about because of reports from Stalin's purging lieutenants. A. A. Andreev, for example, reported to Stalin in late June 1938 that the border areas of the Belorussian SSR still contained from 8 to 10 per cent non-collectivised farmers and that families of arrested Poles had links across the frontier or acted on the orders of Polish intelligence.[61] In the course of the "national" operations, many Russians, by virtue of their contacts with foreign residents, were drawn into these lethal "spying conspiracies". In the course of the NKVD's "Finnish" operation, a "wrecking" or "spying" indictment was also the fate of Russians who, because of their work, had contact with Finnish sailors or railwaymen.[62]

Crude conspiratorial scenarios were also invented to annihilate members of ethnic settlements. Seventy-one Greeks living in the Krymsk tobacco-growing area (Krasnodar territory) were arrested from December 1937 on the charge of belonging to "a Greek counter-revolutionary, nationalistic, terrorist wrecking and insurgent organisation". The arrested (at least 67 were executed) represented a cross-section of the local population, including 23 *kolkhoz* peasants, 20 blue-collar and 13 white-collar workers and 5 local government officials. The proportion of communists was one-sixth.[63] The arrest squads in the town of Bodaibo (Irkutsk Region) went from door to door with lists of Chinese and Koreans in March 1938 and also seized a few Oriental stragglers on the streets. In his oral report to the district commander, the leader of the raids took stock of the results:

> All the Chinese were arrested. There are only a few old men left, seven of whom have been exposed as spies and smugglers. I don't think it's worthwhile wasting our time on them. They're too decrepit. We arrested the more hale-and-hearty ones.[64]

By contrast, in dealing with the "clientele" arrested during the course of Operation 00447, NKVD interrogators usually had evidence of some kind to incriminate the prisoner. In the early stages of the "anti-kulak" drives the nefarious past of the accused sufficed – of kulak origin or a criminal record. At the first sitting of the *troika* in Tatarstan on 23 August 1937, the death sentence was pronounced in all but 2 of the 30 cases – 18 criminals and 12 kulaks.[65] In other cases compromising remarks attributed to the defendant were seen to deserve summary execution, as was the fate of a peasant sentenced to death at the first sitting of the Voronezh triumvirate on 9 August for the following remark: "Soviet power and the Stakhanovite movement have resulted in the peasants staying hungry. They worked all summer in the *kolkhoz*, but when winter came there was nothing to eat."[66]

As the caseload grew in volume, the *troika* hearings (always in the absence of the accused) became yet more perfunctory, as in Omsk on 10 October 1937 (1,301 verdicts), or in Moscow where 500 cases in one night's sitting was the average.[67] Semenov, the chairman of the *troika* in the capital, admitted that he lacked the time to read through the prepared protocols that contained the prisoners' biographical data, charge and proposed sentence. Sittings often lacked a "quorum". In Ivanovo, the local procurator and the Party secretary did not attend (their presence was not obligatory) and were informed later by telephone of the total of red "Rs" (*rasstrelat'* – shoot) written on the protocol by the NKVD chairman.[68] Sittings of the Tomsk *troika* were attended by NKVD officers only – the nominees of the Party and the procuracy were arrested and not replaced.[69]

The Kremlin monitored the implementation of Order 00447 closely, frequently deciding to change its direction, to shift its gears and kick-start a new offensive in one area and let it run down in another. "Foreign" or "national" operations, on the other hand, were driven to the finishing line (November 1938) but recharged less often – by means of blanket extensions sanctioned by Moscow in January, May and September 1938. The dynamics of the "anti-kulak" operation were fired by in-built mechanisms: the possibility of increasing sentencing quotas or changing the composition of the *troika*, i.e. transferring NKVD commanders in order to speed up the repression in "slack" provinces. Both mechanisms often went hand in hand, as is apparent in the work record of Grigorii Gorbach. After taking up office as NKVD chairman in Omsk on 23 July 1937, Gorbach was not satisfied with the "allotment" granted the region on 9 July – 2,438 sentences (including 479 death verdicts) – and wired Moscow on 1 August, that is four days before

Operation 00447 officially started, for a higher quota. His argument was that due to Stakhanovite work practices his men had arrested "3,008 persons for the first category".[70] Twelve days later, as arrests in the region had reached over 5,000, Gorbach requested Moscow to top up his shooting total to 8,000. Stalin wrote on the margin of the telegram: "Comrade Ezhov. I am in favour of raising the quota to 8.000. I. Stalin."[71] Transferred to administer the Western Siberian province of the secret police in mid-August, Gorbach retained his Stakhanovite zeal, outstripping in a matter of weeks the quotas set down in Order 00447 to the extent of 50 per cent in respect of arrests, and three times that in the number of death sentences he had pronounced via the *troika*. His bloody career was terminated by arrest in Khabarovsk (Far East), but not before he had secured a new quota from the Politburo in July 1938 to the amount of 20,000 (75 per cent death verdicts).[72] One sub-operation of the "anti-kulak" campaign was outside the quota framework – the shooting of prison inmates and Gulag slaves. The text of Operation Order 00447 decreed 10,000 executions for this hostile contingent, but three times more were shot, the majority in March–April 1938.[73]

Victims of both kinds of mass operation were executed at night, either in prisons, the cellars of UGB headquarters or in a secluded area, usually a forest. Popashenko, the chief of the NKVD administration in the Kuibyshev Region, issued the following shooting regulations to Captain Korobitsin in Ul'ianovsk on 4 August 1937, on the eve of the "anti-kulak" operation:

> 1) Adapt immediately an area in a building of the NKVD, preferably in the cellar, suitable as a special cell for carrying out death sentences. [...]
> 3) The death sentences are to be carried out at night. Before the sentences are executed the exact identity of the prisoner is to be established by checking carefully his questionnaire with the *troika* verdict.
> 4) After the executions the bodies are to be laid in a pit dug beforehand, then carefully buried and the pit is to be camouflaged.
> 5) Documents on the execution of the death sentences consist of a written form which is to be completed and signed for each prisoner in one copy only and sent in a separate package to the UNKVD [local administration of the secret police], for the attention of the 8th UGB Department [Registrations] UNKVD.
> 6) It is your personal responsibility to ensure that there is complete secrecy concerning time, place and method of execution.

7) Immediately on receipt of this order you are to present a list of NKVD staff permitted to participate in executions. Red Army soldiers or *militsionery* are not to be employed. All persons involved in the work of transporting the bodies and excavating or filling in the pits have to sign a document certifying that they are sworn to secrecy.[74]

Korobitsin's lists of executioners consisted of the three UGB departmental heads and the commander of the normal police in the city.[75] The condemned learned of the death sentence immediately before it was carried out and not any sooner.[76] Frinovskii's directive forbidding the disclosure of capital sentences pronounced by the *dvoika* or *troika* also applied to the families of the victims.[77] At the nocturnal executions, NKVD officers using the standard Nagan pistol shot prisoners in the back of the head or neck, and, sometimes for good measure (*kontrolnyi vystrel*), in the temple.[78] Official requests for the requisite ammunition were made to the *komendant* of the regional NKVD, and the recipient was directed to take stock of expenditure.[79] For the execution of 38 prisoners in Chistopol in August and September 1937, the executioners registered an outlay of 84 projectiles in their report of the killings.[80]

The tempo of mass operations

The campaign of mass arrests unleashed in July 1937 ran on two parallel tracks. The "anti-kulak" Order 00447, directed at "hostile elements" in the native population, predominated repressive policy in the first half of mass operations, up to 1 February 1938. The orgy of violence visited on perceived *antisovetchiki* is reflected in the statistics of the perpetrators, which read like the balance of military war losses:

30 July 1937: 268,950 sentences approved by the Politburo
15 August: 100,990 in custody, 14,305 convicted
31 August: 150,000 in custody, 30,000 shot
August–December: 40,000 additional sentences approved by Moscow
1 February 1938: 600,000 convictions [81]

Raids of the NKVD against foreigners characterised the main thrust of mass repression in 1938. The high figures for August–September 1937 marked the extermination of the first batches arrested in August – kulaks and criminals. Ninety-seven per cent of the criminals executed in the Kalinin region in the years 1937–8, were shot in the last quarter of 1937, for instance.[82] The number of executions dropped subsequently, but peaked again towards the year's close. A reason for the increased shooting totals of December 1937 was a prominent feature of the ubiquitous planning mania – exerting a supreme effort to reach or overfill norms before the old year ended. The NKVD in the Khakassian Autonomous Region (Krasnoiarsk Province) increased the November sentencing totals by two-thirds in December; of the 282 prisoners sentenced to death in that month, 159 were shot in the last four days of the year.[83] The highest execution totals were registered in Moscow for February and March 1938, a result of the mass sentencing of Gulag inmates and Latvians in December. Almost half of the Latvian victim total arrested throughout the country had been apprehended by the end of that month.[84]

A countrywide lull in the activities of the *troiki* followed at the start of the new year. The reasons for this are unclear, perhaps because the 00447 drives were considered completed in some regions, as in Tatarstan,[85] or on account of the deliberations of the Central Committee plenum in January 1938. The respite was short. On 31 January the Politburo approved 48,000 capital and 9,200 Gulag verdicts for Operation 00447 in 22 administrative areas of the USSR, sentencing to be completed by mid-March. The new shooting totals exceeded the death verdicts allotted to these regions in the original text of Operational Order 00447 by 7,600. Another striking feature of the new quotas was the ratio of 5:1 between death and Gulag verdicts, a reversal of the proportionate tallies of 1:2.5 laid down the previous July. The Politburo also ordered the prolongation of ten *natsoperatsii* (sentences to be pronounced by 15 April) against Poles, Latvians, Germans, Iranians, Kharbintsy, Chinese, Romanians and Greeks, and the beginning of mass arrests affecting Bulgarians and Macedonians, in its resolution of 28 January. Such nationals were subject to arrest irrespective of the citizenship they possessed. Four months later, on 26 May, the Politburo ordained a prolongation of operations against persons of Polish, German, Latvian, Estonian, Finnish, Bulgarian, Macedonian, Afghan and Chinese nationality until 1 August.

Operation 00447, in contrast, was being run down. Although new quotas totalling 90,000 were approved by the Politburo in the period 1 February to 29 August, relatively few regions were affected, which signifies an intensification of the killings in western and southern border areas and not countrywide, as in the case of the ubiquitous and unabated annihilation of "national" contingents: Ukraine 30,000 (15 February), Belorussian SSR 18,500 (17 July) the Far East 20,000 (31 July), to mention the largest new approvals.

The Politburo resolution passed on 15 September referred to "national" operations only, and ordered the installation of special triumvirates (*osobye troiki*) at regional, republic and provincial level for the duration of two months only in order to review the unprocessed *dvoiki* cases ("Polish", "Harbin" and "German" operations). The wording of the decision, despite its emphasis that "category one" (execution) verdicts were to be implemented immediately, contains indications that the terror had peaked. The new three-man bodies could only decide on the fates of persons arrested before 1 August; persons seized after that date were to be handed over to "court organs", including normal regional courts. Furthermore, the new *troiki* could refer cases for repeal and order the release of the accused if there was not enough evidence for sentencing. This was a signal that a return to a legality of sorts was already under way. None the less, the decision of mid-September underlines the trend that the terror in 1938 was annihilation by the bullet rather than slow death in the camps, for mass operations ended in an orgy of executions – two-thirds of the verdicts (72,254 as against 105,032) passed by the *osobye troiki* were capital sentences.[86]

Mass operations in Moscow

In the preparatory phase of the "anti-kulak" operation of the NKVD, Moscow Party Secretary Nikita Khrushchev wrote to Stalin that the targeted contingent in the Moscow area numbered 41,305 – 33,436 "criminal elements" and 7,869 returned kulaks. He held that enough "material" existed to warrant the "first category" (shooting) sentencing of 6,500 "criminal elements" (1,500 to be seized in the city districts) and 2,000 "kulaks". He proposed himself for *troika* membership, or the person of his deputy A. A. Volkov in "necessary cases."[87] Khrushchev subsequently kept his head under the parapet, for Volkov took on the compromising role of the Moscow Party nominee in the *troika* chaired by NKVD district commander Redens. The horrendous total suggested by Khrushchev was reduced to 5,000 executions and 30,000 Gulag sentences in Operational Order 00447. At the end of January 1938, the Moscow administration of the secret police was allotted a further 4,000 quota for nocturnal massacres.[88] Roughly 29,200 death sentences were carried out in Moscow in the years 1937 and 1938.[89] Two-thirds of the latter victim tally can be ascribed to verdicts pronounced in the course of mass operations. There is no evidence that the Moscow NKVD administration applied for quota increases over and above the figures granted by the Politburo in August 1937 and January 1938 during operation 00447; Khrushchev's figures suggest that the greater part of arrested *antisovetchiki* comprised the socially marginalised rather than peasants, a plausible supposition for a sprawling urban conglomeration like Moscow. Another specific characteristic of mass operations in the Soviet capital was the relatively high percentage of foreigners, or persons ascribed as such by the NKVD, seized and subsequently shot.

More detailed knowledge of the conduct of these discrete campaigns, based on prisoners' prosecution files, is available for the period following 20 January 1938, when Leonid Zakovskii was appointed chief of the Moscow Regional Administration of the NKVD. Zakovskii was chosen as one of the leading NKVD officers to perform as witnesses for the prosecution against the discredited Iagoda at the February–March 1937 Plenum of the Central Committee.[90] His prominent influence in the Ezhovite secret police is also attested by his appointment as Ezhov's deputy (29 January 1938), by being awarded the Order of Lenin (June 1937), his election to the Supreme Soviet, and by his propagandistic writings.

The date of Zakovskii's appointment (late January 1938) was significant – just before Operation 00447 was restarted by the issue of new *limity* for the regions, including Moscow, and when operational plans needed to be drawn up to conduct the intensification of sweeps against foreigners (Politburo decisions of 28 and 31 January 1938). Robert Conquest is of the opinion that Zakovskii's move to Moscow was "clearly designed to restore the momentum of the Yezhovshchina", and that the new appointee believed that "Moscow had dragged its heels over the purge."[91] This plausible interpretation is indirectly confirmed by a passage in the confession (14 April 1939) of Zakovskii's predecessor in Moscow, Stanislav Redens:

> Minaev and Tsesarskii [leading NKVD officers] said openly, "some regions are achieving such totals, but you are falling behind. You have to apply pressure". At that time [autumn 1937] 2,500–2,700 Poles had been arrested. After my transfer to Kazakhstan, Zakovskii acted in a clearly criminal fashion in this matter, arresting 12,500 persons in two months. The arrests were mainly carried out on the basis of the names in the telephone directory, surnames that were similar to Polish, Latvian, Bulgarian and other names.[92]

Statements from ex-security service officers questioned by the KGB during the 1950s in connection with the rehabilitation of victims dated the commencement of widespread beatings and the forgery of interrogation records in Moscow to February–March 1938, shortly after Zakovskii's arrival.[93] In an assembly of operative staff, one such deposition reads, Zakovskii stated that investigation cases had to be conducted "in a more active manner, the prisoners should be beaten and not treated with white gloves."[94] Zakovskii also introduced the practice of plan quotas for the work of the interrogation teams, and 1,000–1,200 cases were distributed monthly to each UGB department.[95] The pressure to procure confessions, complete indictments and hand the cases over for sentencing was especially intense in the first quarter of 1938, for Frinovskii, Ezhov's deputy, ordained on 1 February 1938 that 4,000 first category (shooting) cases for Operation 00447 were to be completed by 15 March,[96] and "foreigners' files" by 15 April.[97]

Zakovskii's instructions to his over-worked subordinates were unequivocal:

> Zakovskii said openly that we did not have to pussy-foot around with the prisoners, they should be given one on the snout, and that we should not restrain ourselves as regards violence, as permission to beat prisoners was no longer necessary, not even for Taganka prison.[98]

Foreigners were arrested according to place of birth, on the basis of documentation sent by the Comintern,[99] or because their names were among those copied by NKVD operatives from registers of inhabitants kept by the housing administration and janitors in the Moscow municipal districts.[100] Within an enclosed area in the village of Butovo 20,765 *troika* and *dvoika* capital verdicts were executed in the years 1937–8.[101] The proportion of Butovo victims who were born outside the USSR was one-fifth (4,118), persons hailing from 28 countries outside the Soviet Union.[102] The total of Polish victims (1,621) represented 8 per cent of all those shot at the NKVD execution yard, and 40 per cent of executed foreigners. The second largest foreigner victim contingent in the Butovo total comprised Latvian immigrants (one-third of the executed foreigners), a high percentage of whom were VKP(b) members. Although this national group constituted a mere 0.4 per cent of Moscow's inhabitants in 1933, the Latvian death toll in Butovo was proportionally 13 times higher. Most were indicted on the fabricated charge of "belonging to a counter-revolutionary nationalist organisation", and/or espionage for Latvia and other countries. On the evening of 3 February 1938, 229 of the 258 prisoners shot were Latvian nationals.[103]

The two known operations against the physically handicapped that testify to Zakovskii's merciless leadership originated, it would seem, in "operational exigencies" rather than in a motivation based on eugenic theories. In Leningrad Zakovskii sanctioned the arrest of 53 members of the deaf mutes' association; 33 were sentenced to death by the *troika* in December 1937 to January 1938, the others sent to camps in Mordovia and Karaganda. The arrests, carried out during Operation 00447 against a "fascist-terrorist" organisation, were an initiative of the *militsiia* department combating "speculation". It received a denunciation from the Leningrad branch of the All-Union Deaf Mutes' Association that members were engaged in speculation by selling postcards with "counter-revolutionary" content at railway stations and in suburban trains. The counter-revolutionary "evidence" consisted of a cigarette-card with Hitler's portrait given to a deaf and dumb youth by his German neighbour.[104]

In Moscow, clearing communal prison cells of custodial inmates in order to make room for a new intake was the consideration behind the extermination of invalids. By September 1937, in the early stages of mass operations in the capital, the Gulag authorities were refusing to accept over 800 invalid prisoners already sentenced in Moscow to a term in the camps. Due to the massive increase in arrests in the ensuing months, prison space was at a premium.

In February 1938, Shitikov, the officer in charge of Moscow's prisons, requested Zakovskii to direct the Gulag Main Administration to accept such "invalids and persons only partially capable of physical labour". Zakovskii solved the matter as he had when in charge of the Leningrad secret police. Saying that he had taken no trouble with "such contingents" in Leningrad but had them executed to a man, he ordered the cases of the physically and mentally incapacitated to be "reviewed" by the Moscow NKVD three-man board. At several sittings in February and March, 163 invalids waiting to start a camp sentence of 8 to 10 years or already in the Gulag were sentenced to death by shooting. Some of these *troiki* verdicts were sent to the respective Gulag administrations that had reluctantly accepted the less incapacitated, for example Iakov Trifonov. The 55-year-old *kolkhoznik* from the Voronezh Region was arrested in Moscow on 26 November 1937 on his way to visit relatives. Just three days later the Moscow *troika* sentenced him to 5 years in the Gulag as a "socially harmful element".[105] Trifonov's misfortune was that he had no residence permit for Moscow and had been stopped on the street by the *militsiia* for the same reason on two occasions in 1936. He was an invalid "third class" with a withered right arm and a hernia complaint. Although he had started his camp term in Ivdel'lag (Urals), his case was re-examined by the Moscow *troika* and the original sentence changed to a shooting verdict at the sitting of 2 March 1938 because of alleged "criminal activities". He was executed in the camp on 5 May 1938.[106]

A crude rule-of-thumb for UGB operatives was to pin "anti-Soviet agitation" charges on compatriots, and an espionage indictment on those born abroad or having links there. Frequently, the additional "justification" for a shooting sentence demonstrates that no real pre-trial investigation worthy of the name ever took place, the purported state of mind of the prisoners was seen to warrant their final removal from "Soviet life", as the excerpts from the final indictments reproduced in the *Butovskii poligon* martyrology reveal:

"Is hostile to Soviet power."
"Has a terrorist attitude to the leadership of the VKP(b)."
"Is a hostile element."
"Is a de-classed element."
"Has close links to terrorists and spies."
"Knew of her husband's criminal espionage activities."
"Spreads anti-Soviet agitation among neighbours and acquaintances."
"Spreads rumours about a coming war."
"Praises life under the Tsar."
"Expresses sympathy for enemies of the people."
"Agitates against the Stakhanovite movement."
"Agitates against the signing of national loan bonds."
"Leads a suspicious mode of life akin to that of a spy."

Over a fifth of all executions were carried out in August and September 1937 and the victims were almost exclusively native-born peasants and workers, priests, believers and pensioners living in villages. The time between arrest and conviction rarely exceeded two weeks. Executions were usually carried out one or two days after the *troika* lists had been signed. Evidence taken from the prosecution files of peasants arrested in Pirochi village (Kolomna district) show that the NKVD targeted de-kulakised peasants on their returning home after serving the banishment term imposed in the early 1930s. The chairman of the village Soviet was summoned to local NKVD headquarters and interrogated five times over two days. Faced with dire threats, he named families of kulak origin who subsequently featured as members of "a counter-revolutionary conspiracy". They were arrested some days before Operation 00447 began; all were sentenced to death by the *troika* on 19 August and shot the following night in Butovo.[107]

Data on the victims shot in Moscow during the final phase of mass operations presents a totally different picture from the hectic and speedy arrest, conviction and execution tempi of August 1937. Now, by contrast, about 90 per cent of the victims were foreigners (primarily Latvians, Poles and Germans) who had been arrested as far back as autumn 1937 but mostly in February-March 1938 and sentenced to death by the *dvoika* in August or by the *osobaia troika* in October.

How were mass operations in Moscow different from other regions? The last extra-judicial shootings took place in Butovo on 19 October 1938 (52 persons), one month before mass operations were officially curtailed. Why the carnage was ended in Moscow earlier than elsewhere can only be a matter for speculation, given the present fragmented state of our knowledge about the internal decision-making processes of the NKVD. If Stalin and his circle felt that the terror had gone on too long, had destroyed too many valuable cadres or had left Ezhov too much leeway, the obvious place to start the deceleration was in the capital. Secret police cadres there would have been the first to hear of the turn-around and act accordingly. Certainly, the carousel-like appointments and demotions of the Moscow Administration heads suggest that in such an atmosphere nobody at the top knew if he was being too diligent, desultory or "under-achieving" arrest-norms. After a short stint with Lubianka staff following his removal from the Moscow NKVD administration, Zakovskii was demoted in April 1938 to the post of camp commandant in Samarlag (Kuibyshev Region), arrested two weeks later and executed in late August.[108] The former deputies of Zakovskii in the Moscow Administration suffered the same fate – Iakubovich in February and Semenov in September 1939.[109] Vasilii Karutskii, Zakovskii's immediate successor in the capital, killed himself three weeks after being appointed. Vladimir Tsesarskii, the next administration chief, remained only three months in office before being demoted to a Gulag post. He was arrested in December and shot with many other leading *Chekisty* in January 1940. The term of office of Aleksandr Zhurbenko, the next occupant, was of equally short duration – two months, terminated by arrest in November 1938 and the death verdict in February 1940.[110]

In the capital, arrests fell sharply after April[111] and all but 7 per cent of the Butovo execution total had been shot by the end of June. For the Moscow UGB teams, the work schedule from spring 1938 onwards consisted therefore of clearing the accumulated case loads rather than carrying out new waves of arrests. This change in course went hand in hand with the first moves to curb Ezhov's agenda – he was appointed People's Commissar for Water Transport on 8 April and Zakovskii lost his post in Moscow 11 days earlier.[112]

The published statistics on executions during mass operations in Moscow and Leningrad also indicate certain priorities in exterminatory policy.[113] The percentage of foreigners (national affiliation) executed in the Leningrad region between August and December 1937 totalled around 30 per cent. As the corresponding figure (place of birth) for Butovo was one-fifth and encompassed a far longer period (August 1937 to October 1938), it can be stipulated that the repression of foreigners in Leningrad was far more intensive than in the Soviet capital in the early stages of mass operations – the essence of the confession by Redens. Details of the victim toll in both urban conglomerations would suggest that mass operations did not specifically target Party cadres, for while the percentage of executed Communists or ex-Communists ranged from 10 per cent in Leningrad to 17 per cent in Moscow, a substantial number from this victim sub-group were Communists from abroad – 55 per cent in Leningrad (August to October 1937) and 76 per cent in Moscow (August 1937 to October 1938), in the main Latvians, Poles, Balts and Germans.

As regards the approximate social composition of the Butovo victim totals, the operational "results" remained roughly within the parameters suggested by Khrushchev (6,500 "criminals" and 2,000 "kulaks"), as one-third of the 20,765 final toll were charged with a criminal offence.[114] A further 20 per cent were composed of inmates of the DMITLAG camp complex and peasants in their home areas, who were frequently owners of horse transport or private farmers (*edinolichniki*). Mass operations in Moscow, however, decimated proportionately more in the "underworld" constituency (including the socially marginalised) and within the compact foreigner colonies in the capital. The joint category of homeless–unemployed accounted for at least 5 to 10 per cent of all victims executed in the Moscow and Leningrad regions.[115]

The balance of mass operations

The new directive on punitive policy, signed by Stalin and Molotov on 17 November, stated that mass operations were now to cease. Further arrests could be carried out only with the approval of the procuracy, reference being made to the appropriate decision of the Central Committee and Council of People's Commissars (SNK) of 17 June

1935. All *troiki* and *dvoiki* were to be wound up and the NKVD had to establish special investigation teams in the "operative departments". A great amount of the "deficiencies" listed in the document pertained to the alleged negligence of intelligence gathering caused by the preference for "simplified" investigate procedures, in particular the adherence to quotas in carrying out mass arrests. The blame, of course, for such practices lay not with the Party leadership who had initiated and monitored the operations, but with "enemies of the people" who had wormed their way into the NKVD and the Procuracy, arrested innocent Soviet citizens, and falsified evidence. The directive positively acknowledged the destruction of agents of "foreign intelligence services", namely "Poles, Romanians, Finns, Germans, Latvians, Estonians, Kharbintsy and others".[116]

Reading between the lines, one can assume that the criticism was directed first and foremost at how NKVD commanders had conducted Operation 00447 in the second phase, i.e. when the "most active" criminal and kulak groups had been arrested and the mass terror was engulfing members of the general, Russian-speaking population. We may further assume that Party functionaries argued along such lines against the intolerable rule of NKVD potentates in 1938 – too many "honest" Soviet citizens were being repressed. There is evidence for this supposition from the work "culture" of the Ukrainian NKVD. Commanding officers forced their subordinates who were responsible for compiling statistics on the sociological composition of the convicted to falsify the data in the columns "workers" and "peasants". These were the population sectors forming the support base of the regime in the self-perception of the Bolsheviks. These toilers were *blizkie liudi*, "near people", as against persons said to be nostalgic for Tsarism (*byvshie liudi*) or "alien elements" (*chuzhdye elementy*) of suspect social origin. The worker-collectivised peasant totals were transferred to the rubric "former kulaks" in Donetsk, and to the column *byvshie liudi* in Vinnitsa.[117] The secret police were therefore "deceiving" the Party, concealing the true state of affairs from Moscow and acting like an autonomous authority – a charge comparable to "the collusion" of provincial Party cliques, whom Stalin had excoriated at the February–March Central Committee plenum.[118] Another piece of circumstantial evidence that matters had gotten "out of hand" is the fact that Ezhov was confronted in prison with the charge that he had unilaterally sanctioned an increase in arrest quotas when on a visit to the Ukraine.[119]

That blue-collar workers and peasants made up the bulk of the victims of mass operations is borne out by statistical evidence collated by the NKVD, or subsequently computed on the basis of the victims' files – Leningrad 57.2 per cent, Moscow 57 per cent, Novgorod 74 per cent, Kalinin (Tver) 63.8 per cent, Tomsk 64 per cent.[120] The significance of mass operations for studies of the Great Terror is underlined by the victim tolls: 82 per cent of all "political" convictions in 1937–8 were pronounced during the "anti-kulak" (57 per cent) and "national" (25 per cent) operations. As regards death sentences, over nine-tenths of the approximate total (700,000) were executed in the course of mass operations. The ratio of capital to all verdicts was 1:1 in the case of Operation 00447 but 3:1 in "national" campaigns. This rate of attrition was exceeded solely in the sittings of the Military Collegium, which sentenced over 84 per cent of the accused to death by shooting (30,514:36,157) in the biennial beginning on 1 October 1936.[121]

Conclusions

Understanding the Great Terror is to comprehend its multi-faceted nature. Informed speculation as to its origins has to take account of different time-scales and short/long-term causation. Operation 00447 against the peasantry, other traditional foes and the socially "non-integrated" was the culmination of persecution policy as old as the regime itself, with marked repression cycles at the beginning of the 1930s (dekulakisation) and by the middle years of the decade: "passportisation" expulsions from the major cities and the perceptible trend towards harsher sentences for expressions of dissent ("anti-Soviet agitation") and "anti-social" behaviour. For the regime, "social" enemies had become subversives by 1935.

It seems a paradox that the deliberations triggering the decisive and all-inclusive arrest campaigns against "traditional" and "social" enemies from summer 1937 were – apparently – an unforeseen result of the "democratisation" of society as heralded by the new Constitution of 1936: the granting of voting rights to disfranchised and inveterate opponents of Bolshevism. The danger they would pose at election time was referred to time and again in the public discussion on the draft of the new Constitution (autumn 1936), articulated at some length and urgency at the February–March plenum and, as shown above, motivated the annihilation of "the usual suspects" during the first phase of mass operations terminating in mid-December 1937.[122] Since the operational parameters, victim-tolls and targeted groups of the massive offensive against the general population are now known in broad outline, can the Ezhovshchina not be seen as an attempt to remove those from society who did not fit into the few formalised and ascribed class categories of a "homogenised" Soviet state? Future research might also address another paradigm, namely the concept that the Great Terror was a drastic form of Bolshevik problem solving, an attempt to dispose of the hostile human detritus left by the recurring tremors of the industrialisation and collectivisation upheavals.

The motives behind the "national" *massoperatsii* of the NKVD can be interpreted on the basis of proximate and long-term explanatory models. Oleg Khlevniuk has argued the short-term scenario, focussing on tension in the Far East and the Spanish Civil War.[123] Events in Spain, viewed in retrospect, seem to have facilitated the replication or retroactive consolidation of "images of the enemy" propagated in the Russia of 1937–8: a "Fifth Column" of Francoists waiting to seize power in Madrid, chaos and tensions in the Republican government, a dissenting libertarian left ("Trotskyists") and Soviet military advisers directing the Communist-led International Brigades in daily combat with the ideological arch-enemy – German, Italian and Spanish fascists. Attractive as the model is because of its temporal affinity to the outbreak of mass operations, diplomatic mishaps closer to home were perhaps of greater import: the failure of the Kremlin to come to an understanding with hostile European regimes, especially Poland and Germany. A diplomatic setback, and one much closer in time to the inception of mass operations, was the brusque cessation by Berlin in March 1937 of tentative détente discussions with Soviet diplomats that had commenced two years previously. A war on two fronts seemed a distinct prospect following the Japanese invasion of China in July 1937.[124]

Despite whatever weighting one might accord the international situation of 1935–7 in the embryonic state of mass repression strategy,[125] two wider paradigmatic vistas are worthy of consideration. Robert Tucker emphasises Stalin's "statist" and "great power" inclinations that were at variance with classical Marxism (Engels and Lenin) and would lead, in time, from the "imperialist" to the "socialist" encirclement of the USSR.[126] The quantum leap in Soviet foreign policy away from coexistence with the capitalist West ("Popular Front") to collaboration with Nazi Germany was an initiative taken just before the outbreak of the Second World War, after "internal enemies" had been destroyed in the USSR. The turn-around in Soviet foreign affairs made the "Popular Front" and the Communist International, its main propaganda vehicle, redundant within the framework of Stalinist "statism". The repression of the Comintern apparatus, and of foreign-born communists exiled in the Soviet Union, should therefore be perceived not only as the removal of a "Fifth Column", but also of convinced opponents to any rapprochement with fascism.

Terry Martin describes the internal components of the "foreign affairs" argument. He traces the development of internal nationalities policy, the programmatic shift from class to people that, coupled with a "xenophobic attitude towards all influence from abroad, combined to create the category of enemy nations" that "owed their highest loyalty to their 'homelands' abroad and so represented an internal enemy".[127] The link between Operation 00447 and "foreigner" arrest campaigns was that the disaffected in the native population could make common cause with foreign states (or their representatives and subjects residing in the Soviet Union) and non-Russian ethnics in the coming war.[128] Stalin had warned of such a constellation, with some modifications, as early as 1933: "remnants of the dying classes", SRs, Mensheviks and the "bourgeois nationalists in the centre and in the border regions", together with Party oppositionists ("Trotskyists" and "Right deviationists").[129]

Why the rate of extermination (percentage of capital verdicts) was higher in the "national" than in the "traditional" sector of suspects was due to how the Party and the secret police estimated their subversive potential. Operation 00447 was arguably the removal of a disposable mass, the final reckoning with small-time and habitual criminals, or the chronically dissatisfied and vocally disloyal but relatively harmless ordinary folk, including the mostly aged *byvshie liudi* who threatened nobody. Such contingents were destroyed in an orgy of mass shooting in the last quarter of 1937, with four-fifths of operational verdicts passed by 1 February 1938. "Foreigner" repression was of longer duration. Those born abroad, or their relatives, and members of non-Russian ethnic colonies were potential confederates of hostile states.

A final consideration is whether mass operations were influenced by or, in terms of NKVD repression tactics, technically connected to the staged "unmasking", arrest and sentencing of Party functionaries, state or local government officials and industrial managers. While all repressive thrusts during the Great Terror were intertwined to an extent which is open to debate and further examination, there was evidently a division of labour which allowed secret police units a more or less free hand during mass operations. Doomed members of the elite, by contrast, were selected by the Politburo. It is likely that a "spill over" from the persecution of the local *nomenklatura* may have topped up arrest totals for one or other mass operation by including lower bureaucratic or industrial staff in arrest sweeps. Five characteristics of repressive politics, however, distinguish the two forms of terror from one another and seem to belie a close connection between them.

First, the destruction of leading cadres were usually public affairs, whereas mass operations were top secret. Second, and as a corollary, the arrest of local potentates was preceded by a VKP(b) plenum chaired by an emissary of the Politburo or Central Committee, whereas victims of mass operations were seized unceremoniously and without warning. Third, the "trial proceedings" of the Military Collegium, however farcical in hindsight, were fundamentally different – many of the dethroned regional leaders were taken to Moscow for further interrogation and shot there; indicted peasants or workers, on the other hand, were interrogated and condemned *in absentia* within their home area. Fourth, in contrast to the pre-arrest scenarios among the elite poisoned by mutual recriminations and fault-finding, denunciations played apparently little part in mass operations as the victims were arrested on the basis of sociological or national affiliations.[130] This could be termed arrest by questionnaire (*po ankete*), based on the data given by anyone dealing with the Soviet bureaucracy (point 5 denoted nationality, for instance). Fifth, while a "terror from below" was fabricated to give the "unmasking" of the once mighty a popular participatory legitimacy, this phenomenon was absent from, and unnecessary for, mass operations. The victims of the latter campaigns – to paraphrase Hannah Arendt – were "objective enemies" invented to fit a possible crime in the anticipation of "objective developments" (war) and regardless of whether it had been committed or not.[131]

Notes

1. J. Arch Getty and Oleg V. Naumov (eds), *The Road to Terror. Stalin and the Self-Destruction of the Bolsheviks, 1932–1939* (New Haven and London, 1999), p. xi.
2. Ibid, p. 472.
3. For a recent study based on such sources, see R. Binner and M. Junge, 'Wie der Terror "Groß" wurde. Massenmord und Lagerhaft nach Befehl 00447' (Part I), *Cahiers du Monde russe*, vol. 42 (2001); idem , '"S etoj publikoj ne stoit ceremonjatsja". Die Zielgruppen des Befehls 00447' (Part II), *Cahiers du Monde russe*, vol. 43 (2002). At the time of writing neither of these articles had appeared; I am therefore grateful to the authors for the draft of the German text. For details of mass operations collected by the CPSU in the run-up to the Twentieth Party Congress of February 1956, see A. Artisov et al. (eds), *Reabilitatsiia: Kak eto bylo. Dokumenty prezidiuma TsK KPSS i drugie materialy, mart 1953–fevral' 1956* (Moscow, 2000), pp. 317–48.

4 Sarah Davies, 'The Crime of "Anti-Soviet Agitation" in the Soviet Union in the 1930s', *Cahiers du Monde russe*, vol. 39 (1998), pp. 149–68, cited p. 159.
5 Paul M. Hagenloh, '"Socially Harmful Elements" and the Great Terror', in Sheila Fitzpatrick (ed.), *Stalinism: New Directions* (London and New York, 2000), pp. 286–308, cited pp. 286–7. For an earlier study of "social crime" in the 1930s, see David R. Shearer, 'Crime and Disorder in Stalin's Russia. A Reassessment of the Great Retreat and the Origins of Mass Repression', *Cahiers du Monde russe*, vol. 39 (1998), pp. 119–48.
6 Terry Martin, 'The Origins of Soviet Ethnic Cleansing', *Journal of Modern History*, vol. 70 (1998), pp. 813–61.
7 O. V. Khlevniuk, A. V. Kvashonkin, L. P. Kosheleva and L. A. Rogovaia (eds), *Stalinskoe Politbiuro v 30-e gody. Sbornik dokumentov* (Moscow, 1995), p. 58.
8 T. Kuz'micheva, 'Resheniia Osobykh Troek privodit' v ispolnenie nemedlenno', *Istochnik*, no. 5 (1999), pp. 81–5; O. F. Suverinov, 'Voennaia kollegiia Verkhnogo suda SSSR (1937–1939 gg.)', *Voprosy istorii*, no. 4 (1995), pp. 137–46. The *piatërka* became a sextet (*shestërka*) in late 1938, with Beria and Zhdanov replacing the toppled Ezhov.
9 Oleg Khlevnyuk, 'The Objectives of the Great Terror, 1937–1938', in Julian Cooper, Maureen Perrie and E. A. Rees (eds), *Soviet History 1917–1991. Essays in Honour of R. W. Davies* (London, 1995), p. 166. Khlevniuk assigns this role to the commission because Ezhov was a founding-member although he did not join the Politburo, as a candidate, until October 1937.
10 I. V. Pavlova, 'Mekhanizm politicheskoi vlasti v SSSR v 20–30-e gody', *Voprosy istorii*, nos 11–12 (1998), p. 63. According to Mikhail Shreider, later deputy-chairman of the NKVD in Kazakhstan, Stalin chaired important assemblies of prominent NKVD cadres in the Kremlin during the period 1933–4. See Mikhail Shreider, *NKVD iznutri. Zapiski chekista* (Moscow, 1995), p. 22.
11 The number of all Politburo sittings (regular, irregular, closed and joint CC Secretariat-Politburo) dropped from 85 in 1930 to nine in 1936. Due to the compilation of Politburo protocols from 1937 onwards, it is impossible to estimate how often the VKP(b) leading circle actually met. For a discussion on the changes and the number of sittings, see Oleg Khlevniuk, *Politbiuro. Mekhanizmy politicheskoi vlasti v 1930-e gody* (Moscow, 1996), pp. 287–9.
12 G. M. Adibekov, K. M. Anderson and L. A. Rogovaia (eds), *Politbiuro TsK RKP (b)-VKP (b). Povestki dnia zasedanii, tom 2, 1930–1939, katalog* (Moscow, 2001), pp. 876–987.
13 Sheila Fitzpatrick, *Stalin's Peasants. Resistance and Survival in the Russian Village after Collectivization* (Oxford, 1994), pp. 59–62; Gregory L. Freeze, 'The Stalinist Assault on the Parish, 1929–1941', in Manfred Hildermeier and Elisabeth Müller-Luckner (eds), *Stalinismus vor dem Zweiten Weltkrieg. Neue Wege der Forschung* (Munich, 1998), p. 213.
14 Martin, 'Origins of Soviet Ethnic Cleansing', pp. 836–7. For documents on the German emigration movement of 1929–30, see L. P. Kosheleva, L. A. Rogovaia and G. A. Bordiugov, 'Emigratsionnoe dvizhenie nemtsev v kontse 20-kh godov', *Svobodnaia mysl'*, no. 12 (1993), pp. 93–104.
15 V. Khaustov, 'Repressii protiv sovetskikh nemtsev do nachala massovoi operatsii 1937g.', in Irina Shcherbakova (ed.), *Nakazannyi narod. Repressii protiv rossiiskikh nemtsev* (Moscow, 1999), pp. 76–7, 82–3.

16 Markka Kangaspuro, 'Nationalities Policies and Power in Soviet Karelia in the 1920s and 1930s', in Tauno Saarela and Kimmo Rentola (eds), *Communism National and International* (Helsinki, 1998), pp. 129–31.
17 Ivan Chukhin, *Kareliia-37: ideologiia i praktika terrora* (Petrozavodsk, 1999), p. 24.
18 Getty and Naumov, *The Road to Terror*, pp. 422–5, "Lessons of the wrecking, diversionary and espionage activities of the Japanese-German-Trotskyist agents".
19 *Voprosy istorii*, no. 3 (1995), pp. 5–6.
20 I. Stalin, *O nedostatkakh partiinoi raboty i merakh likvidatsii trotskistkikh i inykh dvurushnikov. Doklad i zakliuchitel'noe slovo na plenume TsK VKP (b), 3–5 marta 1937g.* (Moscow, 1937).
21 Oleg Khlevniuk, 'The Reasons for the "Great Terror": The Foreign-Political Aspect', in Silvio Pons and Andrea Romano (eds), *Russia in the Age of Wars 1914–1945, Annali Fondazione Giangiacomo Feltrinelli* (Milan, 2000) p. 167.
22 L. Sakowskii, *Spione und Verschwörer* (Prague, 1937).
23 Artisov, *Reabilitatsiia*, p. 318.
24 A. Ia. Razumov (ed.), *Leningradskii martirolog, tom 3, noiabr' 1937 goda* (St. Petersburg, 1998), pp. 583–5.
25 A. Ia. Razumov (ed.), *Leningradskii martirolog, tom 2, oktiabr' 1937 goda* (St. Petersburg, 1996), pp. 452–3.
26 Chukhin, *Kareliia-37*, pp. 60–1.
27 Nikita Okhotin and Arsenii Roginskii, '"Latyshskaia operatsiia" NKVD 1937–1938 godov. Arkhivnyi kommentarii', *30 Oktiabria* (Bulletin of Memorial), no. 4 (2000), p. 5.
28 Svetlana V. Onegina, 'The Resettlement of Soviet Citizens from Manchuria in 1935–1936: A Research Note', *Europe-Asia Studies*, vol. 47 (1995), pp. 1043–50.
29 Okhotin and Roginskii, '"Latyshskaia operatsiia" NKVD 1937–1938'.
30 Khlevniuk, 'The Reasons for the "Great Terror"', p. 162.
31 N. Okhotin and A. Roginskii, 'Zur Geschichte der "deutschen Operation" des NKWD, 1937–1938', in Hermann Weber (ed.), *Jahrbuch für Historische Kommunismusforschung 2000/2001* (Berlin, 2001), pp. 97, 101.
32 A. N. Dugin, *Neizvestnyi GULAG. Dokumenty i fakty* (Moscow, 1999), p. 76 (Poles and Germans), p. 78 (Kurds); N. F. Bugai and A. M. Gonov, *Kavkaz: narody v eschelonakh, 20–60-e gody* (Moscow, 1998), pp. 103–7 (Iranians); Michael Gelb, 'An Early Soviet Ethnic Deportation: The Far-Eastern Koreans', *Russian Review*, vol. 54 (1995), pp. 389–412.
33 *Voprosy istorii*, no. 6 (1993), pp. 6, 25, 27.
34 *Voprosy istorii*, no. 5 (1993), pp. 4–5.
35 Ibid, pp. 14–15.
36 Calculated on the figures in V. B. Zhiromskaia, I. N. Kiselev and Iu. A. Poliakov, *Podveka pod grifom 'sekretno'. Vsesoiuznaia perepis' naseleniia 1937 goda* (Moscow, 1996), pp. 98, 100.
37 *Trud*, 4 June 1992, p.1.
38 This is a moot point. Getty and Naumov (*The Road to Terror*, p. 471) hold that the tallies from the provinces sent in early July "were higher than the round-number quotas" set down in Order 00447. Binner and Junge, for their part, cannot see any major difference in the two sets of figures: the final quota was lower than that suggested by the VKP(b) in the cases of

Moscow (minus 20 per cent), Mari Republic, Kuibyshev, Far Eastern region, Western Siberia and Cheliabinsk, but higher in Karelia, Omsk, Udmurtien and Saratov (Binner and Junge, 'Wie der Terror "Groß" wurde', ms., p. 14).
39 A. Ia. Razumov (ed.), *Leningradskii martirolog, tom 1* (St. Petersburg, 1995), p. 39.
40 Ibid, pp. 47–8 (extract from Circular No. 61 of 7 August 1937).
41 Khlevniuk, *Stalinskoe Politbiuro*, p. 60.
42 I. I. Strelovka (ed.), *'Khotelos' by vsekh poimenno nazvat'. Kniga-martirolog* (Khabarovsk, n.d.), pp. 15–16 (Instruction no. P-6028 of the Central Committee VKP(b) and Council of People's Commissars, 8 May 1933).
43 V. N. Uimanov and Iu. A. Petrukhin (eds), *Bol' liudskaia, tom 4* (Tomsk, 1994), pp. 195–7 (Order no. 0023 of NKVD and Procuracy USSR, 19 June 1935).
44 RGASPI, f. 17, op. 162, d. 19, l. 24.
45 V. Kudriavtsev and A. Trusov, *Politicheskaia iustitsiia v SSSR* (Moscow, 2000), p. 292.
46 Peter H. Solomon Jr, *Soviet Criminal Justice under Stalin* (Cambridge, 1996), p. 238.
47 O. F. Suverinov, *Tragediia RKKA 1937–1938* (Moscow, 1998), p. 217.
48 V. N. Uimanov and Iu. A. Petrukhkin, *Bol' liudskaia, tom 3* (Tomsk, 1992), p. 65.
49 Chukhin, *Kareliia-37*, p. 58.
50 Other police data available referred to social marginals or the disfranchised who had been refused passports or permission to live in a particular city. See Sheila Fitzpatrick, 'Ascribing class: The construction of social identity in Soviet Russia', in idem, *Stalinism: New Directions*, pp. 34–8; Hagenloh, '"Socially Harmful Elements"', ibid, pp. 296–7.
51 A. F. Stepanov, *Rasstrel po limitu. Iz istorii politicheskikh repressii v TASSR v gody 'ezhovshchiny'* (Kazan, 1999), p. 87.
52 For excerpts from the pertinent telegrams to UGB units in Siberia and the Leningrad Province, see Uimanov and Petrukhin, *Bol' liudskaia, tom 3*, p. 64; P. A. Nikolaev (ed.), *Ne predat' zabveniiu. Kniga pamiati zhertv politicheskikh repressii, tom 1* (Pskov, 1996), p. 18.
53 Stepanov, *Rasstrel po limitu*, p. 34.
54 I. N. Kuznetsov (ed.), *Repressii 30-40khgg. v Tomskom krae* (Tomsk, 1991), p. 14; N. S. Abdin (ed.), *Kniga pamiati zhertv politicheskikh repressii Respublika Khakassiia* (Abakan, 1999), p. 13.
55 As noted in NKVD investigation file no. P-56354 Leopold Brudna, interrogation protocol, 1 April 1938 (GARF, *fond* 10035). I received victim files of Austrian, German and Irish nationals when the NKVD documentation was still held in the Archive of the Moscow Administration of the Ministry of Security of the Russian Federation and cannot therefore give the exact archival reference at present. The victims' files were handed over to GARF in 1995. For a short description of the stocks, see S. V. Mironenko (ed.), *Putevoditel', tom 3. Fondy Gosudarstvennogo arkhiva Rossiiskoi Federatsii po istorii SSSR* (Moscow, 1997), p. 350.
56 A. A. Kulakov et al. (eds), *Zabveniiu ne podlezhit'. Neizvestnye stranitsy nizhnegorodskoi istorii, 1918–1984 gody* (Nizhnii Novgorod, 1994), p. 245.
57 Artisov, *Reabilitatsiia*, pp. 338–9.

58 Stalin's notorious order of 10 January 1939 allowing the use of torture in "exceptional cases" (*Izvestiia TsK KPSS*, no. 3 (1989) referred to such a decree issued in 1937. During the June 1957 plenum of the CPSU, Kaganovich alleged that he and Molotov had counter-signed such a decree drawn up by Stalin in a Politburo sitting sometime in 1937. Khrushchev declared that the document could not be found when he had instigated a search in connection with his speech to the closed session of the 20th Party Congress one year earlier. See N. V. Kovaleva et al. (compilers and commentators), 'Poslednaia "antipartiinaia" gruppa. Stenograficheskii otchet iun'skogo (1957g.) plenuma TsK KPSS', *Istoricheskii arkhiv*, no. 3 (1993), pp. 88–9.
59 Getty and Naumov, *The Road to Terror*, p. 477 (Order 00447).
60 NKVD operative Order no. 00693, 23 October 1937, in Uimanov and Petrukhin, *Bol' liudskaia, tom 4*, p. 182.
61 A. V. Kvashonkin, A. P. Kosheleva, L. A. Rogovaia and O. V Khlevniuk (eds), *Sovetskoe rukovodstvo. Perepiska 1928–1941 gg.* (Moscow, 1999), pp. 393–4.
62 A separate order for the "Finnish" operation was not issued. For a draft version, see Chukhin, *Kareliia-37*, pp. 60–1.
63 N. F. Bugai and A. N. Kozonis, *'Obiazat' NKVD SSSR...vyselit' grekov'. O deportatsii grekov v 1930–1950 gody* (Moscow, 1999), pp. 68–74.
64 Artisov, *Reabilitatsiia*, pp. 336–7.
65 Stepanov, *Rasstrel po limitu*, pp. 56–64.
66 Iu. Iu. Veingol'd (ed.), *Zhivi i pomni. Dokumenty, spiski repressirovannykh, staty* (Belgorod, 1999), p. 27.
67 V. M. Samosudov, *Bolshoi terror v omskom priityh'e 1937–1938* (Omsk, 1998), p. 161; Irina Osipova, 'Piat' del', in Semon Vilenskii (ed.), *Soprotovlenie v GULAGE. Vospominanniia. Pisma. Dokumenty* (Moscow, 1992), p. 120.
68 Shreider, *NKVD iznutri*, pp. 71, 76.
69 Uimanov and Petrukhin, *Bol' liudskaia, tom 3*, p. 66.
70 A. A. Petrushin, *'My ne znaem poshchadu...' Izvestnye, maloizvestnye i neizvestnye sobytiia iz istorii Tiumenskogo kraia po materialiam VChK-GPU-NKVD-KGB* (Tiumen', 1999), p. 137.
71 For a reproduction of the document, see Iu. Feofanov, 'Rasstrel po 1-ii kategorii', *Izvestiia*, no. 62, 3 April 1996, p. 5.
72 Binner and Junge, 'Wie der Terror "Groß" wurde', Part I (Table).
73 S. Kuzmin, 'Lagerinki (GULAG bez retushi)', *Molodaia gvardiia*, no. 4 (1993), p. 211.
74 Iu. M. Zolotov (ed.), *Kniga pamiati zhertv politicheskikh repressii* (Ul'ianovsk, 1996), pp. 797–8.
75 Ibid, p. 801. Unlike mass executions carried out by the Nazis during the Second World War, the shootings performed in the course of Soviet mass operations of the pre-war era were the "prerogative" of NKVD officer staff. Matveev, *komendant* of the Leningrad NKVD, and his assistant Alafer, personally shot 1,111 inmates of the Solovetskii Island Gulag on the mainland in October and November 1937. For reproductions of Matveev's confirmation of the shootings, and of Zakovskii's specific order to him personally, see Arsen Zinchenko et al. (eds), *Ostannia adresa. Do 60-richchia solovets'koï tragedii, tom 1* (Kiev, 1997), p. 32.

Mass Operations of the NKVD, 1937–8 149

76 This is confirmed by researchers in Moscow. See L. A. Golovkova, 'Spetsob"ekt "Butovskii poligon"'. Istoriia, dokumenty, vospominaniia', in idem (ed.), *Butovskii poligon 1937–1938*. *Kniga pamiati zhertv politicheskikh repressii, vypusk pervyi* (Moscow, 1997), pp. 25–6.
77 The families received, if at all, the following answer to their enquiries: "Your [type of family member] was sentenced to ten years without the right of correspondence. Wait". See Stepanov, *Rasstrel po limitu*, p. 30 (NKVD directive no. 424, 8 August 1937).
78 Rafael Gol'dberg, 'Slovo i delo po-sovetski. Poslednii iz NKVD', *Rodina*, no. 9 (1998), pp. 85–7. The article is based on an interview with an anonymous executioner.
79 For reproductions of such letters, see P. M. Podobed (ed.), *Spisok rasstreliannykh v g. Borovichi po resheniiam Osoboi Troiki (avgust 1937g.-mart 1938g.)* (Borovichi, 1994), p. 3.
80 Aleksei Stepanov, 'Rasstrel po limitu', *Volia. Zhurnal uznikov totalitarnykh sistem* (Moscow), nos 6–7 (1997), p. 113.
81 A. I. Kokurin and N. V. Petrov (eds), *GULAG (Glavnoe upravlenie lagerei) 1917–1960. Dokumenty* (Moscow, 2000), p. 99 (full text of Order no. 00447); Artisov, *Reabilitatsiia*, p. 320 (15 August); Okhotin and Roginskii, 'Zur Geschichte der "deutschen Operation" des NKWD', p. 93 (31 August), p. 115 (1 February); O. W. Chlewnjuk, *Das Politbüro. Mechanismen der Macht in der Sowjetunion der dreißiger Jahre* (Hamburg, 1998), p. 275 (August–December).
82 E. I. Kravtsova (ed.), *Kniga pamiati zhertv politicheskikh repressii Kalininskoi oblasti. Martirolog 1937–1938, tom 1* (Tver, 1999), p. 29.
83 Abdin, *Kniga pamiati Respublika Khakassiia*, pp. 13–14.
84 Okhotin and Roginskii, '"Latyshskaia operatsiia"'.
85 Stepanov, *Rasstrel po limitu* (Kazan) p. 15. The author does not state whether the Politburo or NKVD headquarters refused to prolong the life of the Tatarstan *troika* to 1 April or to sanction an increase of 5,000 sentences (ibid, pp. 115–16).
86 Feofanov, 'Rasstrel po 1-i kategorii', (resolutions 31 January, 17 February, 15 September); RGASPI, f. 17, op. 162, d. 22, l. 114 (resolution 28 January); f. 17, op. 162, d. 23, l. 32 (resolution 26 May); Chlewnjuk, *Das Politbüro*, p. 278 (90,000 quota total); Binner and Junge, 'Wie der Terror "Groß" wurde', Part I (Table: Ukraine, Belorussian SSR, Far Eastern Territory); Okhotin and Roginskii, 'Zur Geschichte der "deutschen Operation" des NKWD', p. 116 (statistics of *osobye troiki*).
87 Natalia Gevorkian, 'Vstrechnye plany po unichtozheniiu sobstvennogo naroda', *Moskovskie novosti*, no. 25, 21 June 1992, p. 18.
88 Ibid; Kokurin and Petrov, *GULAG*, p. 99 (full text of Order no. 00447); Feofanov, 'Rasstrel po 1-i kategorii' (text of Politburo decision on supplementary quotas for 22 regions, 31 January 1938).
89 A. B. Roginskii, 'Posleslovie', in L. S. Eremina (ed.) *Rasstrel'nye spiski, Moskva 1937–1941, Kommunarka, Butovo. Kniga pamiati zhertv politicheskikh repressii* (Moscow, 2000), p. 485.
90 For the text of his speech and Iagoda's replies, see Getty & Naumov, *The Road to Terror*, pp. 425–8.
91 Robert Conquest, *Inside Stalin's Secret Police. NKVD Politics, 1936–1939* (London, 1985), p. 56.

92 S. Bilokin', *Masovii teror iak zasib derzhavnogo upravlinnia v SRSR (1917–1941 rr.)* (Kiev, 1999), p. 292.
93 GARF, f. 10035, NKVD investigation file no. P-33337 Richard Altermann, statement of Stefan Skvortsov (9 May 1957), statement of Rudolf Traibman (3 January 1957).
94 GARF, f. 10035, NKVD investigation file no. 24722 Walter Bitter, excerpt from interrogation protocol Maxim Kosyrev, 4 September 1956.
95 Osipova, 'Piat' del', pp. 120–1.
96 Ibid, p. 124.
97 GARF, f. 10035, NKVD investigation file no. 24722 Walter Bitter, Information, 30 April 1955.
98 GARF, f. 10035, NKVD investigation file no. P-24982 Richard Brandt, excerpt from interrogation protocol Arkadii Postel', 11 December 1939.
99 L. A. Golovkova (ed.), *Butovskii poligon, vypusk tretii* (Moscow, 1999), pp. 345–6, excerpt from the confession of former NKVD officer Arkadii Postel', 9 January 1939.
100 Ibid, pp. 348–55, confession of former NKVD cadre Petr Tikhachev, 27 December 1955 and 21 September 1956.
101 Golovkova, *Butovskii poligon, vypusk pervyi*, pp. 346–7 (shooting totals by month, August 1937–October 1938). For articles in English about these killing fields, see Barry McLoughlin, 'Documenting the Death Toll: Research into the Mass Murder of Foreigners in Moscow, 1937–38', *Perspectives. American Historical Association Newsletter*, vol. 37 (1999), pp. 29–33; Andrew Jack, 'In Moscow's Killing Fields', *Financial Times* (Weekend Supplement), 29–30 April 2000, p. 10. I am grateful to John Halstead (Sheffield) for a copy of the latter article.
102 Extracted from the data on place of birth in *Martirolog rasstreliannykh i zakhoronennykh na poligone NKVD " Ob"ekt Butovo", 08.0.8.1937–19.10.1938* (Moscow, 1997). The volume was issued by the Orthodox Church.
103 Vidvud Shtraus, 'O Butovskikh latyshakh', in Golovkova, *Butovskii poligon, vypusk tretii*, pp. 17–24.
104 The group case was reviewed in 1939–40. Nineteen of the convicted were released from the camps and proceedings instigated against several policemen, of whom at least two were subsequently executed. See A. Ia. Razumov (ed.), *Leningradskii martirolog. tom 4, 1937 god* (St. Petersburg, 1999), pp. 675–81.
105 Osipova, 'Piat' del', pp. 114–27.
106 Osobyi Fond, ITs GU MVD MO (Information Centre of the Main Administration of the Ministry of the Interior for the Moscow Region), file SO-38382. I am indebted to Lidia Golovkova for giving me the copies of her notes on the NKVD files of invalids held in this closed archive.
107 A. Vatlin, 'Krest'iane i krest'ianskie sem'i v Butovo', in L. A. Golovkova (ed.), *Butovskii poligon. Kniga pamiati zhertv politicheskikh repressii, vypusk vtoroi* (Moscow, 1998), pp. 5–15.
108 N. Okhotin and A. Roginskii (eds), *Sistema ispravitel'no-trudovykh lagerei v SSSR, 1923–1960. Spravochnik* (Moscow, 1998), p. 370.
109 Golovkova, *Butovskii poligon, vypusk pervyi*, p. 21.
110 N. V. Petrov and K. V. Skorkin (eds), *Kto rukovodil NKVD, 1934–1941. Spravochnik* (Moscow, 1999) pp. 195, 227, 432–3.

111 According to the data in NKVD files of Austrians shot in Butovo (47) and in the author's possession, two-thirds were arrested in February or March 1938, the last arrest taking place in April. See also the contribution by Hans Schafranek and Natalia Musienko in this volume.

112 One Russian account (without footnotes) attributes Zakovskii's downfall to complaints from the Leningrad Party organisation about his murderous tenure in that city, a protest that was acted upon in the aftermath of the January 1938 plenum of the Central Committee. See B. B. Briukhanov and E. N. Shoshkov, *Opravdaniiu ne podlezhit. Ezhov i Ezhovshchina 1936–1938 gg.* (St. Petersburg, 1998), p. 118.

113 Unless otherwise stated, all statistics concerning the social, national and political composition of the victims shot in Leningrad in 1937, and in Moscow in 1937–8, have been extracted from the biographies of the executed: all five volumes of *Butovskii poligon* and volumes one and two of *Leningradskii martirolog*. For the breakdown of victim data for the months November and December 1937 in Leningrad, I have taken the figures from vol. 3 (pp. 587–91) and vol. 4 (pp. 686–9) of *Leningradskii martirolog*.

114 As only those sentenced on the basis of Article 58 ("political crime") are subject to rehabilitation, "criminal" biographies do not feature in *knigi pamiati*. For a discussion of this point, see "Vstuplenie", L. A. Golovkova (ed.), *Butovskii poligon. Kniga pamiati zhertv politicheskikh repressii. Vypusk piatyi* (Moscow, 2001), pp. 3–4.

115 This is a conservative estimate. The unemployed rubric (*bez opredelennykh zaniatii*), often including many homeless (*bez opredelennogo mesta zhitel'stva*), made up 5.2 per cent of the victims shot in the Leningrad Region in November 1937 and 1 per cent in December. See Razumov, *Leningradskii martirolog*, vol. 3, p. 588 and vol. 4, p. 687. My own analysis of the biographies of persons shot in Leningrad in August, September and October 1937 (vols 2 and 3) revealed much higher percentages for the unemployed–homeless category, namely 11.2 and 11.3 per cent, respectively. That this proportion declined in November and December underlines the general trend that the greater part of the social marginalised victim contingent was executed in the first two months of Operation 00447. Among the 9,957 victim biographies of Butovo victims, not including Gulag inmates, published in volumes 1 to 4 of *Butovskii poligon* the percentage lies at 4.7 per cent according to my own calculations. The true percentage is difficult to compute as many "unemployed" were housewives, or on account of the fact that most criminals were never rehabilitated and therefore do not feature in *knigi pamiati*.

116 G. V. Kostyrchenko and B. Ia. Khazanov, 'Konets kareri Ezhova', *Istoricheskii arkhiv*, no. 1 (1992), pp. 125–8; Getty and Naumov, *The Road to Terror*, pp. 532–7.

117 *Z arkhiviv VUChK-GPU-NKVD-KGB* (Kiev), nos 2–4 (2000), pp. 110–11 (Donetsk), pp. 218–19 (Vinnitsa).

118 James R. Harris, 'The Purging of Local Cliques in the Urals Region, 1936–7', in Fitzpatrick, *Stalinism: New Directions*, p. 278.

119 For details of Ezhov's interrogation in Lefortovo prison as depicted by military prosecutor Afanas'ev, who carried out the questioning and was

present at Ezhov's execution, see S. Iu. Ushakov and A. A. Stukalov (eds), *Front voennykh prokurorov* (Moscow, 2000), pp. 6–172, esp. pp. 67, 72–3.

120 *Leningradskii martirolog* and *Butovskii poligon* (see footnote 113 above); L. P. Rychkova (ed.), *Kniga pamiati zhertv politicheskikh repressii Novgorodskoi oblasti, tom 2* (Novgorod, 1994), pp. 11–12; Kravtsova, *Kniga pamiati... Kalininskoi oblasti*, p. 28; Kuznetsov, *Repressii 30-40-kh gg. v Tomskom krae*, p. 18. The Moscow and Leningrad figures refer to the executed, those from the other regions to all convictions.

121 Getty and Naumov, *The Road to Terror*, p. 588 (all convictions; total for executions); Okhotin and Roginskii, 'Iz istorii "nemetskoi operatsii" NKVD 1937–1938 gg.', in Shcherbakova, *Nakazannyi narod*, p. 60 (ratio death sentences to all verdicts for Operation 00447, "foreigner" operations and Military Collegium verdicts); Terry Martin, 'Origins of Soviet Ethnic Cleansing', p. 855 (total number of sentences for Operation 00447 – 767,397); Dugin, *Neizvestnyi GULAG*, p. 16 (Military Collegium statistics, 1 October 1936 to 30 September 1938).

122 J. Arch Getty, 'State and Society under Stalin: Constitutions and Elections in the 1930s', *Slavic Review*, vol. 50 (1991), pp. 18–35.

123 Khlevniuk, 'The Reasons for the "Great Terror"', pp. 163–8.

124 For a concise account of Soviet foreign policy in the 1930s, see Geoffrey Roberts, *The Soviet Union and the Origins of the Second World War: Russo-German Relations and the Road to War, 1933–1941* (Basingstoke, 1995).

125 The recently published excerpts from the Politburo protocols concerning relations with the European powers do not throw much light on the strategy of the Kremlin in key areas of foreign affairs. There is no mention, for example, of the secret negotiations with Germany in 1935–7 and 1939. See G. Adibekov et al., *Politbiuro TsK RKP(b)-VKP(b) i Evropa. Resheniia "osoboi papki" 1923–1939* (Moscow, 2001), pp. 298–304.

126 Robert C. Tucker, 'Stalinism and Stalin. Sources and Outcomes', in Hildermeier, *Stalinismus vor dem Zweiten Weltkrieg*, pp. 1–16.

127 Terry Martin, 'Modernization or Neo-Traditionalism? Ascribed nationality and Soviet primordialism', in Fitzpatrick, *Stalinism: New Directions*, pp. 357–8.

128 Molotov justified the mass slaughter of 1937–8 on precisely these grounds during an interview in his old age. See *Sto sorok besed s Molotovym. Iz dnevnika F. Chueva* (Moscow, 1991), p. 390. See the extract from Dimitrov's diary (7 November 1937), with Stalin's remarks on the dangers posed to the territorial integrity of the Soviet Union, in Fridrikh Firsov's contribution to this volume.

129 J. V. Stalin, *Problems of Leninism* (Moscow, 1947), p. 424 (Central Committee Plenum, 7 January 1933).

130 David Shearer, to my knowledge, was the first to make this essential point. See Shearer, 'Crime and Disorder in Stalin's Russia', p. 140.

131 Hannah Arendt, *The Origins of Totalitarianism. New Edition with added Prefaces* [1951 edn] (San Diego, London and New York, 1976), p. 427.

7
The "Polish Operation" of the NKVD, 1937–8

Nikita Petrov and Arsenii Roginskii[1]

The scope allotted to us merely allows a description of the general contours of the "Polish operation" of the NKVD in the years 1937–8. We place the main emphasis on how it originated, the policy behind it, how it worked and to what extent it was realised. The core document in this connection is Order no. 00485 of the NKVD of the USSR. Order 00485 was confirmed by the Politburo of the Central Committee of the VKP(b) (as the CPSU was then called) on 9 August 1937. It was signed by Ezhov two days later, together with the "sealed" letter "On Fascist-Insurgent, Espionage, Sabotage, Defeatist and Terrorist Activities of Polish Intelligence in the USSR". This letter had also been approved by Stalin beforehand, and was then signed by Ezhov for circulation to all NKVD units.[2]

The necessity of issuing these two documents simultaneously was determined by certain special operations of the secret police then unfolding. For example, operative Order no. 00447, issued on 30 July 1937, had been circulated without any kind of accompanying letter. The order was deemed not to require any supplementary explanations for a variety of reasons. Firstly, because it had been preceded by months of intensive preparation (the calculation of contingents to be arrested, correspondence on the composition of the *troiki*, correcting the quotas to be arrested and shot etc.). Secondly, and more importantly, the purpose of this order had been completely clear not only to the leading officers, but also to ordinary NKVD personnel who were supposed to carry it out. Order 00447 was directed against those people (kulaks, criminals, ex-members of banned political parties and the clergy) who had always been considered "hostile elements" and had been arrested and condemned to detention over the years. The *troika* method of sentencing these victims was not new; it had been tried out in the 1920s and early 1930s, most commonly during the years of collectivisation. In this way Order 00447 seemed a natural stage in development, the final point in the liquidation of "traditional" enemies of Soviet power rather than anything really novel. The precise thrust of the order was underlined not only by the fulfilment quotas it contained and the scope of its application, but also by a time limit: NKVD staff had four months to arrest, investigate and sentence roughly 300,000 persons.

Order no. 00485 had to be grasped completely differently. In spite of the fact that in the text there was no mention of Poles as such but of "Polish spies", it was nevertheless concluded that almost the entire Polish population of the USSR was under suspicion. This attitude was hardly in accord with the officially proclaimed slogan of Internationalism, and there were many Poles working in the ranks of the NKVD. They could not pose questions about the order as such or its separate formulations concerning persons marked down for arrest, e.g. all "defectors" (*perebezhchiki*) or all former ex-POWs, or to put it differently, not just those Poles who were suspected of hostile activities, but namely all Poles. For the practical work of the NKVD this type of directive was a novelty. In a confession after his arrest, A. O. Postel', a staff-member of the NKVD Administration for the Moscow District, stated:

> When we, the departmental heads, learned of Ezhov's order to arrest absolutely all Poles [in the order there is no mention of "all Poles", but it is characteristic of the NKVD that it interpreted the order in such a general sense – N.P./A.R.], former POWs, members of the KPP and others, it aroused not only amazement, but was also a subject of discussion in our corridors. [These doubts] were brought to an end by the statement that we had been told that the directive was issued in agreement with Stalin and the Politburo of the Central Committee of the VKP(b) and that we must destroy the Poles completely.[3]

It seems that it was precisely to take account of such internal reactions that Order 00485 was issued simultaneously with the "sealed letter" which supplemented the order and, in a certain fashion, substantiated it. The 30-page letter, saturated with names and facts, painted a fantastic picture of the activities of Polish Intelligence on the territory of the USSR in the preceding 20 years. This activity was stated to have been directed and carried out by the so-called "Polish Military Organisation" (Pol'skaia voennaia organizatsiia – POV), together with the Second (Intelligence) Department of the Polish General Staff. A long time before, it was alleged, POV had taken over the leadership of the Polish Communist Party (KPP), had penetrated all sections of the Soviet state *apparat*, including the People's Commissariats of Foreign Affairs (NKID) and Internal Affairs (NKVD), and the Red Army (RKKA). With the help of such confederates, thousands of new agents were transported from Poland to the USSR, and, in the guise of political emigrants, many exchanged political prisoners and "defectors" created within their ranks 30,000 new agents and formed a huge number of espionage groups, recruited mainly from the Polish population in the Soviet Union. This vast net was ruled from a Moscow "centre" which acted on orders from Warsaw, and single groups and individuals had frequent contact with the Polish capital, directly or via the Polish Consulate in the USSR.[4]

The "head" of the POV organisation "at this time" (August 1937) was considered to have been exterminated already, and the main task of NKVD organs, as stated in the preamble to the order, was now "the complete liquidation of those insurgent, minor groups of the POV and units of Polish Intelligence still active in the USSR." According to this version of NKVD fantasy, the order defined six categories of persons who were to be arrested:

1) "In the process of investigation to uncover all active members of the POV not yet discovered ..."

The investigation into the "POV case" was carried out intensively by the central *apparat* of the NKVD from the end of 1936. In late July 1937, soon after the receipt of confession statements made by some dozens of the most important prisoners, these extracts were enclosed in special volumes. These materials, together with the theses devoted to the POV in Ezhov's speech to the June 1937 plenum of the Central Committee of the VKP(b), were employed in the composition of Order 00485 and in that of the "sealed letter". Simultaneously, those names which were excerpted from confessions were later included in the list attached to the order and titled "active members of the POV not yet uncovered". Parts of the confessions were also duplicated and distributed, together with Order 00485 and the "sealed letter", to NKVD offices countrywide.

2) "All prisoners of war of the Polish Army who remained in the USSR."

Most of the Polish POWs captured during the Soviet-Polish War returned to Poland in the early 1920s. Only some 1,500 to 2,000, it is estimated, remained in the Soviet Union up to the mid-1930s.

3) "'Defectors' from Poland, regardless of when they entered Soviet territory."

Economic, social or family circumstances caused the flood of refugees from Poland to the USSR to continue over many years. Those who fled eastwards belonged to the poorest sections of the Polish population. The category of what the NKVD termed "defectors" involved all who illegally crossed the Polish-Soviet border, including persons who had been detained by Soviet border guards or had voluntarily confessed to this offence later. Such persons were to undergo an obligatory investigation, in the course of which the following categories were to be determined: first, those previously sent back to Poland ("expellees"); second, those arrested on suspicion of spying, smuggling and other crimes; third, members of revolutionary organisations possessing the suitable recommendation, who had been released from Polish custody and subsequently allowed to live in any part of the USSR they wished; fourth and finally, the biggest group, namely those who, on the one hand, had the right to apply for and who had received political asylum (e.g. deserters from the Polish Army) and, on the other hand, who did not have any dealings with the revolutionary movement but had likewise been released from a Polish gaol, permitted to settle in the Soviet Union and offered work in definite districts. The last mentioned were subject to "operational registration" by the pertinent OGPU-NKVD unit to which they had to present themselves periodically for re-registration. In time they were offered Soviet citizenship and could choose freely their place of residence.

No centralised system of monitoring or counting Polish immigrants was set up, even their approximate number was unknown. In a speech before the leading officers of the Main Administration of State Security (GUGB) of the NKVD in January 1938, Ezhov stated a rough figure of over 100,000. In 1937 many of these had gone "missing", and the search for such "defectors" became one of the many tasks of the NKVD in the course of implementing the "Polish" order.

4) "Political emigrants and political exchange prisoners from Poland."

5) "Former members of the Polish Socialist Party (PPS)."

In accordance with this portion of Order 00485, almost the entire rank-and-file of the KPP emigration in the USSR was exterminated, and also other Polish political activists, especially those who, at some time or other, had had links to the PPS – as far back as 1892 and continuing through the party's troubled history of splits and factionalism. Exchange of political prisoners between Poland and the Soviet Union had taken place in the 1920s and 1930s on the basis of special agreements signed in 1923–4. Polish leftists were exchanged for Catholic priests detained in Russia, for example, and now the "sealed letter" confirmed that such Poles were practically all POV agents and that they had been specially trained in Poland for subsequent missions on Soviet territory.[5]

6) "The most active part of the local anti-Soviet and nationalist elements in the Polish districts."

In effect, this clause meant carrying out arrests in areas where Poles lived in compact settlements. According to the 1937 census, a total of 636,220 Poles lived in the USSR, of whom 417,613 resided in the Ukraine, 119,881 in Belorussia and 92,078 in the Russian Federation.[6] In the Ukraine and Belorussia more than two-thirds of the Poles lived in rural areas, and by the early 1930s there were more than 150 Polish village soviets. Many Poles lived in the Kamenev-Podolsk, Zhitomir and Vinnitsa regions of the Ukraine. In the Russian Federation the majority of Poles dwelt in the Moscow and Leningrad regions and in Western Siberia. In 1936 there were roughly 36,000 – other sources state 45,000 – Poles in Kazakhstan. They had been sent there during the evacuation of the Ukrainian districts bordering on Poland, an operation directly foreshadowing that of 1937–8.[7]

In the regions mentioned, and in the Urals as well, where the NKVD believed many refugees from Poland had settled, Order 00485 was implemented most thoroughly. In addition, Order 00485 categorically laid down that persons who had been convicted of spying for Poland were not to be released from the Gulag on completion of their term. Material on these cases was to be handed over to the Special Boards (OSO) of the NKVD two months before the specific camp sentence ran out in order to impose a new sentence.

A substantial extension of such arrest contingents occurred on 2 October 1937, when Ezhov, in a special directive, widened the scope of the potential victims of Order 00485 by including members of their families. This was the application of Order no. 00486 "On the Repression of Wives of Enemies and Traitors to the Motherland, of Members of Right-Trotskyist Espionage-Sabotage Organisations Sentenced by the Military and by Military Tribunals", which had been issued for the whole country on 15 August 1937.[8] Accordingly, now subject to arrest were the wives of men who had been convicted of "counter-revolutionary activities" by various sentencing bodies. Also to be placed under arrest were children over fifteen years of age if they were considered to be "socially dangerous and capable of committing anti-Soviet acts". The wives were sentenced by Special Boards of the NKVD, and the children over fifteen years, depending on how they were characterised, were dispatched to camps, colonies or children's homes with "special regime". Children aged one to fifteen, now orphans, were sent to nurseries or children's homes of the NKVD. It soon transpired that the directive of 2 October was encountering major technical difficulties: the flood of new prisoners, in this case the wives of Poles and Kharbintsy[9] on whom the order of 15 August was also being enforced, turned out to be far greater than expected, prison space was scarce and the orphanages of the secret police were also overcrowded.

Ezhov was forced to cancel Order No. 00486 on 21 November 1937, directing instead that the wives of Poles and Kharbintsy be exiled. It seems that this measure, too, was realised in a haphazard fashion, affecting only some regions. In this case, reality had defeated the ambitious plans of the NKVD. On the other hand, during the execution of Order no. 00485 some groups not mentioned in the order but a category in their own right were arrested, e.g. those Russians who had links with Polish diplomatic circles. Meanwhile, Ezhov had issued an order under his own name in late October 1937 whereby *all* Soviet citizens were to be taken into custody who had links with, or had visited the staff of foreign consulates at work or in their apartments. Particularly suspicious were contacts with diplomatic personnel from Poland, Germany, Italy and Japan. Foreign citizens suspected of contacts with diplomatic posts were only then to be arrested if the NKVD felt they had committed hostile acts against the USSR.

Corresponding to the idea behind Order no. 00485 (mass arrests per "contingent") and commencing as an independent initiative of local NKVD staff, ex-POWs of the Soviet-Polish War of 1919-20 were quickly arrested, in some regions even Polish ex-POWs of the First World War who had served in the Polish Legion or the Austro-Hungarian army. Red Army men who had been held captive in Poland were arrested at a later stage. This creation of new arrest categories did not provoke any objections from the central NKVD *apparat* and was subsequently legalised in the Ukraine in February 1938, for example. Now targeted were also ex-Red Army men who had gone through POW camps in Poland and had returned home only after the signing of the Treaty of Riga.

What charges were levelled at prisoners arrested on the basis of Order no. 00485? The overwhelming majority of the victims were farmers from border areas, factory workers or railwaymen. One of the aims of the "sealed letter" was to offer a "menu" of possible "crimes": spying in all regions, especially in the military jurisdictions; the plotting of acts of sabotage, biological warfare included; "wrecking" in all sections of the national economy; terrorism on a local and national basis; membership in insurgent groups to plan uprisings in time of war; and anti-Soviet agitation. Furthermore, a long period of residence in the USSR was supposed to "explain" the specific traits of collaboration, and this was reflected in the charges: hostile activities during the Russian Civil War and the conflict with Poland; or close links to various intelligence services, especially German agencies; and finally, cooperation with forces within the country traditionally hostile to Soviet power – joint operations with Socialist Revolutionaries to carry out terrorist acts or setting up insurgent groups with Ukrainian and Belorussian "nationalist elements".

This all-inclusive list, which even surpassed the scope of the "enemies" set down in Order no. 00447 against "anti-Soviet elements and kulaks", was vigorously applied in order to fulfil the quotas fixed in the "Polish" directive. It also served as a model for other "national" contingents, the last repressive mass operations of the NKVD in 1937–8. Order 00485 established new forms in the NKVD's practice of sentencing the accused. Following the conclusion of the investigation into the charges, an information sheet (*spravka*) was drafted containing "a short summary of the investigation and agents' reports characterising the accused's degree of guilt". The separate information sheets had to be collected and then typed as lists every ten days. The papers were presented for examination to two persons: an officer of the local NKVD administration and a public prosecutor. This constellation gave rise to the term *dvoika* (twosome), an appellation that never surfaced in the official correspondence of the period. The task of the *dvoiki* was to sentence the accused to one of two categories: "first" was the death penalty by shooting, and "second" incarceration for five to ten years. Then the list was sent for confirmation to Moscow, where it was examined and sanctioned by the People's Commissar for Internal Affairs, Ezhov, and the General Public Prosecutor, Vyshinskii. The list was afterwards returned to the region so that the sentences could be carried out. This mode of convicting prisoners soon came to be known in the NKVD as the "album" procedure, perhaps because the typed lists were filled in on the page in horizontal entries and bound together at the margin, outwardly resembling entries in an album.

In practice, the local operative officer of the NKVD, after he had composed the information sheet, consulted with members of his group or with his departmental head before determining the verdict to be passed. The leaders of administrative NKVD units and the public prosecutors who had to place their signatures on the lists drawn up specially for the "Finnish" or "Polish" operations did so automatically, usually each on his own, without consulting the other or, indeed, possessing any knowledge of the cases enumerated on the list. Formalistic procedures were also evident in Moscow, the destination of the "albums". In like manner, neither Ezhov nor Vyshinskii nor their respective deputies Frinovskii and Roginskii ever cast a glance into the signed pages of the "albums". The examination of these was entrusted to some departmental heads in the central *apparat*: initially to V. E. Tsesarskii, head of the accounts and statistics department, and to A. M. Minaev-Tsikanovskii of the counter-intelligence department. He was assisted by the head of Ezhov's secretariat, I. I. Shapiro, thus giving grounds for the rumour of "Ezhov's special *troika*". After the "albums" had subsequently become bulkier, other heads of departments, their deputies and even group leaders were drawn into this work.

In the various documents of this type we encounter the names of fifteen or so officials who examined the "albums" at different times. All of them, as can be seen in countless pieces of evidence, considered this work a tiresome additional burden, which they tried to finish as quickly as possible. In the evenings, every one of these officers sanctioned 200–300 information sheets. As a rule they mechanically approved the draft, but occasionally and for a variety of reasons, raised objections or penned remarks on the lists of Poles to be sentenced – for example, changing the verdict or recommending that the file be passed on to a court for review. The list and the supplementary remarks were re-typed without being checked, presented to Ezhov for his signature and then brought by courier to Vyshinskii for signing.

Because of this work pattern it turned out that the only person who really looked at the case in question was the NKVD officer who had led the investigation and, in most cases, also fixed the verdict. In accordance with a directive of the Public Prosecutor of the USSR, complaints about *dvoiki* verdicts were examined only "in exceptional cases."[10] In all remaining cases, as was stated without the slightest explanation, the verdict was final. The great majority of persons arrested during mass operations were convicted by the "album" method, but this does not apply to all victims of the "Polish" operation. The "album" procedure was intended for "lower" cases arrested on the basis of Order 00485.

Many of those charged with spying on behalf of Poland or belonging to higher "spying and sabotage networks" were sentenced by the Military Collegium of the Supreme Court or by military tribunals at a lower level. Sentencing of the "Polish" operation cases was entrusted to Special Boards (OSO) of the NKVD as well, which, as we have already mentioned, examined the prisoners' files and also those of arrested spouses. The repressive role of Special Boards was strengthened by a specific resolution of the Politburo passed on 5 September 1937 (P51/920), according to which such sentencing bodies were empowered, in cases of "anti-Soviet activities" on the part of former Polish "defectors" and "ex-members of the PPS", to pass verdicts of up to 10 years in prison.[11] As far as we can ascertain, this mechanism was rarely used in 1937–8. In any case, another Politburo decision of an earlier date, passed specifically for the "Polish operation" on 8 April 1937 (P48/3), had stated that the maximum sentence to be set by Special Boards was 8 years.

It was originally thought that the "Polish" order would take three months to complete, from 20 August to 20 November 1937. But this time limit was repeatedly extended, along with others fixed for various "national contingent" operations: first to 10 December, then to 1 January, subsequently to 15 April and finally to 1 August 1938. Belorussia was an exception in this context – it was permitted to extend such operations until 1 September 1938. Each prolongation had the same consequence: a further simplification of the methods used to investigate and convict prisoners. It was precisely the "album" method which proved a stumbling-block in conducting the different "national" arrest drives, including the "Polish" one. From January and February 1938 onwards, the "national" operations became the main thrust of NKVD activity, replacing, as a central aim, the activities involved in executing Order 00447 in the autumn and early winter of 1937. By early 1938, more than half a million prisoners had been convicted on the basis of directive no. 00447. Shortly afterwards, when "national" operations were being pursued with special urgency, it transpired that the Centre was not able to "digest" all the "albums" sent in from the regions. Between the dispatch of an "album" to Moscow and it being returned to the original NKVD unit several months could pass.

By summer 1938 "albums" containing over 100,000 verdicts had accumulated in Moscow. As a consequence, the regions sent barrages of complaints about overcrowding in the prisons and the high costs of keeping prisoners who had already been given the death sentence. Possibly for this reason the Politburo passed a motion on 15 September 1938 (P 64/22) abolishing the "album" procedure of convicting those in custody and establishing in each region a special *troika* specifically to pass verdicts on members of "national" contingents in custody, that is on all "album" cases which had not been sanctioned to date. The personal composition of the new *troiki* did not need the confirmation of the Politburo. In another sense this triangle was different from the now more or less defunct *troiki* set up a year previously to sentence those arrested on the basis of Order 00447. The new trio was appointed strictly according to function and comprised the following officials: the local Party leader, the public prosecutor and the local chief of the secret police. The verdicts they agreed on did not need the approval of Moscow, but had to be carried out immediately.

The working life of the new *troiki* was limited to two months and they were expected to examine the cases of all those arrested up to 1 August 1938. The files of prisoners arrested after this date were to be handed over to the courts, military tribunals, the Military Collegium or the Special Boards.[12] On the basis of this decision NKVD Order no. 00606 was issued on 17 September, and in the following two months all "albums" which had not been checked were returned from the Centre to the regions. In the roads and transport department (DTO) of the NKVD, which existed at all main railroads and played an essential part in conducting the "national" operations, *troiki* were not established; "albums" emanating from these units were sent to the pertinent territorial headquarters of the NKVD. Most of the special *troiki* had been set up by early October. The intensity of their workload depended directly on the number of "album" information sheets for checking. The number of cases varied considerably – from some dozens in the Kalmyk, Kuibyshev, Riazan and Iaroslavl' regions to several thousands in the administrative centres around Leningrad (8,000 plus), Novosibirsk, Sverdlovsk, and Cheliabinsk (each more than 4,000). In some regions approximately thirty to fifty cases were examined in a *troika* sitting, in others anything from 300 to 800. As was strict tradition, the special *troiki* did not deal with the original investigation files, but with the entries in the "album", and, in rare cases, with the explanations offered by the chief of the pertinent NKVD-UNKVD department present at the sitting.

In a period of two and a half months the special *troiki* examined and confirmed the sentences of almost 108,000 persons, who were all victims of "national" operations. Only 137 from this huge total were released from custody. The activities of the special *troiki* were subject to an exact time-limit – up to 15 November 1938. At the same time a strict order was issued to suspend the execution of all death sentences passed but not carried out by that date. Despite this order, such shooting quotas were completed in full in some regions. On 17 November 1938 a joint motion of the Central Committee of the VKP(b) and the Council of People's Commissars decreed the cessation of all mass operations. A subsequent order signed by Beria, the new NKVD Commissar, cancelled all operative orders of the NKVD issued in the years 1937 and 1938, those already issued and others awaiting realisation.[13]

Order 00485 became a "model" for all "national" operations launched after August 1937, affecting Romanians, Finns, Latvians and others. Everywhere the hunt began to uncover branches of "spying and sabotage networks" and "insurrectionist groups in the remit of a foreign power"; everywhere similar "contingents" were set down for arrest, especially political immigrants and "defectors"; everywhere the "album" method of convicting became the norm. What this meant was frequently not detailed in the directive. The NKVD teams had to take the laconic statement literally that the verdicts were to ensue "on the basis of Order 00485".

These "national" operations occupy a special place in the general system of oppression in 1937–8. They were clearly shaped by Stalin's conviction that war was looming, by his fear of a "fifth column",[14] by his notion of "hostile encirclement", notably by the "country of the main enemy", Germany, but implying other states as well, particularly those which bordered on the USSR. In Stalin's mind the frontiers of the Soviet Union were a bulwark, and all those who had come over "to our side", as indeed the "defectors" had, were real or potential enemies of the Soviet state, regardless of the motives they arrived with, their capabilities or the length of time they had spent in Russia. Their class affiliations or political past did not have any significance. They were not to be treated as "class brothers" or comrades saved from the "oppression of bourgeois governments", or as comrades-in-arms from the time of the Russian Revolution; that is, not any longer as the political refugees which they had been for over a decade. Instead, all such foreigners were seen exclusively as representatives – and later as "agents" – of foreign states. These states, bent on weakening or destroying the USSR, were conducting a continuous campaign to undermine Soviet power and found themselves in an undeclared state of war with the Communist regime. Such was Stalin's "logic" of interstate relations, especially those between neighbouring countries. It was therefore in his eyes essential to deal with such "agents" as if a state of war did exist.[15]

Such ideas of statehood and of the nation's need for self-defence had come to dominate Stalin's thinking by the mid-1930s, leading him to discard conventional scenarios of class struggle. This new orientation, we believe, determined the course of the "national" operations of the NKVD in the period 1937–8, campaigns directed at all those who had direct or indirect links to "hostile" states which "encircled" the Soviet Union. The especially harsh verdicts handed down to such foreigners must also be seen against this psychological background.

Archival sources reveal that approximately 19 per cent of all convictions passed in 1937–8 by courts, tribunals and the Military Collegium were death sentences. The percentage of those shot on the basis of a *troika* verdict during the course of the mass operation unleashed by Order 00447 was two and a half times higher – 49.3 per cent. As regards mass arrests of foreigners ("national operations"), the number of cases examined by the "album" procedure in the special *troiki* totals 346,713 persons, of whom 247,157 (73.66 per cent) were sentenced to death by shooting. The percentage of those executed in the course of implementing the "Polish" order is even higher: 143,810 persons were examined, 139,835 were sentenced, and of these 111,091 (79.44 per cent) received the death penalty. A still higher ratio between those sentenced and subsequently shot was registered for operations directed against Greeks, Finns and Estonians. The majority of arrested Iranians and Afghans were, by contrast, expelled from the USSR.

There were no special directives concerning the application of the death penalty in any of the "national" operations. In the Polish case, no separate directives concerning the various regions were formulated. In such cases, we believe, everything, including the number of capital verdicts, depended on the mood of the NKVD chief involved, and the percentage ratios mentioned above varied widely. For example, the per centage of capital as against all sentences passed in the course of all "national" operations in the Kuibyshev region was 48.16 per cent, in Vologda region 46.5 per cent, and in Armenia and Georgia the corresponding figure was 31.46 per cent and 21.84 per cent respectively. During the same period the percentage of those shot in the Leningrad region and in Belorussia totalled 87–8 per cent, in the Krasnodarsk and Novosibirsk regions it exceeded 94 per cent. And, finally, in Orenburg region it reached 96.4 per cent. Such wide percentage variations are also discernible in the statistics of the Polish victims (see Table 7.1, below).

Among those repressed during the "national" operations it is possible to isolate certain categories that were subject to exceptional cruelty; for example, the ongoing punitive policy against "defectors", which was reinforced by the decisive special resolution of the Politburo of 31 January 1938 (P57/50). Now all "defectors" who had been re-arrested were to be shot if it could be "proved" that they had crossed the Polish-Soviet border with hostile intent; in cases where no such evidence was available, the "defectors" were to receive a sentence of ten years in prison.[16]

In comparison with other "national" operations, the mass repression against Poles was different not in the numbers of those actually shot, but in the extent to which this minority was decimated. The order against the Poles was not the first aimed at a minority living within the Soviet Union[17], but turned out to be the most devastating of all when measured by the total number of victims. There are many reasons for this. Firstly, because Poland was held, in the inter-war period, to be the most dangerous neighbouring state; secondly, there existed the profound myth of Polish "perfidy"; thirdly, there were more "defectors" from Poland than from any other country; fourthly and finally, because of their presence it was argued that the scope of activities for Polish Intelligence in the USSR was remarkably wide and far more extensive than the espionage activities carried out in the Soviet Union by other states.

The mass repression of the Polish population was determined to a lesser degree by the dislike Stalin is said to have harboured of Poles. He was not interested in Poles as such, but in Poland as a hostile state. Other "national" operations of the NKVD had an analogous background. The "national" operations were conducted on a certain "line", that is, the Stalinist "logic" pertaining to the "hostile intentions" of all countries bordering on the USSR and the "fifth columns" they had infiltrated over the frontier. However, the "nationality" of these foreigners was not criminal in itself, even if it always gave grounds for suspicion. Of decisive importance was whether the individual had been born in a foreign country, had lived there and still had contact with it. This was the principal difference between the "national" operations of 1937–8 and the repression the national minorities in the USSR were subjected to during the Second World War. By using categories that had to be filled in when completing *ankety* – questionnaires – (place of birth, residence abroad, contact to relatives in a foreign country), a purge was carried out within the Red Army in 1937–8. Many were dismissed from the service and usually arrested immediately afterwards. Affected in this way were not only all serving staff and civilian employees of the armed forces with a foreign nationality, but to a lesser extent members of the national minorities within the USSR as well. The "questionnaire" method had quite a tradition in the repressive practices of the OGPU-NKVD, but it hinged usually on class affiliation, and the former social status and political views of the prisoner. During the mass arrests of 1937–8 the entry on the questionnaire on "links with abroad" became the foremost cause of arrest, whereas earlier it had merely given grounds for suspicion.

In initiating "national" operations, Stalin followed another goal distinct from the one aimed at destroying potential sources of support for "hostile countries". If it was not possible to terminate all contacts with foreigners – something attained in later years – the State must endeavour to monitor all kinds of non-sanctioned relations with the world outside the Soviet Union. This policy of hermetically sealing off the native population from foreign influence was not pursued merely by means of repressive measures, but by a plethora of supplementary edicts issued in the late 1930s: jamming foreign radio stations and supervising a close watch over personal communication with other countries (amateur radio operators, philatelists) and enforcing detailed regulations governing the behaviour of Soviet citizens abroad. In the years of the Great Terror this policy led to the growing conviction among ordinary people that any kind of "contact with abroad" was dangerous.

In regard to the Poles with foreign contacts who were subsequently arrested, three categories are now apparent. Firstly, those who had earlier lived abroad and, under whatever circumstances, had later returned to the Soviet Union; secondly, those who still had contacts with Poland; and finally, their immediate family and acquaintances. Not all Poles taken into custody, however, had been arrested during the "Polish" operation, but in the course of other NKVD campaigns as well.

The sources do not provide exact figures on the national composition of the victims arrested and convicted in the years 1937–8, not because documents giving such an estimate were maliciously destroyed or concealed, but for another reason altogether: in the whole course of 1937 and during the first four months of 1938 the central *apparat* of the NKVD did not demand from its local units information concerning the nationality of those arrested. The absence of such a requirement was wholly in keeping with the logic and spirit of mass operations: it was important for Moscow to know how many persons had been arrested during a major NKVD sweep, how many had been condemned and to which category of "enemy" the sentenced prisoners belonged, from what police register or branch of industry they had been "taken", but not which nationality they possessed.

The nationality, of course, was noted down in each investigation file (in the questionnaire filled in by the prisoner, for example), as explanatory data in the lists drawn up under the "album" procedure during "national" operations, in the information sheets for cases heard by *troiki* according to Order 00447, and finally, in the formal indictment in files sent for examination to the courts or a Special Board of the NKVD. However, data on the national composition of prisoners were collated neither at the local NKVD offices nor at the Centre; if it was done at all, then at random and for specific reasons.

Such an eventuality occurred in February 1938 when the chief of the NKVD in Sverdlovsk, D. M. Dmitriev, complained to Ezhov that the active operations were being hindered by the slow process of examining "albums" sent to Moscow. Frinovskii, against whom the complaint was really lodged, counted once more the cases in the Sverdlovsk "albums". He accused Dmitriev, in carrying out a "national" operation, of proceeding on the lines of Order 00447: from a total of 4,218 arrested by the Sverdlovsk NKVD during the "Polish" operation, only 390 were real Poles, and "ex-kulaks" totalled 3,798; furthermore, the 237 prisoners seized during the "Latvian" operation turned out to be "ex-kulaks" in the main, only 12 real Latvians having been taken into custody. For these reasons, then, the Sverdlovsk "album" lists had not been sanctioned.

After a lengthy pause the practice of summarising prisoners' data on the basis of national affiliation was resumed in May 1938 following a directive of the NKVD, mainly because of new regulations pertaining to the nationality of Soviet citizens. According to circular no. 65 of 2 April 1938, a new procedure was established to indicate nationality when issuing or renewing passports. Whereas previously the nationality the applicant stated he or she belonged to was registered, now the authorities had to take account of the nationality of the parents in all cases. This was henceforth to be indicated on passports and other official documents. This regulation remained in force for some decades, and for our theme it had special significance. An explanatory passage in the circular reads:

> If the parents are Germans, Poles etc., [the children], regardless of where they were born, how long they have lived in the USSR or whether they now have a different citizenship or not, may not be registered officially as Russian or Belorussian. In cases where the native language or the surname of the applicant does not correspond to the nationality given, for example, Müller or Popandopulos, and the applicant describes himself as Russian or Belorussian, and if it proves impossible to establish the real nationality of the applicant during the registration, then the nationality column on the form is not to be filled in until documents proving national status can be produced.[18]

It was surely no accident that in this text express mention is made of Poles, Germans and Greeks, that is, those ethnic groups against whom "national" operations were carried out. One of the aims behind establishing new criteria for determining nationality status, and indeed other measures such as having a photograph included in all new

168 *Stalin's Terror*

Table 7.1: Sentencing totals for the "Polish" Operation (Order no. 00485) of the NKVD, August 1937 to November 1938

Area NKVD	Total	Shot	Gulag	Area UNKVD	Total	Shot	Gulag
Azerbaijan SSR	189	100	89	Altai territory	1,540	1,230	310
Armenian SSR	19	7	12	Far Eastern Region	536	376	160
Belorussian SSR	19,931	17,772	2,159	Krasnodarsk territory	1,916	1,807	109
Georgian SSR	89	47	42	Krasnoiarsk territory	2,269	1,859	410
Kazakhstan SSR	1,968	1,777	191	Ordzhonikidze territory	423	214	209
Kirghiz SSR	76	36	40	Archangel region	328	163	165
Tadzhik SSR	30	11	19	Vologda region	193	121	72
Turkmen SSR	157	91	66	Voronezh region	658	345	313
Uzbek SSR	533	121	412	Gorkii region	786	519	267
Ukrainian SSR	55,928	47,327	8,601	Ivanovo region	200	145	55
Bashkir ASSR	450	343	107	Irkutsk region	649	626	23
Buriat-Mongolian ASSR	86	74	12	Kalinin region	140	109	31
Dagestan ASSR	14	12	2	Kirov region	138	108	30
Kabardino-Balkar ASSR	52	48	4	Kuibyshev region	279	132	147
Kalmyk ASSR	9	7	2	Kursk region	314	171	143
Karelian ASSR	146	119	27	Leningrad region	7,404	6,597	807
Komi ASSR	62	44	18	Moscow region	2,875	1,880	995
Crimean ASSR	488	315	173	Murmansk region	51	45	6
Mari ASSR	129	109	20	Novosibirsk region	7,444	7,012	432
Mordvinian ASSR	258	229	29	Omsk region	1,106	430	676
Volga German ASSR	38	21	17	Orenburg region	483	471	12
Northern Ossetian ASSR	137	81	56	Orel region	892	428	464
Tatar ASSR	307	160	147	Rostov region	1,478	847	631
Udmurt ASSR	77	22	55	Riazan region	86	50	36

Table 7.1: Sentencing totals for the "Polish" Operation (Order no. 00485) of the NKVD, August 1937 to November 1938 (*continued*)

Area NKVD	Total	Shot	Gulag	Area UNKVD	Total	Shot	Gulag
Chechen-Ingush ASSR	112	102	10	Saratov region	472	216	256
Chuvash ASSR	36	16	20	Sverdlovsk region	5,988	3,794	2,194
Iakut ASSR	68	34	34	Smolensk region	3,717	2,203	1,514
				Stalingrad region	763	552	211
				Tambov region	395	301	94
				Tula region	976	416	560
				Cheliabinsk region	2,693	2,212	481
				Chita region	130	112	18
				Iaroslavl' region	477	356	121
				Road/Rail Units GUGB/NKVD	10,647	6,219	4,428
Totals for USSR					139,835	111,091	28,744
In Per cent					100.0	79.4	20.6
Totals for dvoiki (album)					103,067	84,160	18,907
Totals for osobye troiki					36,768	26,931	9,837

Source: N. V. Petrov and A. B. Roginskii, '"Pol'skaia operatsiia" NKVD 1937–1938gg.', in L. S. Eremina (ed.), *Repressii protiv poliakov i pol'skikh grazhdan* (Moscow, 1997), pp. 40–3.

passports, was to find persons who, in the view of the NKVD, were suspicious individuals and could be subject to arrest. In fact, if we are to believe the reports based on the questioning of passport applicants at the ZAGS registry offices, an ample number (some thousands) of former Polish "defectors" and ex-POWs were "unmasked" in this way. Only on 16 May 1938 did the NKVD direct its local units to include in reports data about the national composition of the arrested. From this comparatively late date onwards the NKVD leadership began to show special interest in the ethnic aspect of mass repression. However, information about the nationality of those arrested on the basis of Order 00447 was subsequently not sent to the Centre. Moreover, some regions, especially the railroad units of the secret police (DTO), did not systematically report to Moscow. For these reasons, then, even in the last months of mass repression our information about the national affiliation of those taken into custody is perforce incomplete. In our opinion, the sole reliable figures are likewise not complete: they include no final figures for the total numbers arrested, merely those sentenced by special *troiki* in the period September to November 1938. These statistics seem to confirm the thesis that it would be wrong to equate "Poles" with the "Polish" operation.

In these three months, special *troiki* condemned a total of 105,032 persons arrested in the course of all "national" operations. The biggest national group was that of the Poles (21,258), followed by Germans (17,150), Russians (15,684), Ukrainians (8,773) and Belorussians (5,716). "Poles", in this instance, meant those who were so described in their passports and other official documents or declared so on the random decision of the NKVD investigating team, which simply wrote in the prisoner's file that he or she was a Pole. From this total figure of 105,032, those convicted during the "Polish" operation numbered 36,768. This statistic included the following national groups: Poles 20,147, Belorussians 5,215, Ukrainians 4,991, Russians 3,235, Jews 1,122, Germans 490, Lithuanians 396, Latvians 271, Estonians 112, Czechs 97, Gypsies 76, Austrians 59, Bulgarians 53, Hungarians 47, Romanians 29, Greeks 27, Moldavians 26, Tartars 23 and "others" 362. During the same period Poles also fell victim to other "national" operations, roughly 500 during the "German" sweep and 209 during the "Latvian" one.

The interrelation presented here between "Polish" and other nationalities should not be applied mechanically to the implementation of the entire "Polish" operation. It developed unevenly and contributed, in the first stage, to a higher figure of arrested Poles than in the sweeps of spring 1938. Almost 143,000 persons were convicted and 111,000 shot during the "Polish" operation, about 10 per cent of all those condemned during the mass terror of 1937–8. Under convictions we mean the sentences passed by courts, by Special Boards, on the basis of the "album" procedure, and also the verdicts of those *troiki* set up by Orders 00447 and 00606. If one speaks of arrested Poles as distinct from convicted ones, our estimate is even more so an approximation derived from several sources. During the two years of the Great Terror more than 1,600,000 persons were arrested by NKVD staff (excluding the normal police). In this figure is included 118,000 to 123,000 Poles, of whom 96,000 to 99,000 were arrested during diverse "national" operations, especially during the "Polish" one; the remaining 20,000 were arrested on the basis of Order 00447 and other "mass operations" directives.

The limited scope of this article compelled us to neglect many very important subjects directly connected to our theme: people deported from border areas, purges in the NKVD itself or inside the intelligence service of the Red Army, or in the defence and other branches of industry. We barely touched on the specific problems concerning the execution of Order 00485 in the separate regions, but merely mentioned the total number arrested during that operation. In order to investigate the effects of Order 00485 thoroughly, it would be necessary to widen our base of sources with material from Russian, Ukrainian and Belorussian archives. However, it must be remembered that the overwhelming bulk of documents pertaining to political repression remains, as in the past, closed to scholars.

Notes

1 This article has appeared in a somewhat longer format in L. S. Eremina (ed.), *Repressii protiv poliakov i pol'skikh grazhdan* (Moscow, 1997), pp. 22–43.
2 Prikaz (Order) no. 00485 of the NKVD was published, with some abridgements, in A. Ia. Razumov (ed.), *Leningradskii martirolog 1937–1938*, vol. 2 (St. Petersburg, 1996), pp. 454–6, and in full in *Karta* (Warsaw), no. 11 (1993), pp. 27–9. For the text of the sealed letter, see Tsentr Khraneniia sovremennoi dokumentatsii (TsKhSD), Moscow, f. 6, op. 13, d. 6, ll. 8–51.
3 Arkhiv UFSB MO (Archive of the Administration of the Federal Security Service for Moscow and Moscow District), NKVD investigation file no. 52668 A. O. Postel', interrogation protocol of 11 December 1939. This file is now held in GARF, *fond* 10035.
4 See V. N. Khaustov, 'Iz predystorii massovykh repressii protiv poliakov. Seredina 1930-kh gg.', in Eremina, *Repressii protiv poliakov*, pp. 10–21.
5 I. S. Saikina kindly drew our attention to documents of the Polish Red Cross held in the Moscow State Archive of the Russian Federation (GARF, *fond* 8406) that contain statistics on six such prisoner exchanges in the period 1923 to 1932. The Soviet side handed over 425 persons, the Poles roughly half that figure.

6   *Vsesoiuznaia perepis' naseleniia 1937 goda: Kratkie itogi* (Moscow, 1991), pp. 83, 85, 94.
7   See 'Postanovlenie SNK SSR ot 28 aprelia 1936 g.', in N. F. Bugai, *L. Beria – I. Stalinu: 'Soglasno Vashemu ukazaniiu'* (Moscow, 1995), pp. 9–11. There were also deportations of Germans at this time.
8   For Order no. 00446 of the NKVD, see E. A. Zaitsev (ed.), *Sbornik zakonodatel′nykh i normativnykh aktov o repressiiakh i reabilitatsii zhertv politicheskikh repressii* (Moscow, 1993), pp. 86–93. The text of the order was first published by Nikita Okhotin in *Memorial-Aspekt* (Moscow), nos 2–3 (1993). We are obliged to colleague Okhotin for his valuable advice in planning our article.
9   The "Harbin" (sometimes called the "Harbino-Japanese") operation of the NKVD was aimed primarily at former employees of the Chinese Eastern Railway and their families who had returned to the USSR. They were usually charged with spying for Japan. The "Harbin" Order no. 00593 of the NKVD-USSR, dated 20 September 1937, was first published by Nikita Okhotin in *Memorial-Aspekt* (Moscow), no. 1 (1993).
10 For Vyshinskii's directive no. 1/001532 of 17 April 1938, see GARF, f. 81341, op. 28, d. 33, l. 2.
11 Archive of the President of the Russian Federation (APRF), f. 3, op. 58, d. 254, ll. 156–7. The text of this Politburo decision can be viewed in RGASPI, f. 17, op. 162, d. 21, l. 172.
12 The resolution of the Politburo of 15 September 1938, first published in *Moskovskie novosti*, 21 June 1992, can also be found in RGASPI, f. 17, op. 162, d. 24.
13 For the decision of 17 November 1938 see *Organy gosudarstvennoi bezopasnosti SSSR v Velikoi Otechestvennoi voine*, vol. 1, book 1 (Moscow, 1995), pp. 3–8. See pp. 16–18 of the same work for Order no. 00762 of the NKVD (26 November 1938), which followed the Politburo-Sovnarkom decision of 17 November 1938. The text of the joint decision was also reprinted in *Istoricheskii arkhiv*, no. 1 (1992), pp. 125–8.
14 Concerning the liquidation of alleged "fifth columns" and other goals of the Great Terror, see Oleg Khlevniuk, *Politbiuro. Mekhanizmy politicheskoi vlasti v 1930-e gg.* (Moscow, 1996), pp. 196–8.
15 For Stalin's speech at the evening session of 3 March 1937 during the Central Committee plenum of the VKP(b), see *Voprosy istorii*, no. 3 (1995), pp. 5–6.
16 APRF, f. 3, op. 58, d. 6, l. 53.
17 Formally, the "German" operation began earlier than the "Polish" one, and NKVD Order no. 00439 of 25 July 1937 [published in *Leningradskii martirolog*, vol. 2 (St. Petersburg, 1996), pp. 452–3 and in *Neues Leben*, Moscow, no. 16, 11 May 1996, p. 5] affected "German citizens" (i.e. foreigners) who had worked or were working in key defence plants or in transport. Such persons were to be tried before the Military Collegium of the Supreme Court or by a Special Board of the NKVD. The categories liable for arrest were subsequently extended and their conviction followed by the "album" method. The entire operation was to be concluded by November 1937.
18 See 'Raz'iasiaiushchee ukazanie Otdela aktov grazhdanskogo sostoianiia NKVD SSSR no. 146178 ot 29 aprelia 1938', reprinted in *Memorial-Aspekt*, no. 10 (1994).

Part III
Victim Studies

8
Foreign Communists and the Mechanisms of Soviet Cadre Formation in the USSR

Berthold Unfried

Introduction

According to their convictions, foreign communists in Stalin's Russia should have felt at home in Soviet Party life. Although they shared the internationalist *Weltanschauung* of the world movement and consumed the Stalinist culture surrounding them, foreign cadres differed from their Soviet counterparts in how they lived, acted and thought. Adjusting to a strange and mystifying political environment also entailed coming to terms with expressions of ritualised Party life such as purge-sittings and lengthy sessions where "criticism and self-criticism" (*kritika i samokritika*) were on the agenda. For the perplexed foreigner, these meetings seemed to violate Western notions of individuality and ignore boundaries between what were private and public domains, for presenting oneself for intense scrutiny at a public forum was relatively unknown in Western communist parties (CPs) of the period. Apart from the expulsion of so-called oppositionists, the term "purge" (*chistka*) was a vague concept outside the VKP(b), especially in the form it was intended to take: the periodical "self-cleansing" of the Party rank-and-file. Moulding party cadres according to Soviet criteria had not established itself in an organised fashion within Western CPs by the mid-1930s, with the French and German Comintern sections providing possible exceptions to this general rule.[1]

The following pages describe the behaviour of German, Austrian, Swiss, French and British CP militants when confronted by Soviet Party rituals. Documents from the Comintern section of the former Central Party Archive (RGASPI) are the main source for our investigation, papers which demonstrate either the (self) justification and defence put up by individual communists when requested to speak at Party meetings, or what Party functionaries, colleagues and fellow communists wrote or said about the cadre under examination. The documentary material thus generated occasionally surfaces, verbatim or in summary, somewhat later for a second time: in the indictment drawn up by Soviet State Security officers and during the absurd dialogues between tormentor and tormented, when the prisoner was forced to slander himself and others during interrogation. Such documents are used here to demonstrate how mechanisms of repression and of identity (re)construction based on Soviet norms were applied.

"Criticism and self-criticism" were the intrinsic components of Soviet political liturgy which foreigners found most difficult to comprehend or internalise. In many autobiographies this twin formula figures as "a rite of passage" from Western to Russian political realities. Wolfgang Leonhard, a German teenager studying at a secret Comintern school near Ufa in 1942, was shocked to see how, as he saw it, trivial incidents could be exaggerated out of all proportion in order to form the basis for a barrage of strictures brought against him by his teachers and fellow students: "The tone grew harsher and harsher, but there was no flare up, rather cold, factual speeches with clear, strongly worded formulations."

Confronted with this totally unexpected and massive criticism of his person, Leonhard stammered out the first "self-criticism" of his Party career, an act of contrition which was rejected because of its alleged superficiality.[2] Paolo Robotti, a leading Italian communist and the son-in-law of party leader Palmiro Togliatti, saw such tribunals in a positive light – they produced anticipatory unease but strengthened the convictions of those who passed the test: "This event was without doubt an effective means of democratic control coming from below."[3]

During a four-day *chistka* session of the German section of the Soviet Writers' Union held in Moscow in September 1936, the communist theatre director Gustav von Wangenheim admitted that Russian purge rituals had been incomprehensible to him at first:

> When I came here as a German Party member, I saw during a purge [sitting] how comrades beat themselves on the breast and spoke voluntarily of what they had done, the terrible acts [*Schweinerei*] they had committed. I have to admit that I was aghast. [...] During the initial period here I perceived that, wrongly, as a Russian attribute. Now I know that it is a Bolshevik one.[4]

"Self-criticism" was therefore something one had to "learn" when in the USSR.[5]

This painful process of exposing oneself and denouncing others produced crises of conscience in some and psychosomatic disorders in many others. The purge-sittings held for Comintern staff in 1936–7 were purgatives in the literal sense, which left the toilets in Hotel Lux in an indescribable condition, as Ruth von Mayenburg notes in her memoirs.[6] Why were criticism and self-criticism linked together in theory and practice? Their integral connection manifested itself in the standardised forms of almost all self-critical statements uttered at Party meetings. Phrases like "I came to this anti-Party standpoint under the influence of X", or "I made this error because I was encouraged by Y", automatically drew wider circles, involved others and atomised the collective. Sergei Kirov, in a speech in Leningrad in 1928, drew attention to the recoil produced when one fired off a complaint: "If you criticise a Communist working with you, you should not forget that in doing so you are also criticising yourself."[7]

Self-criticism in its Soviet form, therefore, generally meant criticism of third parties as well. Edgar Morin relates a joke in this regard, popular in French communist circles: "He is doing his self-criticism. But against whom?"[8] The twin process, then, was dynamic in a double sense: first, "sound" (acceptable)[9] self-criticism inevitably implicated others; second, the contrite statement could also be a launching pad for a counter-attack or to fend off a more dangerous accusation.[10]

Forms of "self-criticism" and their historical sources

The occasions for demanding contrite statements were many, and the resulting statements varied greatly in content. The venue was usually a meeting of a Party cell (*iacheika*) called during a current purge in the VKP(b). The word "purge" (*chistka*), often given as a synonym for the Great Terror of 1936–8, will be used here in its more specific and narrow sense: ridding the Party of "unworthy elements" of all kinds during the periodic cadre reviews (*proverky*).[11] Kaganovich stated in 1933 that cleansing the VKP(b) ranks was an expression of the Soviet Party's willingness to practice self-criticism.[12] Countrywide Party purges were carried out in 1921, 1929, 1933 and 1935–7. Until the mid-1930s, *chistka* proceedings were pretty unspectacular, with only a handful of the punished condemned because of dissenting views; the great majority received the seal of approval "considered examined" (*schitat' proverennym*).[13] This was a general accounting operation, and not one instigated because of specific charges levelled at Party cadres – the Party cell confrontation scenarios after 1934.

Purge campaigns were supposed to encompass the entire membership, not just "suspicious elements", and all those called to account were expected to give an oral, "self-critical" statement to the assembly. The protocols of such meetings, called in the course of a regular *chistka* or to judge an individual case (*delo*), belong to the most striking testimonials of Stalinist thought-control. Purge sessions, summoned by the Party cell officers and usually held at the place of employment after work, produced thick bundles of records, including the statements of those under fire. Incriminating excerpts were re-typed and included in the cadre file of the suspect, later providing the basis for internal investigations that could lead to expulsion. Fragments of accusatory or self-justifying dialogues also surface during the interrogation of prisoners.

The records of *chistka* sittings vary in length but the self-critical remarks of the purged are usually quoted extensively, sometimes word for word. The results of the purge – the decisions passed at the sitting – were summarised in lists of the verdicts handed out, and in the accompanying characterisations which evaluated the cadre in question and made suggestions for his or her further use. The starting point for the *chistka* meeting of the *iacheika* was written reports sent in beforehand to the Party Committee. These included denunciatory letters and self-critical biographical accounts that were supplemented by oral contributions during the sitting.

The actual agenda of a purge session held by the VKP(b) cell responsible for the staff of the Executive Committee of the Communist International (ECCI) in 1933 ran along the following lines: the evening meeting, called to purge from four to six Party members, was opened by the Purge Commission sitting on a podium before the assembled. Called from the floor, the person to be purged took up position before the audience on the platform and recounted his or her biography, commencing with social origin, family life, work record, Party tasks and voluntary social activities. The statement generally ended with references to political attitudes past and present, in particular if the individual had deviated from the "Party line" at some stage. Questions from the audience then followed, inquiries into every aspect of the member's public and private lives. During the sitting written notes were passed up to the platform from the floor, short statements in favour of the cadre, or denunciations and evaluations.[14] The cadre was also subject to the so-called political examination (*politproverka*) in the "struggle against political illiteracy". A question-and-answer episode ensued to check the knowledge held by the purge candidate of classical

Marxist-Leninist dogma and of contemporary VKP(b) policies, for example:

> What is the essence of Trotskyism?
> What is the meaning of the Law on Socialist Property?
> How is the Party structured?
> What are the tactics of class struggle?
> What is the Party's attitude towards kulaks?
> Who is Stalin, who is Thälmann?
> What did Stalin say at the last Party Congress?

The answers given were reproduced in the protocol in short, standardised form, usually "Answered correctly", "Answered correctly with the assistance of the [Purge] Commission", and rarely, "Did not answer" or "Answered incorrectly". The oral and written contributions from the audience were openly discussed after the cadre had presented his or her biography. The decision on the cadre was made by the Commission in a closed sitting, and could not be contested by the Party cell members, only by a higher authority, in the last resort by the Central Party Control Commission.

In the case of purge procedures staged within the Comintern, both native and foreign communists participated. The quiz on political knowledge was generally confined to the Russian-born technical workers, whereas the foreign-born functionaries were scrutinised on their attitudes to the twists and turns of Comintern policy – in the 1929 purge, whether they had sympathised with the Bukharinist "Right". Comrade Budkiewicz was called upon at a sitting in January 1930 to "analyse" his former sympathy for Trotsky. Some of the questions were traps, but he gave the "correct" answers – "No, Trotskyism is not a deviation but an alien concept going back to 1905". Budkiewicz had also to detail how he had personally "overcome" Trotskyism, namely by issuing a public statement distancing himself from Trotsky and by helping others to the same end.[15]

The outcome of purge sittings or cadre examinations was revealed in the evaluation of the collective, which, as the cliché had it, showed itself to be "politically healthy" or "Bolshevik-strong".[16] The members or candidate-members of the Party sometimes received suggestions as to their betterment, and the collective verdict outlined why the cadre was worthy or unworthy of belonging to the VKP(b). Suggestions to improve the cadre's political profile ranged from voluntary social or political work to compulsory attendance at political instruction classes.

The Party Committee could also direct the collective to offer the cadre direct assistance in overcoming shortcomings.[17]

The reasons given for Party penalties were based on negative aspects of political and private behaviour. As regards the technical staff of ECCI, who were usually Russians, cases of bad work-discipline and drunkenness were frequent; the political functionaries, on the other hand, were charged with ideological deviations such as factionalism or "hesitations in carrying out the general line of the Party".[18] Other charges specifically made against foreign cadres stemmed from an allegedly carefree attitude to the need to maintain strict secrecy (*konspiratsiia*), not learning the Russian language or cutting oneself off from Soviet comrades by leading an individualistic life-style and not participating in "Soviet life". Discussions on such shortcomings were introduced at meetings by the popular phrase – "We don't know the foreign comrades". "Links to abroad" were a common cause for suspicion, and indeed arrest, after 1935: earlier charges that the individual lived isolated from Russian comrades were now supplanted by the murderous slander that the foreigner was, in reality, the agent of a foreign power. "Evidence" in such cases often proceeded from the fact that the accused had relatives abroad and corresponded with them. Suspicion was often shot through with chauvinist or anti-intellectual attitudes. For instance, the daughter of a Polish weaver spoke six languages and the *proverka* in the Marx-Engels Institute held this part of her autobiography worthy of further investigation: how can a worker's daughter come to speak so many foreign languages?[19]

Themes of "criticism and self-criticism"

The themes discussed at Party meeting which provoked "criticism and self-criticism" did not have to be political in the accepted sense of the term. More often than not they dealt with general human failings and cases of outrageous behaviour in social relationships. The sources reveal that all aspects of the cadre's life could be called into question. Especially in the post-1935 period, intercourse with friends or relatives who had been "unmasked as enemies of the people" were grounds for condemnation. Westerners tended to view such contacts as personal matters. The Party cell did not. Women, it was often alleged, infringed rules of "class vigilance" because they were "sentimental petit-bourgeois" who continued to have contact with male "enemies" and had hid this from the Party Committee. A staff-member of the Marx-Engels Institute, the wife of an arrested German, had concealed his arrest from the Party. This was termed "non-Party behaviour".[20] The "correct" attitude in such eventualities was expressed by the wife of a German Party functionary:

> It is an indescribably hard blow for me to learn that I supported an enemy of the Party for so many years. After I heard yesterday that the charges levelled against him are valid, I broke off all contacts with him.[21]

Another accusation from the realm of family life was womanising, termed "non-Communist attitude towards women", a charge which often surprised the Lothario in question who still believed private and Party agendas should not impinge on one another. The fourth – and deserted – wife of a German communist complained about her husband in a letter to the Party Committee in the Frunze district of Moscow. The man had already received a reprimand from the Party because of promiscuity and neglecting his family. In his "self-critical" statement, the German admitted to "petit-bourgeois" behaviour in family life. The Party official in charge of the investigation (*partsledovatel'*) found that the delinquent had such an attitude to all women, and only the good Party record of the accused over fifteen years saved him from expulsion. The Party cell in Hotel Lux was directed to support the aggrieved wife and integrate her into voluntary political activity. Her husband, sacked from ECCI employment, was given an official warning and a reprimand by the VKP(b) committee.[22]

Such cases occurred often, with themes taken from everyday life; political "deviancy" did not yet feature as the usual pretext for "criticism and self-criticism", at least before the onset of the Great Terror. Having private affairs brought into the sphere of Party examinations was sometimes challenged by communists from Western Europe. When a Russian official of the International Lenin School (ILS) attacked a member of the Austrian student group in late 1937 for having three girlfriends in succession and not having obtained permission for the last of these liaisons, he posed the rhetorical question, "Is it correct to raise this matter here?" The students, who had refused to put the matter on the agenda at an earlier meeting, answered in unison "No!"[23]

Learning to practise "self-criticism"

Adults coming from another culture of self-presentation had considerable difficulties in accepting "self-criticism" as one of the main forms of discussion within Soviet Party bodies. At the meeting held by German writers in Moscow in September 1936, the speakers went to great lengths to convince each other that they had "freed themselves from the bad Berlin milieu", and were now immersed, as "good Soviet people", in daily Moscow life. That they attempted to surpass one another in slavishly "self-critical" statements is the point to be noted, not that their avowals seem unconvincing.[24] The process of criticising oneself and others for political motives was something the children of immigrants learned very early. The first step was writing characterisations on fellow-pupils or friends, as the account of life in Children's Home No. 6 (Moscow) for Austrian and German "orphans from Fascism" demonstrates.[25]

Particularly in Comintern schools like the International Lenin School or the Communist University of Western National Minorities (KUNMZ), *kritika i samokritika* were important means of communication and evaluation. They surfaced not only in confrontational situations but also in everyday instruction as the teachers expected the students, leading Party cadres *in spe*, to make such psychological mechanisms their second nature. "Self-evaluation" or "self-accounting" (*samootchët*) in a self-critical sense was the method popular in KUNMZ. Students were thus encouraged to provide unvarnished estimations of their progress in learning, how they carried out voluntary (political) assignments or how they got on with their comrades politically and socially. The self-critical comments often pertained to the charge of "non-Bolshevik conduct". When a German ILS student in the debate about his *samootchët* was accused of behaviour unworthy of a communist in family matters, he defended himself. Later, he admitted to "bad-tempered flare ups" towards his wife, a fellow-student, and that he had struck their child. The ensuing discussion reads like the minutes of a psychological self-help group:

> We must try to help both of them ... We expect a higher standard from married student comrades who are Party members ... Hitting a child is a crime ... We have to inculcate in him a higher cultural standard.

The delinquent "capitulated" fully, saying:

> I make the solemn pledge before the Party group to change my ways, especially in regard to my wife, and not to strike my child again. But the comrades should come and see for themselves whether I have changed or not. Support me![26]

Students from Western democracies often did not even make a pretence of accepting *kritika i samotkritika*. British students, it was alleged in 1933, did not understand this method or had a superficial or irresponsible attitude towards it.[27] The French in the ILS were charged with conducting "l'autocritique à la française"[28]; that is, having "an informal attitude" to the subject as, not wishing to hurt their comrades' feelings, they played down criticisms in a false spirit of comradeship. The criticism expected was therefore not expressed in open meetings but, if at all, during chats in the school corridors. The leading PCF and Comintern functionary André Marty took these students to task. In two speeches on how self-criticism was to be applied correctly, Marty stressed that the method should be used in all situations, and that the comrades had to learn to give up ideas of "tolerance" and to forget about group loyalties. Their "liberal" attitude to date in this question amounted to a non-Bolshevik approach to criticism and self-criticism.[29]

> The fear of self-criticism leads to isolation, to a disparagement of principled discussions, to the formation of groups and to other opportunistic illnesses that represent the greatest hindrance to the bolshevisation of our cadres ... The cleansing [*épuration*] has to be a school of self-criticism for us.[30]

Marty's rebukes provoked a self-critical discussion in the French sector, with the students replying in writing and debating these contributions in a special *Jour du parti*:

> "Damon": We have made an effort to stress the positive sides of our work and to omit the negative aspects. During the cleansing process it was the same. We did not understand that cleansing was the highest form of self-criticism and, simultaneously, a powerful lever to improve our education and to correct our faults. The voice of Comrade Marty was necessary to remind us of these truths.
> "Remy": ... the cleansing of the CP helped us to rectify our faults in the fire of Bolshevik self-criticism.[31]

Finally, the French sector passed a resolution promising to pay careful attention to "criticism and self-criticism" and praising Marty for having imparted how "to make self-criticism a lever in the struggle against rotten liberalism, against group formation and family spirit".[32]

These examples from 1933 show the rôle assigned to self-criticism in educating foreign Party cadres as if they were Russian cadres. The foreigners had been tempered in the fire of "self-criticism" in a double sense: targets of salvoes against Western individualism, and cauterised by the fire which removed the remnants of "petty-bourgeois individualism". Those attributes of the "old" personality considered rotten were exorcised in bouts of criticism and contrition.

The political culture of the home country, it may be argued, had a decisive affect on the extent to which collective Soviet thought-patterns were really internalised. Cadres at the Lenin School from countries where the communist party was illegal were preconditioned to accept strict norms: absolute secrecy was understandable when the cadre was expected to return home to lead an underground movement; his or her very life depended on Soviet institutions who would arrange for the transfer to "illegal work" on the home front and provide the underground Comintern emissary with lodgings and money. Against this background, "criticism and self-criticism" could be seen as an essential part of the "steeling" process for coming, dangerous assignments.

Lenin School trainees from the English-speaking democracies,[33] by contrast, knew that, on return, they could operate in societies with a comparatively low level of political repression. They displayed little understanding of the need to adhere to strict security regulations in Moscow as the legal consequences arising from a sojourn at a Comintern school were minimal, at least in the short term. Differences of opinion between teachers and students in Sector "E" (Britain, Ireland, Australia, New Zealand, South Africa) on "rules of conspiracy" came to a head in 1934. In the mimeographed wall-paper (*stengazeta*) of the sector, the Scottish railwayman Bill Cowe ("Watson") lampooned secrecy directives and complained that "during the May Day parade we had to play deaf mutes as we marched alongside the factory workers of Moscow".[34] The school directorate ascribed Cowe's outburst to the "weak leadership" of the Party secretary and depicted the scandal as an open display of "dangerous counter-revolutionary opinions".[35] When the course terminated in April 1935, the British communist leader Harry Pollitt was directed to "take full responsibility" for the defiant young Scot.[36]

However, when the opportunity did arise at the close of the 7th Comintern Congress (August 1935), Pollitt defended Cowe in a meeting with the school leadership: Cowe, described by his teachers as "a bad student", was "a good Party worker"[37] and in the ensuing discussion, school rector Kirsanova stated that only Pollitt's intervention had saved Cowe from being sent home prematurely and in disgrace.[38] Bill Cowe was deemed such a valuable cadre of the CPGB that he was elected to its Central Committee at the 15th Congress three years later.[39]

"Criticism and self-criticism" as Party dialogue

The cadre was expected to show his "Party countenance" (*partiinoe litso*) during purging sessions. Gustav von Wangenheim began his bout of self-criticism on that note: "Comrades! We, as Communists, have to show our true face, in other words, the whole person."[40] "Showing one's face" meant displaying the *persona* of the Party cadre constituted along Stalinist norms. A *leitmotiv* of the Great Terror comes from the same source – the obsession to "unmask" the foe. "Evil spirits have no faces, they wear masks"[41] is an old Russian proverb, and underlining Stalinist directives on "Party vigilance" was the notion that the enemy was masked to hide his nefarious intentions. "Unmasking" therefore meant finding the enemy, the saboteur or the traitor behind the mask worn by the good Party activist, by the loyal comrade, or by the *udarnik* in the factory. And if "criticism and self-criticism" were properly carried out, so the implicit reasoning went, the comrades would reveal the "true face" behind the mask:

> Only an enemy is afraid of criticism. To criticise a comrade is an honour, a mark of respect, because we believe that he could improve on his work ... We have to raise our vigilance, sharpen it, so that we can discover our enemies no matter what masks they wear.[42]

Communists from abroad had to grasp that the correct reaction to criticism is not self-justification but the search for inadequacies and mistakes in one's own conduct.[43] A German directive in cadre matters spelt this out in some detail:

> Every comrade must therefore account for his weaknesses by [practising] self-criticism ... and he must help others, in a comradely fashion, to overcome their failings. It is a false sense of comradeship to hush up the mistakes made by good friends and this prevents errors being rectified. Allowing errors, no matter how they arise, is a crime committed against the whole Party.[44]

On being criticised by the collective, the correct response from an educated cadre could only be self-criticism. "Honest and Bolshevik" self-criticism, in dialogue with "comradely" criticism, induces in the cadre the wish to admit to errors and brings him or her back on the track of the correct "Party line". Reacting to criticism with self-justification, therefore, hampers this learning process, prevents the correction of false views and is an additional proof of guilt. Justifying one's behaviour thus shows that the cadre has learned nothing, is two-faced and has an anti-Party attitude. Stubbornly sticking to an opinion when under attack during a Party meeting generally led to even more reproaches. Owning up to faults was not sufficient: the cadre had to express regret, analyse past behaviour and characterise it. If this "capitulation" was considered incomplete or inadequate, the collective rejected it ("lack of honesty") and redoubled the onslaught: the comrade uses self-criticism as a camouflage, in order to justify past behaviour and to play down errors; he or she is nothing but a cunning, two-faced enemy who uses self-criticism to portray crimes as mere errors. The delinquent must therefore repent again, and criticise the self-criticism already offered.[45]

The psychological pressure on the cadre under stricture continued for as long as was thought necessary – until the accused gave up resisting and demanded a fitting punishment. The appropriate statement of Arnold Reisberg, an Austrian teacher at the ILS who later served two terms in the Gulag, was unequivocal:

> I made my error only worse by neither admitting to it, nor criticising it in the Party meeting of the Sector [ILS]. Instead, I tried to explain and defend my faults, and not to analyse their roots. I have to admit that the contents and essence of my error were anti-Party and anti-Soviet, that I am not equipped well enough to stop the infiltration of the ideologies of the class-enemy and that I will have to work really hard to rid myself of the remnants of such ideologies ... I am fully aware that I expressed hostile, fascist views. I am fully aware that my crime deserves the most severe punishment from the Party.[46]

A functionary of the German Communist Party (KPD) wrote to the Party committee of KUNMZ after his self-criticism had been rejected: "My statement ... is absolutely inadequate and cannot contribute to helping the Party in its struggle to unmask all anti-Party activities and to liquidate in full all counter-revolutionary groupings."[47]

The Party interrogates

Self-presentation in the framework of *chistka* (purge or cleansing) sessions was a ritual that each party member had to undergo. This was more an educational measure than a tool of political repression. Furthermore, there existed "extraordinary" meetings on the case of a person against whom an accusation had been raised. Such assemblies took the form of a tribunal staged within the "criticism and self-criticism" discourse. It was this form that became the real manifestation of repression within the Party. The proceedings began with a "self-critical" autobiography given orally, which was followed by a cross-examination. The outcome was generally a confession on the part of the cadre under scrutiny, a contrite statement that might not pass muster because of what colleagues had said during the debate. An admission of guilt was the inevitable result of the grilling, but the accused, by the skilled use of "self-criticism", could sometimes influence the imminent verdict.[48]

The room for such manoeuvring, however, was quite limited during the Great Terror. Whereas "criticism and self-criticism" sessions were instigated in the early 1930s because of what a cadre had actually done or said, the accusations levelled some years later had little basis in reality but originated in the nightmarish world of omnipresent enemies and conformed to irrational and stereotype images. The indictments of the three great show trials, for instance, were now regurgitated in the accusatory pandemonium of purge meetings. Harmless incidents or confrontational situations from daily life were interpreted as evidence of crimes against the State and translated into a hallucinatory "political" prose, as the indictment against an Austrian *Schutzbündler* in Kharkov in 1937 indicates:

> Terror (§8): Drunken scenes in the municipal apartment-block and brawls with the local police.
>
> Anti-Soviet agitation (§10): the defendant had spoken about the bad conditions of Soviet life to his work-mates in the factory.
>
> Membership in a counter-revolutionary organisation (§11): the defendant is the leader of all "dissatisfied elements" and is planning their return to Austria.[49]

"Explaining" all manifestations of discord in political terms was also commonplace in the Lenin School. Comrade "Huber", to quote just one case, was under the influence of alcohol when he struck a fellow student in the face during an evening event in September 1936, thereby "revealing" the following: a covert attitude of distrust towards the Party and the Party leadership; the overestimation of his own worth which stemmed from "social democratic and anarchistic" deviations; being dishonest by changing the tactics he adopted at the circle assembly to the ones when confronted in a meeting of the entire sector – admitting what he did was wrong while simultaneously expressing his belief that "the comrades were exaggerating". "Huber" was also accused of not understanding the role of the Party or indeed the concept of "criticism and self-criticism".[50]

Purge rituals, however, while seeming grotesque to foreign cadres who learned to play the rules by adopting a self-critical pose, did have a predictable course, a kind of liturgical logic. Practising "criticism and self-criticism" was sometimes part of a defence strategy, a possibility to hide behind standardised phraseology. The mass arrests of 1936–8, by contrast, as terrified foreign communists learned at their cost, resembled a natural catastrophe: nobody was safe from the arrest-squads, and the best defence, offered earlier to the Purge Commission in a spirit of searing self-criticism, had no apparent influence on the "choice" of victims or their fate. Now, it was no longer "the Party" who was "purging" (or "cleansing") its ranks but a competing organisation, the NKVD, that was arresting party members according to its own logic.

The NKVD interrogates

The purging process, as exemplified in self-critical atonement following cross-examination at Party meetings, contributed to forming the kind of cadre Stalinist organisational structures demanded. The rigours thus imposed on the foreign revolutionary implied that the cadre in question was capable of development, and was, in essence, a "good element". For NKVD interrogators the only personal character traits of interest were negative ones – the prisoner was guilty because the "organs" did not arrest the innocent. The Party biography of the victim was of secondary importance in most cases in the years 1937–8, as the cadre in police custody existed merely as a cipher, a case number, preordained to be shot or incarcerated in the Gulag. The person behind the *persona* in interrogation does not emerge, the questions and answers are standardised formulae dictated by uniformed thugs.

Foreign communists arrested during the *massoperatsii* of the secret police from July 1937 resemble film-extras with vocal roles, faceless players who are forced to repeat a given text mechanically, and to confirm the screenplay with their signatures. The contents of the signed "confessions", unlike the protocols which documented the purge proceedings of the Party cell, tells us nothing about how the victims saw or coped with social reality in the USSR. The documents in the NKVD file are nothing more than the reality as perceived by bureaucrats in the punitive organs, investigators for whom the party cadre under indictment now possessed neither a personal nor a Party identity but one of an "enemy".

A series of interrogations always started with the prisoner recounting his or her biography. The result of the questionings, that is, the final indictment based on the "confession", contained, apart from name, date of birth, occupation and last address, nothing of substance about the doomed prisoner, no inklings of motivations, intentions or hopes.

The structures of NKVD investigative files have, none the less, similarities with those of the cadre-files in a Comintern section or the VKP(b), as both begin with biographical data. Before 1937, as the case of Franz Koritschoner, a veteran Austrian Communist arrested in Kiev in 1936, exemplifies, the interrogating officer found passages in the biographical account which aroused suspicion (K. opposed certain aspects of Comintern policy or was dissatisfied with, and isolated from, "Party life" in the Ukraine). After Koritschoner had admitted that his "main error" was "Left opportunism"[51] he was questioned about personal acquaintances. These links, irrespective of their intensity or duration, became "evidence" of a concerted "counter-revolutionary" plot. The interrogator insisted on a confirmation of this distorted biography, using language, which, in its written form, has a grotesquely polite and proper tone: "The investigating authorities demand that you desist from making untrue statements and begin to tell the truth. Do you intend to begin telling the truth?"[52] Koritschoner's response was more than adequate:

> I stand as a criminal before Soviet power, the laws of which I have broken; as a betrayer of my friends and comrades to whom I pretended that I was a good, conscious Communist, something I had long ceased to be; as a betrayer of my wife who married an honest Communist and now must realise that I have deviated from the path of Communism. I request nothing more than that I be shot as soon as possible as a criminal. My many years of service to the Communist cause are not grounds for mercy.[53]

Such statements seem implausible, grotesquely exaggerated "acts of contrition". However, they can be sometimes re-translated and linked to elements of reality (as perceived by foreign communists). The files opened on Italian anti-fascists seized by the NKVD contain references to "oppositionist" states of mind, both in the Party sense or as evidence of a chronic dissatisfaction with life in Stalin's Russia: social injustice, the miserable conditions for workers, lack of freedom, and disillusionment.[54] Expressions of opinion along these lines were pressed into a political mould, distorted into indictments of anti-communist subversion on an organised basis ("Bordighist-Trotskyist machinations") – a predictable ruse because discussions on the true state of affairs in the country were forbidden. "Mi riconosco colpevole" (I admit that I am guilty) conceded an Italian comrade who had criticised the Soviet industrialisation programme and shared his views with friends abroad. But they denied charges that they had disseminated "anti-Soviet propaganda" among Soviet workers.[55] The arraignment was initially rejected by the prisoner, but the dialogue proceeded until the required answer was provided, a formula adumbrated in the original indictment:

> *Question*: You are continuing to lie. You were, until lately, a member of a Bordighist-Trotskyist espionage organisation. It is futile to deny it.
> *Answer*: Yes, I am going to stop lying now and will answer your questions concerning the activities of this organisation.[56]

The prisoner then supplied the self-incriminating biographical details demanded of him.

Résumé

The language of "criticism and self-criticism" can be interpreted as a form of speaking about oneself that was specific to Stalinism, a tool used in the construction of Soviet-style political cadres. The Party biography offered by the cadre during Purge rituals, along with the "confession" made before the assembled cell members, *could* become permanent constituent elements of identity as such occasions were often the first and only opportunity for the communist in question to speak about himself in public: an attempt to demonstrate conformity with the characterisations of Stalinist cadre formation.[57] Constructing a Party identity in the Soviet sense certainly did not accord with the Western concept of each individual having a unique personality. During the Great Terror formal similarities between "self-criticism", Party autobiography and "confession" were discernible when the victim adopted this Soviet manner of speaking about oneself. In these years "self-criticism" changed from an instrument of Stalinist education into a tool to eradicate the personality of the cadre, and often preceded his physical destruction. This metamorphosis was complete when the prisoner was coerced into adopting a new biography, a new Party identity: that of an agent, a saboteur or a Trotskyist, whose "Party countenance" was now the hideous visage of the "enemy".

Notes

1. The French Communist Party (PCF) had set up a cadres commission by the early 1930s. For details, see Annie Kriegel, *Les communistes français* (Paris, 1968), pp. 158–65; Robert Robrieux, *Histoire intérieure du parti communiste 1920–1945* (Paris, 1980); Claude Pennetier and Bernard Pudal, 'La "vérification" (l'encadrement biographique communiste dans l'entre-deux guerres)', *Genèses* (Paris), no. 23 (1996), pp. 145–63. For insights into cadre control in the German CP before 1933, see Herbert Wehner, *Zeugnis* (Cologne, 1984), pp. 54–70; Reinhard Müller, 'Permanenter Verdacht und "Zivilhinrichtung". Zur Genesis der "Säuberungen" in der KPD', in Hermann Weber and Dietrich Staritz (eds), *Kommunisten verfolgen Kommunisten. Stalinistischer Terror und 'Säuberungen' in den kommunistischen Parteien Europas seit den dreißiger Jahren* (Berlin, 1993), pp. 253–4.
2. Wolfgang Leonhard, *Die Revolution entlässt ihre Kinder*, 16th edn (Frankfurt am Main, 1978), pp. 182–6, here p. 182.
3. Paolo Robotti, *La Prova* (Bari, 1965), p. 60f.
4. Reinhard Müller (ed.), *Die Säuberung. Moskau 1936: Stenogramm einer geschlossenen Parteiversammlung* (Reinbek bei Hamburg, 1991), p. 422.
5. This was also the opinion of the Austrian Lenin School student "Reif" when participating in the kangaroo court mounted against his teacher Arnold Reisberg in 1937 (RGASPI, f. 495, op. 187, d. 3003, protocol of the Party meeting in Sector "Ia" of the International Lenin School, 27 February 1937).
6. Ruth von Mayenburg, *Hotel Lux* (Munich, 1978), p. 37. For a detailed description of such *chistka* sessions in Moscow during the Great Terror, see also Margarete Buber-Neumann, *Von Potsdam nach Moskau. Stationen eines Irrweges* (Frankfurt am Main, 1990), pp. 394–5.
7. S. M. Kirov, *Selected Articles and Speeches* (in Russian), (Moscow, 1944), p. 103.
8. Edgar Morin, *Autocritique* (Paris, 1975), p. 254.
9. In a programmatic speech to activists of the Moscow organisation of the VKP(b) on 18 April 1928 on "self-criticism", Stalin laid down that criticism must come only from "Soviet people" and not from "counter-revolutionaries" (J. W. Stalin, *Werke*, vol. 11 (East Berlin, 1954), pp. 26–35, esp. p. 31).
10. This was the tactic adopted by Johann Koplenig, the chairman of the Communist Party of Austria (KPÖ), when accused of having sent the "enemy" Arnold Reisberg to teach at the Lenin School. Koplenig admitted to this "grave error", but then turned on school director Kirsanova who, he alleged, had refused to remove Braun-Reisberg at an earlier stage when requested by the KPÖ to do so, thereby confirming that she had "an unhealthy attitude" to the Austrian Comintern section (RGASPI, f. 495, op. 73, d. 88, ll. 109–11).
11. For a strict distinction between party purges and State terror, see the theses in J. Arch Getty, *Origins of the Great Purges. The Soviet Communist Party Reconsidered, 1933–1938* (Cambridge, 1985).
12. L. M. Kaganowitsch, *Über die Parteireinigung* (Moscow–Leningrad, 1933), p. 30.
13. The results of the 1933 *chistka* showed that the expulsion rate countrywide was 18 per cent of Party members. Passivity, moral corruption, careerism and "bureaucratism" accounted for 40 per cent of the expulsions and violation of Party discipline for 20 per cent (Getty, *Origins*, pp. 53–4).

14 These scribbled slips of paper are still extant in the files of the *partkom* of the VKP(b) within ECCI (RGASPI, f. 546, op. 1, d. 228).
15 RGASPI, f. 546, op. 1, d. 110, protocol of closed meeting of the VKP(b) cell within ECCI, 5 January 1930.
16 The concepts of "sound" or "unhealthy" attitudes were used by the NKVD when reporting to the Politburo on popular opinion. See Sarah Davies, *Popular Opinion in Stalin's Russia. Terror, Propaganda and Dissent, 1934–1941* (Cambridge, 1997), p. 11.
17 For such examples from 1936, see RGASPI, f. 546, op. 1, d. 335.
18 The charges against those punished in 1929–30 centred on dishonest attitudes to the Purge Commission (hiding one's past or distorting it) or the local Party cell (not paying Party dues promptly, greed, individualism and political illiteracy). See RGASPI, f. 546, op. 1, d. 146.
19 Tsentralnyi Arkhiv Obshchestvennykh Dvizhenii, Moscow (TsAOD), f. 212, op. 1 , d. 41, protocol (no. 19) of the closed Party meeting in IML, 22 December 1937.
20 TsAOD, f. 212, op. 1, d. 42, protocol no. 11 of the sitting of the Party Committee of IML, 17 May 1937.
21 RGASPI, f. 546, op. 1, d. 252, letter from A. Heinrich , 29 January 1935.
22 RGASPI, f. 546, op. 1, d. 252, complaint of 24 June 1932.
23 RGASPI, f. 531, op. 1, d. 227, ll. 56–61 (Minutes of Sector "Ia" meeting, 27–8 November 1937). As the assembly took place in connection with the dismissal of Klavdia Kirsanova as school rector, the students used the opportunity to take revenge on her and her officials, condemning in particular the high-handed and bureaucratic nature of her rule.
24 For examples, see Müller, *Die Säuberung*.
25 Hans Schafranek (in co-operation with Natalia Mussienko), *Kinderheim Nr6. Österreichische und deutsche Kinder im sowjetischen Exil* (Vienna, 1998), pp. 74–5.
26 RGASPI, f. 529, op. 2, d. 454, protocol of meeting of German section KUNMZ, 13 April 1935.
27 RGASPI, f. 531, op. 1, d. 169, ll. 7–15 (Sector Meeting of 23 October 1933 on Comrade Alexandrov's Report on Purge).
28 As the French student "Célestin" admitted – RGASPI, f. 531, op. 2, d. 67, Discussion sur le rapport du cam. Yablonsky, Sector "I" of ILS, 14 October 1933.
29 RGASPI, f. 531, op. 2, d. 67, Discours du cam. Marty le 10 octobre 1933; ibid., Speech Marty to Sector "I", 23 November 1933.
30 Speech Marty, 23 November 1933.
31 RGASPI, f. 531, op. 2, d. 67, Jour du Parti, 4 December 1933.
32 Ibid.
33 For examples of recalcitrance on the part of Irish ILS students, see Barry McLoughlin, 'Proletarian Academics or Party Functionaries? Irish Communists at the International Lenin School, Moscow, 1927–1937', *Saothar* (Dublin), no. 22 (1997), pp. 63–79.
34 RGASPI, f. 531, op. 2, d. 62, l. 17.
35 RGASPI, f. 531, op. 1, d. 172, l. 14.
36 Public Records Office (London), HW 17/18, radio telegram London–Moscow, 8 April 1935.
37 RGASPI, f. 531, op. 1, d. 171, l. 27.
38 RGASPI, f. 531, op. 1, d. 171, l. 32.

39 Noreen Branson, *History of the Communist Party of Great Britain 1927–1941* (London, 1985), p. 342.
40 Müller, *Säuberung*, p. 390.
41 Hans Günther, 'Der Feind in der totalitären Kultur', in Gabriele Gorzka (ed.), *Kultur im Stalinismus. Sowjetische Kultur und Kunst der 30er bis 50er Jahre* (Bremen, 1994), p. 93.
42 RGASPI, f. 495, op. 187, d. 3003, Stellungnahme Vadim, Protokoll der Sektorversammlung im Sektor "Ja" der ILS, 27 February 1937.
43 For further discussions on this point, see Berthold Unfried, 'Die Konstituierung des stalinistischen Kaders in "Kritik und Selbstkritik"', *Traverse* (Zürich), no. 3 (1995), pp. 71–88.
44 RGASPI, f. 495, op. 74, d. 124, Entwurf der auf der Brüsseler Konferenz gewählten Zentralen Kontrollkommission zu Kaderfragen (der KPD).
45 "Comrade Hansen practised self-criticism by admitting that the self-criticism she practised last year was dishonest" (RGASPI, f. 529, op. 1, d. 553, Protokoll der Sektorversammlung des deutschen Sektors der KUNMZ, 4 February 1936).
46 RGASPI, f. 495, op. 187, d. 3003, autobiography of Bruno Braun (=Arnold Reisberg), 7 March 1937.
47 RGASPI, f. 546, op. 1, d. 282, Erklärung "Fritz Winter" an das Partkom, 9 February 1935.
48 The KPD member Frida Rubiner was successful in fending off the charge of contacts to "a counter-revolutionary organisational centre" when it had been established that she had met former oppositionists for tea. She escaped with a "severe reprimand" (*strogii vygovor*) – RGASPI, f. 546, op. 1, d. 282, Protokoll Nr. 10 der Sitzung des Parteikomitees des EKKI, 13 February 1935.
49 Barry McLoughlin, Hans Schafranek and Walter Szevera, *Aufbruch-Hoffnung-Endstation. Österreicherinnen und Österreicher in der Sowjetunion 1925–1945* (Vienna, 1997), p. 357.
50 RGASPI, f. 531, op. 2, d. 117, ll. 18–19.
51 NKVD investigation file no. 52160 Franz Koritschoner, interrogation protocol, 2 April 1936. The file is kept in the Central Archive of the Ukrainian Security Service in Kiev.
52 Ibid., interrogation protocol, 26 January 1937.
53 Ibid., Letter of Franz Koritschoner to NKVD, 10 April 1936. Koritschoner later recanted, but received a ten-year sentence to the Pechora Gulag none the less. He was gassed in Auschwitz in June 1941, following his extradition to Nazi Germany at the request of the Gestapo. For details of the case, see Hans Schafranek, *Zwischen NKWD und Gestapo. Die Auslieferung deutscher und österreichischer Antifaschisten aus der Sowjetunion an Nazideutschland 1937–1941* (Frankfurt am Main, 1990), pp. 76–7.
54 Francesco Bigazzi and Giancarlo Lehner, *Dialoghi del Terrore. I processi ai comunisti italiani in Unione Sovietica 1930–1940* (Florence, 1991).
55 Ibid., p. 113 (Gaggi).
56 Ibid., pp. 152–3 (Gorelli).
57 An analysis of this process of identification could be based on excerpts from cadre files in RGASPI, by drawing on the countless hand-written autobiographies or pre-printed forms and questionnaires which foreign communists were obliged to complete while living in the USSR. Unfortunately, the limited scope of this contribution does not allow for such an examination.

9
Stalinist Terror in the Moscow District of Kuntsevo, 1937–8

Aleksandr Vatlin and Natalia Musienko

The very mention of the Stalinist terror conjures up pictures of the show trials, Stalin and his cohorts in the Politburo signing death-lists, the forbidding Lubianka and its landlord, "Iron People's Commissar" Nikolai Ezhov. These images are influenced by the urban dweller's perspective and concentrate on the main perpetrators. Western historians have written about Stalin's secret police from this vantage point.[1] While this approach produced valuable insights when access to the pertinent Soviet archives was closed, it does not contribute very much to our understanding of the aims and methods of the NKVD during the Great Terror of 1937–8. Furthermore, recent publications on the activities of subordinate NKVD bodies contain little about how the mass repression was organised and carried out from the district NKVD headquarters.[2] An analysis of this micro-level is essential in order to comprehend how the NKVD set about fulfilling the operational targets drawn up by Ezhov's staff and confirmed by the Politburo in the summer of 1937.[3]

The offices of the Administration of State Security (UGB) of the NKVD at republic and provincial level directed the work of its subordinate units in the urban and rural districts.[4] The latter had inadequate staff for "operative work" (arrest and interrogation) and also lacked the facilities needed to carry out mass operations – prison cells and transport in sufficient quantities. The NKVD chiefs in the districts were expected to send informers' reports and the lists of those in custody to headquarters in Moscow, conduct arrests and the ensuing investigations. These formal duties were of secondary interest to the Lubianka, which insisted that the "plan" was adhered to, that is, the fulfilment of arrest quotas. When these were reached or even surpassed, especially the total of confessions acquired, the district officers could hope to escape arrest themselves and attain, perhaps, promotion.

The absurdity of Stalinist repression was most crass at this subordinate level of the NKVD hierarchy, where the data written on the questionnaire (*anketa*) completed by all residents, and other arbitrary factors, decided a citizen's fate. The terror in the localities was not mentioned in Khrushchev's famous "Secret Speech" to the 20th Party Congress in February 1956, nor is it frequently mentioned in the memoirs of Gulag survivors. Engraved in mass-consciousness are the arrests of family members, friends and relatives, not the abstract category of "enemies of the people" prescribed by Stalin and his entourage.

The "purging" of the NKVD by Ezhov's successor Beria in late 1938 and early 1939, hit the *apparat* at local level hard. The statements or "confessions" extracted from State Security staff arrested at that time sometimes surface in the investigation files of the victims they tormented. Such documents were used as evidence to prove that "illegal methods" of investigation had been in place in 1937-8, providing KGB officers reviewing the cases of the civilian victims in the 1950s with vital arguments to accelerate the process of rehabilitation. As most of the NKVD archival material extant is still inaccessible to historians, these portions of investigation files are the best source available to document the ghastly practices of the secret police under Ezhov.

Our study concerns the activities of the Kuntsevo district office of the NKVD (Moscow Region) during the month of March 1938, when the terror reached its peak.[5] The centre of Kuntsevo district, now just inside the city boundary on the highway to Minsk, was then 11 kilometres to the west of Moscow. The town of Kuntsevo had received legal status as late as 1925 and had over 40,000 inhabitants in 1937. The flagship of local industry was the factory named after the Communist Youth International (Zavod Imeni Kommunisticheskogo Internatsionala Molodezhi), an enterprise which produced sewing needles. The area around Kuntsevo was where Stalin and other members of the *nomenklatura* had their summer residences. The locality was therefore under the special surveillance of the central *apparat* of the NKVD. It is also no coincidence that Ivan Sorokin, the head of the NKVD administration in the Kuntsevo district, succeeded in being transferred to the Lubianka in January 1937. He was henceforth commanding officer of the 3rd Department of the Administration for State Security (UGB), the unit responsible for counter-espionage in urban Moscow. The man who replaced him in Kuntsevo, Lieutenant Kuznetsov, along with his assistant Sergeant Karetnikov, soon learned what was expected of them when mass operations commenced seven months later. Even before the main directive (no. 00447) against "enemies" in the native population was issued in early August, the NKVD staff in Kuntsevo were preparing: cells were built in the cellar of the district headquarters, the offices were renovated for interrogation purposes, lorries were commandeered for the transport of prisoners and young cadres were mobilised by the VKP(b) for "operative work in the higher organs". These recruits were usually students at Moscow third-level colleges and universities, persons with a basic knowledge of law.

During the daily pep-talks in the Moscow administration of the NKVD, the Kuntsevo colleagues were often praised for their diligence in "unmasking enemies of the people". Sorokin frequently visited his successors, urging them to surpass the plan quotas. The head of the NKVD administration in Mytyshi (Moscow Region), Kharlakevich, ordered that all district offices be issued with arrest quotas (*limity*) and that each officer had to complete at least one case daily. Any staff member who did not agree with this directive should write a report which would be sent to headquarters in Moscow. Kharlakevich also mentioned that the district head of the NKVD in Pushkino had refused to carry out mass arrests and was immediately taken into custody.[6] The pressure exerted from above was bolstered by Party propaganda encouraging denunciations and informers. The countless number of informers recruited by the NKVD, the so-called *seksoty* (*sekretnye sotrudniki*), were expected to deliver every kind of "negative" information. Paradoxically, the regular system of reporting by police agents suffered. Their NKVD "handlers" were fully engaged in chasing operational goals, and the system could not deal with the flood of denunciatory reports. In 1937–8, the charges to be subsequently levelled at the prisoner were decided by the highest echelons. Up to 1937 the accusation usually read "anti-Soviet propaganda" and "wrecking" (sabotage at the workplace). Indictments on this basis were invented for the hundreds of thousands arrested according to Order no. 00447. A year later, the indictment had changed to "spying", "preparing a terrorist act" and "sabotage", and these charges were employed predominantly against non-Russians, in particular Poles, Lithuanians, Latvians, Germans and Finns.

The huge arrest raids to "unmask counter-revolutionary organisations working hand-in-hand with the Gestapo and Trotskyists"[7] were at the heart of all directives emanating from the Lubianka during Ezhov's term of office (1936–8), thus determining how the mass terror proceeded, its "technology". In a political system based on collectivism and periodical "self-cleansing", the content of repressive policies was perforce based on primitive stereotypes. In exploiting the propaganda value of "the giant conspiracies unmasked by the NKVD", the Stalinist leadership resorted to scapegoat tactics, shifting the blame for the disastrous manifestations of social and economic policies onto the shoulders of the defendants, as the indictments in the great show trials of 1936 to 1938 amply demonstrate. NKVD staff read the trial accounts in *Pravda* closely and adopted the Stalinist scapegoat logic in their own fiefdoms, at district, regional and republic level.

Sergei Konstantinovich Muralov,[8] chairman of the regional executive committee in Kuntsevo since 1933, had survived "criticism and self-criticism" campaigns and the examination of his reports to higher authorities mainly by virtue of his spotless revolutionary record. He was a worker by origin, had served in the First Cavalry Army as commissar in the Civil War and earned himself the "Red Banner" award for participating in the crushing of the Kronstadt rebellion. His surname, however, was a stumbling block – another Muralov, Nikolai, was one of Trotsky's most loyal followers. Muralov's downfall began in 1937 when his former regimental commander remembered that Muralov had suffered from "Trotskyist deviations" in 1923. It is still a mystery why the army officer, then living in the Irkutsk Region, penned a letter denouncing Muralov to the Commission for Party Control in the Central Committee of the VKP(b). This letter was the first document enclosed in Muralov's party dossier. The compromising report was put aside for the time being, to be used later as evidence in judging the "vigilance" of this member of the Kuntsevo *nomenklatura*. The opportunity soon presented itself. Muralov had a dispute with Moscow bureaucrats in regard to the management of local agriculture. During the altercations Muralov obviously overestimated his rank. The investigation commission sent from Moscow found that Kuntsevo's leading executive bodies were "full of alien social elements" who were to blame for the setbacks in collective agricultural production: a decrease in harvest yields and animal husbandry figures, and the presence of "wrecking" in producing new seed cultures. The *kolkhoz* peasants in Teplyi Stan, Khoroshevo and Krylatskoye, it was alleged, were neglecting their collective duties in favour of tending their own plots and travelling to Moscow to earn extra money. The commission also found that this situation had arisen because state supervision was insufficient. Furthermore, the commission's findings also provided the basis for legal charges:

> In the Kuntsevo district wrecking is widespread in order to destroy the *kolkhoz*. It is necessary to hand the evidence over to the investigative organs so that those responsible be brought to justice.

The results of the examination reflected the relative strengths of competing bureaucracies – the Party would always win out in a confrontation with the Executive Committee, which was made responsible for all setbacks in rural areas, mishaps it was supposed to solve on a day-to-day basis. The Chairman of the District Executive Committee was often the first important official to be dismissed. In December 1937, for instance, the Chairman of the Moscow Executive Committee N. A. Filatov was arrested. Anyone who had worked with him was now under suspicion of having "links to an enemy of the people". The regional state prosecutor received, from the party regional committee, the thick Muralov file. It contained three serious allegations: "Trotskyist" deviations in 1923, restricting the democratic rights of *kolkhoz* members and bad relations with his family. The first two imputations were enough to open criminal proceedings. Muralov's biography came to his rescue once more. He was transferred to Leningrad. However, when he came home on a short visit in March 1938, he was arrested at the railway station. His relatives did not know of his whereabouts until Karetnikov, the deputy commander of the NKVD office in Kuntsevo, arrived to search the family flat. Ekaterina Stepanova, Muralov's wife, described the scene years later:

> During the house search they found nothing to incriminate my husband. When it was over, Karetnikov made a telephone call in my presence and reported the negative results of the search. He then informed me that I and my son had to confine ourselves to one room, the other two were being taken from us and sealed. The next day Karetnikov told me that my husband was in trouble and advised me to look for work.

The house search had been delayed because Muralov refused to make a statement, but a description of his family's plight persuaded him to adopt a more "cooperative" attitude towards his interrogators. Karetnikov had not found any incriminating material at Muralov's home, but none the less he confiscated documents, letters and the "Red Banner" award. The NKVD man pocketed the latter, a common practice at the time, and the sealed rooms were reserved for NKVD personnel. Muralov's file contains dozens of appeals to leading personalities. Ekaterina's first petition to Ezhov, written a week after her husband's arrest, reads:

> I am not writing to you as a wife, but as a Soviet citizen, and declare that in the twenty years of our marriage I would not have hesitated

to report to the NKVD even the slightest indication of a deviation on the part of my husband.

Muralov was kept in Taganka prison and probably still suffered from the shock of being arrested. He was therefore brought to interrogation straight away in the expectation that the prisoner could be forced to sign the "confession" which had been formulated by the NKVD in advance. If this surprise tactic did not work, the prisoner was questioned night and day – the "conveyor" method in the jargon of the secret police. On 14 March, three days after his arrest, Muralov began to "confess". Eight years later, after his release from the Kolyma Gulag system, Muralov still believed that he was the victim of "a distortion of the Party line" in Kuntsevo. Psychologically he was still the "Party soldier", despite incarceration, a common phenomenon that helped to bolster the Stalinist system. In a letter to Stalin he wrote:

> I consider myself guilty, for although I have been a Party member for twenty years and went through a hard political schooling, I grew weak when confronted with the beatings and threats from my interrogators. They forced me to confirm by signature the most outrageous lies and self-denunciations, saying, "If you love the Party, then you have to sign this protocol. Today, our country needs such confessions".

The first interrogation began with the obligatory question "What political views do you have?" The answer was also stereotype: "My political views on the existing order and the Party are negative ones". Further questioning proceeded from this point:

> I was not a supporter of VKP(b) policies as far back as 1923, when I supported the Right-Trotskyist elements (Bukharin, Rykov and Trotsky). For the sake of appearances I kept in line, pretending I was a true Party member and behaving in a two-faced fashion.

The interrogators had only to adhere to a fictitious "screenplay": the third great show trial had ended on 13 March; Bukharin, formerly the most prominent "Right deviationist", was portrayed in the courtroom as one of Trotsky's confidantes. How could primitive NKVD personnel, when superimposing this scenario on to their own "investigations", have known that Bukharin and Trotsky had been irreconcilable opponents during the disputes in the Party leadership a decade previously?

The direction Muralov's case subsequently took was therefore influenced by the reports of Bukharin's trial as published in *Pravda*. One of the co-defendants in the show trial was N. A. Chernov, the former People's Commissar for Agriculture. He was found guilty of "wrecking during the sowing campaign". The verdicts were published on the day Muralov was compelled to sign the first interrogation protocol. The NKVD staff grilling him in Kuntsevo knew about the state of agriculture in the district, and the setbacks in this sector played a prominent role in subsequent questioning. The file passed on by the Party committee was to provide excellent evidence. Most of the denunciations it contained came from a man called Gogol, an inspector for statistics in the district administration. The similarity between him and his famous namesake was striking. The "literary efforts" of the statistician showed that he understood the need on the part of his superiors to have "wreckers unmasked". Once the NKVD interrogators had pored over Gogol's statistics and tables, they understood the fall in the number of farm animals and why harvest yields were deteriorating. Their conclusion was simple: hidden enemies had undermined agricultural production in the district, thus jeopardising the supply of foodstuffs to the capital. All that needed to be done was to find the cadres of the "wrecking organisation" and assign them roles in this fictitious conspiracy.

The protocols in Muralov's file demonstrate that the NKVD staff went to no great pains to make their scenario plausible. One of the accused was portrayed as "the statistician of the terrorist organisation". His job was to keep a tally of the prominent state and party leaders marked down for liquidation. Rukodanov, a member of the NKVD operative unit in Kuntsevo, managed to extract twelve confessions from Muralov's "conspirators" by the end of March. This Stakhanovite work record produced the following plot: due to the vigilance of the Cheka, a Right-Trotskyist All-Union Centre had been smashed; its structure resembled that of the VKP(b), with Muralov as district leader; he built up an extensive network of "wreckers" in all sectors of the economy.

The membership list of this organisation was exactly the same as the names of alleged "socially alien elements" compiled by the land commission in Kuntsevo. According to this fantasy product of the NKVD, the sabotage activities planned by Muralov's group would have disrupted the hitherto peaceful life of Kuntsevo's inhabitants. But not only were their lives in danger, the targets for terrorist attacks also included Stalin and other Politburo members who had summer houses there, as Muralov confessed during the third protocolled interrogation.

In March 1938 alone, over twenty persons prominent in the district were arrested – factory directors, members of the planning commission, veterinary surgeons, agricultural experts etc. In a statement made later when faced with trumped-up charges, NKVD Sergeant Karetnikov disclosed:

> Muralov gave details of the counter-revolutionary activities of the district Party secretary Morozov, his deputy Krylov and other leading functionaries. When Muralov signed this statement I said to my subordinate Rukodanov that the former was doing this to incriminate honest Party officials. I forbade that these names be included in the protocol and so saved a portion of the illegal organisation from being found out.[9]

The respect Chekists usually showed towards members of the local Party committee seemed to have remained intact in the Kuntsevo case as well, even at the height of the repression. Both bodies exchanged incriminating material, and NKVD officers also took part in the Party purges of the late 1930s. In some instances, however, the Party secretary wanted to exert supervision over the work of the punitive organs, sometimes complaining of the arbitrary methods the latter employed. Sukurov, head of the NKVD district office in Voskresensk (south Moscow Region),[10] forbade his staff to inform the Party committee about cases under investigation. In this episode the NKVD man won out. In September 1937, when the mass arrests were beginning, Gorbulskii, the first secretary of the VKP(b), was taken into custody. The arrest and house search were carried out by staff of the 8th UGB (counter-espionage) Department, under the command of Kaversnev.[11] Brutal pressure was also exerted on the area's *nomenklatura*. Factory directors, for example, were obliged to supply lorries and staff for the operations of the NKVD, and also to participate in the falsification of evidence. N. S. Oparin, the director of the chemical *kombinat* in Voskresensk district, was summoned to the NKVD offices to make an incriminating statement against his deputy. Oparin's account reads:

> After Ottomer had been arrested, Sukurov demanded that I write a negative characterisation of the prisoner. I knew Ottomer's work well and described him accordingly. Sukurov tore up the page in my presence and said I could "wipe my arse" with the scraps of paper.[12]

Oparin was delivered to the Lubianka one year later, Sukurov went the same way six months after that. Victim and tormentor both received ten years in the camps. In Kuntsevo, however, the arrests were directed at the local government elite and not at that of the VKP(b). In violation of the penal code, the sentences were decided on an individual basis during internal meetings of the local NKVD staff. Everything depended on whether the prisoner in question was needed as the first defendant to supply other names in the construction of a "conspiracy". This was apparently not the case with Muralov. He was given a protracted grilling in March, but was left in peace for the ensuing nine months. The NKVD in Kuntsevo also endeavoured to create cases of "espionage activity". Their starting point was a perusal of the questionnaires containing details about the local inhabitants. Persons who had a foreign name or worked in the defence industry were categorised as "spies". Kuznetsov, who was himself arrested in July 1938, described how the "spy teams" were compiled:

> During the operation against kulaks and members of non-Russian nationalities we processed over 1,000 cases, including defendants or convicted prisoners who had confessed under torture. I arrested non-Russians on the basis of lists sent to me by factories or institutes situated in our district. The accused, who had previously worked in these plants or institutes, were grouped together by me into counter-revolutionary conspiracies. The charges we levelled were in accordance with the product of the plant where the defendant worked. If he had been employed in a factory producing military hardware, he was accused of spying and sabotage.[13]

As there were not many factories attached to the defence industry situated in the Kuntsevo district, the NKVD took recourse to institutions or plants that were secret to some degree. Near Sukovo village, for example, was located "Facility (Ob"ekt) No. 1" of the Department for International Communications (OMS) of the Comintern, a country house where OMS staff lived and held meetings. Festivities also took place in the building and were sometimes attended by ECCI members who also spent their summer holidays there. The house garden supplied Comintern headquarters in Moscow with fresh fruit and vegetables. The manager of "Facility No. 1" was the German communist Arthur Gohlke ("Arden"), a 50-year-old later to be executed in Butovo.[14] In the 1920s he had belonged to the Central Committee of the KPD, and was responsible for the party's finances. He was also a popular speaker in the Prussian provincial parliament (Landtag). Gohlke lost office in the course of inter-party squabbling and subsequently emigrated to the USSR. Abramov-Mirov, the head of

OMS, offered him the manager's post at Sukovo. When OMS employees were later arrested, Gohlke was accused of "links to enemies of the people" and dismissed from Comintern employment.

This was often the background to the repression of foreign communists, some of whom naively thought that they might escape arrest in a village near Moscow or by taking up work on a large building-site. However, by doing precisely that they came to the notice of the local NKVD. By 1937 a small colony of Germans was resident in the village of Sukovo, Kuntsevo District, in the vicinity of "Facility No. 1". Many were the wives of arrested German refugees, like the sisters Bertha and Lydia Feyerherd. The tragic fate of the six Feyerherd siblings – employees, at one time or another, of the Soviet Embassy in Berlin or of the Soviet Intelligence Service – warrants a study in its own right. They emigrated to the Soviet Union after Hitler's accession to power and later became victims of the system they thought protected them. Bertha and Lydia waited too long before applying for the Soviet passport they needed for further employment or a place at a third-level institution. Their desolate situation persuaded Bertha to return to Germany, and she travelled to Moscow in January 1938 to apply for a visa from the German Embassy. The next day the secret police arrested her and took her sister Lydia soon afterwards. Lydia, the youngest sister, was arrested because of what Bertha had said. It was not difficult to extract a confession of "spying" from the frightened young woman. In all probability she had been advised to do so by her cell-mates: a confession shortened the time in prison custody and brought the day of departure to the Gulag nearer.

How the final indictment was compiled can be reconstructed by following the line of the interrogation with Lydia Feyerherd:

Question: Did you know, when you lived in Sukovo, that there was an airfield nearby?
Answer: Yes, I knew that there was an airfield in Sukovo when I lived there. I saw aeroplanes and tents.
Question: Were you on the airfield territory, and if so, why?
Answer: I was never there.
Question: The investigation has shown that you often took walks in the vicinity of the airfield. Who was with you and what was the goal of your walks there?
Answer: Yes, that's right. I often went walking there in my free time with my sister Bertha Karlovna Feyerherd, and with my brothers Alexander, Wilhelm, Friedrich and their wives and children. We wanted to enjoy our free time, it was an area with summer houses.[15]

This dialogue contained the implicit charge that sufficed for an indictment. According to the final charge sheet, the sisters got to know the young, inexperienced flying personnel and prised secret information from them. The statements made by the sisters unleashed a series of arrests – acquaintances and others who could be termed "enemies of the people" in a NKVD scenario. The leading role in the "conspiracy" was ascribed to Arthur Gohlke. On the night of 13–14 March 1938, just after Sergei Muralov had made his first confession, the NKVD district unit launched the operation "to destroy a nationalistic espionage group". Arrested were the unemployed Gohlke, the lorry-driver Alexander Feyerherd, some pensioners, two cooks, a book-keeper and a man from the Fire Brigade. All eight were non-Russians.

As none of them had any connection to State secrets or defence plants, the NKVD invented a "plot" based on the jobs previously held by the prisoners. The lorry-driver was supposed to have sent information to Berlin on the condition of Moscow's roads, the cooks were expected to start an anti-Soviet rebellion once war broke out, and the man in charge of ordering sugar was said to have sabotaged the supply of this product to the capital. It was more difficult to falsify charges against pensioners, the unemployed and housewives. Vera Kolbuta, a Polish woman "amalgamated" into the group indictment because there were no more Germans to arrest, was forced to state the following:

> Because I knew the district well and had plenty of free time I could go for extended walks. In this way I saw the state of the roads where important buildings were located. I handed over this information to Alexander Feyerherd. He then gave me seeds of weeds which I strewed over the *kolkhoz* field to reduce crop yields and thus contribute to the dissatisfaction felt by the peasants.[16]

Even more ridiculous statements were beaten out of the suspects. Apart from the beatings and the constant questionings, the NKVD interrogators also tried to convince the German prisoners of the "need" for the indictment. Lydia Feyerherd stated in 1939 that her interrogator tried to convince her that the evidence must be confirmed in order to "liquidate" the German Consulate. And she, Lydia, had to help the NKVD to this end.[17] The staff at "Facility No. 1" were questioned in the course of the case against Arthur Gohlke. As they could not supply evidence that he had conducted espionage activities, they signed a passage invented by the interrogating officer: "Gohlke introduced a fascist system of running the facility and was contemptuous of his

Russian co-workers." In addition, he was said to have "intentionally neglected" to learn the Russian language. The only true part of the statement was that Gohlke had ruled out drinking during working hours, confiscated the bottles and locked in Russian workers overnight so that they could sleep off their intoxication. The main charge directed at Gohlke was that he had known V. N. Melnikov (Müller), an official of OMS shot in 1937. Seeing that the "ringleaders of the conspiracy" were now dead, Gohlke could not be charged in connection with Melnikov, but instead was confronted with "spying", the most common form of indictment brought in cases involving foreigners in the years 1937-8. The NKVD officer Tsyganov was in charge of the Gohlke case. The indictment was completed within the month. Gohlke, Alexander and Willi Feyerherd and A. Koleskinkov-Tikki were shot, the remaining defendants sent to the Gulag.

By mid-1938 the practice of mass shootings was tapering off, and now it was the turn of the killers and the torturers to be put through the mill. Karetnikov, arrested on 13 July 1938, was quick to point the finger at his bosses in Moscow. He and his immediate superior Kuznetsov were charged with "membership in a Trotskyist conspiracy within the NKVD". The investigator wrote: "The leading staff in the NKVD offices in Kuntsevo went so far in violating revolutionary legal norms that they demanded that 45-50 cases be completed each week. During the day the interrogation protocols were forged, and at night the confessions were extracted. Arrests were carried out without warrants, these were issued later." In order to reach the fixed quotas Karetnikov assigned persons to operative duties who had no knowledge of such activities. Some of Muralov's protocols were counter-signed by Kukhalskii, a man "mobilised" from the local fire brigade. NKVD officer Rukodanov, also under arrest, described the conditions prevailing in the Kuntsevo district group of the NKVD in the spring of 1938:

> Beatings were carried out during questioning. On his return from service trips to the Main Administration of State Security (GUGB) in Moscow, Karetnikov told us that Zakovskii, the head of GUGB, personally beat prisoners under interrogation. If I did not do just that, Karetnikov reprimanded me as follows: "Look, Rukodanov, you are not able to conduct interrogations properly. Be careful not to be accused of showing a mild attitude towards our enemies".[18]

Tsyganov, a former student at the Moscow Institute of Civil Law, was taken into NKVD service in late 1937. He participated in the Gohlke case and admitted later: "We arrested on the basis of lists, without warrants or evidence. It sufficed that the suspect was either a Pole or a German."[19]

Some NKVD officers protested at the methods used to extract evidence or to compile indictments. The arrest of Karetnikov and Kuznetsov can be ascribed to such complaints, which also came from the public at large. Such a complaint is contained in the file of Khvatov, a staff member of the NKVD in Serpukhov. Six female workers of the Sanara factory wrote to Beria: "Khvatov and his people are rough types. They shout, curse and threaten people with arrest". An anonymous letter contains the charge that Khvatov bought a motor-bike from a photographer, but instead of paying him the NKVD officer had the man arrested and convicted.[20]

The leaders of the NKVD units in the Moscow Region were sentenced by the Military Tribunals of NKVD Troops. Their subordinate staff usually escaped prosecution, being merely transferred or dismissed from the service. Muralov's case, too, was decided in the period after Ezhov's removal. Witnesses were now compelled to confirm that he had "undermined *kolkhoz* management"; the sabotage and spying charges were dropped. However, despite protestations that confessions had been extracted under duress, the remaining pending cases went before a Special Board (OSO) of the NKVD. No more death sentences were passed. Muralov ended up in Kolyma, and Lydia Feyerherd was handed over to the Gestapo at Brest-Litovsk in December 1939.[21]

The review of such cases was not carried to its logical conclusion – release – by the new man in the Lubianka, Ezhov's successor Beria. It was still far too early and too dangerous to openly question the policy of mass arrests or the rehabilitation of the victims. New officers took up their posts in the Kuntsevo office of the NKVD, and the planned quota of arrests was reduced to "normal" proportions.

Notes

1 Robert Conquest, *Inside Stalin's Secret Police. NKVD Politics, 1936–1939* (London, 1985).
2 A. G. Tepliakov, 'Personal i podsednevnost' Novosibirskogo UNKVD v 1936–1946 gg.', in *Minuvshee. Istoricheskii al'manakh. Vypusk 21* (Moscow and St. Petersburg, 1997), pp. 240–93.
3 Oleg Khlevniuk, *Politbiuro. Mekhanizmy politicheskoi vlasti v 30-e gody* (Moscow, 1996), pp. 188–90.
4 The unit in Kuntsevo was named in the correspondence of the time as "*Raiotdel upravleniia gosudarstvennoi bezopasnosti UNKVD Moskovskoi oblasti*" – District Department of the Administration of State Security in the Administration of the NKVD for the Moscow Region.

Stalinist Terror in Kuntsevo, 1937–8   207

5 In March 1938 2,335 persons were executed in Butovo, the highest monthly figure for this execution ground in the period August 1937 to October 1938. See Orthodox Church (eds), *Martirolog rasstreliannykh i zakhoronennykh na poligone NKVD 'Ob"ekt Butovo' 08.08.1937–19.10.1938* (Moscow, 1997), p. 6. Our research to date indicates that at least 500 inhabitants of Kuntsevo were arrested in 1937–8.
6 GARF, *fond* 10035, NKVD investigation file no. P-59971 N.D. Petrov.
7 Alexander Weißberg-Cybulski, *Im Verhör. Ein Überlebender der stalinistischen Säuberungen berichtet* (Vienna and Zürich, 1993), p. 183.
8 All details of the case against Sergei Muralov are taken from his NKVD investigation file no. P-25777 (GARF, *fond* 10035).
9 GARF, *fond* 10035, NKVD investigation file no. P-23556 Arthur Gohlke.
10 For an account of the terror of 1937–8 in the Voskresensk region, see Aleksandr Vatlin, 'Bolshaia khimiia i bolshoi terror', *Moskovskaia pravda*, 25 November 1997 (p.14) and 16 December 1997 (p.14).
11 GARF, *fond* 10035, NKVD investigation file no. P-22682 Solomon Gorbulskii.
12 GARF, *fond* 10035, NKVD investigation file no. P-41792 August Ottomer. Ottomer, a 40-year-old Latvian, was shot in Butovo on 25 October 1937. See *Martirolog rasstreliannykh*, p. 256.
13 GARF, *fond* 10035, NKVD investigation file no. P-23556 Arthur Gohlke, interrogation protocol A. V. Kuznetsov, 3 February 1939.
14 For an account of the NKVD persecution of Arthur Gohlke and the Feyerherd family, see Aleksandr Vatlin and Natalia Musienko, 'Krovavaia propolka', *Vechernaia moskva*, 27 June 1997, p. 5.
15 GARF, *fond* 10035, NKVD investigation file no. P-23478 Bertha Feyerherd, interrogation protocol (copy) Lydia Feyerherd, 25 January 1938.
16 GARF, *fond* 10035, NKVD investigation file no. P-25071 Vera Kolbuta.
17 GARF, *fond* 10035, NKVD investigation file no. P-23478 Bertha Feyerherd, statement of Lydia Feyerherd, 22 February 1939.
18 GARF, *fond* 10035, NKVD investigation file no. P-23556 Arthur Gohlke.
19 Ibid.
20 GARF, *fond* 10035, NKVD investigation file no. 531402 V. V. Khvatov.
21 Hans Schafranek, *Zwischen NKWD und Gestapo. Die Auslieferung deutscher und österreichischer Antifaschisten aus der Sowjetunion an Nazideutschland 1937–1941* (Frankfurt am Main, 1990), p. 132.

10
The Fictitious "Hitler-Jugend" Conspiracy of the Moscow NKVD

Hans Schafranek and Natalia Musienko

Introduction

When the Soviet intelligence agent Walter Krivitsky looked down one morning in May 1934 from NKVD headquarters at the columns of singing Schutzbündler, the defeated militants of the Austrian Civil War fought three months before marching now in step across Lubianka Square, his reverie on international solidarity was sharply interrupted. His colleague Volynskii, a counter-intelligence officer, expressed the opinion that "in six or seven months seventy percent" of the receding marchers would find themselves in custody.[1] The prediction was somewhat off the mark – the Austrian political refugees remained relatively unscathed till the Comintern cadre reviews of 1936.[2] None the less, Volynskii, a section leader in the Special Department of the GUGB, was correct in intimating that German-speakers were a "suspect category" after Hitler's accession to power.

Targeting Germans as a specific subversive minority first gained momentum with the issue of the Politburo resolution of 4 November 1934, "On the Work among the German Population". The document asserted that anti-Soviet activities had increased among German-speakers, and that both the Party and the secret police had "reacted weakly" to this development.[3] Nine months later, an internal circular signed by Volynskii warned UGB units of "an increase in the activities of the Gestapo on our territory". His main recommendation for prophylactic action reveals the undifferentiated nature of Chekist enemy categorisation:

> The work of agency observation among German and Austrian political immigrants is to be increased as they are being used by the Gestapo as a conduit to infiltrate our country and also because, due

to the falling number of German specialists working here, German intelligence agencies will pay greater attention to the recruitment and use of political immigrants for espionage purposes.[4]

Fictional plots concocted by the NKVD at the time against Germans led to arrests in the Karl-Liebknecht secondary school in Moscow and the editorial offices of the German daily newspaper *Deutsche Zentral-Zeitung*.[5] Countless "fascist elements" of German nationality were arrested during the VKP(b) purges from 1935 onwards. Roughly 3,000 of the 4,600 strong German political refugee colony disappeared during the terror of the 1930s,[6] as did an unknown number of the 5,000–6,000 skilled workers from Germany who had arrived on a contract basis in 1930–1 and chose to remain in the USSR.[7]

Many German refugees were categorised as suspects because they had been released, or had escaped, from Gestapo custody, others on account of their Party record: KPD members who had been followers of dissident or discredited Party leaders in the 1920s, especially the adherents of the "conciliatory Right" accused of Bukharinist sympathies. The Cadres Department of ECCI subsumed such communists under the lethal appellation "Trotskyist" and expelled them collectively through the decisions of the compliant rump of the German Central Committee in exile in Moscow.[8] Prominent KPD leaders purged – the majority was later shot – included 15 serving or former members of the Central Committee and thirteen ex-members of the Reichstag. The corresponding figures for those murdered by the Nazis were 18 and 36, respectively.[9]

Most Germans arrested during the Great Terror, however, belonged to the German minority in the USSR. Of the 70,000 plus ethnic Germans convicted in 1937–8, 40,000 were sentenced during "national" operations of the NKVD, twenty thousand during the "anti-kulak operation" and the remainder by the Special Board of the NKVD and courts. Over 55,000 verdicts were passed in the course of the "German" operation of the secret police and 76 per cent were death sentences (see Table 10.1). Just over two-thirds of the victim toll were registered German nationals (not citizens), with the others being, as was the case during the "Polish" operation, Soviet citizens who had been POWs during World War One, had contacts to German diplomats or businessmen, or corresponded with friends and relatives in a German-speaking country. As regards German citizens proper arrested during 1937 and 1938, the subject of this micro-study, Russian historians well acquainted with original documents of the NKVD calculate that the total lies between 750 and 820.[10] The figure is higher, of

Table 10.1: Sentencing totals for the "German" operation (Order no. 00439) of the NKVD, August 1937 to November 1938

Area NKVD	Total	Shot	Gulag	Area UNKVD	Total	Shot	Gulag
Azerbaijan SSR	146	70	76	Altai territory	3,171	2,412	759
Armenian SSR	47	34	13	Far Eastern Region	41	30	11
Belorussian SSR	355	243	112	Krasnodarsk territory	2,895	2,784	111
Georgian SSR	152	37	115	Krasnoiarsk territory	658	546	112
Kazakhstan SSR	1,471	1,410	61	Ordzhonikidze territory	547	241	306
Kirghiz SSR	255	158	97	Archangel region	261	153	108
Tadzhik SSR	12	4	8	Vologda region	147	77	70
Turkmen SSR	85	63	22	Voronezh region	130	80	50
Uzbek SSR	284	114	170	Gorkii region	608	234	374
Ukrainian SSR	21,229	18,005	3,224	Ivanovo region	137	112	25
Bashkir ASSR	386	282	104	Irkutsk region	149	134	15
Buriat-Mongolian ASSR	10	7	3	Kalinin region	8	8	0
Dagestan ASSR	?	?	?	Kirov region	60	48	12
Kabardino-Balkar ASSR	85	73	12	Kuibyshev region	0	0	0
Kalmyk ASSR	13	6	7	Kursk region	98	71	27
Karelian ASSR	8	8	0	Leningrad region	2,919	2,536	383
Komi ASSR	8	7	1	Moscow region	1,220	863	357
Crimean ASSR	1,625	1,391	234	Murmansk region	29	28	1
Mari ASSR	92	68	24	Novosibirsk region	2,645	2,548	97
Mordvinian ASSR	138	114	24	Omsk region	539	128	411
Volga German ASSR	1,002	567	435	Orenburg region	193	187	6
Northern Ossetian ASSR	82	51	31	Orel region	136	54	82
Tatar ASSR	98	60	38	Rostov region	666	339	327
Udmurt ASSR	3	2	1	Riazan region	37	24	13
Chechen-Ingush ASSR	38	32	6	Saratov region	394	201	193

Table 10.1: Sentencing totals for the "German" operation (Order no. 00439) of the NKVD, August 1937 to November 1938 (*continued*)

Area NKVD	Total	Shot	Gulag	Area UNKVD	Total	Shot	Gulag
Chuvash ASSR	19	9	10	Sverdlovsk region	4,379	1,467	2,912
Iakut ASSR	1	1	0	Smolensk region	242	76	166
				Stalingrad region	1,271	1,019	252
				Tambov region	85	65	20
				Tula region	171	46	125
				Cheliabinsk region	1,626	1,434	192
				Chita region	94	86	8
				Iaroslavl' region	117	83	34
				Road/Rail Units GUGB/NKVD	1,688	968	720
Totals for USSR					*55,005*	*41,898*	*13,107*
In per cent					*100.0*	*76.2*	*23.8*
Totals for dvoiki (album)					*30,534*	*24,910*	*5,624*
Totals for osobye troiki					*24,471*	*16,988*	*7,483*

Source: N. Okhotin and A. Roginskii, 'Iz istorii "nemetskoi operatsii" NKVD 1937–1938gg.', in I. L. Shcherbakova (ed.), *Nakazannyi narod. Repressii protiv rossiiskikh nemtsev* (Moscow, 1999), pp. 63–6.

course, if one takes into account the unknown total of those numerous German political refugees or skilled craftsmen who had returned their German passports and acquired Soviet citizenship.

A substantial number of German citizens arrested in the USSR were expelled from the USSR, 858 between November 1937 and January 1940.[11] This policy had been suspended for most of 1937, when the arrested Germans were shot or sent to a labour camp. Subject to arbitrary "suspension" was also the Politburo decision of 5 January 1936 that foreigners residing in the USSR could not be arrested without the approval of Molotov or the Secretariat of the Central Committee.[12] Only in October 1938, in the last weeks of *massoperatsii*, did Beria remind his subordinates that permission to arrest foreigners must be "obtained in each single case".[13]

Although NKVD Operative Order No. 00439 of 25 July 1937 that launched the "German" arrest raids restricted the victim spectrum to German citizens working in military plants, those under the aegis of the Defence Ministry or on the railway system and specifically excluded political refugees of German origin who no longer possessed a German passport, these provisos were dispensed with in the course of the sweeps. Moreover, the operational arrests should have been completed within five days but continued for more than a year.[14] Similarly, the Politburo decision of 20 July 1937 ordering Ezhov to draw up the directive for the blanket arrest of Germans had proposed the seizure of "all Germans working in defence plants" that produced artillery, rockets, rifles, machine-guns, ammunition and gunpowder. Ezhov understood, in this case as well, that the spirit behind the measures was more important than the actual wording, for Stalin had enclosed a handwritten note, an unequivocal message: "All Germans in our military, semi-military and chemical plants, in electro-generating stations and on building sites, are *all* to be arrested in *all* regions."[15]

The arrest of "Hitler-Jugend" suspects in Moscow, January to March 1938

The "investigation into case no. 8842" was the internal cipher to denote the "Hitler-Jugend plot" hatched by officers of the Moscow administration of the NKVD. The "operative work" in this complex was assigned to the 7th Group of the 4th UGB department, the sub-unit responsible for observing foreign teenagers (workers and students) in the capital. Mikhail Persits, chief of the 4th UGB, had overall responsibility for supervising the arrests and interrogations; Vasilii

Smirnov, his subordinate in charge of the 7th Group, directed the conduct of questionings, which were carried out by a dozen or so junior ranks, often relatively new recruits to secret police work. A score of the "Hitler-Jugend" indictments were processed in the 3rd UGB Department under Captain Ivan Sorokin. When, on one occasion, UGB departmental chiefs brought sheaves of arrest warrants to NKVD administration deputy commander Iakubovich, the latter put his watch on the table, began to scribble his initials on the papers in red pencil and said, "Let's see how many warrants I can sign in a minute".[16]

The warrants so presented for signature by Smirnov's 7th Group were compiled on the basis of lists obtained from factories, technical schools and learned institutes.[17] Additional names of "suspects" were extracted from the Austrian and German students and apprentices already in custody, with some arrests being carried out merely on the principle of "guilt by association", or on the strength of a common address (House For Political Immigrants, Ulitsa Obukha 3, for instance) and family ties. When a detachment from the 7th Group arrived at a Moscow apartment to arrest a young German factory worker, they found he was on night shift, arrested his younger brother instead and left a policeman in the room to seize the older sibling on his return.[18]

As Moscow's prisons were full to overflowing in early 1938, many of the 80-90 "Hitler-Jugend" suspects subsequently condemned were interrogated on the third floor, and kept in the cellar cells, of the NKVD Administration building at Bolshaia Lubianka 11.[19] The biographical data of the 75 victims known to date prove that an inner logic was missing from this fabricated case. The age of the victims ranged from 17 to 62, and a third was over 30 years of age. A minority comprised experienced metalworkers, actors from the German theatre group "Kolonne Links", residents of the House for Political Immigrants, Austrians who had fled from fascist terror, teachers from the Karl-Liebknecht School and other persons whose only common characteristic was German as a native tongue and political refugee status. The greater portion was made up of teenagers studying at medical, technical and sport institutes, or apprentices employed in the "Stalin" automobile plant and other factories, and at the Scientific Research Institute for the Car and Tractor Industry (NATI). Only 6 were released from investigative custody, the remainder were either shot in Butovo (40) or sentenced to long stretches in the camps (25).

The foremost consideration for the interrogation teams was the imperative to complete inter-departmental work quotas as quickly as possible; that is, to obtain an ordained number of "confessions" daily. The text of three documents along the chain of command illustrates the pressure imposed on the NKVD interrogation teams:

Politburo decision of 31 January 1938
Permit the NKVD until 15 April 1938 to continue operations to smash the spying-sabotage contingents of Poles, Latvians, Germans, Estonians, Finns, Greeks, Iranians, Kharbintsy, Chinese and Romanians, whether Soviet or foreign citizens and in accordance with the appropriate orders of the NKVD.[20]

Memorandum from Iakubovich to Sorokin, head of 3rd UGB, Moscow, 19 March 1938
The number of confessions attained by your department has fallen sharply – 34 on 16 March, 33 on 17 March. The fifth department reached the figure of 51 confessions on 17 March. I request you to apply more pressure.[21]

Sorokin's orders, statement by Zakharov of 4th UGB, 13 June 1938
When we were to pick up the real foreigners I went to Sorokin and said that I had arrested none. He abused me and asked whether there were persons in my city district – Russians or Jews – who had lived in Germany, Poland and other foreign states. I said that we had a lot of such cases. Referring to this, Sorokin declared: 'It's always possible to make them Germans and Poles, but this has to be done accurately in order to avoid failure". After having received this directive, Karetnikov and I began the practice, when writing the arrest warrants [*spravki na arest*], interrogation protocols and other standardised documents, to denote Russians or Jews who had lived in Poland and Latvia as Poles and Latvians.[22]

The obligation to complete unrealistic "production targets" was challenged by Rudolf Traibman, a young NKVD cadre who translated during the interrogation sessions with the German youths. Twenty years later he asserted that he had cast doubts on the validity of the proffered charges in a complaint to Smirnov. The group leader threatened him with a transfer from the third-floor offices to a cell in the cellar, showing him Iakubovich's written order that a "nationalistic, counter-revolutionary group among young Germans had to be discovered within two days".[23]

Another consequence of the primacy of "norm-fulfilment" was that the final indictment could be based on any one paragraph of Article 58, usually "espionage" (§6), coupled with one or more of the following: "wrecking"(§7), "terrorism"(§8), "anti-Soviet agitation"(§10) or "membership in a counter-revolutionary organisation"(§11). The imaginary criminal scenarios subsequently underpinned by statements made under duress of all kinds concentrated on spying on behalf of the German or Austrian embassies, the formation of sabotage units in factories for operations in time of war and plans to assassinate Soviet leaders such as Stalin, Molotov and Voroshilov. The principal actors in the grotesque arraignments were changed at will by the interrogators, with a former employee of the German Embassy, a pensioner, receiving a leading role.[24] That fragments of reality surface in the absurd dialogue between torturer and victim can be seen, for example, in the insinuation that the alleged sabotage planned by the accused might go unheeded as "the plant management was of the opinion that machinery breakdowns were attributable to the inability of Russian workers to operate foreign equipment."[25] Most "investigations", however, took little account of how the prisoner had behaved in the past, and were carried out at maximum speed. The accused generally gave in fairly soon, terrified and intimated by protracted beatings and sleep deprivation. They also succumbed to the inevitable on the advice of their cellmates who had more experience of prevalent Chekist "investigation methods". The interrogators, in turn, were informed of such conversations by the stool pigeons they had placed in the packed communal cells.[26]

Wilhelm Klug, a 17-year-old political refugee from Linz arrested in March 1938, enquired why he was in custody and refused to sign a pre-typed confession. He was beaten for four hours, fell unconscious and was to spend months in the prison hospital because of injuries to his lumbar vertebra.[27] Another "Hitler-Jugend" defendant was Helmut Damerius, the leader of the theatre troupe Kolonne Links. He was punched and whipped with a wet towel.[28] Gustav Sobottka, the son of a German Reichstag deputy of the same name, tried to commit suicide by slashing his wrists during a break in the torture sessions. Transferred to the sick-bay of Taganka prison, Sobottka concluded that further resistance was futile; his fellow-patients, bed-ridden because of smashed ribs or severe spinal injuries, asserted that signing the dictated confession was the only strategy which would bring the torture to an end.[29] The first of the executions in the "Hitler-Jugend" conspiracy took place in Butovo on 20 February 1938; at least 39 further capital sentences in the case were executed at the same place between March and May.

Reaction to the arrests and their aftermath

An internal report of the KPD compiled in Moscow in late April 1938 detailed the sharp rise in arrests among German Communists:

> 70% of all registered KPD cadres in the USSR, 842 in all, of whom 470 had been seized in the period October 1937 to March 1938; 100 were arrested in Moscow in the month of March alone, including all male German political refugees living in Dom Politemigrantov in Ultisa Obukha; the German party group had ceased to exist in Engels, capital of the Volga German Republic, and the membership of the KPD cell in Leningrad had sunk from 103 to 12 between January 1937 and February 1938.[30]

Paul Jakl, the writer of this chronicle of despair, ascribed the onslaught to state-sponsored xenophobia. He repeated what the Party secretary in a military plant had said in late March to the communist wife of an arrested German employee: as a member of the VKP(b) she should know that all Germans in the USSR are spies. Jakl believed that this was official policy, especially following the leading article of *Le Journal de Moscou* of 12 April: "It is no exaggeration to say that every Japanese living outside Japan is a spy, just as every German citizen living abroad is working for the Gestapo."[31]

Dimitrov complained to Central Committee secretary Zhdanov about this "ridiculous" and "politically harmful" characterisation of people forced to live outside their country, including the political immigrants in the Soviet Union.[32] The protest from Eugen Varga, the famous Marxist economist and Hungarian refugee, was more forthright and addressed to Stalin personally. He saw a narrow-minded nationalism gaining ground in the USSR, with widespread hatred against foreigners, who were now collectively seen as spies. Varga divided the exiled communist groups in three groups: volunteers of the International Brigades in Spain, those arrested by the NKVD and the "demoralised and discouraged" remainder who had a "great part to play in the coming war". Noting that ten of the fourteen commissars of the Hungarian Soviet Republic who had found exile in the USSR were now imprisoned, Varga urged a review of the arrested cadres with the assistance of the Comintern.[33]

These appeals had no discernable effect, primarily because the undifferentiated portrayal of foreigners as actively hostile and dangerous had become part of official "discourse": Stalin's remarks in this connection to the Central Committee of the previous year (3 March 1937) had been widely publicised in the press and booklets, namely the presence of "wreckers, spies, saboteurs and murderers, sent into our hinterland by agents of foreign states".[34]

It is naturally impossible to quantify the extent of public support for this total reversal of the principles of internationalist solidarity. One example suggests that some not forced by the exigencies of Party or State office to regurgitate Stalinist propaganda were, at the very least, perplexed and disturbed by the shameless foreigner-baiting. Maria Simenova, a Muscovite factory worker and Stakhanovite, wrote to Dimitrov in May 1938:

> Comrade Dimitrov!
> You may find it strange that I am writing to you and not to Comrade Stalin. I have written to him, and not only once, but they obviously don't pass on the letters from small, semi-literate people ... One week ago ... my little boy came home from school and said that all the boys are preparing a pogrom and would beat up all nationals, Poles, Latvians and Germans [pupils] because all their parents are spies. When I tried to find out who had said that, [my son] said it was from another boy whose brother is in the Komsomol and works in the NKVD and had told him that all foreign spies living in Moscow would soon be convicted and that their families and children would be beaten up like the Jews were under the Tsar. I went to see the director of the school, but he only said that the parents were to blame but I could not follow [the logic] of all these conversations. Today in the factory I heard again from a group of women that someone had written on the factory fence in the morning, "Beat up the Poles and the Latvians". This is an unpleasant business. I wrote to Comrade Stalin as well, and fellow women workers said I should report to you what can be heard daily in similar conversations. Even Party people are afraid of everything and they said that the wives and children really were guilty, that they will be beaten up and driven out of their homes.[35]

Perhaps the reaction of Dimitrov to such letters led to the release of four of the accused "Hitler-Jugend" group from investigative custody that same month. Hans Beimler and Max Maddalena were the sons of prominent KPD functionaries of the same names. Beimler senior, a member of the KPD Central Committee and the Reichstag, had escaped from Dachau Concentration Camp and was killed on the Madrid front in December 1936.[36] Maddalena's father had served in the KPD inner circle in underground and was serving a life sentence in a German prison when his son was seized in Moscow. Wilhelm Pieck, the provisional chairman of the KPD in Moscow exile, intervened for young Maddalena and fifteen other German communists in a petition to Dimitrov.[37] NKVD documents pertaining to their release stated that both Beimler and Maddalena had withdrawn their original statements and were no longer considered members of "a counter-revolutionary, fascist organisation".[38] Pieck's deputy Walter Ulbricht, however, believed the teenagers were set free only after they had signed a commitment to spy on leading KPD cadres.[39] Pieck's applications to Dimitrov also led to the release of the young Germans Harry Schmitt and Günther Schramm in 1940, after two years' imprisonment on false charges.[40]

Such appeals on behalf of the German, Austrian, Italian and Hungarian Communist Parties had to be addressed to Dimitrov in his capacity as General Secretary of the Comintern. If he supported the case, Dimitrov sent the appeals, as enclosures, with a covering letter to the Central Committee of the VKP(b), the State Prosecutor's office or the NKVD. Considering the atmosphere of the times, Dimitrov knew he could do little to help the aggrieved, and he rebuffed those colleagues he considered too insistent in this matter.[41] The total number of petitions he forwarded is unknown, at least 30 depositions in 1939 and 131 interventions for fellow-Bulgarians in 1938.[42] Dimitrov, as Fridrikh Firsov documents above, was also an accomplice. In connection with the assistance offered by the German Embassy to repatriate the families of victims, Walter Ulbricht sent a denunciatory report to Dimitrov in October 1940: the women were negotiating with a "German agent", spreading slander about the USSR, and "as enemies of the Soviet Union" should be forbidden to live any longer in Moscow. This recommendation to banish the wives and children of the victims deep into the Soviet interior, thus preventing their return to Germany, found Dimitrov's acceptance. He forwarded Ulbricht's denunciation to Beria, stating in the covering letter that "you [Beria] naturally are in a better position to judge what measures should be taken in this matter by the organs of the NKVD."[43]

Following the signing of the German-Soviet Non-Aggression Pact of 23 August 1939, the secret police of both states cooperated in occupied Poland, especially in the transfer of ethnic minorities from one side to the other, or trying to expel Jewish refugees over the demarcation line. Between November 1939 and May 1941, at least 350 German and

Austrian survivors of the Gulag were handed over to the Gestapo at Brest-Litovsk. In contrast to the expulsions of earlier years, these contingents contained a higher proportion of Jews and communists.[44] In the Soviet transports to Brest-Litovsk were merely three former "Hitler-Jugend" defendants.[45]

In other areas affecting German native-speakers in the USSR, the Hitler-Stalin Pact was not so much a caesura, rather a new phase in a current development. A Politburo decision of 17 December 1937, for instance, directed that German districts in many Soviet republics be abolished. German-language institutes of learning and newspapers were closed down, with *Deutsche Zentral-Zeitung* appearing for the last time in July 1939.[46] Children's Home no. 6 in Moscow, the model orphanage for 130 Austrian and German children including many teenagers implicated in the "Hitler-Jugend" conspiracy, was threatened with closure in 1938. A supplication from the Austrian Communist Party (KPÖ) to keep the home open was supported by Dimitrov, but the closure became final and official a week after Ribbentrop's visit to the Russian capital to sign the Pact.[47]

While the condemned "Hitler-Jugend" teenagers were in transit to the work camps, their tormentors were subjected to double indictments: they had used "illegal methods of investigation" and belonged to a clandestine "counter-revolutionary, Trotskyist organisation" within the Moscow NKVD. Mikhail Persits, former commandant of the 4th UGB department, was removed from his post and put at the disposal of the Lubianka's Cadres Department before being arrested in April 1939. Indicted on three paragraphs of Article 58, Persits confessed his guilt under torture, but later recanted. That did not convince his fellow-officers trying him in the NKVD Troops Tribunal: he was found guilty on all charges and shot on 2 February 1940. His assistant Petr Sheidin was arrested earlier, in July 1938. The arrest warrant signed by Ezhov alleged that Sheidin had shown "Trotskyist hesitations in 1924" and was acquainted with Zinoviev's secretary. Arraigned before the Military Collegium of the Supreme Court on 2 March 1939, Sheidin pleaded not guilty. He was executed the next day.[48] Vasilii Smirnov, the leader of the 7th Group, was charged with "protecting Trotskyist cadres" within the secret police and employing "physical methods of influence during the interrogation of prisoners".[49] Condemned in 1939 to ten years in the Gulag, Smirnov received a second sentence (six years) in 1946, but this was halved on appeal. He was released from the Gulag near Sverdlovsk in 1949.[50] The factual evidence collated against Ivan Sorokin, chief of the 3rd UGB in Moscow, centred on mishandling prisoners and fabricating charges, such as the espionage indictment that a prisoner had collected data about the movement of the ice-masses in the Barents Sea. Sorokin admitted his guilt at a sitting of the NKVD Troops Tribunal in August 1939, but rejected the fictitious part of the indictment (belonging to a counter-revolutionary organisation in the NKVD). The Military Collegium and the Supreme Soviet confirmed his death sentence.[51]

Most of the subordinate staff, it seems, came through relatively unscathed. Some were dismissed in 1939, others after 1956, when the rehabilitation of the victims sometimes led to disciplinary measures or criminal charges against their erstwhile tormentors. Rudolf Traibman was working for state railways in Kiev when he gave the KGB in 1957 a long and plausible account of his time in the Moscow administration of the NKVD. He had been dismissed from the "organs" five years previously.[52] His ex-colleague Skvortsov, a colonel in the Gulag Administration of the Ministry of the Interior, when questioned by KGB officers in 1957, was unconvincing: neither he nor any other of Vasilii Smirnov's underlings had ever struck a prisoner.[53]

In the course of reviewing the case of survivor Helmut Damerius in 1955, military jurists ordered the interrogation of Nikolai Mitrofanov, the officer in charge of the "investigation" against the German in 1938.[54] Mitrofanov, pensioned off on health grounds in 1951,[55] was traced to Simferopol. When questioned there, he bewailed his state of health and denied that he had beaten Damerius: torture was unheard of in the Moscow NKVD, and the German had incriminated himself on the advice of fellow prisoners in order to expedite his case.[56] Such reviews also revealed that some charges in the "Hitler-Jugend" case were amalgamated with arraignments against more prominent prisoners, even *after* Ezhov's henchmen had been removed. Young Sobottka, for instance, was tied into the "Anti-Comintern Conspiracy" indictment brought against the Comintern leaders Béla Kun, Osip Piatnitskii and Waldemar Knorin. The ludicrous supplementary charge read that a leading KPD functionary had "assigned" the 23-year-old the task of assassinating Molotov. Sobottka's case was never concluded. He died in the Butyrka prison in September 1940, presumably due to the injuries he had received during interrogation. His mother, who had lost a second son in a Nazi concentration camp, went mad.[57]

Few young Germans released from custody remained at liberty for very long. Max Maddalena junior was arrested a second time three months after the German invasion, this time on a charge of "anti-Soviet agitation". He died in a prison hospital ten months after arrest.[58]

Günther Schramm left the prison with chronic TBC and died during the war. Like many political immigrants, he had been conscripted as a work-slave by the military labour force (Trudovaia armiia).[59] Dimitrov intervened for some of the press-ganged, but not for Schramm, who was not considered "an active Party cadre".[60]

The results of internal enquiries in the post-Stalin era were naturally not revealed to outsiders. The grounds for issuing a rehabilitation decree also remained a State secret, and relatives seeking information were not told the full truth, or issued with a proper death certificate, until 1989. The Russian wife of Kurt Rinkovsky (shot in Butovo) was told by the authorities in 1954 that her husband had died in a fire at Kiev prison 13 years before.[61] When Charlotte Silbermann wrote from Germany in 1965 to enquire about the fate of her son Kurt, the KGB told the Soviet Red Cross to answer that nothing was known about this missing person as the old woman "lives in the capitalist West and does not know that her son was arrested".[62] Kurt Silbermann was 27 when sentenced to death on a "Hitler-Jugend" indictment in April 1938.

Although the Soviet Ministry of the Interior had established shortly after Stalin's demise that a "Hitler-Jugend" subversive group had never existed in Moscow[63], the last of the victims were not rehabilitated until 1989. Shortly afterwards the surviving victims or their relatives gained access to the investigation files of the NKVD.

Notes

1 Walter Krivitsky, *I Was Stalin's Agent* (Cambridge, 1992), pp. 39–40.
2 Barry McLoughlin, Hans Schafranek and Walter Szevera, *Aufbruch-Hoffnung-Endstation. Österreicherinnen und Österreicher in der UdSSR, 1925–1945* (Vienna, 1997), pp. 352–90.
3 Holger Dehl, 'Deutsche Politemigranten in der UdSSR: Von Illusionen zur Tragödie', *Utopie Kreativ* (Berlin), January 1997, p. 53. Dehl's article is based on archival material held in RGASPI and GARF (Moscow and Novosibirsk).
4 Russian State Military Archive, Moscow (RGVA), f. 500, op. 1, d. 1050a, ll. 196–202. The document is in German, part of the archive of Gestapo headquarters (Reichssicherheitshauptamt) that was confiscated by the Red Army in Berlin at the end of the war. The Russian original was found in the NKVD building in Smolensk after the German invasion of the Soviet Union.
5 Dehl, 'Deutsche Politemigranten', pp. 53–4.
6 Carola Tischler, *Flucht in die Verfolgung. Deutsche Emigranten im sowjetischen Exil* (Münster, 1996), pp. 97, 108.
7 Hans Schafranek, *Zwischen NKWD und Gestapo. Die Auslieferung deutscher und österreichischer Antifaschisten aus der Sowjetunion an Nazideutschland 1937–1941* (Frankfurt am Main, 1990), p. 11.

8 Over 1,000 victims' biographies (KPD) were published by the successor institute of the East German Institute of Marxism-Leninism in the last months of the Gorbachev era. See Institut für Geschichte der Arbeiterbewegung (eds), *In den Fängen des NKWD. Deutsche Opfer des stalinistischen Terrors in der UdSSR* (Berlin, 1991). In respect of the gruesome "cadre-screening" to which KPD members in Russia were subjected, see the following by Reinhard Müller, *Die Säuberung. Moskau 1936: Stenogramm einer geschlossenen Parteiversammlung* (Reinbeck bei Hamburg, 1991); *Die Akte Wehner, Moskau 1937–1941* (Berlin, 1993); and 'Unentwegte Disziplin und permanenter Verdacht. Zur Genesis der "Säuberungen" in der KPD', in Wolfgang Neugebauer (ed.), *Von der Utopie zum Terror. Stalinismus-Analysen* (Vienna, 1994), pp. 71–95.

9 Hermann Weber, *"Weiße Flecken" in der Geschichte. Die KPD-Opfer der Stalinschen Säuberungen und ihre Rehabilitierung* (new enlarged edition, Frankfurt am Main, 1990), pp. 19–21.

10 Unless stated otherwise, all statistics relating to German victims are taken from N. Okhotin and A. Roginskii, 'Iz istorii "nemetskoi operatsii" NKVD 1937–1938 gg.', in I. L. Shcherbakova (ed.), *Nakazannyi narod. Repressi protiv rossiiskikh nemtsev* (Moscow, 1999), pp. 35–75, especially the tables, pp. 63–6.

11 Schafranek, *Zwischen NKWD und Gestapo*, pp. 190–1.

12 RGASPI, f. 17, op. 162, d. 19, l. 24.

13 Okhotin and Roginskii, 'Iz istorii "nemetskoi operatsii"', p. 47.

14 For the text of the "German" order, see A. Ia. Razumov (ed.), *Leningradskii martirolog, tom 2, oktiabr' 1937 goda* (St. Petersburg, 1996), pp. 452–3.

15 Underlined in the original. For the full text of the Politburo decision and Stalin's note, see Okhotin and Roginskii, 'Iz istorii "nemetskoi operatsii"', p. 35.

16 *Volia* (Moscow), nos 2–3 (1994), p. 76 (excerpt from NKVD investigation-file no. 716060 Ivan G. Sorokin).

17 GARF, f. 10035, NKVD investigation file no. 476428 Kurt Bertram, statement of Stepan Skvortsov, 18 January 1957.

18 GARF, f. 10035, NKVD investigation file no. P-33334 Richard Altermann, statement of Rudolf Traibman, 3 January 1957.

19 GARF, f. 10035, NKVD file Kurt Bertram, statement of Skvortsov.

20 Natalia Gevorkian, 'Vstrechnye plany po unichtozheniiu sobstvennogo naroda', *Moskovskie novosti*, no. 25, 21 June 1992, p. 19 (excerpt).

21 *Volia*, nos 2–3 (1994), p. 77.

22 L. A. Golovkova (ed.), *Butovskii poligon. Kniga pamiati zhertv politicheskikh repressii. Vypusk chetvertyi* (Moscow, 2000) p. 353 (extract from report on NKVD officer Ivan Sorokin, GARF, f. 10035, NKVD investigation-file no. P-55763). Excerpts from the documentation assembled to prosecute UGB departmental and group leaders were copied many times and inserted in the files of the prisoners these units had interrogated – in Sorokin's case the 3rd UGB.

23 GARF, f. 10035, NKVD file Richard Altermann, statement Traibman.

24 GARF, f. 10035, NKVD investigation file Wilhelm Reich, interrogation protocol of 15 February 1938.

25 GARF, f. 10035, NKVD investigation file Willi Zoschke, interrogation protocol of 14 January 1938.

26 GARF, f. 10035, NKVD file Richard Altermann, statement Traibman.
27 GARF, f. 10035, NKVD investigation file no. P-20591 Wilhelm Klug, appeal to the Supreme Soviet of the USSR, n.d. [December 1953].
28 GARF, f. 10035, NKVD investigation file no. P-20440 Helmut Damerius, letter to Public Prosecutor of USSR, n.d. [1940].
29 Reinhard Müller, 'Der Fall des "Antikomintern-Blocks" – Ein vierter Moskauer Schauprozeß?', in Hermann Weber, Dietrich Staritz et al. (eds), *Jahrbuch für Historische Kommunismusforschung 1996* (Berlin, 1996), pp. 200–1.
30 L. G. Babichenko, '"Esli aresty budut prodolzhat'sia, to ... ne ostanetsia ni odnogo nemtsa – chlena partii". Stalinskie "chistki" nemetskoi politemigratsii v 1937–1938 godakh', *Istoricheskii arkhiv*, no. 1 (1992), pp. 119–20.
31 Ibid, p. 119.
32 Fridrikh Firsov, 'Mut gegen Ungesetzlichkeit. Dokumente aus dem Archiv der Komintern über den Kampf für die Rettung von Kommunisten und Internationalisten vor Stalinischen Repressalien', *Probleme des Friedens und des Sozialismus* (Prague), no. 7 (1989), p. 1000. The journal was the German edition of *World Marxist Review*.
33 Ibid, pp. 999–1000.
34 *Voprosy istorii*, no. 3 (1995), pp. 5–6.
35 Oleg Del', *Ot illiuzii k tragedii. Nemetskie emigranty v SSSR v 30-e gody* (Moscow, 1997), p. 90 (RGASPI, f. 495, op. 73, d. 61, l. 18).
36 For the controversy on the mysterious circumstances of Beimler's death, see Hugh Thomas, *The Spanish Civil War*, third edn (Harmondsworth, 1977), pp. 366, 482, 488; Patrik v. zur Mühlen, *Spanien war ihre Hoffnung. Die deutsche Linke im Spanischen Bürgerkrieg* (Berlin and Bonn, 1985), pp. 148–52, 247–62.
37 For a reproduction of this document, see *In den Fängen*, pp. 333–41.
38 GARF, f. 10035, NKVD investigation file Hans Beimler, interrogation protocol of 8 May 1938; decision to release from custody, 15 May 1938.
39 Herbert Wehner, *Zeugnis* (Cologne, 1984), pp. 251–3.
40 *Neues Leben* (Moscow), no. 31, 10 August 1994, pp. 6–7.
41 For the remarks of the ECCI representative from Austria concerning such interventions, see Ernst Fischer, *Erinnerungen und Reflexionen* (Reinbek bei Hamburg, 1969), pp. 358–9.
42 Firsov, 'Mut gegen Ungesetzlichkeit', p. 1001.
43 K. M. Anderson and A. O. Chubar'ian (eds), *Komintern i vtoraia mirovaia voina, chast' I, do 22 iiunia 1941 g.* (Moscow, 1994), pp. 508–10.
44 Schafranek, *Zwischen NKWD und Gestapo*, pp. 54–9.
45 Hans Petersen, Erwin Turra and Wilhelm Reich.
46 Holger Dehl, 'Stalins Regime contra Rußlanddeutsche. Aus der Geschichte eines unerklärten Krieges', *Neues Leben*, no. 12, 23 March 1994, p. 5.
47 Hans Schafranek (in co-operation with Natalia Mussienko), *Kinderheim Nr 6. Österreichische und deutsche Kinder im sowjetischen Exil* (Vienna, 1998), pp. 129–36.
48 GARF, f. 10035, NKVD investigation file no. 478570 Karl Buren, examination report, 11 April 1955; NKVD investigation file no. P-72766 Kurt Rinkovsky, information, 3 January 1985.
49 GARF, f. 10035, NKVD investigation file Johannes Huth, Sentence no. 82, 17 October 1939.
50 Ibid, information, 3 January 1985.

51 See note 16.
52 GARF, f. 10035, NKVD investigation file no. P-33334 Richard Altermann, statement of Rudolf Traibman, 3 January 1957; NKVD investigation file no. 478570 Karl Buren, information, 18 October 1956.
53 GARF, f. 10035, NKVD investigation file no. 476428 Kurt Bertram, confession of Stepan Skvortsov, 18 January 1957.
54 GARF, f. 10035, NKVD investigation file no. P-20440 Helmut Damerius, decision of Military Tribunal, Moscow Military District, 22 September 1955.
55 Ibid, information, 25 March 1956.
56 Ibid, declaration, 27 June 1956.
57 Müller, 'Der Fall des "Antikomintern-Blocks"', p. 207; Holger Dehl and Natalia Musienko, '"Hitler-Jugend" in der UdSSR. Zur Geschichte einer Fälschung', *Neues Leben*, no. 31, 10 August 1994, pp. 6–7; Reinhard Müller, '"Schrecken ohne Ende". Eingaben deutscher NKWD-Häftlinge und ihrer Verwandten an Stalin, Jeshow u.a.', *Exil. Forschung, Erkenntnisse, Ergebnisse* (Hamburg), no. 2 (1997), p. 71.
58 GARF, f. 10035, NKVD investigation file no. 4179 Max Maddalena, excerpt from investigation file no. 13678.
59 Such conscripts were called up by the Red Army, but remained under NKVD supervision until release.
60 Tischler, *Flucht in die Verfolgung*, pp. 187–92.
61 *Neues Deutschland* (Berlin), 28 August 1995, p. 12.
62 Natalia Musienko, 'Kinder im Exil. Kinder der Karl-Liebknecht-Schule in Moskau während der stalinistischen Säuberungen', in Ernst Heinrich Meyer-Stiens (ed.), *Opfer wofür? Deutsche Emigranten in Moskau – ihr Leben und Schicksal* (Worpswede, 1996), p. 77.
63 GARF, f. 10035, NKVD investigation file Wilhelm Klug, letter from 3rd Department Main Archival Administration of the Ministry of the Interior to Investigation Department KGB of the Moscow Region, 7 July 1954.

11
Terror against Foreign Workers in the Moscow Elektrozavod Plant, 1937–8

Sergei Zhuravlev

The hiring of foreign expertise for Soviet industry, contemporaneous with the First Five-Year Plan, led to the formation of a foreigner colony (*inokolonia*) in the Moscow electro-technical combine Elektrozavod.[1] The craftsmen and engineers from abroad, in total scarcely 1 per cent of the huge workforce (23,000 in 1933), were recruited usually on an individual basis and were predominantly German by nationality. The majority of the German metalworkers in Elektrozavod consisted of members of the German Communist Party (KPD), the most powerful Comintern section after the Soviet one. They comprised a tightly knit social and political group whose members often had long experience in similar Berlin enterprises, most notably with the electric bulb manufacturer Osram or the electrical equipment company AEG.

Elektrozavod, officially opened on the eleventh anniversary of the October Revolution, was the result of a merger between the Union of the Moscow Region Electric Light Bulb Factories (MOFEL) and a series of enterprises which manufactured transformers, film-projectors, turbines, headlamps, electric starters, magnetos and other electrical equipment. The first director of Elektrozavod was Nikolai Bulganin, who advanced to the office of Soviet Prime Minister in the early Khrushchev years. The factory's name was changed to Elektrokombinat in 1933, by which time it was producing one-fifth of all electrical goods in the USSR. The plant was a showpiece of the feverish industrialisation programme and completed the tasks assigned to it in the First Five-Year Plan within two and a half years. For this achievement it was awarded the Order of Lenin, the second enterprise in the Soviet Union to receive this distinction.[2]

Elektrozavod also attained prominence because of the near monopoly status it secured in the manufacture of electric lighting,[3] and in the processing and export of tungsten, platinum and other heavy metals,[4] inventions which later proved essential for the development of the nuclear and electronic industries, and the space programme. The electric light bulbs and lamps turned out by Elektrozavod were employed in anti-aircraft defence, the operation theatres of hospitals, in the manufacture of lorries and cars, and in the apartments of millions of Soviet citizens. The plant's engineers also developed the powerful lighting needed to illuminate the bright red stars on top of the Kremlin's towers. The electro-technical complex was broken up in 1938, and five separate factories took its place.[5] According to figures compiled in 1932, the *inokolonia* in Elektrozavod totalled 180 employees, the third largest contingent of foreign staff in a Russian factory behind the Kharkov Tractor Works (328) and the GAZ automobile plant in Gorkii (221).[6]

Prior to the first large influx of skilled workers from Germany in October 1930, the number of foreigners employed at Elektrozavod stood at roughly twenty. This pioneering group was made up of political refugees, engineers on short contracts and a nucleus of German communists who had arrived in 1925 through the mediation of the KPD.[7] The latter group had worked in AEG or Osram so that their experience was essential for the further development of electric light bulb production. At the request of the management they changed their names in Moscow to avoid possible German accusations of industrial espionage or not paying for patents. A large number of the Germans arriving in Elektrozavod in the early 1930s were personally recruited by Elektrozavod engineers or by director Bulganin on trips to Germany and the USA, or hired after applying to the special office (*spetsbiuro*) of the Soviet Trade Delegation in one of the Central European capitals. Their services were sought by the All-Union Electro-Technical Combine (VEO), the authority supervising production in Elektrozavod for the People's Commissariat of Heavy Industry (NKTP).

Regardless of the mode of recruitment, all contracts entered into with engineers and skilled tradesmen from abroad were subject to confirmation by the Supreme Economic Council (VSNKh) and registered at the People's Commissariat of Labour.[8] Wage agreements concluded with skilled operatives were valid for one year and could be renewed. In some cases the provisions of the agreement promised part-payment in a foreign currency (*valiuta*). By contrast, the terms offered to American, British or German qualified engineers were valid for half a year to two and a half years, and the salaries were 100 per cent *valiuta* ones in all but a handful of cases. Despite the increase in the number of foreigners recruited in 1930–1, the *inokolonia* remained predominantly a reserve of the Germans:

> February 1931: total 94, 29 engineers, 65 skilled men; 83 Germans, 8 Americans, 1 Czech, 1 Briton.
> October 1931: total 168, 16 engineers, 152 skilled men; 132 Germans, 20 Americans, political refugees etc.
> April 1932: total 170, 33 engineers, 137 skilled men; 106 Germans, 24 Americans etc.[9]

The newcomers worked in practically all departments of the plant, with the greatest number in the transformer and automobile-tractor workshops.[10] The craftsmen most in demand were turners, fitters, tool-makers and welders, who, knowing no Russian at first, were put to work on their own. They were later organised in foreign brigades. While this kind of production unit complied with their own wishes and made best use of the skills they possessed, it isolated them even more from their Russian workmates. Russian apprentices were later attached to such teams.

In late 1931 a Foreign Bureau (*Inobiuro*) was set up within the trade union committee (*profkom*) of Elektrozavod in order to observe the fulfilment of contractual obligations. The office was also responsible for providing the foreign employees with visas, accommodation and foodstuffs. It also served as a conduit in supplying the factory's rationalisation department with pertinent suggestions and inventions on the part of foreign engineers and craftsmen. Intelligence gathering, especially on the political views of the foreigner staff, was to become an increasingly important part of the *Inobiuro* remit.

A quarter of all foreigner employees were bachelors, and the married ones, especially the craftsmen, arranged for the transfer of their wives and children to Moscow in the course of 1931. In some cases they were forced to do so because of unilateral changes in the terms of employment (abolition of the foreign currency clause in their contracts). While the arrival of their families may have served as a stabilising factor in a difficult period of acclimatisation, the family reunion frequently entailed a host of other problems in regard to accommodation, food and medical care. The high cost of living in the Soviet capital during the early 1930s forced not a few German housewives to join their husbands on the wage-lists of Elektrozavod.

At the top of the salary scales ranged US and British engineers with maximum salaries of $1,200–1,300 per month. Swiss or German engineers settled for roughly half this amount. Representatives of the

American firms "General Electric Co." or "Sperry Giroscope" were afforded special privileges: domestic servants, reimbursement of the costs of importing their Ford automobiles and other personal possessions, a free supply of tyres and other spare parts, or the service of an interpreter while on holidays.[11] Other engineers, often ideologically committed experts with service in the KPD or the American Communist Party (CPUSA), worked on "rouble only" contracts, earning roughly twice what their skilled countrymen were obtaining as machinists. An analysis of what Elektrozavod paid its employees from abroad in March 1931 shows that the average monthly earnings for craftsmen was 171 roubles, with engineers receiving 814 roubles. The engineers were divided into trainees, who were usually German craftsmen aspiring to engineer rank and earning 200–300 roubles monthly, and "real" engineers who could reach a salary of $1,300 (2,500 roubles).[12]

A guaranteed wage and part-payment in a foreign currency, the most striking features of individual contracts signed with skilled metalworkers in 1929-30, were soon abolished. The Soviet authorities involved, knowing that they were in a buyer's market in seeking skilled machinists among the millions in German dole-queues, lowered the guaranteed monthly wage from 250 to 150 roubles between December 1930 and October 1931.[13] The fixed wage was gradually phased out, as were percentage payments in Reichsmarks (RM) or dollars. The situation thus arose that foreign craftsmen doing basically comparative or identical work-tasks were not remunerated according to strict production criteria but on the basis of the contract they had signed or when they had joined Elektrozavod.

These unforeseen developments, anathema to workers proud of their skills and with a long tradition of trade union militancy, put considerable strains on internalised loyalties, both to the communist ideology and to the idea of a personal contribution to "building socialism". The ensuing conflicts must also be seen in the general wages-prices framework. First, during the initial three years of the First Five-Year Plan living costs rose between 150 and 200 percent, while nominal industrial earnings increased by merely a third, thus leading to a decline in real wages of about 50 percent.[14] Second, individual piece-rates rather than collective ones for brigades became the norm, and the *progressivka*, the scale of determining rates of pay once the work-norm had been reached, was introduced.[15] However, a unified system of progressive piece-rates never emerged, and the "time and motion man" (*normirovshchik*), who rarely had any technical education, could set the norms quite arbitrarily and thus manipulate the payment of piecework.

Preferential treatment for some kinds of foreigners was also evident in the supply of foodstuffs in Elektrozavod during the early 1930s, at a time of strict rationing and general shortages. All grades of employees could share the simple fare of the factory canteen (*stolovaia*), but the midday meal on offer often drew caustic comments from the Germans who missed their beloved beer.[16] Until March 1931 all foreigners, regardless of position in the factory hierarchy, were entitled to buy groceries in a closed cooperative store on the factory premises. The supply of goods, however, was erratic and the amount of items one could buy, while unlimited for engineers, was rationed for the craftsmen on the basis of their norm-fulfilment. Further restrictions of a later date excluded foreigners working on "roubles only" contracts from shopping in this closed system. As they did not possess the valued booklet for the INSNAB (shops reserved for foreigners) retail-chain either, they were not permitted to shop in these outlets, which sold groceries and clothes to foreigners at reduced rates in central Moscow. This discrimination was a source of deep resentment to class-conscious German metalworkers. Pleas to be issued with a special booklet for a closed food supply unit were usually turned down by VSNKh or VEO, despite proof that the scarce item, often meat or milk, was needed not for the worker himself but for his children who had caught infectious diseases like TB or were recovering from bouts of diphtheria and scarlet fever.[17] Further complaints arose when the closed cooperative in Elektrozavod raised its prices by 40 percent in 1931, at a time of falling piece-rates and, consequently, reduced wages.[18]

In order to alleviate the chronic food shortage, the People's Commissariat for Foreign Trade issued decrees in 1930 allowing all foreigners to receive, tax-free, a package from abroad every month: generous amounts of tinned foods, coffee, cocoa, tobacco, sugar, dairy products, soap, toothpaste and certain items of clothing and footwear.[19] This concession, an admission by the Soviet state that, despite all propaganda to the contrary, it could not cater for the most elementary needs of its foreign workforce, did not lead to any great improvements in the short term. The persons who made use of the duty-free food parcels were usually the American engineers, who, in any case, could shop at INSNAB with roubles or at the TORGSIN chain if they wished to expend foreign currency. The skilled workers, on the other hand, coming from industrial areas of Central Europe deep in economic depression, could not expect their pauperised relatives or friends in the homeland to send foodstuffs on a regular basis to Russia. Indeed, the plight of those left behind in Germany, Austria or

Czechoslovakia was sometimes so dire that they subsequently joined their husbands, sons or brothers in Moscow.

The abolition of the rationing system in 1935, while easing the supply situation, led to a sharp increase in the prices of basic foodstuffs, including bread. A modest improvement in the level of real wages at a time of continuing inflation took place in 1936–7: wages were increased during and after the Stakhanovite productivity campaigns, but the standard of living for most workers still fell behind that of 1928, the starting point of massive industrialisation.[20]

As in wage policy and food distribution, the accommodation offered to foreign staff at Elektrozavod was far better than the Russian mean, but contained strong differential elements which once again underlined the division within the *inokolonia* into qualified engineers and skilled metalworkers. Between 1926 and 1933 the amount of living space occupied by one person in the Soviet capital fell from $5.3m^2$ to $4.15m^2$, a consequence of the massive migration from the land to find work in the metropolis.[21] By 1935 only a half of all Moscow tenants – single persons or families – had one room or more at their disposal, with the remainder sharing one room, a kitchen or corridor floor, or a dormitory, with other parties.[22] The accommodation offered to the members of the Elektrozavod *inokolonia* was far superior, even if it fell well behind American or Central European standards. In the initial stage after arrival the German skilled workers found a place to sleep in the rooms occupied by their friends or colleagues; the engineers were put up in central Moscow hotels while a suitable apartment was being renovated.[23] This temporary arrangement, if prolonged, was frustrating as hotel guests were not allowed to cook in their rooms and found the meals in the hotel restaurant inordinately dear.[24] Some American engineers soon rejected the flat offered, complaining about the noise, dirt and untidy state of the courtyards.[25]

Most of the craftsmen from abroad were housed in a modern building (90 rooms) erected by Elektrozavod at Ulitsa Matrosskaia tishina 16, beside the famous Moscow prison of the same name. Almost 75,000 roubles were expended by Elektrozavod in 1931 to repair and furnish accommodation for its foreign employees, with average expenditure per engineer totalling 2,000-4,000 roubles, and 600-700 roubles for skilled men.[26] Nevertheless, conditions at Matrosskaia tishina were unbearable during the first winter (1930–1): some windows had no glass, plumbing and sanitation did not work properly and the central heating system broke down.[27] Another drawback was that the factory management had issued only one front-door key per apartment. As these flats were communal dwellings (*kommunalka*) with two to three families (or bachelors) in single rooms and sharing kitchen, bathroom and toilet, disputes were common. The tenants, mainly German, used to living in flats or houses with a separate entrance for each tenant, found that the *kommunalka* solution undermined privacy and family life.

Complaints from German shift-workers hindered from sleeping by drunken Russian neighbours were not taken seriously by the Elektrozavod management.[28] Equally unheeded were the expressions of disgust on the part of a German metalworker that the hallway of the house was being used as a public toilet because the lock of the front door was smashed.[29] Conditions in the other housing block put at the disposal of the factory's foreign workforce, at Pochtovaia ulitsa 18, were no better. Russian neighbours revelled night and day, the windows were defective, and, as putty was not available in Moscow stores, the German families were chronically sick in winter.[30]

The number of foreigners employed at Elektrozavod peaked at 170–180 in 1932 and declined subsequently, primarily because the practice of hiring staff from abroad on a contract basis was discontinued. Other reasons for the drop in numbers were the transfer of skilled staff to other enterprises and the decision of many craftsmen, especially Germans, to curtail or refuse to renew their contracts. That many of the latter returned home in the early years of Nazi power testifies to the process of disillusionment many had undergone since their arrival in Moscow – from dedicated communists to disillusioned returnees to the "New Order" in Germany which promised work for all. The shortfall in skilled operatives was offset to a certain degree by the arrival of a fresh intake – Austrian political immigrants (*Schutzbündler*), the defeated leftists of the Austrian Civil War (February 1934). Over 20 of their number took up employment in Elektrozavod from mid-1934, working mainly in the automobile and tractor electro-technical department (ATE). The majority were experienced craftsmen who had worked as turners, fitters or welders in prominent Viennese firms like Siemens-Schuckert, Waagner-Biró or Austro-Fiat.

The first noticeable wave of re-emigration began when the initial batch of one-year contracts expired in late 1931. By December of that year 25 contract workers from abroad had left the Soviet Union. Seventeen had terminated their agreements prematurely, the remaining eight refused to renew them.[31] Their more ideologically committed fellow-countrymen dubbed them "deserters from the front of Socialist construction".[32] As those who decided to leave Moscow sooner than expected had to give notice to management, we know the grounds they gave for leaving:

"political motives", "fear of an international war", and, more commonly, dissatisfaction with terms of employment or living conditions. A handful was given notice because of "professional incompetence", and at least two were sacked for holding "fascist views".[33] Some of these cases came before a general assembly of the workforce, the "comradely court" (*tovarishcheskii sud*), where their real problems (alcoholism or low earnings) were ignored and the poor work-record of the individual under scrutiny was put down to hostile political motives.[34]

Many Germans turned their back on the Soviet Union because their wives could not adjust to prevailing conditions, in particular the erratic supply and high prices for groceries, low family income or the intolerable life in the *kommunalka*. Paul Baumhart, a 54-year-old German communist, was dissatisfied with the drop in real wages after the introduction of differential piece-rates. He was transferred to another workshop, and although highly prized as a skilled operative, he returned home because the *Inobiuro* had treated him as a "troublemaker" and shuttled him back and forth between departments without his consent.[35]

Once privileges for foreign machinists had been abolished and they were employed on general terms, the amount of direct political interference increased. The foreign workers' cell of the VKP(b) in Elektrozavod, totalling 66 members in April 1932,[36] attempted to persuade the "unreliable elements" to stay. A campaign was also started to renounce German citizenship and take out Soviet naturalisation papers. From 1933 those who resisted all blandishments and bought tickets for the return journey were expelled from the VKP(b) cell.[37] Max Schmor and Rudolf Mühlberg, key workers in electric light bulb production since 1925, relented and became Soviet citizens in 1935, as did Erich Wittenberg, one of the authors of a German-language propaganda brochure on life in Elektrozavod (*Berliner Proleten erzählen vom Moskauer Elektrozawod*). His co-authors Fritz Pose and Erich Matte, however, had left the USSR one year before. Others prominent in the *inokolonia* followed this example: Otto Thiele, an elected member of Moscow City Council, gave notice in November 1935; Otto Horn, an ex-Osram employee who was regarded as one of the best "shock worker-inventors" voted with his feet after a series of clashes with the factory bureaucracy, the last being a dispute over the payment of a bonus for two inventions – an apparatus for pouring molten tin and a device to test electric light bulbs.[38] Veterans of the foreigner colony also departed because they refused to relinquish their German passports and others because their applications for Soviet citizenship had been turned down[39] – an example of the contradictory policies pursued by different bureaucracies of the Stalinist state.

Voluntary repatriation to fascist Germany was also motivated by the increasingly xenophobic tone of Russian propaganda. A hidden aspect of the widespread suspicion against foreigners regardless of their political views was the exchange of information between Inobiuro or *partkom* on the one hand, and NKTP or NKVD on the other. For example, a confidential directive from the Main Directorate of the Electrical Industry within NKTP (GET) demanded from the Inobiuro of Elektrozavod in May 1935 that it send data on the political opinions of all its foreign employees.[40] In accordance with the Central Committee decisions ordering the mass expulsion of foreigners in 1937, the *inokolonia* of Elektrozavod was informed that its members would be dismissed if they did not take out Soviet citizenship papers. The justification given for this ultimatum was the increasing importance of military hardware within the range of goods being produced in the electro-technical conglomerate.[41]

The few operatives from the original group of ex-Osram and AEG employees were all arrested by the NKVD and convicted in 1937–8. Some survived. Max Schmor served two camp terms. In 1955 he was released, a sick man who was united with his Russian wife in Moscow and managed to return to his old workplace. He died in Moscow in the 1960s.[42] His friend Rudolf Mühlberg was sentenced in 1938 to 10 years, but was released from banishment only in 1955. He emigrated to the GDR. His wife, Gertrude, had committed suicide after his arrest in 1938 by throwing herself from a fifth-storey window of Matrosskaia tishina 16.[43] Mental and physical torture was used to force the friends to incriminate themselves and others ("spying for Germany"). Included in the indictment against Schmor and Mühlberg was their Russian friend Moishe Zhelezniak, a leading Elektrozavod engineer who had supervised the activity and integration of the Osram group 13 years previously. He valued the Germans highly, praising openly their punctuality, exactitude, diligence and inventive skills. He was wont to say that the operatives from Berlin were "our best people". They were always welcome guests in his family apartment.[44] Such close links to Germans were grounds for arrest in 1937 and remarks of this kind could be distorted at will, providing the basis for an espionage charge. Zhelezniak died of tuberculosis in 1945 in Siberia shortly after his release ahead of schedule as "a terminally ill person". That he had survived the brutal prison and Gulag regime for such a long time, Zhelezniak told his daughter in 1945, could be attributed to the selflessness of his friend and fellow-prisoner Max Schmor: Zhelezniak was arrested in his summer suit on a warm autumn day in 1937, and suffering from the cold in the ensuing months, he was delighted to be given the present of a heavy woollen sweater by Schmor during a meeting in the exercise-yard of the Butyrka prison.[45]

That the invented indictment ("spying") in the Schmor-Mühlberg-Zhelezniak case did not end with capital sentences for the trio may have been due to the fact that they were arrested relatively early, in late August and early September 1937. Prior to arrest Zhelezniak was summoned twice to the Stalinsk District Committee of the VKP(b), for the second time on 17 August along with his friend Mühlberg. They faced a barrage of questions from the District Party secretary, his counterpart in the Elektrozavod Party cell and from a plain-clothes NKVD man. They wanted to know about those Germans from the plant who had already left the country. The District VKP(b) committee immediately issued the NKVD with the sanction to arrest Zhelezniak. The bureaucratic procedure to expel him from the Party began with a hastily convened lunchtime meeting of the factory VKP(b) committee on 19 August, and the expulsion resolution was confirmed at a general meeting of Party members at the factory 10 days later. Zhelezniak, arrested on 4 September, defended himself skilfully during the questioning sessions in Butyrka prison, demanding confrontations with Mühlberg who, according to the interrogator, had admitted that Zhelezniak had supplied him with details of Elektrozavod's production programme for espionage purposes. As this was a complete fabrication, the confrontation between the two friends in the presence of their interrogators in the Lubianka was called off. Included in Zhelezniak's NKVD file are some school copybooks in which the engineer had planned his defence strategy for the nightly interrogation sessions. He was confident of proving his innocence in an open court, but was denied the opportunity and sentenced *in absentia* by the Special Board at the end of December 1937. From his prison cell and Gulag camp Moishe Zhelezniak sent many petitions protesting his innocence. Bulganin, who had known Zhelezniak as the engineer in charge of the tungsten department when he himself was the managing director of Elektrozavod and took him on business trips abroad, did not answer the pleas. By the late 1930s, when Bulganin held the post of Deputy Chairman of the Council of People's Commissars, Zhelezniak's wife managed to overcome all bureaucratic barriers and was granted an audience with him. Bulganin insisted that he could not remember ever meeting his talented engineer.[46]

Other staff at Elektrozavod arrested in the Ezhov years fell victim to the *massoperatsii* of the Soviet secret police launched in late summer 1937, in particular following the issue of "German Order no. 00439 of the NKVD" (25 July 1937). Families of German, Jewish, Polish and Baltic origin were torn apart and the male breadwinners shot or sent to the camps. Alfons Huth, a founding-member of the KPD who knew Rosa Luxemburg and Karl Liebknecht, was a highly respected operative in the plant since 1931. His sons soon joined him in Moscow and all family members became Soviet citizens. Two worked with their father in Elektrozavod, another two studied medicine and Karl, the youngest, attended the Karl Liebknecht secondary school in the capital. Bernhard, Johannes, Paul and Bruno Huth were arrested in early 1938 and accused of complicity in the fictitious "Hitler-Jugend" plot. Paul, Bernhard and Johannes were executed in Butovo on 28 February 1938. Bruno disappeared into the Gulag system. Karl was not arrested, presumably because he was only 16 years of age when his brothers were taken into custody. Two years later, their father Alfons was arrested on the charge of "counter-revolutionary activities". He died in confinement and his wife Julia, banished from Moscow, starved to death in Siberia.[47]

The fate of the Zint family was similar. Bernhard, the father, had joined the KPD at its inception and moved with his family to Moscow in 1931. He was arrested in 1938 and sentenced to eight years. Bernhard Zint died in prison; his son Otto was shot in Butovo in February 1938.[48] Erich Wittenberg, an employee of Elektrozavod since 1930, was expelled by the Party committee in the factory in late 1937 because of links with "enemies of the people" and because he corresponded with relatives in his native Germany. He was sentenced on an espionage charge to eight years in the camps and died in Kolyma within the year. Peter Holm, a fellow German, relented under torture and incriminated Wittenberg. The interrogator on the case was questioned in 1956. He described the investigation "methods" he used in early 1938:

> When I was interrogating Peter Holm in Taganka prison Deputy Narkom Zakovskii and the Deputy Head of the Moscow Administration Iakubovich paid a visit to my office. Holm was standing by the wall, and Zakovskii came up to me. He abused me in foul language and screamed, "So this is how you are carrying on!" He then kicked Holm in the stomach and said, "That's the way to interrogate, none of your persuasion". Iakubovich added, "Show him the ABC of Communism" and then left.[49]

Among the victims from the electrical combine workforce were also the remnants of the group of skilled workers recruited in the USA in

1931. Michael Martinson, shot in Butovo on 29 May 1938,[50] had emigrated from Estonia to New York with his parents. As a qualified fitter with over 20 years' experience and a good command of the Russian language, Martinson was promoted several times within the plant, achieved *udarnik* (shockworker) status, joined the VKP(b) and became a Soviet citizen.[51] Adam Hayer, a brigadeer in Elektrozavod, was from a similar background. A native of Bobruisk (Belorussia), Hayer joined the socialist Jewish Bund at an early age, and, in order to escape another prison sentence or term of banishment in Tsarist Russia, emigrated with his family to America. He subsequently took out naturalisation papers, joined the CPUSA and also made the acquaintance of the New York police in the pursuit of his political goals. Hayer exchanged his US passport for a Soviet one in 1933, but the charges levelled at him by NKVD tormentors five years later had nothing to do with past or present loyalties: he was accused of "spying for Germany" and sentenced to eight years in a "corrective work camp". Adam Hayer died in January 1939, shortly after his arrival in Kolyma.[52]

Karl Schreder from Berlin, arrested on 3 March 1938, was a typical victim of mass operations. The welding instructor, who had been characterised in 1933 by the Elektrozavod management as "a good and valuable operative",[53] was forced under torture to admit being an agent of German Intelligence ordered to collect details of production at his workplace. This was supplemented some days later by another fictitious "commission" which echoed the Kremlin's fear of a "Fifth Column", namely planning sabotage in the factory after the war with Germany had broken out. Sentenced to eight years in the Kotlas Gulag complex in June 1938, Schreder died two years later.[54] His daughter remembers what she subsequently found out about her father's time in prison:

> One man, a Czech by nationality, shared the same cell as my father but was released. He told us of the state my father was in when he was pushed back into the cell after the final interrogation bout before being sent to the camps – he was not a human being, more a piece of bloody meat.[55]

Further micro-studies on foreigners working in Soviet factories during the 1930s are required before assessing the comparability of the experiences shared by the foreigner contingent in Elektrozavod. The relatively high proportion of Germans employed in the electro-technical complex was not unusual and conforms to the overall national composition of foreign staff employed by NKTP.[56] What was specific in the recruitment of foreign labour by Elektrozavod was that it began relatively early (mid-1920s) and was a concerted effort to use the latest developments in German electrical technology to expand a nascent production sector. Acquiring German craftsmen with the specific skills through the mediation of the communist movement suggests that the indirect method of industrial espionage employed by the Elektrozavod management may have been more common than imagined.

Comparative studies might also show that the conditions of employment for foreigners in Elektrozavod were the best available in Moscow and surpassed what could be offered in other urban centres and new industrial sites.[57] The electrical factory combine, however, suffered from the general disorganisation caused by lack of spare parts and raw materials, by constantly revised production limits and changing work-schedules. In 1933, for instance, twenty percent of the electric light bulb production had to be rejected, and the functioning bulbs, it was found, burned for only 400–500 instead of the intended 800–900 hours.[58] Low productivity – the average Soviet worker in 1933 spent only five to five and a half hours of his working day actually working[59] – was due in part to lax discipline. As late as 1937 one observer noted that Elektrozavod resembled more a department store than a factory, with long queues at any time of the day stretching from the book kiosk or the ice-cream seller.[60]

While the general factory-floor atmosphere of stop-go and improvisation may have caused frustration among foreign staff in Elektrozavod or encouraged the inventive skills of the more ideologically committed, the sources are unequivocal that the unilateral, and illegal, changes in the terms of employment led to the first breach of trust. The piece-rate remuneration system, the bane of trade unionists everywhere at that time, was a further example of how the needs of Soviet industry (raising productivity levels) clashed with Western Marxist conceptions of working-class solidarity. In the end, this contradiction outweighed the incontestably privileged status enjoyed by the foreigners in other spheres.

Finally, as regards the terror, the core adherents of the *inokolonia* in Elektrozavod had left the country before the onset of mass arrests. Their replacements, political refugees, having no choice but to remain, were arrested in 1937–8 along with the German craftsmen who had become Soviet citizens. David Hoffman holds that "the purges" in Moscow factories "remained very much an elite phenomenon ... while few rank-and file workers were victimized".[61] This is what Party dossiers indicate, but the files of prisoners in NKVD custody recount a different strategy: the arrest of most foreign-born workers somewhat later, when mass operations commenced in the summer of 1937. Charges based on factory affairs, production mishaps or political "deviation", however, rarely surface in the files opened by the NKVD on the foreign employees of Elektrozavod taken into custody in 1937–8: they were repressed solely on "national" criteria, victims of a prophylactic policy of mass repression in a pre-war emergency.

Notes

1. This chapter is a summary of my study of foreign workers in Elektrozavod – Sergei Zhuravlev, *'Malen'kie liudi' i 'bolshaia istoriia'. Inostrantsy moskovskogo Elektrozavoda v sovetskom obshchestve 1920-kh-1930-kh gg.* (Moscow, 2000).
2. A. Gambarov, *Sovetskaia elektrolampa* (Moscow, 1932); *Zavod i liudi* (Moscow, 1968); *Pravda*, 5 November 1928.
3. *Zavod i liudi*, p. 71.
4. The plant signed a trade agreement to supply British buyers with tungsten filament in 1937. See Central Municipal Archive for the City of Moscow, (TsMAM), f. 2090, op. 1, d. 1870.
5. *Zavod i liudi*, p. 80.
6. *Izmeneniia v chislennosti i sostave sovetskogo rabochego klassa* (Moscow, 1961), pp. 38–9.
7. F. Pose, E. Matte and E. Wittenberg, *Berliner Proleten erzählen vom Moskauer Elektrozawod* (Moscow, 1932), pp. 8–9.
8. Such contracts are held in the *lichnyi sostav* (personal file of the foreigner, hereafter: LS) in TsMAM, f. 2090, op. 2.
9. GARF, f. 5451, op. 39, d. 5, ll. 22–7; TsMAM, f. 2090, op. 1, d. 637, ll. 1, 19–25; f. 2090, op. 1, d. 833.
10. TsMAM, f. 2090, op. 1, d. 637, l. 52. This was the situation in March 1931.
11. TsMAM, f. 2090, op. 2, LS 95, l. 5; LS 76, l. 31.
12. TsMAM, f. 2090, op. 1, d. 637, l. 52.
13. TsMAM, f. 2090, op. 1, d. 637, l. 25.
14. Solomon M. Schwarz, *Labor in the Soviet Union* (New York, 1952), pp. 137–9.
15. Lewis H. Siegelbaum, *Stakhanovism and the Politics of Productivity in the USSR, 1935–1941* (Cambridge, 1988), p. 48.
16. TsMAM, f. 2090, op. 2, LS 80 , l. 4.
17. TsMAM, f. 2090, op. 2, LS 14, ll. 11–13, 21.
18. TsMAM, f. 2090, op. 2, LS 89, l. 4; f. 2090, op. 1, d. 832, ll. 2–4.
19. Copies of these decrees are contained in the LS files.
20. See the discussion on these points in Schwarz, *Labor*, pp.157–63; Alec Nove, *An Economic History of the USSR* (Harmondsworth, 1978), pp. 248–50.
21. Timothy Sosnovsky, *The Housing Problem in the Soviet Union* (New York, 1954), p. 112.
22. Nove, *Economic History*, pp. 250–1.
23. TsMAM, f. 2090, op. 2, LS 37, l. 48; LS 92, l. 7.
24. TsMAM, f. 2090, op. 2, LS 44.

25 TsMAM, f. 2090, op. 2, LS 125, ll. 13–14.
26 TsMAM, f. 2090, op. 1, d. 637, ll. 3–4.
27 TsMAM, f. 2090, op. 1, d. 637, l. 23; f. 2090, op. 2, LS 7, l. 18; LS 37, l. 48.
28 TsMAM, f. 2090, op. 2, LS 49, l. 34.
29 TsMAM, f. 2090, op. 2, LS 82, l. 7.
30 TsMAM, f. 2090, op. 2, LS 49, l. 34; LS 50, l. 4.
31 TsMAM, f. 2090, op. 1, d. 637, ll. 19–25; f. 2090, op. 1, d. 833, l. 27; GARF, f. 5451, op. 39, d. 5, ll. 22–47.
32 Wilhelm Baumert, 'Inostrannye rabochie na Elektrozavode', *Dogonim i peregonim* (factory magazine), October 1932, pp. 66–7; RGASPI, f. 17, op. 98, d. 2115.
33 TsMAM, f. 2090, op. 1, d. 637, ll. 19–25; f. 2090, op. 1, d. 833, l. 27; GARF, f. 5351, op. 39, d. 5, ll. 22–47.
34 TsMAM, f. 2090, op. 2, LS 80; LS 95, ll. 3, 11, 11 reverse.
35 TsMAM, f. 2090, op. 2, LS 5.
36 GARF, f. 5451, op. 39, d. 5, ll. 22–47; TsMAM, f. 2090, op. 1, d. 637.
37 See, for example, the case of Richard Michaelis: TsMAM, f. 2090, op. 2, LS 84, l. 3; RGASPI, f. 17, op. 98, d. 3306.
38 TsMAM, f. 2090, op. 1, d. 824, ll. 19–23, 35; f. 2090, op. 1, d. 825, l. 11; f. 2090, op. 2, LS 37, ll. 7, 8, 17, 21; LS 21; LS 108; RGASPI, f. 17, op. 98, d. 3728 and d. 3730.
39 TsMAM, f. 2090, op. 2, LS 54, 66, 72, 75, 123, 128, 140, 141.
40 TsMAM, f. 2090, op. 2, LS 99, l. 114.
41 TsMAM, f. 2090, op. 2, LS 66, l. 5.
42 TsMAM, f. 2090, op. 2, LS 133; f. 2090, op. 1, d. 825, l. 1; Interview with Indebor Zhelezniak, 25 April 1994.
43 RGASPI, f. 495, op. 292, d. 101, l. 10; GARF, f. 10035, NKVD investigation file no. P-40522 (Schmor, Muhlberg, Zhelezniak).
44 GARF, f. 10035, NKVD investigation files no. P-61307 Paul Schweitzer, p. 27 and P-40522 (Schmor, Muhlberg, Zhelezniak).
45 Interview with Indebor Zhelezniak, 25 April 1994.
46 Ibid; GARF, f. 10035, NKVD investigation file no. P-40522.
47 TsMAM, f. 2090, op. 2, LS 41; L. A. Golovkova (ed.) *Butovskii poligon 1937–38. Kniga pamiati zhertv politicheskikh repressii. Vypusk vtoroi* (Moscow, 1998), p. 150.
48 TsMAM, f. 2090, op. 2, LS 124; *Martirolog rasstreliannykh i zakhoronennykh na poligone NKVD 'Ob"ekt Butovo', 08.08.1937–19.10.1938* (Moscow, 1997), p. 371.
49 GARF, f. 10035, NKVD investigation file no. P-32590 Erich Wittenberg, pp. 39, 43.
50 *Martirolog rasstreliannykh*, p. 218.
51 GARF, f. 5451, op. 75, d. 11, ll. 216–17. Biographical information on Martinson can also be found in L. A. Golovkova (ed.) *Butovskii poligon 1937–38. Kniga pamiati zhertv politicheskikh repressii. Vypusk chetvertyi* (Moscow, 2000), p. 137; and Hoover Institution Archives (Stanford University, USA), Adam Hochschild Collection.
52 For a copy of Adam Hayer's NKVD investigation file, see Hoover Institution Archives, Adam Hochschild Collection.
53 TsMAM, f. 2090, op. 21s, d. 136, l. 10.

54 GARF, f. 10035, NKVD investigation file no. P-48416 Karl Schreder, pp. 13–17.
55 Letter of Irma Schreder to Natalia Musienko, 7 May 1994.
56 Seventy employees, attached to the Soviet consular service, were employed in Germany during the early 1930s to recruit foreign expertise. See S. Zhuravlev and V. Tiazhel'nikova, 'Inostrannaia koloniia v sovetskoi rossii v 1920-1930-e gody', *Otechestvennaia istoriia*, no. 1 (1994), p. 181.
57 Better than those prevailing in Magnitogorsk in the early 1930s. See John Scott, *Behind the Urals: An American Worker in Russia's City of Steel. Enlarged edition prepared by Stephen Kotkin* (Bloomington, 1989).
58 Hans-Henning Schroeder, *Industrialisierung und Parteibürokratie in der Sowjetunion. Ein sozialgeschichtlicher Versuch über die Anfangsphase des Stalinismus, 1928–1934* (Berlin, 1988), p. 301.
59 Robert Maier, *Die Stachanow-Bewegung* (Stuttgart, 1990), p. 29.
60 Donald Filtzer, 'Labor Discipline, the Use of Work Time, and the Decline of the Soviet System, 1928–1991', *International Labor and Working Class History*, no. 50 (1996), p. 18.
61 David L. Hoffman, 'The Great Terror on the Local Level: Purges in Moscow Factories, 1936–1938', in J. Arch Getty and Roberta T. Manning (eds), *Stalinist Terror: New Perspectives* (Cambridge, 1993), p. 165.

Select Bibliography

We have included only English-language sources and have concentrated on those books and articles that have appeared since the opening of the Russian archives in the early 1990s. Please consult the notes to the chapters for the voluminous Russian- and German-language literature on Stalinist Terror.

Banac, I. (ed.), *The Diary of Georgi Dimitrov, 1933–1949* (New Haven and London, 2003).
Benvenuti, F., 'Industry and Purge in the Donbas, 1936–37', *Europe-Asia Studies*, vol. 45 (1993), pp. 57–78.
Binner, R. and Junge, M., 'The Great Terror in the Provinces of the USSR, 1937–1938: A Cooperative Bibliography', *Cahiers du Monde russe*, vol. 42 (2001), pp. 679–96.
Blitstein, P. A., 'Selected Bibliography of Recently Published Document Collections on Soviet History', *Cahiers du Monde russe*, vol. 40 (1999), pp. 307–26.
Chase, W. J., *Enemies within the Gates?: The Comintern and the Stalinist Repression, 1934–1939* (New Haven and London, 2001).
Conquest, R., *Inside Stalin's Secret Police: NKVD Politics, 1936–39* (London, 1985).
Conquest, R., *The Great Terror: Stalin's Purges of the Thirties* (Harmondsworth, 1971), up-dated as *The Great Terror: A Reassessment* (London, 1990).
Davies, S., *Popular Opinion in Stalin's Russia: Terror, Propaganda and Dissent, 1934–1941* (Cambridge, 1997).
Davies, S., 'The Crime of "Anti-Soviet Agitation" in the Soviet Union in the 1930s', *Cahiers du Monde russe*, vol. 39 (1998), pp. 149–68.
Davies, S., '"Us" against "Them": Social Identity in Soviet Russia, 1934–41', in S. Fitzpatrick (ed.), *Stalinism: New Directions* (London, 2000), pp. 47–70.
Ellman, M., 'The Soviet 1937 Provincial Show Trials: Carnival or Terror?', *Europe-Asia Studies*, vol. 53 (2001), pp. 1221–33.
Fitzpatrick, S., 'New Perspectives on Stalinism', *Russian Review*, vol. 45 (1986), pp. 357–73.
Fitzpatrick, S., 'How the Mice Buried the Cat. Scenes from the Great Purges of 1937 in the Russian Provinces', *Russian Review*, vol. 52 (1993), pp. 299–320.
Fitzpatrick, S., *Stalin's Peasants: Resistance and Survival in the Russian Village after Collectivisation* (Oxford, 1994).
Fitzpatrick, S., *Everyday Stalinism: Ordinary Life in Extraordinary Times: Soviet Russia in the 1930s* (Oxford, 1999).
Fitzpatrick, S., (ed.), *Stalinism: New Directions* (London, 2000).
Freeze, G., 'The Stalinist Assault on the Parish, 1929–1941', in M. Hildermeier and E. Müller-Luckner (eds), *Stalinismus vor dem Zweiten Weltkrieg. Neue Wege der Forschung* (Munich, 1998), pp. 209–32.
Gelb, M., '"Karelian Fever": The Finnish Immigrant Community during Stalin's Purges', *Europe-Asia Studies*, vol. 45 (1993), pp. 1091–116.

Gelb, M., 'An Early Soviet Ethnic Deportation: The Far-Eastern Koreans', *Russian Review*, vol. 54 (1995), pp. 389–412.
Gelb, M., 'Ethnicity during the Ezhovshchina: A Historiography', in J. D. Morison (ed.), *Ethnic and National Issues in Russian and East European History* (Basingstoke, 2000), pp. 192–213.
Getty, J. A., 'Party and Purge in Smolensk, 1933–1937', *Slavic Review*, vol. 42 (1983), pp. 60–79.
Getty, J. A., *Origins of the Great Purges: The Soviet Communist Party Reconsidered, 1933–1938* (Cambridge, 1985).
Getty, J. A. and Manning, R. T. (eds), *Stalinist Terror: New Perspectives* (Cambridge, 1993).
Getty, J. A., Rittersporn, G. T. and Zemskov, V. N., 'Victims of the Soviet Penal System in the Prewar Years: A First Approach on the Basis of Archival Evidence', *American Historical Review*, vol. 98 (1993), pp. 1017–49.
Getty, J. A., 'Afraid of Their Shadows: The Bolshevik Recourse to Terror, 1932–1938', in M. Hildermeier and E. Müller-Luckner (eds), *Stalinismus vor dem Zweiten Weltkrieg: Neue Wege der Forschung* (Munich, 1998), pp. 169–91.
Getty, J. A., and Naumov, O. V., *The Road to Terror: Stalin and the Self-destruction of the Bolsheriks, 1932–1939* (New Haven and London, 1999)
Getty, J. A., '"Excesses are not permitted": Mass Terror and Stalinist Governance in the Late 1930s', *Russian Review*, vol. 61 (2002), pp. 113–38.
Hagenloh, P., '"Socially Harmful Elements" and the Great Terror', in Fitzpatrick (ed.), *Stalinism: New Directions*, pp. 286–308.
Harris, J. R., 'The Purging of Local Cliques in the Urals Region, 1936–7', in Fitzpatrick (ed.), *Stalinism: New Directions*, pp. 262–85.
Ilic, M., 'The Great Terror in Leningrad: A Quantitative Analysis', *Europe-Asia Studies*, vol. 52 (2000), pp. 1515–34.
Jansen, M. and Petrov, N., *Stalin's Loyal Executioner: People's Commissar Nikolai Ezhov, 1895–1940* (Stanford, 2002).
Kershaw, I. and Lewin, M. (eds), *Stalinism and Nazism: Dictatorships in Comparison* (Cambridge, 1997).
Khlevniuk, O. V., 'The Reasons for the "Great Terror": The Foreign-Political Aspect', in S. Pons and A. Romano (eds), *Russia in the Age of Wars, 1914–1945* (Milan, 2000), pp. 159–69.
Khlevnyuk, O. V., 'The Objectives of the Great Terror, 1937–1938', in J. Cooper, E. A. Rees and M. Perrie, (eds), *Soviet History, 1917–1953: Essays in Honour of R. W. Davies* (Basingstoke, 1995) pp. 158–76.
Khrushchev, N., *The Secret Speech Delivered to the Closed Session of the Twentieth Congress of the Communist Party of the Soviet Union* (London, 1976).
Kotkin, S., *Magnetic Mountain: Stalinism as a Civilization* (Berkeley, 1995).
Kun, M., *Stalin: An Unknown Portrait* (Budapest, 2003).
Kuromiya, H., 'Stalinist Terror in the Donbas: A Note', in J. A. Getty and R. A. Manning (eds), *Stalinist Terror*, pp. 215–22.
Kuromiya, H., *Freedom and Terror in the Donbas: A Ukrainian-Russian Borderland, 1870s-1990s* (Cambridge, 1998).
Lih, L. T., Naumov, O. V. and Khlevniuk, O. V. (eds), *Stalin's Letters to Molotov, 1925–1936* (New Haven and London, 1995).
Manning, R. T., 'The Great Purges in a Rural District: Belyi Raion Revisited', in Getty and Manning (eds), *Stalinist Terror*, pp. 168–97.

Martin, T., 'The Origins of Soviet Ethnic Cleansing', *Journal of Modern History*, vol. 70 (1998), pp. 813–61.
Martin, T., *The Affirmative Action Empire: Nations and Nationalism in the Soviet Union, 1923–1939* (Ithaca, 2001).
McDermott, K. and Agnew, J., *The Comintern: A History of International Communism from Lenin to Stalin* (Basingstoke, 1996).
McLoughlin, B., 'Documenting the Death Toll: Research into the Mass Murder of Foreigners in Moscow, 1937–1938', *Perspectives* (American Historical Association Newsletter), vol. 37 (1999), pp. 29–33.
McLoughlin, B., 'Visitors and Victims: British Communists in Russia between the Wars', in J. McIlroy, K. Morgan and A. Campbell (eds), *Party People, Communist Lives. Explorations in Biography* (London, 2001), pp. 210–30.
Medvedev, R. A., *Let History Judge: The Origins and Consequences of Stalinism*, 2nd edn (Oxford, 1989).
Medvedev, Z. and Medvedev, R., *The Unknown Stalin*, (London, 2003).
Pohl, J. O., *The Stalinist Penal System. A Statistical History of Soviet Repression and Terror, 1930–1953* (North Carolina and London, 1997).
Pohl, O., *Ethnic Cleansing in the USSR, 1937–49* (Westport, 1999).
Popov, V. P., 'State Terror in Soviet Russia, 1923–1953', *Russian Social Science Review*, vol. 35 (1994), pp. 48–70.
Rees, E. A. 'The Great Terror: Suicide or Mass Murder?', *Russian Review*, vol. 59 (2000), pp. 446–50.
Rees, E. A. (ed.), *The Nature of Stalin's Dictatorship: The Politburo, 1924–1953* (Basingstoke, 2004).
Rimmel, L. A., 'A Microcosm of Terror, or Class Warfare in Leningrad: The March 1935 Exile of "Alien Elements"', *Jahrbucher für Geschichte Osteuropas*, vol. 48 (2000), pp. 528–51.
Rittersporn, G. T., *Stalinist Simplifications and Soviet Complications: Social Tensions and Political Conflicts in the USSR, 1933–1953* (Chur, 1991).
Rittersporn, G. T., 'The Omnipresent Conspiracy: On Soviet Imagery of Politics and Social Relations in the 1930s', in Getty and Manning (eds), *Stalinist Terror*, pp. 99–115.
Rogovin, V. Z., *1937: Stalin's Year of Terror* (Oak Park, 1998).
Sanukov, K., 'Stalinist Terror in the Mari Republic. The Attack on "Finno-Ugrian Bourgeois Nationalism"', *Slavonic and East European Review*, vol. 74 (1996), pp. 658–82.
Sebag Montefiore, S., *Stalin: The Court of the Red Tsar* (London, 2003).
Shearer, D. R., 'Crime and Social Disorder in Stalin's Russia: A Reassessment of the Great Retreat and the Origins of Mass Repression', *Cahiers du Monde russe*, vol. 39 (1998), pp. 119–48.
Shearer, D., 'Policing the Soviet Frontier: Social Disorder and Repression in Western Siberia during the 1930s', unpublished paper, 1998.
Siegelbaum, L. H. and Suny, R. G. (eds), *Making Workers Soviet: Power, Class and Identity* (Ithaca, 1994).
Siegelbaum, L. and Sokolov, A. (eds), *Stalinism as a Way of Life: A Narrative in Documents* (New Haven and London, 2000).
Solomon, P. H. Jr, *Soviet Criminal Justice under Stalin* (Cambridge, 1996).
Starkov, B. A., 'Narkom Ezhov', in Getty and Manning (eds), *Stalinist Terror*, pp. 21–39.

Starkov, B. A., 'The Trial That Was Not Held', *Europe-Asia Studies*, vol. 46 (1994), pp. 1297–315.
Thurston, R. W., *Life and Terror in Stalin's Russia, 1934–1941* (New Haven and London, 1996).
Tucker, R. C., *Stalin in Power: The Revolution from Above, 1928–1941* (New York, 1990).
Volkogonov, D., *Stalin: Triumph and Tragedy* (London, 1991).
Weinberg, R., 'Purge and Politics in the Periphery: Birobidzhan in 1937', *Slavic Review*, vol. 52 (1993), pp. 13–27.
Weitz, E. D., 'Racial Politics without the Concept of Race: Reevaluating Soviet Ethnic and National Purges', *Slavic Review*, vol. 61 (2002), pp. 1–29.

Index

Abramov-Mirov, A. L., 202–3
Afghan nationals, 123
Agranov, Iakov, 41, 93
agriculture
  collectivisation, 36, 65–6, 88–9
  de-kulakisation operations, 86, 88, 93, 99, 106
  sabotage and wrecking charges, 12, 42, 197–8, 200, 204
  see also kulaks
"album" procedure, 11, 159–63, 164, 166–7, 171
American experts at Elektrozavod plant, 227–8, 235–6
Andreev, A. A., 128
Angaretis, Zigmas, 75
Anglo-American studies of Stalinism, 3–4
"anti-Soviet" suspects, 51, 93, 119
  lists of suspects, 126–7
  Order No. 00447, 24, 42, 103–111, 112, 119, 120, 123–44, 153–4, 195–6
  see also counter-revolution; kulaks
archives, 1
  access to, 2, 3, 5, 17n
  on Comintern, 56–7, 175–6
  on mass operations, 118–19, 164
  of NKVD, 3, 35, 195
  on show trials, 34–6
Arendt, Hannah, 144
arrest quotas (limity), 125, 133–4, 140, 194, 196, 205
  authorisation of, 120, 129–30
  confession quotas, 135, 194, 213–14
  lists and arbitrary choice of suspects, 126–7, 134, 206, 214
  quotas for death sentences, 129–30, 132, 133
atheist movement, 124
Austrian Communist Party, 175, 189, 191n
  see also "Hitler-Jugend conspiracy"

Austrian political immigrants (Schutzbündler), 208, 231

Barkov, I. I., 98–9
Baumhart, Paul, 232
Beimler, Hans, Jr, 217, 218
Beimler, Hans, Sr, 217–18
Belov see Damianov, Georgii
Bel'skii, L. N., 112
Berg, Bronislaw (Witold Salzberg), 71–2
Beria, Lavrentii, 29, 31, 32, 206, 218
  appointed Ezhov's deputy, 27
  and deceleration of mass operations, 76, 163, 206, 212
  purge of NKVD, 195
  succeeds Ezhov, 49, 103
Bessonov, S. A., 43, 48
Braude, Ilia, 47
Brest-Litovsk transfers, 218–19
British Communist Party, 175, 183, 184
British Secret Service, 46
Brückmann, Georg (Albert Müller), 71
Bukharin, Nikolai Ivanovich, 38, 39, 61, 62, 64
  allegations of plans to assassinate Lenin, 42, 43, 44, 46
  correspondence and writings archive, 35
  execution, 50
  family tribulations, 50
  indictment details, 43–5
  show trial, 8, 24, 40–50, 67, 199–200
Bukharin, Vladimir, 50
Bulatov, D. A., 25
Bulganin, Nikolai, 225, 226, 234
Bulgarian Socialist Party archive, 57
Burkhardt (Commissar of Polish State Intelligence), 73

Butovo village
  executions at, 75, 135, 138
  mass graves at, 1
  see also death sentences

cadre reviews, 9, 177–80, 209
  self-criticism ritual, 11–12, 175–90, 197
Cadres Department of the Central Committee, 36, 38, 209
Cadres Department of Executive Committee of the Communist International, 9, 68, 69–74, 209
capital punishment *see* death sentences
Carr, E. H., 77*n*
Central Archive of the Federal Security Service of the Russian Federation (TsAFSBRF), 34
Central Committee of the All-Union Communist Party (Bolsheviks) *see* VKP(b)
Central Party Archive (RGASPI), 17*n*, 34, 175–6
Cheka, 96
  see also GUGB; NKVD; OGPU
Chernomordik, Moisei, 70
Chernov, N. A., 200
children
  mass round-ups of orphans, 100
  of Polish suspects, 158
Children's Home No. 6, Moscow, 219
Chinese nationals, 128
Chobianu, Maria (Helena Filipovic), 75
Chuianov, A. S., 29
Cichowski, Kazimierz, 72
class struggle, 88, 113
clergy: mass operations against, 120, 123–4
collectivisation, 36, 65–6, 88–9
  accusations of wrecking in Kuntsevo district, 197–8, 200, 204
  de-kulakisation operations, 86, 88, 93, 99, 106
Comintern (Communist International)
  anti-Trotskyist campaign, 57, 63–7
  archival evidence, 3, 56–7, 175–6
  involvement in mass operations, 6, 8, 9, 57, 67–75, 77, 135
  operations against, 56, 66, 74, 75–7, 142–3
  role in "Hitler-Jugend" operation, 216–21
  schools, 74, 176, 182
  show-trial propaganda, 57–61, 63–4, 67
  see also Executive Committee of the Communist International; foreign communists
Commissariat... *see* People's Commissariat...
Communist International, 59, 65, 67
Communist Party *see* VKP(b)
Communist University of Western National Minorities (KUNMZ), 74, 182, 186
confessions
  biographical details, 189–90
  "conveyor" method, 199
  of foreign communists, 188–9, 235
  of "Hitler-Jugend" suspects, 213–14, 215, 220
  NKVD techniques for extracting, 72, 127–8, 134–5, 199, 205, 215, 220, 235, 236
  quotas for, 135, 194, 213–14
  of show-trial defendants, 62, 63–4
Conquest, Robert, 134
counter-revolution
  mass operations against, 107–13, 119, 121, 135–6
  threat from socially harmful elements, 92–3, 96–7, 104–5, 124
  underground movements, 105
  see also anti-Soviet suspects; espionage; "Hitler-Jugend conspiracy"
Cowe, Bill (Watson), 184
CPGB *see* British Communist Party
criminal population, 85, 86, 92–3, 101, 104, 124, 131–2, 139
  Order No. 00192, 97–9
  organised crime, 90–1
  regulation of passport violations by, 96–7

criticism and self-criticism ritual,
    11–12, 175–90, 197
  learning experience for foreign
    communists, 181–8
  protocol for, 178–9
  as tool in mass operations, 188–90
  as "unmasking" process, 185–6

Damerius, Helmut, 215, 220
Damianov, Georgii (Belov), 71
Davies, Sarah, 119
de-kulakisation operations, 86, 88, 93,
  99, 106
deaf mutes' association, 136
death sentences, 135–9, 141, 143
  of agricultural wreckers, 42
  for German nationals, 209–12
  for "Hitler-Jugend" suspects, 215
  for invalids, 136–7
  nationalities of victims, 135, 138,
    139, 164
  for Polish nationals, 162–3, 170–71
  quotas for, 129–30, 132, 133
  "shooting regulations", 130–1
  under Order No. 00447, 131–4,
    141
defectors, 156, 164–5
Deutsche Zentral-Zeitung, 209, 219
"deviationists", 36, 37, 38–9, 41
Dimitrov, Georgi, 9, 56–77, 216, 219,
  221
  anti-Trotskyist campaign, 63–7
  appeals to, 217
  clemency for "Hitler-Jugend"
    suspects, 217–18
  diary archive, 56–7
  repression of foreign communists,
    67–75, 218
  support for show trials, 58–62
disabled people, 136–7
Dmitriev, D. M., 167
dvoiki, 119, 159, 160

Eikhe, Robert, 104, 105, 108
Eisen, Erich, 74
Elektrozavod plant, Moscow, 13,
  225–38
  background and status of plant,
    225–6

foreign expertise at, 225, 226–8
  living conditions, 229–31, 232
  naturalisation campaign, 232–3
  piecework system, 228, 232, 237
  productivity deficit, 237
  wage ranges, 227–8, 232
elite purges, 3, 6, 8, 10, 107
  comparison with mass operations,
    119–20, 143–4
  ECCI members, 9, 56, 68, 74, 75–7
  in Kuntsevo district, 197–206
  of NKVD, 27–32, 39, 41, 88, 103,
    195, 219–20
  VKP(b) members, 23–4, 26, 27,
    36–9, 49, 178–80
  see also cadre reviews; show trials
Enukidze, Abel, 23
Ercoli *see* Togliatti, Palmiro
espionage
  fear of foreigners, 12–13, 68–70,
    120–2, 163–4, 165, 216
  Germans accused of, 120, 122, 123,
    202–6, 208–12, 233–8
  Poles accused of, 154–5, 159, 161,
    165
  show-trial allegations of, 44, 45, 46,
    47
  see also "Hitler-Jugend conspiracy"
ethnic minorities *see* "national"
  operations
executions *see* death sentences
Executive Committee of the
  Communist International (ECCI)
  anti-Trotskyist campaign, 57, 64–6
  Cadre Department/cadre reviews, 9,
    68, 69–74, 178–9, 180, 209
  supportive role in terror, 9, 57, 58,
    67–75, 77
  as victims of terror, 9, 56, 68, 74,
    75–7
Ezhov, Nikolai, 8, 21
  appeals to, 198–9
  becomes NKVD Commissar, 39,
    102, 103
  career path, 36
  elevation to Politburo, 26
  end of reign of terror, 14, 32, 49,
    139, 206
  expulsion of Trotskyist supporters, 38

"From Fractionalism", 8, 34–5, 40, 46
on mass operations against foreigners, 122, 128, 212
NKVD/GUGB reform, 102–3
Order No. 00447 (anti-Soviet elements), 103–11, 119
Order No. 00485 (Polish Order), 153, 154, 158
sanctions "album" procedure, 11, 159, 160
stages show trials, 8, 34–52
at VKP(b) plenum and speech, 24, 25, 61, 87–9
Ezhovshchina see mass operations

families see victims' families
Federal Security Service (FSB), 2
Feuchtwanger, Lion, 59–60, 62–3
Feyerherd, Alexander, 204, 205
Feyerherd, Bertha, 203
Feyerherd, Lydia, 203–4, 206
Feyerherd, Willi, 205
"fifth column" paranoia, 8, 10, 12–13, 37, 104–5, 107–11, 142–3, 163, 165
Filatov, N. A., 198
Filipovic, Helena (Maria Chobianu), 75
Finnish nationals: mass operations against, 120, 121, 122, 123, 128
Firsov, Fridrikh, 218
Fitzpatrick, Sheila, 54*n*
Fleischer, Stefan (Ivan Grzetic), 75
Fokin, F. (head of police passport department), 93–4
foreign communists
archival evidence, 56
cadre formation and self-criticism, 11–12, 175–90
Comintern assists repression of, 67–75, 77, 135
defectors as victims, 156, 164–5
Elektrozavod Plant operation, 225–38
Gohlke case, 202–3, 204–6
"Hitler-Jugend conspiracy", 12–13, 212–21, 235
operations against, 6, 10, 12–13, 67–75, 135, 142–3, 155, 188–90

as suspects, 3, 68–9, 163–4, 165
see also Comintern; national operations; Polish operation
fraternal communist parties, 68, 69
French Communist Party (PCF), 175, 183
Frinovskii, M. P., 124, 131, 135, 160, 167

Gamarnik, I., 23
Gasov, L., 26
Gavrilovich, Ivan, 50
German Communist Party (KPD), 74–5, 175, 180–1, 185, 225, 235
denunciations of German communists, 68, 70, 71
Gohlke case, 202–3, 204–6
"Hitler-Jugend conspiracy", 12–13, 212–21, 235
German national minority
"Hitler-Jugend conspiracy", 12–13, 212–21, 235
mass operations against, 12–13, 120, 122, 123, 128, 208–12, 234–5
operation at Elektrozavod plant, 13, 225–38
Order No. 00439, 122, 123, 209–12, 234–5
German-language research on Stalinism, 3, 56
Gestapo, 74, 208–9, 218–19
Getty, John Arch, 118
Gikalo, M. F., 25
Gogol (inspector of statistics), 200
Gohlke, Arthur (Arden), 202–3, 204–6
Goncharov, 26, 30
Gorbach, Grigorii, 128–9
Gorbulskii, Solomon E., 201
Great Terror
ending of, 14
"intentionalist" interpretations, 8
motivations for, 6–7, 8, 14, 65–6
structure of, 2–3, 6
see also elite purges; mass operations
Greek nationals
mass operations against, 128
resettlement operation, 99–100

Grzetic, Ivan (Stefan Fleischer), 75
GUGB (Main Administration of State Security)
  archives on, 34
  Ezhov's criticisms and reform of, 87–8, 102–3
  functions of, 85
  interrogation techniques, 205
  mass operations, 100, 101–2, 103–4, 118–44
  transport department, 102
  see also NKVD; OGPU; UGB
Gulag system
  execution of kulak inmates, 130, 132, 148*n*
  refusal of invalids and consequences, 136–7
  sentences for German operation, 209–12
  sentences for Polish Operation, 169–70
  survivors' rehabilitation benefits, 2
Gurvich, Esfir, 50

Hagenloh, Paul, 119
Hanecki, Jakob, 71
Harbin re-emigrants (Kharbintsy), 122, 123, 128, 158
Hayer, Adam, 236
Hengst, Paul, 68
Hess, Rudolf, 61, 62
"Hitler-Jugend conspiracy", 12–13, 212–21, 235
  arrest and sentencing of suspects, 212–15
  reactions to arrests, 216–21
  rehabilitation for victims and families, 221
Hoffman, David, 237
Holm, Peter, 235
Holocaust: motivation for, 6–7
homeless people, 139, 151*n*
  orphans, 100
hooliganism, 91
Horn, Otto, 232
House for Political Immigrants, Moscow, 213
Huth, Alfons and family, 235

Iagoda, Genrikh, 22, 36, 43, 111
  criticism of "conciliatory" attitude, 38–9
  demotion, 39, 41, 102, 114*n*
  denunciation, 87–9, 102, 134
  execution, 50
  passportisation regulation, 95
  reform of police administration under, 89–90
  repression of socially harmful elements, 92–3, 96–103, 104, 106
  show trial, 35, 48, 49–50
Iakubovich, G. M., 138, 213, 214, 235
Iaroslavskii, E. M., 35, 40, 124
Ignatiev, S. P., 29
Ikramov, Akmal', 40, 42
industry *see* Elektrozavod plant
informers, 196
"intentionalist" interpretations, 8
international communist movement
  Stalinisation of, 9
  see also Comintern; foreign communists
International Lenin School (ILS), 181, 182, 183, 184, 186, 187–8
invalids, 136–7
Iranian nationals, 123
Italian Communist Party (PCI), 71, 189–90
Ivanov, V. I., 48

Jakl, Paul, 216
Japan as counter-revolutionary threat, 105, 122, 123, 216
  see also Harbin re-emigrants
Journal de Moscou, Le, 216
judicial staff: conflict with NVKD, 22

Kaganovich, Lazar, 5, 35, 38, 39, 61, 91, 119, 177
Kamenev, Lev, 34–5, 37, 38, 57, 59
Kaminskii, G. N., 24
Karavkina, D., 59
Karelian ASSR, 121, 123, 126
Karetnikov, Sergeant (NKVD deputy commander, Kuntsevo), 195–6, 198, 201, 205, 206, 214
Karl-Liebknecht school, 209, 213, 235

Karutskii, Vasilii, 138
Kautsky (Stoian Minev), 72, 80*n*
Kaversnev (commander of 8th UGB department), 201
Kharbintsy operation, 122, 123, 128, 158
Kharlakevich (head of NKVD administration in Mytyshi), 196
Khlevniuk, Oleg, 104–5, 111, 142
Khodzhaev, Faizulla, 42
Khrushchev, Nikita, 27, 133–4, 139, 195
Khvatov (NKVD staff-member, Serpukhov), 206
Kirov, Sergei
  assassination, 44, 51, 52, 57
  on self-criticism, 177
Kirsanova, Klavdia, 184, 191*n*, 192*n*
Klug, Wilhelm, 215
Knorin, Waldemar, 35, 66, 220
Kogan, Lazar, 41
Kolbuta, Vera, 204
Koleskinkov-Tikki, A., 205
Kolonne Links (theatre group), 213, 215
Kommodov, Nikolai, 47
Koplenig, Johann, 191*n*
Korean nationals, 128
Koritschoner, Franz, 189, 193*n*
Korobitsin, Captain, 130–1
Kraevskii, Anton, 68–9
Kravchuk, Alexander, 74
Krestinskii, N. N., 46, 48
Krivitsky, Walter, 208
Kruminš-Pilat, Janis, 75
Krylenko, N. V., 39
Kuibyshev, V. V., 44, 52
kulaks
  de-kulakisation operations, 86, 88, 93, 99, 106
  execution of prison and Gulag inmates, 130, 132, 148*n*
  repression as threat to state security, 105–6, 107, 108, 109–10, 111–12, 120, 123–4, 129, 130, 131–2, 137–8, 140–1
Kun, Béla, 66, 220
KUNMZ (Comintern school), 74, 182, 186

Kuntsevo district office of NKVD, Moscow, 12, 195–206
Kuromiya, Hiroaki, 6
Kurskii, V. M., 41
Kuznetsov, Lieutenant (NKVD commander, Kuntsevo), 195–6, 202, 205, 206

Larina, Anna, 50
Latvian nationals: mass operations against, 122, 123, 132, 135, 167
Lenin, Vladimir Ilyich: assassination allegations, 42, 43, 44, 46
Leningrad: mass operations in, 139, 148*n*
Lenski, Julian, 72, 73
Leonhard, Wolfgang, 176
limity see arrest quotas
log-book for Kremlin visitors, 35
Lubianka building, Moscow, 1
Lubiniecki, Jan (Rylsky), 72, 73
Lukin, Mikhail, 50
Lukina, Nadezhda, 50

McLoughlin, Barry, 3
Maddalena, Max, Jr, 217, 218, 220–1
Maddalena, Max, Sr, 217, 218
Maggo, Petr, 50
Malenkov, Georgii, 29, 35
Mantsev, Vasilii, 43
Manuilskii, Dmitrii, 9, 69, 72, 73, 75, 80*n*
marginal populations: mass repression, 86–113, 134
Marker, Wilhelm Theo (Alfred Rohde), 74–5
Martens, Edna (Greta Wilde), 71
Martin, Terry, 112, 119, 143
Martinson, Martin, 236
Marty, André, 183
mass operations, 2–3, 7, 10, 118–44
  categories of victims, 97–8
  comparison with elite purges, 119–20, 143–4
  deceleration of, 138–40, 162–3, 206
  Elektrozavod plant operation, 225–38
  flexibility of time limits, 125, 132
  in Kuntsevo district, Moscow, 12, 195–206

in Moscow, 133–9
organisation of operations, 119–24, 194
Polish operation, 153–71
quotas and targets, 3, 120, 127, 129–30, 133–4, 214
social order through repression, 85–113
suspension of judicial procedure, 125–6, 129
technology of operations, 125–31, 196
time-scale of, 131–3
see also death sentences
mass shootings, 130–2, 133, 141, 205
location of graves, 1
"shooting regulations", 130–1
see also death sentences
Matte, Erich, 232
Matveev (Komendant), 148n
Mayenburg, Ruth von, 177
Mehring, Richard, 75
Mekhlis, L. Z., 35
Mekkinen, Hannes (Mathias Stein), 75
Melnikov, V. N. (Boris) (Müller), 71, 75, 205
Menzhinskii, V. R., 22, 44, 52
Merkulov, V. N., 75
Mertens, Stanislaw, 72
Military Collegium of the Supreme Court
elite purges, 119–20, 144, 219, 220
scene of third show trial, 43–50
sentencing of foreign spies, 161
Minaev-Tsikanovskii, A. M., 134, 160
Minev, Stoian ("Kautsky"), 72, 80n
Ministry of Security for Moscow City and Region: archive, 1
Mironov, Aleksandr, 48
Mironov, Sergei, 105, 107, 110
Mitrofanov, Nikolai, 220
Molotov, V. M., 26, 35, 39, 45, 61, 119, 125, 152n, 212, 220
Morin, Edgar, 177
Moscow: mass operations in, 133–9
Elektrozavod plant, 13, 225–38
executions see Butovo village
"Hitler-Jugend" operation, 12–13, 212–21
Kuntsevo district office of NKVD, 12, 195–206
Moskvin see Trilisser, Meer
Mühlberg, Rudolf, 232, 233, 234
Müller see Melnikov
Müller, Albert (Georg Brückmann), 71
Munk-Petersen, Arne, 75
Münzenberg, Willi, 65, 71
Muralov, Nikolai, 197
Muralov, Sergei Konstantinovich, 204, 205, 206
arrest after denunciation, 197–9
confession, 199–201, 202

Nagovizina, Polia, 51
namesakes, danger of, 197
"national" operations, 3, 6, 42, 86, 101, 119, 120–3, 128, 132–3, 140
album system as model for, 163
arbitrary choice of victims, 134, 214
control of foreign influence, 166
death sentences for, 135, 138, 139, 141, 162–3, 164
deportations, 123
fuelled by xenophobia, 10, 12–13, 112–13, 121–2, 143, 163–4, 165, 216–17
high percentage of Poles arrested, 170–71
production targets, 214
resettlement of Greek nationals, 99–100
see also espionage; foreign communists; German national minority; Polish operation
nationality status: evidence requirement, 167–8
Nazi Germany: motivation for Holocaust, 6–7
Nevskii, A., 43
NKVD (People's Commissariat of Internal Affairs)
"album" procedure, 11, 159–63, 164, 166–7, 171
archival evidence on, 3, 35, 195
Elektrozavod operation, 233–8

NKVD, (continued)
  foreign communists arrested and interrogated by, 188–90, 215, 235
  formation of, 89
  "Hitler-Jugend" conspiracy fiction, 212–21, 235
  interrogations for show trials, 48, 49
  judicial staff in dispute with, 22
  Kuntsevo district office, 12, 195–206
  local operations, 194–5
  mass shootings, 1, 130–2, 133
  Order No. 00192, 97–9, 101
  Order No. 00439, 122, 123, 209–12, 234–5
  Order No. 00447, 103–11, 112, 119, 120, 123–44, 153–4, 195–6
  Order No. 00485, 10–11, 153–71
  passportisation system, 93–7, 106
  post-terror purge of, 27–32, 195, 219–20
  pre-terror purge of, 39, 41, 88, 103
  social order through mass repression, 9–10, 85–113
  Special Boards, 161, 171, 206, 234
  staging of show trials, 40–50
  survey of mass repressions, 118–44
  suspicion of political emigrants, 68–75
  techniques for extracting confessions, 72, 127–8, 134–5, 199, 205, 215, 220, 235, 236
  torture allegations dismissed by Stalin, 31
  Troops Tribunals, 206, 219–20
  VKP(b) purges, 36–9
  VKP(b) relationship with, 21–32
"non-party behaviour", 181, 182
"normalisation" process, 49
Norwegian Communist Party, 61

OBKhSS (Department for the Struggle against the Misappropriation of State Property), 102
OGPU (Unified State Political Administration), 85, 88
  passportisation system, 93–7

railroad operations, 91
  see also GUGB; NKVD; UGB
Okhrana, 45, 46, 48, 66
Oparin, N. S., 201–2
"oppositionist" suspects, 21, 23, 37, 38–9
Order No. 00192 (socially harmful elements), 97–9, 101
Order No. 00439 (German Order), 122, 123, 209–12, 234–5
Order No. 00447 (anti-Soviet elements), 24, 42, 103–111, 112, 119, 120, 123–44, 153–4
  death sentences, 130–2, 133–4, 141, 143
  preparations in localities, 195–6
Order No. 00485 (Polish order), 10–11, 24, 123, 153–71
  album procedure, 159–63, 164, 166–7, 171
  duration, 161–2
Order No. 00486 ("wives of enemies"), 157–8
Order No. 00606, 162
"ordinary" people as victims, 6, 10
  see also mass operations
Ordzhonikidze, Sergo, 23, 38
organised crime, 90–1
orphans
  mass round-ups of homeless, 100
  of sentenced foreign nationals, 158
ORPO (Department for Leading Party Organs), 28, 29, 37
Osten, Maria (Maria Greßhöner), 59

passport applications: nationality status, 167–8
passportisation, 93–7, 106
  troiki regulation of, 95–7
peasants see agriculture; kulaks
People's Commissariat of Foreign Affairs (NKID), 5, 155
People's Commissariat for Heavy Industry (NKTP), 23, 38
People's Commissariat of Internal Affairs see NKVD
Persits, Mikhail, 212, 219
Peshkov, Maxim, 44, 52

"petit-bourgeois" behaviour, 11, 181, 182
Petrov, Nikita, 24
physically handicapped people, 136–7
Piatakov, Georgii, 23, 39, 40, 41, 57–8, 60–1, 62, 64
Piatnitskii, Osip, 24, 66, 220
Pieck, Wilhelm, 73, 77, 218
Pilsudski, J. K., 71, 72
police
  roles of civil and political police in repression of social disorder, 85–113
  see also GUGB; NKVD; OGPU
Polish Communist Party (KPP), 71–3, 155
Polish Military Organisation (POV), 71–3, 154–5, 157
Polish operation, 10–11, 13, 24, 71–3, 123, 128, 153–71
  album procedure, 159–63, 164, 166–7, 171
  categories of victims, 155–9
  death sentences, 135, 170–71
  issuance of Polish Order with "sealed letter", 153–5
  sentencing totals, 170–71
Polish Socialist Party (PPS), 156–7
Politburo
  elite purges, 143–4
  procedure for mass operations, 119, 120
  supervision of NKVD, 22, 27–8
  Trotskyist purges, 38
Pollitt, Harry, 58, 184
Popashenko, I. P., 130–1
Popov, B. S., 73
Pose, Fritz, 232
Postel', A. O., 154
Postyshev, P. P., 23, 27
POUM party (Spain), 60–1
POV (Polish Military Organisation), 71–3, 154–5, 157
Pozdniakov, N., 108
Pravda, 41, 43, 51, 52, 121–2, 197, 200
Presidential Archive of the Russian Federation (APRF), 17n, 34
prison inmates: execution, 130, 136
prisoners of war, 155, 158

Próchniak, Edward, 72
propaganda
  Comintern campaign, 57–61, 63–4, 67
  on mass operations against foreigners, 121–2
  sabotage accusations, 36–7, 41, 51
  surrounding show trials, 39, 57–61, 63–4, 67, 199–200
"purge" (*chistka*)
  meaning and use of term, 175, 177
  see also criticism and self-criticism ritual; elite purges; mass operations

"questionnaire" method, 165, 194–5
quotas see arrest quotas

Radek, Karl, 38, 40, 41, 57–8, 60, 62
railroad operations, 91, 102
Rakovskii, Christian, 43, 57–8
Raskolnikov, Fedor, 71
Reck, Julie, 68
Red Army: purge by questionnaire, 165
Redens, Stanislav, 133, 134, 139
"regime" cities: passportisation, 93–7, 106
registration system see passportisation
Rehabilitation Group: Ministry of Security for Moscow City and Region, 1
Rehabilitation Law (1991), 2
rehabilitation process, 1, 2, 195, 221
Reicher, Gustav (Rwal'), 72
Reisberg, Arnold, 186, 191n
religion: mass operations against, 120, 123–4
remembrance books, 2, 118
"revisionist" school of Soviet history, 4, 14
"Right deviationists", 36, 37, 38–9, 41
Rinkovsky, Kurt, 221
Riutin platform, 40, 42, 46
RKM (Raboche-krest'ianskaia militsiia), 89, 90
Roasio, Antonio, 71
Robotti, Paolo, 176
Roginskii, Arsenii, 24

Roginskii, G. K., 160
Rohde, Alfred (Wilhelm Theo Marker), 74–5
"Romanian" operation, 123
Rozengolts, A. P., 49
Rubiner, Frida, 193n
Rukodanov (NKVD officer, Kuntsevo), 200, 201, 205
rural areas
  mass operations in, 105–6, 107, 108–10, 111–12, 120, 137–8
  see also agriculture; kulaks
Russian General Military Union (ROVS), 105
Russian State Archive of Socio-Political History (RGASPI), 17n, 34, 175–6
Rwal' see Reicher, Gustav
Rykov, A. I. : show trial, 8, 24, 40–50, 61, 62, 64, 67
  indictment details, 43–5
Rylsky see Lubiniecki, Jan

sabotage, 12, 36–7, 38, 39, 41, 128
  accusations of, 36–7, 38, 41, 42, 48, 51, 52, 236
  police protection against, 91, 102
  Stalin's fears of, 92
  see also "wreckers of socialist construction"
Salzberg, Witold (Bronislaw Berg), 71–2
"scapegoat" logic, 12, 35, 197
Schmitt, Harry, 218
Schmor, Max, 232, 233–4
Schramm, Günther, 218, 221
Schreder, Karl, 236
Schutzbündler (Austrian political immigrants), 208, 231
secret police see GUGB; NKVD; OGPU
self-criticism see criticism and self-criticism ritual
Semenov, M. I., 129, 138
sentences see death sentences; Gulag system
Shapiro, I. I., 160
Sharangovich, V. F., 42, 43
Shearer, David, 119
Sheboldaev, B. P., 23

Sheidin, Petr, 219
Shitikov (Senior Lieutenant of State Security), 136
shootings see death sentences; mass shootings
show trials, 34–52
  archives relating to, 34–6
  Comintern propaganda campaign, 57–61, 63–4, 67
  evidence of falsification, 61
  first show trial (Zinoviev–Kamenev), 37, 39, 51, 57, 58–60
  second show trial, 40, 51, 57–8, 60–1
  stenogram record of third trial, 45–6, 47, 48–9
  strategic recesses, 48–9
  third show trial (Bukharin–Rykov), 8, 35, 40–50, 67, 199–200
  third trial indictments, 43–5
Silbermann, Charlotte, 221
Silbermann, Kurt, 221
Simenova, Maria, 217
Skulski, Stefan, 72
Skvortsov, Colonel, 220
Smirnov, Vasilii, 212–13, 214, 219, 220
Sobottka, Gustav, 215, 220
social order and mass repressions, 6, 7, 9–10, 85–113
  categories of socially harmful elements, 97–8
  Order No. 00192 (socially harmful elements), 97–9, 101
  Order No. 00447 (anti-Soviet elements), 103–11, 112, 119, 120, 123–4
  passportisation system, 93–7, 106
Sokolnikov, G., 23, 40, 43, 61, 62
Sorokin, Ivan, 195, 196, 213, 214, 219–20
Sosnovskii, Ignats, 68
Sovnarkom, 100–1, 104
Spanish Civil War, 14, 142
Spanish Communist Party (PCE), 60–1
"special folders" archive, 35
speculators, 100, 101, 136
spies see espionage

Index 255

Stalin, Josef
  allegations of plans to assassinate, 42, 43, 49, 200
  appeals to, 217
  control of foreign influence, 166
  directs Comintern propaganda, 63–5
  encirclement paranoia, 12–13, 121, 163, 165
  exasperation with bureaucracy, 5–6, 14
  manipulation of organs of power, 21, 32
  and mass operations, 119, 120, 212
  motivation for terror, 8, 14, 65–6
  "normalisation" process, 49
  personal supervision of Great Terror, 4, 5, 8, 13–14
  on repression of social disorder, 91–2, 96–7
  stages show trials with Ezhov, 34–52
  on unity of Soviet state, 66–7
  use of torture approved, 31, 128, 148*n*
VKP(b) plenum (June 1937) instructions, 25
State Archive of the Russian Federation (GARF), 17*n*
State Farm Kommunarka site of mass graves, 1
State Security Administration *see* GUGB; UGB
Stein, Mathias (Hannes Mekkinen), 75
Stepanova, Ekaterina, 198–9
"street children": mass round-ups, 100
Sukurov (head of NKVD district office, Voskresensk), 201–2
Suslov, Mikhail, 31–2
Sverdlov, I., 42, 43
Swiss Communist Party, 175

TASS, 43
Teleshev, G. G., 26
Thiele, Otto, 232
Thorez, Maurice, 58
Togliatti, Palmiro (Ercoli), 58, 60, 61, 77, 176
Tomskii, M. P., 23, 41, 49, 61

torture
  in anti-Soviet operations, 127–8
  of Elektrozavod foreign employees, 236
  of "Hitler-Jugend" suspects, 215, 220
  in Kuntsevo district, 12, 195
  Stalin's absolution of NKVD, 31, 128, 148*n*
  Zakovskii's promotion of, 134–5, 235
"totalitarian" school of Soviet history, 4
Traibmann, Rudolf, 214, 220
transport
  police protection of, 91, 102
  sabotage accusations, 51
Trifonov, Iakov, 136–7
Trilisser, Meer (Moskvin), 73, 74, 75–6
troiki
  for anti-Soviet elements, 107, 108, 109, 120, 124, 125, 129, 130, 137–8, 153–4
  for national operations, 133, 162–3, 164, 171
  for passportisation regulation, 95–6
  for violations by undesirables, 96–9, 100–1
Trotsky, Leon, 35, 66
  and Hess, 61, 62
  supporters purged, 38–9, 43–50, 51, 57, 63–7
Tsesarskii, Vladimir, 134, 138, 160
Tsyganov (NKVD officer in charge of Gohlke case), 205–6
Tucker, Robert, 13–14, 142
Tukhachevskii, M. N., 41–2, 47

UGB (State Security Administration)
  access to archive files, 2
  Ezhov's criticisms of, 88
  "Hitler-Jugend" operation, 212–21
  interrogation techniques, 127–8
  repression of socially harmful elements, 98–111
  see also GUGB; NKVD; OGPU
ugolovnyi rozysk, 90–1
Ukraine: Polish emigrants in, 157–8
Ulbricht, Walter, 218
Ulrikh, V. V., 43, 45–6, 48
unemployed people, 151*n*

Valukhin, K. N., 26, 30
Varga, Eugen, 216
"victim studies", 3, 4
victims' families
  and archival access, 3, 118, 221
  loyalty to party not partner, 180–1
  as suspects, 50, 157–8
VKP(b) All-Union Communist Party (Bolsheviks)
  archives of minutes, 35
  internal elections (1937), 23
  and NKVD purges, 27–32
  NKVD relations with, 21–32
  plenum (December 1936), 61–2
  plenum (Feb.–March 1937), 40–1, 64, 75, 87–9, 102, 103, 123
  plenum (June 1937), 23–6, 35
  plenum (January 1938), 27, 49
  purges of members, 23–4, 26, 27, 36–9, 49, 178–80
  reinstatement of expelled members, 27, 49
  staging of show trials, 34–52
Volkogonov, Dmitrii, 77*n*
Volkov, A. A., 133
Volynskii (NKVD counter-intelligence officer), 208–9
Voroshilov, K. E., 119
Vyshinskii, Andrei, 29, 57–8
  conduct during show trials, 62
  role in national operations, 119
  sanctions "album" procedure, 11, 160
  show-trial indictments, 38–9, 41, 43, 44, 45, 47, 51
  troiki formation for socially harmful elements, 96–7, 100–1

Walecki, Henryk, 71, 72
Walter, Helena, 61
Wangenheim, Gustav von, 176, 185
war, threat of, 13, 86, 104–5, 106–7, 112, 142, 163
Weber, Hermann, 56
Weinberg, Erich (Erich Eisen), 74
Western Siberia: mass repression in, 87, 98–9, 105, 107–10
Wilde, Greta (Edna Martens), 71
Wittenberg, Erich, 232, 235
wives
  loyalty to party not partner, 180–1
  as suspects, 157–8
womanising: "non-party behaviour", 181; *see also* RKM
Worker-Peasant Militia, 89
"wreckers of socialist construction", 12, 36–7, 38, 39, 41, 128
  accusations in Kuntsevo district, 197–8, 200, 204
  Poles accused of, 159
  trials of, 42, 45, 51
  see also sabotage

xenophobia, 10, 12–13, 112–13, 121, 143, 163–5, 216–17

Yeltsin, Boris, 2

Zakharov, P., 214
Zakovskii, Leonid, 92–3, 138, 139, 205, 235
  appointment as director of mass operations in Moscow, 134–6
  demotion and execution, 138
  propaganda production, 121–2
Zhdanov, A. A., 123–4, 216
Zhelezniak, Moishe, 233–4
Zhurbenko, Aleksandr, 138
Zinoviev, Grigorii, 34–5, 37, 38, 39, 57–9
Zint, Bernhard and family, 235